ABOUT THE TYPE

This book was set in Times Roman, designed by Stanley Morison specifically for *The Times* of London. The typeface was introduced in the newspaper in 1932. Times Roman has had its greatest success in the United States as a book and commercial typeface, rather than one used in newspapers.

BOILING POINT

KEVIN PHILLIPS

BOILING POINT

□   □   □

Republicans, Democrats,
and the Decline of
Middle-Class Prosperity

RANDOM HOUSE 🏠 NEW YORK

*To Brent, Emily
and Andrew*

Preface

For a contest that pivoted on middle-class anger and fear of the economic future—emotions that victor Bill Clinton tapped better than any other Democrat since Franklin D. Roosevelt and that Ross Perot rode to a stronger showing than any other third party candidate since Theodore Roosevelt—the presidential election of 1992 produced surprisingly little discussion of just what changes the new president would make. And the candidates offered only a superficial analysis of what had caused the economic mess in the first place.

As the voters firmed against George Bush and his administration, there was less need for Clinton to explain his purpose in detail, and as the campaign wore on, the Democratic nominee seemed to retreat further into vagueness. He was, after all, going to be in charge of the economy from 1993 to 1996, and detailed commitments made in the heat of the campaign were unwise. From the huge federal budget deficit to the vulnerability of important U.S. manufacturing sectors, serious economic dangers confronted ordinary Americans and menaced their future standard of living. Glib political promises to restore the opportunity of the Truman, Eisenhower and Kennedy years—the kind of commitment that Reagan made so lightly in 1980—could now seem as futile as the Sioux dances a hundred years earlier to bring back the vanishing American buffalo. Voters sensed that major dislocations were ahead.

Yet the evidence of widespread fears was so pronounced, raising the prospect of a watershed change in national politics, economics and culture, that it seems worthwhile to spell out, as I shall do in this book, some of the reasons for this fear, reasons that were insufficiently detailed during the campaign itself. Sixty-two percent of Americans voted to replace the president, which suggested that the economic damage to middle-class America was real enough. One purpose of this book is simply to describe this damage—to tell middle-class householders and voters just what happened to them over the last thirty years (but especially over the last fifteen), what happened to their disposable income, their taxes, their home values, their earnings, their job prospects, their services from government, their assets and net worth, their safety net of pensions, health care and insurance, and their children's prospect of enjoying the same upward mobility and living standard as they themselves had enjoyed. I believe that it is also important to explain a critical change in national political fashion: how opinion-molders and officials who, from the New Deal to the Nixon years, had spoken up for the common people and fought for the "little guy" transformed their outlooks, so that by the 1980s the country's leaders were embracing or flirting with an elitist philosophy that celebrated investors, entrepreneurs and the rich while neglecting the interests of a middle class that found itself increasingly threatened. The Bush administration, in particular, left itself wide open to Democratic accusations that it had betrayed the middle class in favor of the top 1 percent of wealthy Americans. Even for many Republicans, this was an uncomfortable truth. In 1992 economic transformation brought its political reckoning.

Because recent U.S. presidential candidates have too often avoided uncomfortable issues during the campaign, postelection periods may be the best times to raise urgent questions for national discussion. Perhaps this will be true again in 1993, when informed debate can build rather than dissipate in a few sound bites and autumn tactical compulsions, as it did during the election. Back in late 1967 I finished a book, whose analyses would be used in the 1968 Republican campaign. The book was then released in 1969 as *The Emerging Republican Majority.* Publication seven months after the election turned out to provide a perfect context for confirmation of its thesis—that the worn-out New Deal Democratic coalition was breaking up in favor of a new Republican presidential majority based on a new middle-class populism and a new Southern-Western alignment, which I called the Sun Belt. One newsmagazine labeled the book "the political bible of the Nixon Era," and its arguments influenced Republican strategy not only in 1972 but right through 1980.

Two decades later, *The Politics of Rich and Poor,* which I began to write in 1987 but published in 1990, crystallized issues that Michael Dukakis touched only hesitantly in the 1988 campaign. However, its message fell on fertile ground in June 1990, and its portrait of the rich as the major beneficiaries of the Reagan and Bush eras quickly became a pivot of the 1990 congressional elections and grew from there. In 1992, as the presidential campaign began, *Newsweek* described *The*

Politics of Rich and Poor as a "founding document." *The New York Times* noted that Democratic strategists "revere" the book's thesis that the 1990s are marked by a populist reaction to the economic excesses of the 1980s.

Most of the Democratic presidential hopefuls and contenders of 1991–92—from Bill Clinton to Mario Cuomo, Lloyd Bentsen, Dick Gephardt, Tom Harkin, Douglas Wilder and Jerry Brown—had read *The Politics of Rich and Poor* or drawn on its theses. So had Pat Buchanan on the Republican side; and in December 1991, well before Ross Perot went public, I received an unexpected telephone call from *The Dallas Morning News.* The Texas billionaire was supposedly blue-printing a 1992 presidential campaign based in part on *The Politics of Rich and Poor.* Was I involved? the reporter asked. I was not.

Although that famous cloth-coat Republican Richard Nixon gave me a laudatory comment for the dust jacket of *The Politics of Rich and Poor.* George Bush and his political advisers chose to ignore the book. However, as the dissatisfaction closed in around the president's men, some of them complained to the media that I had given the Democrats the arguments with which Bush could be beaten. Several GOP loyalists who introduced me to public audiences announced that some Republicans regarded me as a traitor. In fact, the same convictions that led to my part in helping to define the populist-infused new GOP majority of 1968–72 were outraged by the Bush administration. Too many of its officials had no interest in the swing voters from the small-town South, blue-collar Peoria, Levittown or the ends of Northern urban subway lines who had rallied first to Nixon and then later to Reagan—constituencies and shifts I had discussed in *The Emerging Republican Majority.* As Pat Buchanan and Ross Perot insisted in their own blunt language, Skull and Bones and the prep schools and country clubs were once again in charge. When Bush lost an Iowa straw poll in 1987, he suggested that his absent supporters were too busy on the golf course or at air shows or debutante parties to come out and vote. It was a revealing glimpse—and a revealing prophecy of Bush economic loyalties to come. Nixon's cloth-coat coalition of earlier years was abandoned during the Bush years; some Democrats would even say it had been betrayed.

For many Americans, including significant numbers of Republicans, the sense that old constituencies and causes had been abandoned led to disapproval of Bush and ultimately to his defeat. Favoritism to the rich and imploding speculative bubbles had been devastating to Republican national coalitions before, in the late-nineteenth-century

Gilded Age and in the early 1930s, and in 1992 it happened again. Large chunks of the GOP coalition, especially those recruited in the Nixon and Reagan years, abandoned Bush for Buchanan, for Perot and even for Clinton. Network exit polls on November 3 showed over one quarter of self-identified Republicans voting against their incumbent president.

In 1990 I wrote that Bush was vulnerable to losing the support of the Middle American swing constituencies that backed Nixon and Reagan. I felt this even more strongly in 1991 and 1992 as I worked on this book and saw the severe damage that the circumstances and policies since 1973 inflicted on middle-class voters. Small wonder that U.S. politics turned sour in 1990–92 just as it had following previous periods of excessive debt and speculation and subsequent downturns. Herbert Hoover's share of the total presidential vote plummeted 18 points between 1928 and the mid-Depression election of 1932; Bush's percentage dropped a nearly comparable 16 points between 1988 and 1992.

In examining this explosion, where it came from and where it's going, *Boiling Point* picks up where *The Politics of Rich and Poor* left off. It explains how and why much of the middle class stagnated economically (or worse) while those at the top did so well, why this was politically disastrous for the GOP, and why remedial policies have now become the key to the 1996 elections. Many of the gruesome details are drawn from the nation's major metropolitan areas—New York, Los Angeles, Chicago, Philadelphia, Boston, Dallas–Fort Worth, the San Francisco Bay Area and South Florida. To read of this quiet devastation is to understand what undercut Bush, fueled Perot's populist insurgency and gave Bill Clinton his winning appeal to a middle class whose interests had, in fact, been forgotten much as Clinton said they were. Yet this same populist thrust that brought Clinton to the White House also set the new Democratic president on a razor's edge.

Angry middle-class voters mobilized in record numbers to defeat a man whose approval rating they had cut from an extraordinary 90 percent in the spring of 1991 to a ghostly 30 percent in mid-1992. No other president has ever fallen so far, and the plummeting of the Republican presidential vote from 54 percent in 1988 to just 38 percent in 1992 was another rare tumble. Previous convulsions of this magnitude have been few and far between, the stuff of once-a-generation watershed upheavals. The caution, of course, is that if middle-class anger could destroy Bush and his presidency in eighteen months, his successor can also be destroyed by the same angry electorate, and just as quickly. In this regard, the restoration of middle-class confidence and stability is probably the key to the 1996 election. In October's final presidential debate, Clinton told the huge national audience that he would keep his commitments to the middle class. If he does not, if budget pressures make it impossible for him to do so, his failure could unleash demons. Over the next four years, this will be the new battleground of American politics—and perhaps of America's future.

No book, of course, is solely the product of its author. My wife and sons put up with the deadlines and dislocations; my assistants Michelle Klein, Rebecca Palmer and Lynn Murray provided important research and word-processing assistance; my agent, Bill Leigh, and his associates provided counseling; and my editor at Random House, Jason Epstein, was as usual the critical spur to the book's evolution and polish.

—Kevin Phillips
Bethesda, Maryland
November 1992

Contents

Introduction: The Legitimacy of Middle-Class Frustration

The rich get the gold mine and the middle class gets the shaft. It's wrong and it's going to ruin the country.
> —Democratic presidential nominee Bill Clinton, 1992

I want a revolution where the working class and the middle class take back control of the Republican Party.
> —Republican presidential candidate Patrick Buchanan, 1992

The American people can't afford it themselves, so I'm buying the country back for them.
> —Independent presidential candidate Ross Perot, 1992

The ruling class has lost touch with the American people. They have lost touch because they swim in a world of privilege, power and wealth.
> —Democratic presidential candidate Jerry Brown, 1992

Statements like these defined the 1992 presidential race as a watershed, spurred unexpected millions to go to the polls and made George Bush the first popularly chosen Republican president to be defeated for reelection since 1932. Voters told survey-takers there was "no chance" that things could get better in the United States if Bush was reelected—and he was not. For six weeks in late spring and early summer, Ross Perot, the independent presidential contender, moved ahead of the Democratic and Republican contenders in national polls though he had not yet announced his candidacy. Nobody had seen anything like it before.

Americans had reached their boiling point. In 1964 a mere 29 percent had told polltakers that government was run for the benefit of a few big interests. Following Watergate, that surged to 66 percent, and climbed to 70 percent in 1980 after disenchantment with the Carter presidency. By 1992 the proportion of Americans who felt that government favored the rich and powerful had reached 80 percent. Unprecedented numbers of citizens also believed that "quite a few" of the people running the government were crooked. A mere 24 percent had said so in 1958, 45 percent in 1976 and 49 percent in 1980. No *majority* had said so, though—until 1992, when the percentage soared to 65 percent. Political analyst William Schneider combined these measures of indignation along with three others into what he called a "P.O. Index." The conclusion, Schneider argued, was unmistakable: postwar Americans had never been so angry.

By condemning the Reagan-Bush administrations for favoritism to the rich and neglect of the middle class, Clinton tapped a historic Republican vulnerability and took a strong lead over Bush from July onward. True, many voters still doubted the Arkansas governor's trustworthiness. His last rival for the Democratic nomination, former California governor Jerry Brown, had insisted that Clinton couldn't be believed because he was financed by the same elites he purported to deplore. Many voters, however, felt they had no choice. The Iran-Contra and Iraqgate scandals had called the president's own good faith into question, and no independent candidate had cracked the Democratic-Republican monopoly of the presidency in one hundred thirty-six years. By November 3 many Americans were applauding Perot, and a surprising 19 percent voted for him. But of the candidates demanding change, only one was electable.

When the dust settled, an angry and frustrated middle class, displaying marked populist tendencies, had defeated one president and chosen another, making Clinton the first Democrat since Franklin D. Roosevelt to enter the White House propelled by a major election victory instead of a close race or by succession to the presidency from the vice presidency. Hopeful Democrats saluted a watershed and predicted that a new era was beginning. Yet America's economic and fiscal difficulties were in some ways the worst since the 1930s, which meant that the frustration politics that brought down George Bush would not abate until the challenge was met. Besides, middle-class Americans were just beginning to realize how much they had to be unhappy about. They would hold the new president—and his campaign promises, vague as they were—to account.

Because this book is about the dynamics and, yes, the *legitimacy* of middle-class frustration, I will not revisit—except in scattered pages and footnotes—the account of the concentration of wealth that I set forth in *The Politics of Rich and Poor* three years ago. With each year, fewer doubted that upper-income Americans had hugely profited in the previous decade. The allegations bitterly disputed when *The Politics of Rich and Poor* was published had become almost common wisdom by 1992, even though the trend toward even greater concentration was finally slackening. Clinton himself waved copies of *America: What Went Wrong,* a compilation of newspaper articles detailing how the decade had favored the rich at the expense of the middle class, and brandished a parallel *New York Times* analysis suggesting that the top 1 percent had received over half of the additional income generated in the United States from 1977 to 1989. Voters were not the only ones aroused; even skeptical economists were starting to pay attention. After reading the Federal Reserve Board's own survey research, Fed chairman Alan Greenspan told several meetings in early 1992 what had been obvious to millions of his fellow Americans: that growing weakness in family income distribution might help explain low consumer confidence. Then came spring's Los Angeles riots, reflecting economic as well as racial tensions, which further illustrated the destructive effects of declining economic expectations.

Republicans had been indignant over earlier Congressional Budget Office calculations, derived from federal income tax returns, that the wealthiest 1 percent had received roughly 60 percent of the after-tax income gains realized by all U.S. families from 1977 to 1989. But the Federal Reserve Board's studies provided nonpartisan but similar documentation for the 1983–89 period, which coincided with the Reagan boom years. Between 1962 and 1983 the share of total private net worth held by the top 1 percent had barely budged. From 1983 to 1989, it surged from 31 percent to 37 percent, reaching heights unseen since 1929! Economist Paul Krugman noted "a big unprecedented jump in inequality to Great Gatsby levels," while Harvard economic historian Claudia Goldin found "inequality at its highest since the great leveling of wages and wealth during the New Deal and World War Two."

So much for the rich. The middle class, in the meantime, had stalled. The Fed found that the average pretax family income, adjusted for inflation, did indeed rise from $33,400 in 1983 to $35,700 in 1989, but this was an *average* inflated by huge gains at the top. *Median* family income—a more revealing measurement of the yearly receipts of the family smack in the middle—increased by only 0.4 percent on an inflation-adjusted basis during those six years. In the face of such evidence, defensive commentators began falling back to a new line of ideological trenches: Yes, America's rich *were* amassing a disproportionate share of wealth and income; however, the pattern was worldwide, reflecting a global economic shift that concentrated rewards among those with capital, skills and education, so that government biases were not important.

Whatever the general trends might have been, willful governmental actions—direct and indirect—probably accounted for 30 to 50 percent of this upward shift. It is true that inequality and polarization had begun intensifying in the 1970s, years in which Democratic, Liberal and Labour regimes governed the United States, Canada and Britain, so that Ronald Reagan and Margaret Thatcher were not the initial or sole perpetrators. And during the 1980s, even socialist-run nations, from Scandinavia to New Zealand, produced somewhat similar economic behavior. Nevertheless, the key, which too many observers ignore—and which we shall examine in more depth in Chapter 2—is that economics, politics and ideology run in broadly similar patterns, and that during the 1980s the broad pattern of government and politics in the prosperous Western nations was conservative. The result was to intensify favoritism to the upper brackets.

Most of the global economic effects that emerged in the mid-1970s—inflation, the increasing unpopularity of big government, the growing competitive weakness of old-line industry, anger at labor unions—had aided this political change by strengthening conservative critiques and the opposition parties that promoted them. The victories of Thatcher and Reagan in 1979–80 in the West's two leading financial centers launched what conservatives excitedly called "revolutions"—transformations that were supposed to unleash capitalist energies and market economies on a grand scale. By 1986–87 the Group of Seven leading economic nations had undergone startling political realignments: aggressive free-market conservatism was in style, more so than at any other time since World War I. The ensuing policy changes, ranging from tax reductions to financial deregulation, regulatory permissiveness, strict treatment of labor and glorification of the rich, proved to be an elixir for global stock markets, property values and business opportunities, just as supply-side economists had predicted. The drawback in the United States, however, was that as the 1980s boom crested, rising taxes and other costs were gobbling up much of the nominal income gain of the middle class, while public services and the government safety net were starting to deteriorate. By the end of the decade, these economic effects were producing political unrest.

In addition to the Federal Reserve Board's analysis that middle incomes stagnated from 1983 to 1989, the Joint Economic Committee of Congress pointed out that for the nation's two-parent families, on average, the relatively meager gains of the 1980s came from the paychecks of working wives. Two thirds of the increase came from more hours worked, *not* from higher real wages earned. While there is no clear cause-and-effect, we shall see repeatedly in future chapters that the wider the gates of opportunity opened for the top 1 percent of Americans, the more they seemed to shut for the average household.

Such trends were new in the American experience. So a critical question arises: Did the 1980s represent the first U.S. boom in which the interests of the middle class—not those of subordinate groups like farmers or labor-union members, but America's powerful and idealized middle-class majority—were pushed aside for the interests of the nation's several hundred thousand richest families?

No one, including Ronald Reagan, had intended this. However, the 1983–89 boom itself was far from uniform; all too frequently, one sector's gain was another's loss. As the Dow-Jones industrial average soared between 1980 and 1986, the value of U.S. farmland simultaneously dropped from $712 billion to $392 billion as collapsing commodity prices put more farmers out of business. Corporate chief executives' compensation set new records as workers' real hourly wages declined. Young workers watched their inflation-adjusted wages and net worth fall behind what their fathers had at a similar age. And while financial assets like stocks and bonds were surging, the value of family homes in roughly half of the nation's metropolitan areas shrank during the 1980s on an inflation-adjusted basis. It was not an equal-opportunity decade.

Middle-class householders found themselves sitting down more and more often with a figurative pencil and piece of paper. *Somebody* had profited enormously in the 1980s, with all that whipped cream and meringue in the financial markets, boardrooms and lawyers' offices, and now *somebody* else—a lot of somebodies—would lose their jobs, pay higher taxes on incomes with lower real purchasing power and otherwise foot the bills for the decline that followed (as declines usually do) the debt-and-speculative boom. What made the 1990s hangover even worse, though, was that the United States was losing its postwar global economic advantage so critical to earlier middle-class prosperity and expansion. Voters were worried, and began to ask whom to blame for the unequal gains and losses.

The new conservatism, which shaped the political economies of the major industrial nations, began as a move to limit big government, but by the late 1980s had revealed a less popular aspect: a developing inattentiveness to public-sector functions, economic fairness and jobs. Voters now saw this threatening the interests of the middle class, not just the poor. By 1992, as we shall see, many of these changes had further weakened the economy and helped produce a populist counter-tide among frustrated individuals.

Glorification of the unfettered marketplace soon came to include a permissiveness toward securities markets, real estate speculation and corporate reorganizations that helped bring about a level of speculative tremors and financial jitters unseen since the 1930s. But while speculators and corporate raiders took home huge sums, the average American family wound up fearing for the safety of its bank accounts, insurance coverage, home values and pension coverage.

Meanwhile, the postwar middle-class "social contract" broke down. The most successful Americans—baseball players, money managers, entertainers and corporate executives—negotiated huge salaries or compensation packages that increasingly dwarfed what other Americans received, distantly echoing late-nineteenth-century "survival of the fittest" excesses. By 1990 corporate chief executives, whose 1980 compensation had been 30 to 40 times higher than that of their average worker, were being paid sums 130 to 140 times greater. In this climate, top executives lost compunctions about terminating blue-collar and middle-class jobs in order to make their companies "competitive." They moved production to Taiwan and Mexico, liquidated company pension plans and reduced other employee benefits. Upper-middle-class professionals and vendors of private services were also able to charge rapidly escalating prices for health care, legal costs, banking services, college tuition, entertainment tickets, cable television charges and the like.

Securities markets also moved ahead as ordinary folk lost ground. After 1929, Wall Street and Main Street had crashed together. In 1991–92, when unprecedented numbers of Americans went on public assistance and personal bankruptcies set an all-time record, the Dow-Jones Industrial Average reached new highs. As corporations purged their white-collar staffs and cut their costs, they often bolstered their stock prices.

Financial booms that produce the great new fortunes inevitably bring record levels of debt, leverage and speculation. At the crest, captains of industry give way to financial manipulators and paper plunderers—as in the late 1980s, when the Horatio Alger figures of American industry were overshadowed by the Charles Keatings, Michael Milkens and Ivan Boeskys. Then the boom disappears in an implosion of assets—crumbling savings and loan institutions, banks and commercial rent estate—and pain spreads to the real economy, where ordinary families live and work. Popular bitterness grows.

Long before the presidential election, it was clear that the economy had become stagnant, producing the weakest growth since the Hoover years. Unfortunately, as we shall see in later chapters, previous world economic powers as they begin to ebb have shown the same pattern: stagnation develops as wealth and income bunch at the top while rising taxes, ballooning debt and declining purchasing power weigh down the middle. In the United States, merely to service the $4 trillion national debt of 1992—up fourfold from $1 trillion in 1980—required some $235 billion a year in net interest payments, most of which went to high-income bondholders (and some went abroad) while the money to make the payments was raised from broad-based taxes.

Even as the middle class was shrinking, the "top 1 percent economy" marshaled its own well-funded intellectual champions, ever ready to contend that critical studies or statistics were wrong, that America's true weakness lay in eroded family values or a pernicious politics of "envy," or to argue that the rich hadn't really done that well (or that if they had, it made no difference because the ranks of "the rich" were always changing). Some of these champions were in Congress, but many hung their hats at conservative foundations— the Heritage Foundation, the Hudson Institute, the American Enterprise Institute and the Manhattan Institute, as well as other lesser centers.

The aim of this book, by contrast, is to focus on the factors and predicaments that many defenders of the status quo have tried to sidestep—middle-class decline as a national danger signal, rising economic polarization, the irony of tax rates that hit record highs for average families and record lows for millionaires, the inadequacy and even misrepresentation of government statistics, and the citizenry's worry over endangered pensions, home values and future living standards, deteriorating public services and the rapidly increasing cost of private services, including health care. Taken together, these issues and the public's legitimate complaints about them go a long way to explain yet another symptom—*the dangerous rise of middle-class frustration politics.*

Kindred attitudes were also visible in other G-7 nations, but the United States of the 1990s was unique in one important dimension— the special discomfort and trauma that overtakes a fading great economic power, less and less able to sustain the unique affluence once bestowed on its ordinary middle-rank citizenry. In 1992 major policy changes to deal with that future finally began to weigh in the national debate. But that is for the final chapter. Let us now begin at the beginning: Within just two generations after the triumph of 1945, what had happened to middle-class America—to its taxes and purchasing power, pensions and neighborhoods, hopes and dreams—and how had it come to pass?

PART ONE

THE MIDDLE CLASS
IN PERIL

C H A P T E R 1

America's Crisis—The Decline of the Middle Class

Whatever the promise of higher incomes in the mid-80's, it is gone now. Instead of continuing to rise, real incomes—that is, wages and salaries adjusted for inflation—have declined over the last three years, with the decline becoming particularly noticeable this fall, as the national economy slowed. The upshot is that most Americans are entering the 1990's worse off than they were in the early 1970's. Only those Americans whose incomes are in the top 20 percent have escaped stagnation; their incomes have grown significantly.

—*The New York Times,* December 1990

Any substantial decline of the middle class—even if it is partially psychological—would be ominous for the U.S. as a whole. It is the middle class whose values and ambitions set the tone for the country. Without it the U.S. could become a house divided in which middle Americans would no longer serve as a powerful voice for political compromise. . . . Virtually everyone agrees that America needs to maintain its middle class.

—*Time* magazine, November 1986

The middle class in this country is in far worse shape than most people really have any idea. That's the big casino, and that's what's going to change the course of this country.

—Former Democratic national chairman Robert Strauss, 1991

As the American middle class shrank in the early 1990s, its members had reason to be nervous. Survey after survey showed that middle-income ranks, while not precisely definable by dollars or purchasing power, had thinned by 8 to 15 percentage points of the nation's population from the days of John F. Kennedy, Lyndon Johnson and Richard Nixon, an unprecedented decline.[1] Each year, especially in the late 1980s, a little more of what citizens perceived as the legacy of America's postwar zenith—great corporations, downtown office towers, famous landmarks and even colleges—was being deeded over to investors in London, Paris, Frankfurt and Tokyo, cities the average

American tourist, in turn, couldn't afford to visit because the U.S. dollar bought so little. Meanwhile, the blue-collar middle class, once large, was receding with disturbing rapidity from the old steel, rubber and auto towns that had earlier symbolized U.S. industrial prowess— places like Detroit, Pittsburgh, Youngstown, Akron and Flint, now themselves fading. Some of these workers could remember, from their own long-ago military service in postwar Germany and Austria, when U.S. captains and corporals had barracked in Bavarian castles, when the dollar was king and when a pack of American cigarettes brought even more than dollars could buy. Only a little more than a generation later, families of U.S. enlisted personnel stationed locally were poor enough to qualify for public assistance in some parts of the booming German Federal Republic.

Even in the United States, the median U.S. family income, $35,000 in 1990, no longer assured the middle-class status and life-style that median earnings had brought ordinary households twenty or thirty years earlier. The end of American exceptionalism—of the unique advantages of being American—was closing in on more and more of those without capital, skills or education who still dreamed yesteryear's dream. Household purchasing power was eroding more than federal inflation statistics acknowledged. For more and more families, educational and medical costs were climbing faster than incomes, and together with rising federal, state and local taxes, they ravaged nominal earnings figures and turned the middle-class "squeeze" into something worse: a slow, economic retreat that most of its victims could not comprehend. Worry about this slippage and what it might foreshadow for future prosperity was unfocused, although discussion began to intensify during the 1992 elections. Optimists pointed out that America had survived crises before—it would survive this one, too.

Besides, many middle-class Americans were not entirely comfortable with the idea that their problems had become the nation's new bellwether. Images from television and Hollywood—and even the 1980s reassurances of a Hollywood president—reinforced this uncertainty. So did the renewed concern about the poor focused by 1992's urban riots. For most of the twentieth century, the middle class had grown larger and stronger; the conventional images of economic hardship and need were mostly low-income cityscapes—immigrants packed nine to a room, women dead in Manhattan's 1911 Triangle fire clutching $10-a-week pay envelopes, four-generation families in the rat-and-cockroach-infested galleries of the South Bronx. Since the Depression, to be sure, rural portraits also qualified: California agricultural labor camps overcrowded with migrants from the Oklahoma dust bowl, Kentucky's coal-seamed Cumberland Mountains, and the flat, heat-shimmered poverty of the Mississippi Delta. Fear in Mall City didn't really count. No one ever repossessed the future on Maplewood Terrace. Tree-lined suburban streets were a land of plenty.

Yet the 1980s and 1990s began to produce some surprisingly different pictures. Across broad swaths of charcoal-grill and lawnmower America, the middle class was in trouble. Decay and even poverty were expanding into new precincts. Suburbia, now home for the first time to a majority of the national population, was exactly where the American Dream was increasingly at risk. In late 1989 and 1990, real family income and purchasing power began to decline. By the end of 1992 it was clear that the economic stagnation of the Bush years had wiped out the small gains of the 1980s; median household income fell 3.5 percent in 1991, after adjustment for inflation, leaving the average family worse off than it was when George Bush took office in January 1989. The statistics of middle-class erosion were startling, as we shall see. Welfare, food stamps and unemployment lines soon came to suburbs and high-tech centers, where a few years earlier such pain had seemed impossible.

The unlucky Bush administration presided over the lowest economic growth rate of any four-year regime since Herbert Hoover's. In February 1992 the California State Department of Finance contended that the state's 1990–91 job decline, the worst since the 1930s, had been misrepresented by federal authorities, who said only 160,000 jobs had been lost. State records showed that the true loss had been over 500,000 jobs. Similar figures in New York showed 400,000 jobs lost in 1990–91 beyond what had been acknowledged by Washington.[2] During the 1992 presidential election, real unemployment in these states was probably in double digits, though official calculations remained artificially low. Wall Street economists were predicting the nineties would have the lowest overall expansion rate since the Depression thirties. Citizens heard experts repeatedly warn that many of the jobs were lost forever, even with nominal recovery. Economic polarization and discomfort were seeping further into the life of the average American family, and as the future of the middle class slowly became a political issue, warnings abounded.

Fear in the Urbanoid Village

Economists, urbanologists, demographers and sociologists all added their voices. Dire forecasts of some Cassandras would prove premature or wrong, but they were not implausible. Something new *was* in the wind.

As the post-1989 economy stagnated, with the recession deepening into what some described as the longest downturn since the 1930s, polltakers reported an extraordinary degree of popular concern about America's prospects. In late 1991, 63 percent told NBC sample-takers that the United States was in decline. Survey after survey reported citizens' concern that the next generation—their own children—would not live as well as theirs. Then in 1992 another sampling reported a more immediate disquiet: 55 percent of Americans said that children in America now were worse off than when the person asked was growing up.[3]

Economically or technologically, that simply wasn't true. But there were other measurements by which it *was* true, which fanned the concerns of parents and social scientists alike. Marc Miringoff, director of New York's Fordham University Institute for Innovation in Social Policy, announced in 1992 that his national Index of Social Health—a monitor of seventeen problems ranging from child abuse to the percentage of Americans without health insurance—had dropped to record lows. On a scale of 100, it had fallen from 68 when the numbers were first compiled in 1970 to 39 in 1988 and 33 in 1989. Five problems, said Miringoff, had never been worse: child abuse, teen suicide, the chasm between rich and poor, the percentage of people who have no health insurance and the portion of their own money that people over sixty-five were obliged to spend on doctors' bills.[4] A month later, Berry Brazelton, professor emeritus of pediatrics at the Harvard School of Medicine, told the World Congress on Child Health that society in the United States was breaking down, with children in poorer communities becoming infected with a sense of self-destruction while middle-class two-earner families were pushed beyond their capacities to function.[5]

Consumer specialists, in turn, had begun predicting an end to the Age of Consumption that had begun around 1900 in favor of a new, subdued spending ethic. Increased dependence on proliferating discount stores would be an important hallmark of the new frugality. Pawnshops were also booming, as chains like Texas-based Cash America Investments set up facilities in middle- and lower-middle-class shopping centers across the no-longer-buoyant Sun Belt.

More and more people, experts said, would be bunking in and commuting from remote stucco dormitories like Moreno Valley, California, seventy miles east of Los Angeles along a clogged freeway. One local urbanologist called Moreno Valley "the cruelest suburb of them all."[6] Between 1980 and 1990 its population had soared from 28,000 to 119,000, lured by comparatively cheap (and adequate) family housing. But the amenities in such places were so limited—mostly food markets, fast-food emporia, auto-parts and hardware stores—that Mayor Barbara Sigmund of affluent Princeton, New Jersey, called them "urbanoid villages." The young breadwinners, just twenty-eight years old on average and with $35,000–$50,000 family incomes, spent so much travel time in their cars that some child-care centers were open from 4:00 A.M. to midnight to accommodate the estimated 71 percent of the work force who were commuters. "People come to Moreno Valley for the American Dream, but for a lot of them it becomes the American nightmare," said Theresa Canady, vice chair of the city Planning Commission. "A lot of people hardly get to spend any time with their families."[7]

Established, close-in suburbia—the big, roomy houses on cheery tree-lined streets—was becoming unaffordable, especially for young families. In some of the most fashionable areas, from New York to California, the 1990 Census found the populations aging—and declining. Frank Levy, the incomes demographer, reported in 1991 that Americans aged thirty-five to forty-four, moving into middle age, were only half as wealthy, on an inflation-adjusted basis, as their parents had been at the same age. That disparity in assets, he predicted, would *worsen* as the United States moved into the twenty-first century.[8]

Many economists predicted that family income data for the early- to mid-1990s would extend the polarization of the 1980s, when the prime beneficiaries, the top 1 percent of Americans, a million families, increased their inflation-adjusted income by a whopping 50 to 75 percent. The next 4 percent gained a respectable 25 percent, but below that, gains tapered toward stagnation. Worse still, these were *nominal* gains; gains that had been further reduced—or turned into losses—by state and federal taxes and other increased costs exceeding the official calculations.

The erosion of the middle class cataloged during the 1980s was projected to continue. In early 1992 the Joint Economic Committee of Congress reported that while two-parent families on average had made slight gains from 1979 to 1989, "fully 80% of these families are on a treadmill—they saw their net family income decline over the past decade, or grow by a smaller percentage than did their hours of work."[9] The Congressional Budget Office calculated that middle-income families with children would have lower inflation-adjusted after-tax incomes in 1992—$29,500—than they had in 1980 ($30,900).[10] And the University of Michigan's Survey Research Center Panel Study of Income Dynamics forecast continued middle-class slippage: "The probability of falling from middle-income to lower-income status increased significantly after 1980. . . . The middle-class decline documented in our study may well continue into the 1990s. The recession of 1990–92 should further retard upward mobility for lower-income adults, while causing many borderline cases to fall into poverty."[11]

State-level analyses produced more negative results. From New York and Massachusetts to Illinois and California, official tax compilations published in 1991 and 1992 showed that in the 1980s the share of income going to the top 1 percent, 5 percent or 10 percent ballooned while what went to the middle 40 percent or 60 percent shrank. And as these statistics built up, concern about the disparities grew, and so did local demand for more progressive state income taxes.*

According to a study by three Census Bureau economists, the United States by the mid-1980s had the largest gap between rich and poor among the major Western nations.[12] Still another survey found that the United States had a much smaller middle-income group than countries like Sweden, Norway, Germany, Switzerland and Holland.[13] The irony was heavy: Was the once-egalitarian United States becoming more stratified and polarized than Europe—and what would it mean?

Housing analysts, in turn, warned that home ownership was losing its half-century meaning as a piggy bank for the American dream. In many parts of the country, single-family homes, the principal repository of middle-class net worth, were either (a) continuing to lose value in absolute terms or (b) gaining nominal value but lagging behind the rate of inflation. The Mortgage Bankers Association reported that in 1990 the amount borrowed against the average American home rose to 57.5 percent of its value, possibly the highest ever, reducing homeowners' equity by $300 billion or 16 percent—the biggest drop on record.[14] Price declines were also steep in some areas—in places like Southern California home values fell 20 to 40 percent from their 1989 peaks to 1992, especially when adjusted for inflation.

Large, aging chunks of suburbia were forecast to rot. Urbanologists like Roosevelt University's Pierre DeVise predicted that more older,

*See Chapter 5.

declining locales would swell the list of 500 suburban jurisdictions (out of 6,500) characterized as poor in 1989. This could expand the 9.5 million suburbanites already below the poverty line, a majority of them white and 36 percent of them children.[15]

Residents of even affluent suburbs began to see a new uncertainty and risk. In late 1990, 23 percent of the unemployment claims in Massachusetts were being filed by workers with a college education and a technical or professional background; and in the high-tech corridor along once-fabled Route 128, 37 percent of the jobless were such workers—a rate officials said they had never seen before.[16] In greater Phoenix, Arizona, 54 percent of new welfare applicants had never received assistance before.[17] Laid-off executives in high-tech Salem, New Hampshire, forced to borrow money to pay their real estate taxes from the town welfare officers, found themselves repaying the loans with blue-collar municipal labor. As winter set in in late 1991, Philadelphia authorities reported thousands of middle-class families they'd never seen before applying for public assistance to pay their heating bills. In the warmer suburbs of Southern California, mortgage foreclosures set all-time records. "This is the worst I've ever seen it in Southern California," said James Cornwall, president of a trustee firm that handles foreclosures for Home Savings of America. "Even during the recessions of the early '70s and '80s, we never saw this many homes going under."[18] In early 1992 greater Chicago suburban homeless shelters reported 50 percent increases in use over the previous year. The director of the Illinois Coalition to End Homelessness said, "Homelessness has finally caught up with the suburbs. All indications say that the problem has only begun its cycle stages."[19] In the suburbs of Atlanta the Horseshoe Bend Country Club launched a job-hunting program to aid unemployed members.[20]

Circumstances like these, unseen in prior post–World War II recessions, created a sense of foreboding. Suburbia was no longer economic high ground, relatively safe from the cyclical storms that moved through factory and farm districts; this time, in some metropolitan areas, suburbia—which now, after all, housed a majority of the nation's population—was bearing the brunt. Local analyses by *The Philadelphia Inquirer* made just that case. Between January 1990 and January 1992, unemployment rose by 39.6 percent in the city but grew by over 50 percent in suburban Bucks, Delaware and Montgomery counties. Meanwhile, 1991 applications for state mortgage assistance rose by 16 percent in Philadelphia versus 58 percent to 107 percent in the three suburban counties. Sheriff's foreclosures in Philadelphia were up 13 percent from the last quarter of 1990 to the last quarter of 1991; in suburban counties, the increase ranged from 48 percent to 146 percent.[21]

Times were tougher in suburbia, experts said, for three reasons: the greater vulnerability of companies and jobs there than in the already weakened cities, the indebtedness and financial precariousness of the mobile middle class after the expansion of the 1980s, and the perils of owning houses bought at peak prices just as values began to sink. Timothy Smeeding, author of *Whither the Middle Class?*, suggested that "the blow may have fallen hardest in the suburbs because white-collar professionals who live in the city 'are much more likely to be working for governments, or businesses closely related to governments, like bankruptcy lawyers or lawyers helping people refinance their house, or in the health-care sector, which is the only growing set of jobs.' "[22]

In metropolitan Chicago, the biggest proportionate surge in aid to families with dependent children and medical assistance came in the suburbs. During 1991 AFDC payments rose an average of 16.4 percent in Chicago's so-called collar counties compared with 7.8 percent in Cook County, which includes the city itself. "It's more than humiliation. It's close to devastation," said Nanci Vanderwell, president of the board of directors of Northwest Community Services in Elk Grove Village. "This is the thing that could not happen. They think 'we're out in the suburbs, we have a home or a condo or a nice apartment, this isn't supposed to happen to us.' "[23] Polling in suburban Maricopa County, Arizona, encompassing Phoenix, found that by early 1992 the highest ratio of complaints about job losses or income declines were coming among the affluent upper-middle class.[24] And in Texas, as a middle-class wave expanded the state's welfare, food stamp and Medicaid rolls, some of the biggest 1991 increases came in the Dallas area, with suburban counties like Denton and Rockwall leading the way. "What we're seeing is a lot of previously middle-class people coming to our offices," said Jerome Lindsay, regional administrator for the Human Services Department. "They considered themselves taxpayers and didn't think they would ever need our services."[25]

Other suburban areas worried about turning into prosperous but embarrassed Du Page County, Illinois, where stunned officials in late 1990 counted 363 homeless young people between the ages of sixteen and twenty.[26] And then there was suburban Jefferson County, Colorado, outside Denver, where emergency shelters and food banks were swamped in the winter of 1990–91: "People are living in homes they can't sell," said Nancy Osborne, Jeffco Action Center director. "They have no furniture. They have no food."[27]

Food itself was increasingly becoming a mainstay of public assistance. By November 1991, 24.56 million Americans—virtually one in ten—were receiving federal food stamps. "This litany of need," said the chairman of the House of Representatives Select Committee on Hunger, "continues to document the erosion of the American middle class."[28] In many prosperous suburbs of Boston, unprecedented numbers of unemployed engineers and executives found themselves turning for assistance to charitable food pantries—some of which set up hidden side entrances for those humiliated and embarrassed.[29] Outside Washington, D.C., rich suburban Fairfax County charted the area's largest 1991 rise in free hot lunches and in applications to qualify for them. The county's food-services director said, "Some of the people coming in today are people who never thought they would end up in this situation. They probably had a good job and were laid off. The first thing they try to take care of is their children."[30]

Many restaurateurs, especially fast-food purveyors, announced plans to move downscale during the nineties, tailoring lower-priced menus to families needing cheap food but having no time to prepare it themselves. Marketers warned their corporate clients: The stereotyped middle class is shrinking; the sub-middle class is growing. Marissa Piesman, coauthor of *The Yuppie Handbook,* predicted the emergence of the "schleppy"—a person off the fast track who is "living with less grandiose expectations and accepting limitations."[31]

Demographers offered yet another warning. Millions of women—mothers, wives and sisters—had entered the work force during the 1980s, sacrificing leisure time within the family and accepting a reduced quality of life in order to provide additional paychecks essential to keeping their families afloat. The problem in the 1990s, the experts said, was that few families still had nonworking women available to bolster purchasing power for another weak decade.

Personnel experts had their own dire predictions. Even before General Motors announced that 15,000 of its 99,000 salaried positions would be eliminated between 1991 and 1993, placement firms calculated that millions more white-collar workers, professionals and managers in companies all across the country would lose their jobs during the 1990s, following the 1.5 million discharged in the 1980s. Moreover, worsening international competitiveness pressures meant most of the jobs lost would never come back. As the corporate hemorrhage accelerated, the authoritative newsletter *Workplace Trends* reported that, on average, 2,700 permanent jobs had been cut each day in the third quarter of 1991.[32] Editor Dan Lacey prophesied that corporate downsizing would continue through the decade: "This is not just a recession. This is the end of a 40-year boom. Everything we consider to be a normal workplace relationship is not—it is a postwar boom relationship."[33] He predicted that by the year 2000 the nation's top 500 companies would reduce their payrolls by an additional several million workers. Fortune 500 corporations would be lopping off assistant vice presidents and marketing coordinators as cold-bloodedly as they had discharged highly paid blue-collar and production-line workers in the early 1980s.

Young people, in particular, would face a new and harsher employment world, experts said. Pay and prospects for high school graduates had been eroding for over a decade, and wages for white-collar workers were beginning to follow blue-collar wages in decline. In 1992 the Economic Policy Institute reported that wages of college graduates fell 3.1 percent in real terms between 1987 and 1991. "Having a college degree," the institute said, "no longer affords protection against falling wage trends."[34] Against the competition of so many unemployed older persons competing for jobs, Samuel Ehrenhalt, regional director of the Bureau of Labor Statistics, warned in 1992 that "College graduates are facing the toughest job market in a half-century in the New York region."[35]

There were plenty of upbeat counterassertions as well. The overall U.S. economy and per capita incomes were certain to expand, economists said. The improved productivity painfully achieved in manufacturing could spread to services. It wouldn't be hard for the decade's growth rate to exceed low expectations, and even some relative pessimists predicted a boom in the second half of the nineties. Most Americans still believed they had greater opportunities than their parents had. Polls made that clear. And even declining housing prices had a silver lining; they would make home ownership more affordable.

But the near-term picture was definitely a shade of gray. For almost three decades after World War II a rising tide had lifted virtually all boats. However, from the late 1970s to the early 1990s, a more discriminatory international economic realignment occurred, one that favored persons with capital, education and skills at the expense of those less well endowed. And with two thirds of Americans psychologically self-enlisted in the middle class, a significant minority faced a real threat of downward mobility. Jobs and Maplewood Terrace were at stake together. Yet the traumas of economic slippage cataloged by authors like Barbara Ehrenreich and Katherine Newman were only starting to translate into politics.[36] At first, people affected didn't know which party or ideology to blame, just as those losing ground in the boom years of 1927 or 1928—and there were many—hadn't known until the battering of the Great Depression provided the answer.

The new decade's first confrontation over emergent wealth issues came in October 1990, when the Bush administration, having agreed to higher taxes, found itself on the defensive over *whose* taxes were going to go up. Republicans found themselves labeled protectors of the rich, fell into temporary disrepute with some of those who were not rich, and lost ten points in some party-identification surveys.* That image, an old Republican weakness, angered voters until it was super-seded by the excitement over the Persian Gulf.

But autumn's budget acrimony had raised questions that would persist and grow in the larger political debate of the 1990s. Was the unfolding crisis of the middle class unavoidable, the relentless corol-lary of global economic and technological change, or was it aggravated by Republican favoritism to the top 1 percent of the population? Were Americans suffering the effects of a historic shift in wealth and its distribution, or were their politicians to blame for mishandling na-tional assets? When the middle class finally decided, the political impli-cations would not end in Washington (or Albany and Sacramento); they would echo around the world.

That was because the middle classes of great economic powers have a special significance. A generation earlier, the size and wealth of the postwar American middle class had matched and then surpassed those of history's two previous bourgeois zeniths—seventeenth-century Hol-land and late-nineteenth-century England. At its peak, back in the "happy days" of the 1950s and the early 1960s, the American middle class was hardly an expression of high culture, but neither was the Holland of smug, pipe-smoking Calvinist burghers nor the England of Victorian frumpery and humming new machinery whose beneficiaries, in the title of R. F. Delderfield's famous novel, assumed that "God is an Englishman." The suburbs of Detroit and Kansas City, equally sure in 1954 that He was an American, played a similar historical role. All three middle-class societies were world-class successes, and just as important, the weakening and polarization of the earlier two had been ill omens for their countries' international as well as domestic effec-

---

*The damage was severe enough that from roughly October 15 to October 25, when Con-gress finished the budget agreement and left town, media reports had begun to speak of Republican candidates being in "free fall."

tiveness. Against this backdrop, the erosion and deepening frustration of the U.S. middle class as the 1990s began suggested a national trend that also had global importance.

The Post–World War II Heyday
of the U.S. Middle Class

Nearly a half century earlier the American middle class of the late 1940s was the economic wonder of a still-war-ravaged world and dwarfed any predecessors, even the boom-fed U.S. middle class of the 1920s. Victory in World War II had been its crucible. The upbeat Americans flooding into such new postwar suburbs as Levittown, New York, and Oak Lawn, Illinois, celebrating a victory over Adolf Hitler, imperial Japan *and* the Great Depression, represented a milestone: the most broadly based middle class that the world had ever seen. Its emergence and America's zenith went together.

In his mid-century best-seller *The Big Change: 1900–1950,* social historian Frederick Lewis Allen looked back on the prosperity of the Roaring Twenties and dismissed it, by comparison, as small potatoes. For most Americans in the 1920s the money for stocks, refrigerators and new Dodge cars really hadn't been there. Compilations by the Brookings Institution showed a mere 2.3 percent of American families with incomes over $10,000 a year in 1929, and only 8 percent in the broader but still-comfortable category of those earning over $5,000. On the dark side, 71 percent had family incomes below $2,500, 60 percent under $2,000, 42 percent below $1,500 and 21 percent under $1,000.[37] What made this inadequate, Brookings researchers emphasized, was that "at 1929 prices, a family income of $2,000 may be regarded as sufficient to supply only basic necessities."[38] This estimate exaggerated cash requirements for the many Americans still living on farms, but the purchasing-power caveat was valid: the America of flappers, bathtub gin and Pierce-Arrows had been more middle-class in its dreams than in its disposable dollars. Too large a percentage of households was still poor. Middle-class incomes were a small minority.

By 1950 this was no longer true. Data published by the Joint Economic Committee of Congress for 1948, when prices were only a third above 1929 levels, found that the percentage of families with annual incomes below $1,000 had dropped by half to 10.6 percent. Those subsisting in the $1,000–$2,000 yearly range shrank from just under 40 percent to 14.5 percent. Upward movement was everywhere. Some 20.6 percent of 1948 families had yearly receipts between $2,000 and

$3,000, and a much larger 33.6 percent earned $3,000 to $5,000.[39] The latter group, growing rapidly, from 1.2 million in 1928 to 14 million in 1948, was the foundation of an incipient middle-class majority.[40]

At the top, families making over $5,000 a year nearly tripled from 8 percent to 20.8 percent. Within that category, though, the surprising revelation was that the upper-middle and upper-class component, the Packard-and-country-club group making over $10,000, had remained almost constant—2.3 percent in 1929, 2.9 percent in 1948. The real explosion—the one that would redefine America and affect the entire world—occurred among the solid, stereotypical middle-class families with $5,000 to $10,000 a year. From just 5.7 percent in 1929, they swelled to 17.9 percent in 1948.[41]

Social chronicler Allen called this new alignment "the central fact of prosperity [in 1952] . . . Millions of families in our industrial cities and towns, and on the farms, have been lifted from poverty or near poverty to a status where they can enjoy what has traditionally been considered a middle-class way of life."[42] The National Bureau of Economic Research called it "one of the great social revolutions of history."[43] Fleshing out over another two decades, it would carry hundreds of millions of children and grandchildren of Alabama sharecroppers, Montana copper miners, Boston Irish policemen and Hungarian-American steelworkers in Pittsburgh to scarcely imagined affluence. By 1973 inflation-adjusted U.S. median family incomes had doubled those of 1948. Not even the richest European countries could come close. America's middle-class Golden Era was under way.

While no single factor explains this phenomenon, America's all-powerful postwar economy—the massive industrial, financial and trade supremacy that followed America's success in arms—was the decisive prerequisite. From mid-Depression 1932 to 1950, the U.S. share of world manufacturing ballooned from 31.8 percent to 44.7 percent, and trade followed suit. Such lopsided international economic preeminence, whether Britain's global trade and industrial dominance of the 1850s and the 1860s or Holland's trade leadership two centuries earlier (when New York was still New Amsterdam), is an unmistakable dynamo of middle-class expansion.* The achievement of the U.S. mid-

---

*Chapter 8 describes the peak years of U.S., British and Dutch economic, industrial and commercial power and how these golden eras overlapped with middle-class values and prosperity. Books like Paul Kennedy's *The Rise and Fall of the Great Powers* have singled out the precedents of Holland and Britain, along with (sixteenth-century) Hapsburg Spain, from a strategic, military and fiscal standpoint. But the vital importance of the zenith and then erosion of the middle class as great powers rise and fall deserves more attention. Even

dle class in the late 1940s was a wonder, but it wasn't unique. Neither was the vulnerability that would be so apparent by the 1990s.

The Central Role of the Middle Class in Great-Power Zeniths

Not only has the global success of a great economic power been a catalyst for the expansion of its middle class, but the reverse also has been true. Outbursts of bourgeois spirit and inventiveness, the triumph of middle-class values over those of established elites, have often prodded countries toward peaks of economic and political achievement. When these same nations have later turned away from these values, when the elites have again triumphed over the middle classes, the results have been inauspicious.

The rise of the Dutch republic of the early seventeenth century reflected the revolution a generation earlier that had liberated Holland's Protestant merchants, traders and sea captains from Catholic, aristocratic Hapsburg Spain. In *The Embarrassment of Riches,* historian Simon Schama explains Holland's golden-era culture as "shared, in large measure, by that very broad stratum of the populations between artisans and trading merchants that in England would have been known as 'the middling sort'; in Holland the *brede middenstand.*"[44] "The Republic was an island of plenty in an ocean of want. Its artisans, even its unskilled workers and its farmers (for it seems a misnomer to call them peasants) enjoyed higher real incomes, better diets and safer livelihoods than [people] anywhere else on the continent."[45] Another scholar, noting that the "neatness, order, cleanliness of their urban life and its physical sophistication entranced and amazed Europe," credited the "prudent, self-satisfied, unostentatious" Calvinist merchants and burgomasters for indelibly stamping the persona of their class on Dutch society.[46]

A triumphant middle class also characterized mid-nineteenth-century Britain. By 1860, "with 2% of the world's population and 10 percent of Europe's, the United Kingdom . . . had a capacity in modern industries equal to 40–45 percent of the world's potential and 55–60 percent of that in Europe."[47] Industrial workers naturally predominated, so that one 1867 estimate identified just one citizen in five as middle-class (and even this calculus included all artisans, officeworkers

Spain was starting to generate a significant middle class in its early- to mid-sixteenth-century zenith, but soon lost it—at great long-term cost.

and supervisory workers).[48] But in spirit, mid-century Britain was indisputably Europe's preeminent middle-class country. Not only was its middle-class population proportionately larger than elsewhere in Europe, but, more important, the values of this class dominated British government and opinion. Continental visitors had long characterized Britain as a "nation of shopkeepers" or marveled at the importance of "the honest middle class, that precious portion of nations."[49] And this tendency increased in the 1840s and 1850s after Sir Robert Peel, son of a Lancashire cotton master, and William E. Gladstone, son of a Liverpool merchant, became prime ministers.

A painful reconfirmation of the cultural and economic stimulus provided by the Dutch of the "golden era" and the British middle class of the mid-nineteenth century came years later when entrepreneurs in both countries gave way to speculators, rentiers and other passive investors who lived off capital, not enterprise. Whether in Holland circa 1700 or Britain circa 1900, this class was not reluctant to invest its guilders and pounds sterling abroad when more money could be made from the industry of a rival nation. As I shall show in Chapter 8, such transitions in a nation's history often foreshadow trouble—declining manufacturing competitiveness, stagnant real wages, increased economic polarization and early worries over declining world-power status.

In the United States of the Reagan boom years, the analogy was self-evident yet broadly dismissed. Too few policymakers, caught up in the new enthusiasm for wealth, investment and financial elites, wanted to remember that America's own golden era, spanning the "good war" of 1941–45, the "best years" of 1945–50, and the "happy days" of 1950–60 had been marked by an aggressive, even egalitarian middle-class culture. Once the 1929 Crash had soured the reputation of Republican politicians, speculative finance, established wealth and what would later be called "trickle-down" economics, more assertive democratic values took hold in the 1930s, and they continued to dominate U.S. politics and society for a quarter century after the war.

In short, the crucial transformation of the United States, which made it possible for Americans to overcome the Depression and then secure the benefits of World War II, was political and social as well as economic. We have seen how the income gap between rich and poor narrowed between 1929 and 1948 as some 20 to 30 percent of the U.S. population climbed into the middle class, roughly doubling its ranks. By 1950, class differences were also declining in clothing, automobiles, food and even personal hygiene. Revealingly, and despite the postwar boom, the great rich (with incomes over $1 million a year), estimated at 600 in 1929, declined to approximately 130 by 1948.[50] The rich were now Hollywood's villains, while the heroes were usually honest middle-class achievers. Popular culture in the United States, Frederick Lewis Allen wrote, had learned to express popular recriminations over the Crash and the Depression:

> Among the sons and daughters of the rich there is a vague, surviving guilt complex: an embarrassed consciousness that during the Depression great numbers of people were resentful of their way of life and suspicious of the origin of the funds that made it possible. This guilt complex takes many forms, and one of them is a preference for the sort of entertainment which won't seem to involve putting on airs. The same is true in some degree of people in the upper echelons of a business organization: so aware are they of the distrust of them which unionism fosters that they go out of their way at a company party to show that they have no princely delusions.[51]

Such anti-elite attitudes held the maximum U.S. personal income tax bracket at or near 91 percent from World War II until 1964, and partly as a result, between 1929 and 1945, the share of U.S. national income going to the top 1 percent of Americans—over $16,000 a year—shrank from 13 percent to 7 percent, and that of the top 5 percent—over $8,000—dipped from 28 percent to 17 percent.[52] As the rich were squeezed, the middle class advanced.* Egalitarianism and economic growth seem to have gone together. Meanwhile, the puritanical emphasis introduced into politics by the Depression also helped keep down both interest rates and financial speculation. And even when the Republicans captured Congress and the presidency in 1952, White House strategists declined to seek reduction of the 91 percent top personal income tax rate. The United States, at the heart of the mid-twentieth-century world, was militantly middle-class, bourgeois, burgerlijk, in the style of early Victorian Britain and seventeenth-century Holland. Few people wanted to bring back the well-remembered extremes—either the undertaxed, overspeculating millionaires of the 1920s or the lines of unemployed waiting at the soup kitchens of the 1930s. A generation later, as these values eroded, as the middle class lost ground and stratification returned, the United States began to lose a vital national force.

---

*By 1990, conversely, as the middle class declined, the top 1 percent of Americans *regained* the 13 percent of national income they had in 1929.

First Whiffs of "Middle-Class Decline"

The 1950s were the last indisputably "good decade" for the American middle class. Economically, the middle class continued to expand in the 1960s, particularly in the rapidly urbanizing South and Sun Belt. But the culture of the new decade was propelled by a reemerging national desire for excitement, by youthful rebellion against smug middle-class mores, by the civil rights revolution and by a rekindling fascination with elites, sparked by the new president, John F. Kennedy, his Vassar-educated, Social Register wife, and a White House full of Harvard's best and brightest. Sophisticates dismissed the Eisenhower 1950s for suburban dullness and stagnation.

The excitability of the 1960s spread even to Wall Street. The stock market was one institution the Eisenhower years had energized, and speculation crept back with go-go money managers, men like Jim Ling and the conglomerate movement, accelerating as the Dow-Jones Industrial Average touched the 1000 mark for the first time in 1966. Poverty became a chic social cause (and less of a chastening family memory), and by the end of the sixties Southampton and Manhattan millionaires were holding cocktail parties for grape pickers and Black Panthers. Cosmopolitan secret agent James Bond, with his insistence on shaken, not stirred, martinis, had displaced beer-drinking private eye Mike Hammer. *The Saturday Evening Post*—with its Norman Rockwell covers of quilt-robed, hair-curlered wives in station wagons dropping husbands at suburban railroad stations—went out of business.

But if the middle class of the 1960s had gone out of fashion, if it was under siege by the Vietnam War protesters and the other youthful rebels, it was still prosperous, still getting richer and bigger. Yet here, too, important storm clouds were gathering. Inflation resulting from the war in Vietnam and other federal borrowing and the consequent budget deficits was about to bring the steady postwar economic gains to a halt. In 1973 petroleum producers from Arabia to Latin America, unwilling to watch 5–6 percent annual inflation erode the $4 per barrel they were being paid for their oil, doubled their price over the next two years and helped throw the United States into a severe recession.

We now know that the resulting stagflation brought real family income growth more or less to an end. Figure 1, a picture worth a page of technical explanations, shows how median family income, climbing since the end of World War II, began to flatten in 1973. And with some ups and downs, family and household income has remained on that

Figure 1. The Stagnation of American Prosperity Since 1973

Median Family Income, 1967–1990 (in 1991 Dollars)

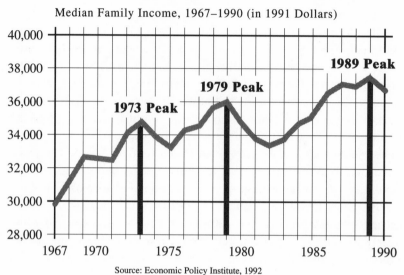

Source: Economic Policy Institute, 1992

Perception and Reality in Household Incomes

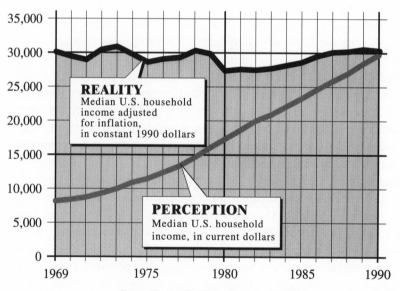

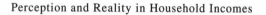

Source: *The New York Times*, November 17, 1991

Figure 1. (continued)

Private-Production Workers' Average Weekly Earnings, 1947–1989
(in 1982 Dollars)

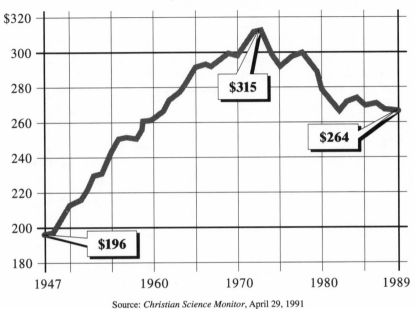

Source: *Christian Science Monitor*, April 29, 1991

plateau ever since.* Calculations of after-tax income were even more dismaying, as we shall see. Other yardsticks—such as real manufacturing wages—began showing outright decline. Moreover, stagflation fed social disruption, so that by the late 1960s and early 1970s, divorces, drug use and hemlines were rising alongside inflation, interest rates and debt. To a sizable minority of Americans, middle-class values were something to be mocked, although the Republican party was starting to discover and build a contrary-minded presidential "new majority" determined to hold fast to the values under siege.

Unfortunately, 1960s America was turning down a familiar pathway. Great prosperity and the cosmopolitanism that accompanied it had undercut middle-class values and initiative before: certainly in Holland's eighteenth-century "periwig" era, then again in luxury-craving Edwardian England, weary of Victorian pieties. The precedents for the United States were all too relevant, as Chapter 8 will show.

*Median family income does have shortcomings as a measurement, which are discussed in Chapter 4. Unfortunately, as that discussion will amplify, the alternative measurements also have weaknesses.

By the late 1980s some concerned Americans had begun to invoke the warnings made in the early twentieth century by former British colonial secretary Joseph Chamberlain, who had judged his own country at risk for reorienting itself toward finance, distribution and other services instead of manufacturing, and for becoming more divided between rich and poor and less self-sufficient.[53] Nor, he said, could a great power avoid competitive deterioration simply because its people had new leisure-time opportunities and conveniences and were richer. Spain and Holland, he added, were richer in the early twentieth century than they had been during their great years, but had lost their once-unique importance.[54]

Many of the new pressures that Americans were feeling in their household accounts were related to a somewhat similar transformation and relative decline of the United States as a great economic power. While no one could directly blame the decade's "middle-class squeeze"—from tax revolts in Massachusetts to the pain of automobile insurance rates in New Jersey, runaway college tuition and health-care costs everywhere and a federal income tax system that put suburban lawyers and dentists in a higher marginal bracket than millionaires— on America's loss of mid-century economic omnipotence, on its declining egalitarian commitment or on its rising tolerance of debt and speculation, there *was* a link.

The Two-Decade Middle-Class Plateau

By the 1990s, as it became unmistakable that recurrent slow growth was in its third decade, a broader apprehension began taking shape. The American dream had rarely, if ever, languished for so long without a clear sign of revitalization.

At first, to be sure, diminished middle-class headway in the United States after Vietnam and the oil shock had seemed merely temporary. But oil prices and inflation ratcheted up again in 1978–80, raising interest rates and spurring two recessions in 1980 and 1981–82. Real household incomes stagnated. Then, even as business recovered in 1983 and thereafter, economists noticed an unanticipated corollary: wage levels were not rebounding at their usual rate. From the rubber plants of Akron, Ohio, to the copper smelters of Montana, more and more of manufacturing's regional emergency wards began to look like graveyards. More mothers, wives and sisters were obliged to enter the work force to keep their families afloat (or to maintain their halves of broken families). By the mid-1980s, statisticians were mapping another significant negative: this was the first postwar recovery period in which economic inequality continued to *worsen.*

By several other measures, the 1970s marked the onset of a weakness that continued into the 1980s despite the apparent boom. Productivity, one key determinant of prosperity, decelerated in the 1970s, then grew during the 1980s at only one third the improvement rate reached in the 1960s. Unemployment, too, had spiked higher in the seventies than in the sixties; then in the 1980s, the *average* unemployment rate—more than 7 percent—exceeded the annual U.S. rate in all but two of the years between 1950 and 1979. Back in the sixties, 5 percent unemployment had meant recession; the jobless rates of the eighties never dropped that low, even at the peak of the boom.[55] Capacity utilization, the government's yardstick of how fully U.S. factories and facilities are working, fell on a decade-to-decade basis in the seventies and then again in the eighties. As for decade-to-decade growth in real average annual GNP, that had ebbed and flowed as follows: 1940s—4.3 percent; 1950s—3.2 percent; 1960s—3.9 percent; 1970s—2.8 percent; 1980s—2.6 percent.[56] Measured against strong growth periods, the 1980s were substandard, as the 1970s had been. Merrill Lynch's early forecast for the entire 1990s anticipated even more sluggishness—a weak real GNP growth rate in the 2.0 percent range, lowest since the Depression-troubled 1930s.

By late 1990, with a new recession starting to bite, *The New York Times* observed that "for a brief moment in the mid-1980s, it looked as if Americans would again know how it feels to get ahead." Instead, wage and income gains proved short-lived, and in the early 1990s real incomes dropped again.[57] The median family incomes for 1990 and 1991 fell back to late-1970s levels when adjusted for inflation and taxes. According to other measurements, households were losing headway not only in terms of income but in *wealth*—this even before the real estate and financial-assets implosion of 1990–92. In a 1991 study entitled *The Economic Future of American Families,* incomes experts Frank Levy and Richard Michel calculated that during the 1970s and 1980s, real new wealth per family had expanded at only a 0.4 percent average annual rate, with gains concentrated among mature home-owning and stock-owning upper-bracket families.[58] The Federal Reserve Board study published in 1992 made the same point. As we have seen, members of the thirty-five–forty-four age group, collectively, were little more than half as wealthy (in constant dollars) as their parents—postwar America's prime beneficiaries—had been at the same age. Those younger were worse off. And Levy and Michel predicted the disparity would widen as the "baby boomers" approached retirement age in 2020 or 2025. For the 1984–88 period alone, the Census Bureau reported that the median net worth of all households—assets minus debts—declined by 4 percent.[59] Rising household debt was an important negative. The most prosperous Americans, of course, greatly increased their net worth during this period.*

Levy and other scholars have taken 1973 as the year when family and household income began to flatten, giving the stagnation process a generally accepted starting point. The weakness of the 1970s is little disputed; the economic circumstances of the 1980s, however, are far more complex, the stuff from which long debates and intense statistical disputes flow. For example, the small 1980–89 increase in inflation-adjusted middle-class incomes, at first much emphasized by the Bush administration, required discounting in two ways: first, because further adjustments for federal, state and local taxes combined to produce a *decline*, and second, because the *overall* nationwide increase, especially in averages, disguised important variations among component income groups. Growth in after-tax disposable family income was concentrated in a way that made the decade difficult for people in the middle. As we shall later see in more detail, for the 1980s as a whole, those near the top prospered (and the top 1 percent soared), the 40th to 80th percentiles ran in place, and the bottom two fifths lost ground.

On the other hand, too much can be made of how real weekly wages for production and nonsupervisory workers, the principal sustenance of ordinary families, fell slightly in the 1980s, according to data from the federal Bureau of Labor Statistics. Not only were supervisors excluded, but BLS data failed to recognize that many individuals worked second jobs or put in longer hours to avoid economic losses. In circumstance after circumstance, leisure was sacrificed to maintain purchasing power. In 1987 the average U.S. worker put in ninety-five more hours of work per year than in 1979—the equivalent of three and a half extra weeks.[60] Some extended their regular job hours; others moonlighted. To keep ahead, more households needed two workers, and not all had them. Wage earners obviously were not the decade's gainers; that reward went to upper-bracket families who transcended wage or salary dependence with financial and real estate assets that brought in rents, interest, dividends and capital gains.

A high percentage of individual U.S. households simply lost ground. Researchers at the University of Michigan, who had begun tracking

---

*A little bit of math makes the point. Between 1984 and 1988, the net worth of the Forbes 400 richest Americans roughly *doubled,* while the median net worth of the overall population stagnated or declined.

the fortunes of a representative cross section of five thousand American families in 1968, tabulated an ever-larger share that reported a creeping deterioration in purchasing power. Between 1968 and 1972, the earnings of 39 percent of these families fell behind inflation, a share that rose to 43 percent in the period from 1973 to 1977. Then in the tougher years from 1978 to 1982, fully 56 percent of the population fell behind.[61] By the end of the 1980s, according to the Michigan researchers, middle-income ranks were shrinking rapidly. Timothy Smeeding, one of the economists involved in the study, said that "what we are looking at is a permanent decline in the size of the middle class."[62]

Because the rich, in the meantime, were steadily boosting their income and assets, official tabulations revealed an extraordinary trend: the collective income of the elite top 1 percent of Americans was overtaking the combined income of the entire middle 20 percent of the population! In 1977, according to the Congressional Budget Office, the top 1 percent had enjoyed 8.3 percent of national pretax family income versus 16.3 percent for the entire middle quintile. Then by 1980 the top 1 percent commanded 9.2 percent and the middle quintile 16.0 percent. In 1985 the two figures were 11.6 percent and 15.1 percent, and by 1989 the split was 13.0 percent and 14.7 percent.[63] Other tabulations emphasizing capital gains put the share of the top 1 percent in the 14 percent range. For these shares nearly to converge was striking. (Full details appear in Appendix A.)

Explanations of why the top 1 percent had so greatly outpaced the middle ranged from the effect of federal tax cuts favoring the rich to the buoyant influence of conservative economics on financial markets and the inevitable effect of worldwide demand for capital, education and skills. Labor leaders, not surprisingly, emphasized the loss of America's postwar concentration of highly paid manufacturing jobs—the shut doors and shrinking employment in western Pennsylvania steel mills, St. Louis auto plants and Louisiana petrochemical producers as foreign producers invaded one market after another. The loss may or may not have been inevitable, but it surely influenced income distribution. During the postwar quarter century, and even into the 1980s, major unionized manufacturing areas, with their mid-range wage scales, enjoyed less economic inequality than other parts of the country.[64] By contrast, from Miami to Los Angeles, many wealthy service-industry areas—whose economies were based on finance, data processing, communications and retirement—registered local rich-poor gaps approaching those of India and other Third World countries.[65] Services and finance meant polarization, a pattern that Chapter 8 will amplify.

Borrowing

Still other economists tied middle-class stagnation to America's excessive borrowing in the 1980s, when household, corporate and national debt soared. This, too, was a factor. The weight of U.S. family indebtedness, and the consequent reduction of disposable income, will be examined in Chapter 7. As for *national* indebtedness, the combination of heavy U.S. international borrowing, high real interest rates, the overvalued dollar and the rising trade deficit of the early 1980s undercut U.S. manufacturing and blue-collar employment—and this was merely an early effect. The burden that future repayment of debt would have on U.S. living standards was still years from its peak. After calculating that U.S. international indebtedness would reach nearly a trillion dollars by the mid-1990s, Harvard economist Benjamin Friedman indicated that to pay down those obligations, Americans would have to divert overseas 1 to 2 percentage points of national income otherwise spendable at home.[66] Parents found themselves confiding worries to pollsters about a decline in the next generation's living standard, something unprecedented for Americans. To many worried Americans, the economic plateau was starting to look like a downslope.

Admittedly, public economic fears have not been a reliable *long-term* barometer. Historians participating in the debates of the 1970s and 1980s pointed out that America had undergone crises of confidence almost from the start, although there *was* an economic logic to the ebb and flow: pessimism deepened in the 1840s and 1850s, following the economic crash of 1837; it intensified again during the years from 1893 to 1914, and once more in the decade after 1929. David Donald, chairman of Harvard's graduate program on the history of American civilization, summed up the frustrations of 1893–97 and thereafter: "Those in the middle felt threatened, and not just financially, either. There was a sense of squeezed opportunities and expectations, a sense that the rules of the game had changed. The flood of immigrants were Eastern European and Mediterranean, many Jews, and they threatened to be unassimilable. The big gas and oil interests were growing. People had a sense of no longer feeling at home, of not having control."[67] Somewhat similar frustrations returned during the hard times of the 1930s.* For the short term, then, public frustrations have been revealing; it is in the long term that they have been misleading. Bernard Bailyn, a Harvard expert on the colonial period, pointed out that even the Pilgrims thought the American dream was unraveling thirty years after they landed on Plymouth Rock![68]

*Chapter 9 will discuss the frustration politics of the 1890s and 1930s—and how many of those same themes and issues recurred in the early 1990s.

Nevertheless, the apprehension that began in the mid-1970s is probably modern America's most enduring; it surged again at the end of the
decade, and then again in 1983–84 following the recession and a series
of attention-getting books and articles by such liberal economists as
Lester Thurow and Robert Kuttner. To be sure, serious debate during
the 1988 presidential campaign was inhibited by the income gains of
1983–87, as well as by Democratic nominee Michael Dukakis's naive
self-congratulation for an already imploding Massachusetts Miracle.
But by 1990–92 another recession brought new real-income declines
and the plight of the middle class became a central if only superficially
discussed ingredient of the 1992 presidential contest. America's uncertain global economic status added to public nervousness. Nations *do*
peak. Ebbing hegemonies *do* bring stagnation. So let us now turn to
the shaky American middle class of the early 1990s: just who belonged
to it—and, in addition, who had already slid from its ranks or was
about to slide.

The Eroding Middle Class of the Early 1990s

How convenient if neat government statistics could tell political or
market researchers that the middle-class population of Illinois had
dropped from 54 percent in 1980 to 45 percent in 1990, or that Collier
County, Florida, had the nation's highest ratio of middle-class residents—or that middle-class percentages for the United States were
falling well below those for Norway (after being higher in 1950). But
such data don't exist, partly because middle-class status—especially in
the late-twentieth-century United States—depends at least as much on
one's state of mind as on one's bank balance.

Most attempts to calculate the historical emergence of the middle
class have built their guesswork on vocational or income categories.
Such broad estimates have described the middle class as growing from
10 to 20 percent of the population after the Civil War to 20 to 30
percent in 1940. Public opinion polls have also been a source, beginning in the 1930s, and since the 1970s these samplings have generally
shown 55 to 75 percent of Americans categorizing themselves as middle-class, although results vary with the phrasing of the questions.[69]

Imprecision is unavoidable. Surveys in the late 1940s, still swayed by
class consciousness and lingering economic insecurity, found only
37 percent of Americans who identified themselves as middle-class;
even among many of those with obvious upward mobility, working-

class self-identification still prevailed. By the 1990s the problem was the opposite: too many people called themselves middle-class because belonging had become almost obligatory in the national culture. More and more of them were being unrealistic. A look at the changing dollar incomes of the various U.S. economic strata in the late 1970s and 1980s—the top 1 percent, top 5 percent, top 10 percent and the remaining deciles—not only confirms stagnation below the top, but suggests that, for a growing minority of Americans, middle-class self-assessments were becoming illusions.

During the 1980s, as Table 1 shows, the 1 million households in the top 1 percent roared ahead, becoming an increasingly distant "upper," especially in statistical series that included capital gains income, thereby increasing the advantage of the rich.* This is Upper America— or, as one phrasemaker called it, the nation's "overclass." The "class" status of the next 9 percent is harder to call; its upper portions gained substantially, in some ways transcending "the middle class" during the 1980s. But for most Americans in this $80,000–$200,000 category, their incomes were too small to be upper-class compared with the top 1 percent. "Upper-middle class" is a better description.

Table 1. Average Income Level and Effective Federal Tax Rates in Each
Family Decile by Year
[Corporate income tax allocated to capital income]

Decile	1977	1980	1985	1990	1977– 90	1980– 90	1985– 90
		Average income level (in 1988 dollars)			Percent Change		
First	4,277	3,852	3,568	3,805	−11.0	1.2	6.7
Second	8,663	7,982	7,717	8,251	−4.8	3.4	6.9
Third	13,510	12,530	12,230	13,110	−3.7	4.6	7.2
Fourth	18,980	17,240	17,010	18,200	−4.1	5.6	7.0
Fifth	24,520	22,380	22,070	23,580	−3.8	5.4	6.9
Sixth	30,430	28,100	27,620	29,490	−3.1	5.0	6.8
Seventh	36,880	34,370	34,620	36,890	0.0	7.3	6.5
Eighth	44,820	42,050	43,370	46,280	3.3	10.1	6.7
Ninth	56,360	53,660	56,190	59,860	6.2	11.6	6.5
Tenth	111,100	107,900	123,200	133,200	19.9	23.4	8.2
Top 5 percent	149,500	146,000	172,100	187,400	25.4	28.3	8.9
Top 1 percent	319,100	321,400	415,700	463,800	45.4	44.3	11.6
All deciles	34,830	32,850	34,480	37,050	6.4	12.8	7.4

Source: Congressional Budget Office, House Ways and Means Committee, 1992 Green Book.

*Capital gains were not included in the standard calculations of income made by the Census Bureau.

The next 10 percentiles (80th to 89th), spanning 1990 incomes in the $60,000–$80,000 range, constituted the upper reaches of the traditional middle class (especially for residents of metropolitan New York, Washington, Los Angeles or San Francisco, where such incomes did not support upper-middle-class status). Incomes in the lower reaches of this group were precarious for a family with children in Manhattan, but qualified for the solid Oldsmobile-and-charcoal-grill middle class in burgeoning new Sun Belt suburbia. The 60th to 79th percentiles, further down the income ladder at $40,000 to $60,000 a year, could be called "middle-middle class," although such families found it hard to live in affluent locales where housing costs and taxes were punitive.*

As the 1990s got under way, the mid-rank 40th to 59th percentiles posed the most obvious problem of slow attrition: had the median family with its median income actually lost middle-class status and purchasing power? In Nampa, Idaho, or Spartanburg, South Carolina, probably not. But in the richer metropolitan areas, a family of four with an income in the $28,000–$40,000 range simply didn't command the local equivalent of a middle-class life-style. As early as the mid-1980s, incomes experts like Frank Levy were concluding that "being in the middle of the distribution *no longer guaranteed a middle-class income,*" which he calculated was enjoyed by only 45 percent of Americans.[70] In the 20th to 39th deciles, middle-class status was rare; incomes here were stagnating while the costs of maintaining a middle-class life-style were rising. Chapter 7 will further pursue the evidence that the true U.S. middle class has been shrinking, as incomes polarized toward either end of the scale, and as many families at and below the median-income range slipped from middle-class ranks.

Critics do have a point, as we will see, in calling family-income statistics misleading because declining family size has, to a limited extent, enabled these units to make the same money go further. They are likewise correct in contending that median family-income numbers "lose" some of the growth shown in faster-rising per capita income calculations for the same period. Profiles by private marketing firms of the top 20 percent to 25 percent of U.S. households, those enjoying most of the nation's disposable income, unmistakably confirmed the increased buying power so visible circa 1987 in the aisles of Neiman-Marcus, Bloomingdale's and luxury-car dealerships. But very little of this benefited people in the middle. Income growth at the top was big

---

*According to one study, for a 1990 family to match the standard of living $100,000 brought in Minneapolis would have required $112,700 in New York City, $111,600 in San Francisco, $110,000 in Los Angeles and $106,200 in Boston, but only $93,300 in Miami or $90,000 in New Orleans ("How Rich Is Rich? Locale Plays Big Role," *USA Today,* October 22, 1990).

enough to boost economic averages, but had much less effect on actual average *families*.

Meanwhile, some of the same calculations that revealed the income surge for the top 1 percent and the moderate gains for the upper-middle class concurred that further down, unusual numbers of Americans *were* dropping out of the lower-middle class. The University of Michigan study provided the best documentation—and by cultural and historical yardsticks, this widespread slippage was more significant than the ongoing upward mobility of a small elite. Polarization, as we shall see, has generally meant bad news for nations, and worriers began to ponder a new question: Was the bottom starting to fall out of Middle America?

Demographers were already explaining who was slipping—and why. Several million highly paid, unionized blue-collar production workers had lost their jobs in manufacturing in the early and mid-1980s, especially in the Great Lakes industrial heartland, and many of the jobs remaining were paying less. For a brief moment—a historical crest— America in the quarter century after the war was rich enough for steel-mill or production-line workers in Flint, Michigan, or south St. Louis to enjoy higher incomes and better living standards than branch bank managers in London or shop supervisors in Stuttgart. Policy changes aggravated their decline, but part of the blue-collar Middle America of the 1960s and early 1970s *was* living higher on the international scale than the U.S. economy could sustain once world prosperity resumed a more normal distribution.

Withering farm areas and dying small towns also became impossible to ignore during the 1980s, especially in the Midwest and Rocky Mountains. In a dozen states, areas covering ten and fifteen counties lost at least 10 percent of their population between 1980 and 1990. In five entire states—Montana, Wisconsin, Louisiana, West Virginia and Wyoming—real median family income *declined* by 11 to 20 percent from the 1980 to the 1990 Census. The rural and small-town component of the middle class shrank (or migrated) as farms were sold or foreclosed and merchants gave in and boarded up their stores.

Even family acrimony and dissolution added to middle-class erosion. Although divorce rates started coming down in the eighties, they remained high enough to make divorced women (and the children in their custody) another group of losers, falling out of the middle class as so many others did. Sudden, steep income drops could make 1990's affluent Elizabeth Arden customer a surprise 1991 statistic in the "feminization of poverty."

Young families, in addition, were whipsawed by low starting salaries, by declining career prospects and wealth opportunities relative to those their parents had enjoyed and by the inability to afford a home (or even to afford marriage as opposed to cohabitation).* Incomeswatcher Frank Levy had no doubt that "it is much harder for a male high school graduate to be in 'the Middle Class' now than it was ten years ago."[71]

And, finally, the 1990s counted millions of middle managers from business and the professions, who had already lost jobs or were fearful that they would, caught in the white-collar, suburban aftermath of corporate America's bloody early 1980s downsizing of blue-collar employment in response to foreign competition and changed world circumstances. The postwar social contract was being breached; major U.S. corporations were giving up their earlier roles as providers of a uniquely American prosperity. Now their horizons and loyalties were increasingly global. Even the downsizing of U.S. military defenses became a factor, as chills spread across the Sun Belt when hundreds of thousands of aerospace engineers, defense workers and military personnel lost their jobs.

By 1992, the nation's most painful income declines were coming in a *new* set of states—service, financial, aerospace and high-technology centers racked by the economic downturn. In Massachusetts and Connecticut, median household incomes had dropped almost 10 percent from 1989 to 1991. In California, the UCLA Business Forecasting Project confirmed the worst economic downturn since the 1930s, and editorialists pondered the hitherto unthinkable: the end of middle-class optimism.

A few years into the decade, then, the middle class was approximately 45 percent of the population, including perhaps half the 40th to 59th percentiles, and virtually everyone in the 60th to 98th percentiles, below the "upper" 1 percent. But despite unprecedented prosperity at the top, the proportion of people whose purchasing power or defined incomes made them "middle-class" was certainly 5 to 10 percentage points smaller than it had been ten or twenty years earlier. Americans on the margin were more nervous, more harried and more politically volatile. And they had reason to be, because during the 1980s many policymakers in Washington and state capitals and county seats had adopted a very different philosophy from the middle-class commitment that had underpinned America's mid-century rise.

*Chapter 7 will provide more detail.

C H A P T E R 2

The New Political Economics of the 1980s: "Soaking the Middle Class"

In the '30s we had the New Deal. In the '40s and '50s we had the Fair Deal. And in the '80s, middle-income Americans got the raw deal.

—U.S. Senate Budget Committee Chairman James Sasser, 1991

Those people in Washington who write the complex tangle of rules by which the economy operates have, over the last 20 years, rigged the game—by design and default—to favor the privileged, the powerful and the influential. At the expense of everyone else.

—"America: What Went Wrong," *The Philadelphia Inquirer,* 1991

Americans' surrender of the ideal of equal sacrifice has occurred without much public debate or even awareness that we were doing it. It has come rather as a byproduct of discrete policies that seemed otherwise perfectly sensible.

—Political economist Robert Reich, 1986

To some extent, the erosion of the U.S. middle class in the 1980s and early 1990s reflected technological change and global economic upheaval. But politics was also involved. The Reagan administration introduced new philosophies, tentative and little understood at first, to justify policies of redistributing tax burdens, exalting markets, overrewarding the rich and the manipulations of finance, cutting back public services and then pointing with a cynical shrug toward exchequers emptied by selective tax cuts and tax expenditures to favored groups. As these trends intensified, to the great benefit of the financial markets, so did economic polarization—and so did the pressure on families in the humdrum middle and lower middle, as well as those at the bottom.

This national transformation was no accident. Economic circumstances had begun souring for Americans in the 1970s, and in 1980 the U.S. electorate had embraced new leaders who, as we shall see, unleashed the third of America's Republican-led capitalist booms in which income and wealth were realigned upward.* Some of these same economic forces worked to the detriment of ordinary Americans by encouraging speculation, shifting tax burdens and redistributing income in ways that eventually became controversial in the nineties. In retrospect, what would become "Soak the middle" policies that led to rising Social Security taxes, as well as an income tax system that imposed higher marginal rates on middle managers than on corporate CEOs, had been nobody's 1980 political platform—obviously—and most swing voters that year, preoccupied with liberal social and economic failures, took at face value conservatism's renewed emphasis on tax reduction, markets and incentive economics. Not until the mid- to late 1980s was it clear that a more ambitious new ideology was developing—in Europe as well as the United States—to shift economic burdens *toward* society's low- and middle-income users of products and services and *away* from capitalism's investors and other lions of the corporate veldt. At first, of course, the objective had been a familiar, broad renewal of American enterprise, and policy components like lower taxes and less regulation were eminently sensible.

Meanwhile, the conservatives who held up Washington's free-market banners in the early 1980s had relatively few questions to answer. American voters were frazzled by bracket creep and resentful of big government. For them, economic redistribution involved "Tax and spend," the liberal Democratic politics that had recycled upper- and middle-class tax revenues downward from Franklin D. Roosevelt's 1930s New Deal to Lyndon Johnson's 1960s Great Society. Opposition to more such welfare statism—some of which was linked to racial fear—stoked Middle America's fiscal conservatism and spurred its preference for a Republican president in 1980.

Equally to the point, rival political memories of conservatives using government policy to transfer wealth *upward* had grown dim, becoming little more than storybook plots of twelfth-century sheriffs of Nottingham and arrogant French Bourbon kings. This, after all, was not *American* practice—unless one recalled how U.S. Treasury Secretary Alexander Hamilton, in 1794, sent troops to force western Pennsylvania farmers to pay new taxes on corn liquor, partly so that the federal government could fund the Revolutionary War debt held by speculators. Or how the federal government, in the quarter century after the Civil War, used the gold standard as a vehicle to impose nationwide money-supply deflation, rewarding bondholders while

*The details of this process are described in *The Politics of Rich and Poor.*

commodity prices collapsed and farmers lost their lands. Even as recently as the 1930s, sour memories of the pro-wealth Republican policies of the Roaring Twenties were immediate enough that when Hollywood released its spectacular 1939 version of *Robin Hood,* starring dashing Errol Flynn as Robin and Basil Rathbone as the arrogant sheriff of Nottingham, few doubted that the hero of Sherwood Forest was the good guy, the Franklin D. Roosevelt of medieval England. By the mid-1980s, however, Robin Hood had become a negative symbol, an ideological villain to *Wall Street Journal* editorialists *and* their avid readers in the White House. Philosophically, the drawbridge of Nottingham Castle was creaking down. The sheriff was ready to ride again.

The Significance of America's Third Capitalist Heyday

To the average American family of 1980, cultural issues were important, but economics were probably a greater preoccupation. Too much regulation and a sense of excessive, heavy-handed government placed near the top of the list, polls showed. Labor unions, many people felt, were pushing the costs of U.S. products too high. Taxes had to come down, especially because inflation, people's top concern, was lifting middle-income people into ever-steeper brackets. And inflation itself had to be stopped.

When disdain for expanding bureaucracy converges with worry about overregulation and dislike of labor unions, inflation and higher taxes, the middle class usually opts for strongly conservative politics. This was the voters' response during the 1980s to the excesses of the late 1970s, just as it had been the reaction in the 1920s to the price rises and expanded regulation accompanying World War I, and, before that, to the explosion of prices and bureaucracy brought about by the Civil War. Beyond any coincidence, all three countertides of anti-tax, antigovernment and anti-inflation sentiment produced strong enough ideological currents—and corollary financial booms—to suggest that the Gilded Age (from the mid-1870s to the mid-1890s), the Roaring Twenties and the 1980s were what I have called "capitalist heydays."

These three heydays, described at some length in *The Politics of Rich and Poor,* each involved ten common elements.

*Shared "Capitalist Heyday" Circumstances of the 1980s,
1920s and the Gilded Age*

1. Republican presidents and dominant conservative politics;
2. Popular and elite belief that government had previously become too big and that there should be less of it;
3. Exaltation of business, with philosophic emphasis on the *private* sector rather than the *public* sector;
4. Low national regard for organized labor;
5. Major restructuring of the U.S. economy, accompanied by merger waves and innovations in business reorganization;
6. Tax reduction, especially high-bracket income taxes;
7. Pursuit of disinflation in response to prior inflation;
8. Economic weakness in the commodity-producing U.S. heartland, with stronger prosperity in the coastal areas;
9. Concentration of wealth and increasing inequality of income;
10. Rising and increasingly precarious levels of speculation, leverage and debt.

Collectively, it was not the sort of rising tide that lifted all boats. This mix of conservatism, skepticism about government, enthusiasm for business, deregulation, tax cuts, disinflation and leveraged corporate restructuring has always concentrated its high yields on the top 1 percent of Americans. But despite this inherent bias toward the rich, much of the middle class—smaller and more elite back then—also shared in the boom of the Gilded Age and the Roaring Twenties, albeit often marginally.* The downside was that, after 1893 and 1929—and then again during 1987–91—middle-class Americans suffered in the inevitable subsequent collapse of banks, credit and asset values. However, in the first two periods, no long-term slippage resulted, because after the boom and bust, the middle class, along with the country itself, bounced back more strongly than ever.

Skeptics like MIT's Lester Thurow and Harvard professor Benjamin Friedman argued that the 1980s, by contrast, threatened a *lasting* decline, that the unique recklessness of public finance in the 1980s posed a critical difference. Whereas during the Gilded Age and the 1920s a careful federal government had maintained regular budget

*Federal economic data for these periods are minimal. The principal benefits went to the rich, and the 10 to 20 percent of Americans in the middle class also improved their income and wealth. Below these levels, the boom petered out. Part Two of this book opens with a look at the "squeezes" on Middle America and its income in the two previous heydays.

surpluses, the several administrations of the 1980s ran up huge deficits that tripled the national debt yet simultaneously provoked new budgetary processes that kept forcing revenue increases. Worse still, the two previous boom-bust periods had come when American economic power was still ascending internationally. The boom of the 1980s, by contrast, was staged as U.S. global economic decline took hold, but under the premise that the go-go policies and attitudes involved were a revitalization process. This time some of the huge new debt load and intensifying economic polarization did have longer-term implications.

These pages will argue that America's heyday practices of the 1980s were, for the first time, those of a weakening great economic power, risking its credit and its future and abusing its middle-class citizenry for the benefit of elites and special interests. But "Soak the middle" practices were not unique to the United States. Similar patterns were also apparent in other major nations that had shifted to the right during the 1980s and chosen governments philosophically akin to the Reagan administration. The interests of Middle Britain, Middle Japan and Middle Canada were also being subordinated to those of economic elites—or so local critics would be charging as the 1980s ended.

The International Supremacy of Conservative Political Economics: From Exuberance to Excess?

Squeezing the ordinary people is one of history's oldest fiscal practices. Sixteenth-century Spain and eighteenth-century France, for example, largely excused the nobility from taxes, levying them principally on the peasants and middle classes, provoking some of the anger that ultimately led to revolution and its philosophical rationalization by Karl Marx. Socialism in Europe temporarily created a reverse set of abuses in the middle third of the twentieth century, but, all the while, conservative preference for cutting government programs and shifting taxes back to the average citizen smoldered in still-warm embers, ready to reignite. This happened in the 1980s as conservative tax and deregulation philosophies spread, and as the political right took control of most governments in the Group of Seven nations—the United States, Japan, Canada, Britain, France, Germany and Italy. Moreover, the conservatism involved was far more crusading and aggressive than at any other time in the previous fifty years. In Europe, as in the United States, tax cuts and deregulation were at first energizing. More controversial policies that burdened the middle—for the sake of unburdening those at the top—were to come later, when conservative governments were surer of their power and ideology.

This militant new conservatism was ideologically powerful enough to spread far beyond the major financial powers, swaying even nominally Labor or Socialist governments in nations like Australia, New Zealand and Spain. Upward redistribution of wealth became global, and the rich became objects of emulation almost everywhere. Nevertheless, the most aggressive ideology and results seem to have come in the United States and Britain, the principal seedbeds of the new free-market religion. A survey conducted by three U.S. Census Bureau economists, which compared early- and mid-1980s household earnings for the United States, Canada, Sweden, Australia and West Germany, found that the gap between rich and poor was the greatest in the United States. The highest percentage of income was going to the top 10 percent of households, and they had also enjoyed the greatest increase in their share. Canada was second. Socialist Sweden was at the low end, with the upper-income quintile holding roughly constant in its share of income during 1981–87.[1]

But if ideology was a brake in Sweden, it was an accelerator in Margaret Thatcher's Britain. In 1991 the Central Statistical Office of the British Treasury released new income data documenting a sharp rise in household income inequality. In 1979 the poorest fifth had accounted for 9.5 percent of after-tax income; by 1988 that dropped to 6.9 percent. Meanwhile the share of the top fifth rose from 37 percent to 44 percent.[2]

The reign of uninhibited conservative economics within the Group of Seven probably peaked in 1987–88, when the ruling governments of Britain, Canada and the United States scored strong—and somewhat unexpected—reelection victories. By 1988 and 1989 conservative British, Japanese and Canadian regimes had begun pursuing regressive tax policies that would soon arouse middle-class anger, with predictable political consequences.

British prime minister Margaret Thatcher had overcome familiar charges of favoring the rich to win a third straight Conservative party victory in 1987. However, she quickly followed up in 1988 by proposing bold new reductions in the popular national health service, urging further cuts in Britain's top income tax rate (trimming it from 60 percent to 40 percent) and then topping both with a fiscal stunner: the replacement of property taxes at the local government level by a "community service charge" or head tax levied equally on each individual, rich or poor. Tory stalwarts hoped the per capita charge would force a tax-aroused citizenry to take pruning shears to local government, but debate soon came to pivot on unfairness—on how a cleaning woman in a low-income council house would now pay the same as the belted earl down the lane in his Jacobean manor. Critics enjoyed pointing out how Thatcher herself would pay $3,600 a year less in poll taxes than she currently paid in property taxes on her retirement home in Dulwich.[3]

Tory economic self-interest notwithstanding, Thatcher's boldness represented historical bravado. The last time a British government imposed a uniform poll tax on its people—back in 1381—a mob forced its way into the Tower of London, seized royal ministers and beheaded the chancellor of the exchequer.[4] And sure enough, by the time the poll tax went into effect on April 1, 1990, London's streets once again echoed to riots and marching feet. The prime minister herself was never threatened physically, but the political peril was consuming. No sooner had Conservatives been drubbed in May's local elections, thanks to the poll tax and a spreading recession, than opposition Labourites went ahead by 12 to 15 points in trial heats for a future general election. To save the party, many back-bench Conservative parliamentarians said both Thatcher and the poll tax would have to go. A November insurrection forced the embattled prime minister to step down, then the second decision—whether and how to replace the poll tax—hung fire until March 1991, when the Conservatives lost a hitherto safe seat in a by-election in northwest England's Ribble Valley. The winning candidate, Michael Carr of the small third-party Liberal Democrats, boasted that "When the poll tax is finally put to rest in its grave, its epitaph will read: 'Here lies the poll tax. Killed in Ribble Valley!' "[5]

The execution was announced a few days later by John Major, the new prime minister who had replaced Thatcher. But the party continued to disagree over how to replace the tax until substitute measures were spelled out in April—a hybrid of a seven-bracket property tax, an adjustment for family size and a further 2-percentage-point increase in the regressive value-added (consumption) tax. It was not a popular solution, but with Thatcher gone, the poll tax repudiated and John Major, whose origins were lower-middle class, forsaking Thatcher-type rhetoric, escalating public spending on services and promising a "classless" society, the Conservatives lost forty seats but kept a narrow majority in the 1992 national elections.

Canada's ruling Conservatives made their own fiscal miscalculation in 1988 after winning lopsided control of Parliament for five more years. That year, the top individual tax rate had been cut from 34 percent to 29 percent and the top corporate rate from 36 percent to 28 percent. Then in April 1989, reflecting the general Western ideological movement toward taxing consumption rather than income, Prime Minister Brian Mulroney proposed a new 9 percent "goods and services tax" (GST), quickly labeled the cribs-to-coffins tax, which applied to just about all goods except food—and also to piano lessons, lawyer fees and even sending a fax. In part, the GST was to replace a sixty-five-year-old manufacturers' sales tax, then levied at a rate of 12 percent on only about a third of goods and services purchased by Canadians. But the basis of vulnerability was obvious. Ed Broadbent, leader of the opposition New Democratic party, quickly attacked the proposal as "extraordinarily regressive," because the "poor pay the same rate as the rich."[6]

Polls taken when Parliament reconvened in autumn showed 75 percent of the electorate opposed to the GST, and by December, when the government backtracked by reducing its proposed 9 percent rate to 7 percent, public support for the Conservatives had dropped to just 21 percent in Canada's Gallup Poll. A year later, when after an energetic filibuster Canada's Senate finally approved the GST for January 1991 start-up, support for Mulroney and the Conservatives had sunk to a rock-bottom 15 percent! Before the final vote, opposition Liberals blew kazoos and waved polls that showed 80 percent of Canadians didn't want the tax, and the *Toronto Star* ran an editorial cartoon showing the prime minister as a menacing, fanged vampire and a caption that read: "I want to suck your wallet."[7]

The unfairness theme continued, with critics saying it would be better to return the corporate tax rate to 36 percent, or at least to set up a corporate minimum tax (to get $8 billion a year from 60,000 concerns that managed to pay no federal tax at all).[8] Middle-class Canadians agreed. Voters in the $30,000–$50,000 bracket condemned the new GST (after it had gone into effect) by 76 percent to 23 percent in 1991 polls.[9] In September 1990, influenced by recession, the GST controversy and threats to the country's social safety net, a surprising number of middle-class voters had joined in electing Ontario's first-ever socialist provincial government.

In Japan, anger at Japan's (conservative) Liberal Democratic party for pairing a new 3 percent consumption tax with top-income-tax-bracket reduction had already come to a head in 1989. Over the previous two years, soaring stock and real estate prices had, perversely, begun to shred Japan's self-image as a broadly middle-class society.

The record real estate prices were making property owners rich while people without property found themselves in a hole, unable to buy homes or to keep up with the Japanese equivalent of the Joneses. In response to a 1988 survey by the Government Economy Planning Agency, 74 percent of Japanese went so far as to call their country's economic system basically unfair.[10] And to add to voters' disenchantment, the governing LDP was embroiled in the infamous Recruit Corporation scandal, which caught leading politicians in a web of bribes, greed and easy-money stock deals.

So when the government proposed a new 3 percent tax on consumption, while lowering the top income-tax rate from 60 percent to 50 percent and cutting the top corporate rate from 42 percent to 37.5 percent, public indignation crystallized. Japan's Socialists won a surprise victory in the July 1989 elections for the upper house of parliament, making big gains among housewives and the elderly after attacking the unpopular consumption levy and suggesting that the revenues would be better raised by taxing stock market and real estate profits.*

LDP leaders understood that some changes were necessary. Modifications in the consumption tax were set forth in time for the early 1990 elections to parliament's lower house, and the LDP easily retained power despite gains by the Socialist minority. However, as the speculative bubble in the Japanese real estate and stock markets— Japan's even frothier equivalent of the Reagan boom—fell apart in 1991–92, with new scandals adding to government woes, LDP fortunes remained uncertain and the opposition maintained its control of the upper house of parliament in mid-1992 elections.

The common denominator was obvious: conservative governments, consistent in their capitalist and free-market assertiveness, were trying to manage markets and raise revenues in ways that would least interfere with business, investment, property and the rich, a goal that frequently involved increasing the burden on those who were not rich. In Britain, where Conservative free-market ideology was purest, the infuriating poll tax was a logical extension of the dismantling of the public sector and enlargement of the private sector already under way

*Voter concern was justified. Economists at S. G. Warburg in Tokyo calculated in 1992 that since tax "reform" in April 1989 the amount a Japanese paid in income tax had grown, on average, by 14.5 percent a year, while the average household income had risen only 7.7 percent a year. Worse still, because Social Security contributions had also climbed an average of 11.7 percent a year, total household income was also lower in mid-1992 than it would have been without tax reform ("So Rich, So Poor," *The Economist,* June 20, 1992, p. 32).

through privatization, deregulation, taxation of consumption (to reduce taxes on income that might become investment), cuts in social services and attempts to finance public services by narrow user fees instead of broad general revenues. The problem, simply, was that it angered ordinary Britons. The British middle class never opposed selling off stale socialist enterprises or restoring economic incentive. But by 1989–90, following the Thatcher regime's announcement of the poll tax and plans to curb the National Health Service, opinion surveys showed the average middle-class voter increasingly concerned about where this new ideology might lead: to the rich getting richer, to more uncertainty for the middle class and to cutbacks in services for the average family (not just the poor). In the major financial capitals of the West, the 1980s ended as economic conservatism overplayed its political hand and voters began to look to the center.

"Soak the Middle" Economics in the United States

Many of the same philosophies also guided Washington, although not to the extent of such a huge symbolic error as Britain's poll tax. Following Ronald Reagan's election in 1980, the ultraconservative Heritage Foundation had presented incoming Republican officeholders with a blueprint (*Mandate for Leadership*) for greatly reducing the cost and size of the federal government, including abolition of several government departments and functions and large-scale privatization. However, if only a few agencies were actually shuttered (such as the Civil Aeronautics Board and the Office of Economic Opportunity), and if relatively little was privatized beyond Conrail and the Federal National Mortgage Association, that was in part because the Reagan administration, from the beginning, was preoccupied elsewhere: with tax cuts and what quickly became the Economic Recovery Tax Act of 1981.

Hostility to progressive income taxation was a mainstay of the Reagan wing of the Republican party. The new president's personal appetite for switching to a flat-rate personal income tax and abolishing the corporate income tax, whetted by the punitive 91 percent top rate of his movie-star years, told only part of the story. For two centuries of American fiscal history, the GOP and its antecedent upper-bracket parties, the eighteenth-century Federalists and nineteenth-century Whigs, had usually been reluctant to tax income or wealth; they generally preferred to tax production or consumption.

Under Federalist and Whig governance, the early United States raised most of its national revenue from excise taxes and import tariffs. The new Republican party continued this tilt, after its formation in the mid-1850s, despite inaugurating a temporary income tax to fight the Civil War (and then ending it in 1872). The *permanent* progressive income tax was not enacted until 1913 under Democratic president Woodrow Wilson, although reform-minded GOP president Theodore Roosevelt had also urged it. The conservative Republican presidents of the 1920s were less sympathetic. Income tax rates had soared (to a top rate of 77 percent) during World War I, but Presidents Harding and Coolidge brought the top rate down to 25 percent by 1925. In 1920 income taxes had produced 66 percent of federal government revenues versus 15 percent for excise taxes and tariffs; by 1928 that proportion had shifted to 56 percent versus 27 percent. Because the average American family was not rich enough to have to pay income taxes in the 1920s, in some ways it was better off when they predominated.

When Franklin D. Roosevelt, the New Deal and World War II restored the primacy of the income tax, Republicans were unhappy—and especially unhappy with a top rate that briefly reached 94 percent in 1944. However, after GOP-led attempts to reduce the upper-rate structure backfired politically in the 1948 elections, the Republicans made no real effort to rewrite the rate tables during the 1950s. Nor did Richard Nixon, after his 1969 inauguration, respond to conservative arguments for bracket reduction that would go beyond the cuts made by Democrats in 1964. Once inflation rekindled in the mid-1970s, though, so did Republican sentiment for reducing income taxes again and increasing the burden on wages and consumption. One spur was the persuasive argument of lobbyists for capital formation and investment that U.S. entrepreneurialism was being diminished; a second was the extent to which price rises were souring Middle America on income taxation. Bracket creep had long since forced average families to become income tax payers; now it was relentlessly saddling ordinary householders with rates once reserved for the top 5 percent of earners. For all these reasons, the Reagan years would become the first period since the 1920s when Republicans could think about displacing the old *progressive* income tax with *regressive* revenue devices, such as (1) a minimally progressive or even flat income tax; (2) a broadened, higher-rate flat tax on employees (FICA); and (3) user fees, excise taxes and consumption taxes.

In retrospect, conservative economic strategists would fail only with the boldest of their new ideas—a flat-rate, single-bracket income tax and a national consumption tax. Otherwise, by the end of the 1980s, renascent U.S. conservatism had all but dismantled the progressive rate structure of the New Deal, creating a system that applied virtually the same top rates to Los Angeles high school principals as to millionaires. Back in 1950 a salaried $100,000-a-year family in the top 1 percent income group would have paid combined federal taxes at an approximately 50 percent rate that was eight times the 5 to 6 percent effective rate paid by a $3,000-a-year median-income family.* But by 1990 a $500,000-a-year family paid an effective overall federal tax rate of about 29 percent, only slightly higher than the 28 percent paid by the $50,000-a-year two-earner household identified as the "average family" by the Tax Foundation.

Following the first Reagan-era tax cuts in 1981, middle-class families, pleased that their own income taxes were being reduced by 25 percent (over three years) and simultaneously indexed against inflation, scarcely worried that much bigger reductions were going to corporations and upper-bracket taxpayers. By 1986, however, alert voters could identify a half-dozen instances in which the decade's emerging theology leaned hardest on middle-class taxpayers. In Chapter 5, I will lay out these matters in detail; here I simply want to document the importance of the *political* and *ideological* upheaval.

A good place to begin is the overhaul of the Social Security retirement system following the 1983 recommendations of a bipartisan commission headed by former Republican Council of Economic Advisers chairman Alan Greenspan. The commission was spurred by fears of insufficient revenues to finance the expected huge costs of baby-boomer retirement after 2010. As a solution, it recommended—and Congress accepted—a rapid escalation of the single-rate Social Security (FICA) tax. Back in 1980, earnings up to $25,000 had been taxable at a rate of 6.13 percent, for a maximum yearly individual contribution of $1,588. The new plan, by contrast, expanded planned FICA increases to make earnings up to $51,300 taxable as of 1990 at an annual rate of 7.65 percent, requiring a maximum individual contribution of $3,924. With so many more wives working, this represented—as we shall see—a very large federal tax increase on two-earner couples in the middle and upper-middle class. For the top 1 percent of taxpayers, with over $200,000 a year, FICA increases were proportionately minor; what often became a $2,000–$4,000 additional annual burden fell hardest in the middle.

In ideological terms, Washington was raising *regressive* Social Secu-

---

*See page 1112 of *The Statistical History of the United States* (New York: Basic Books, 1976) for the effective income tax rates that year—47 percent on the $100,000 family, 3.5 percent on the $3,000 family. My increases are to allow for FICA taxes (1 percent each from employer and employee on $3,000) and excise taxes.

rity taxes even as *progressive* income taxes were being cut—especially for those at the top. Quietly but steadily, the federal revenue-raising burden was shifting away from the income tax (corporate and individual), which had produced 60 percent of total receipts in 1980 but just 55 percent in 1990, and toward FICA levies, which had brought in 31 percent of the total in 1980 but a larger 37 percent in 1990. Table 2 suggests that for families in the middle quintile, by the end of the decade the net easing of federal income tax burdens was canceled out by increased Social Security taxes.

In addition, a slick use of surplus Social Security dollars—*not* legally required to be set aside for future retirees—served to reduce pressures for a higher top income tax rate. In 1985 the architects of the Gramm-Rudman deficit-reduction act succeeded in specifying that any annual Social Security tax surplus—by 1991, it was $75 billion—could be used to reduce the official federal deficit calculation. This jeopardized the original purpose of the 1983 FICA tax increase, and when one member of the U.S. Senate Finance Committee, Daniel P. Moynihan of New York, later referred to it as "robbery," a second member, John Heinz of Pennsylvania, was more precise: No, he pointed out, it was closer to embezzlement.[11] One of Reagan's Social Security commissioners, Dorcas Hardy, would later write a book making the same point.*

Then in 1986, the president and Congress agreed on yet another far-reaching federal tax overhaul in the name of "fairness and simplification." These changes further reduced income tax rates, but while taking away many tax shelters important to the rich, also took away popular deductions and credits long cherished by the middle class. Opinion surveys found voters skeptical: the newest reform, they thought, only made the federal income tax more complex and less fair.

Table 2. Federal Effective Tax Rates for All of
the Middle Quintile (combined) Families

	1977	1980	1985	1988	1993 (est.)
Individual Income Tax	6.9%	7.9%	6.7%	6.4%	6.2%
Social Security Tax (FICA)	8.1%	8.6%	9.7%	10.1%	10.1%

Source: Congressional Budget Office tax simulation model, cited in U.S. House Ways and Means Committee 1992 Green Book, p. 1529.

Note: A second computation by several CBO economists found combined federal income Social Security and excise taxes as a percentage of average family income rising from 20.4% in 1980 to 20.9% in 1990 (*New York Times*, October 1, 1992).

*See p. 184.

Before long, one unusual legislative wrinkle would become particularly infamous. In addition to the two statutory rates of 15 percent and 28 percent, which was the new top bracket (reduced from 50 percent), Washington legislative draftsmen introduced "the bubble," a special 33 percent marginal rate that applied not to the *richest* taxpayers but to the *upper-middle class* in the $70,000–$170,000 bracket.* Although supporters insisted that this made the new tax structure more progressive, the effect on the upper-middle class and on the truly rich was just the opposite: the 33 percent marginal rate imposed on a $125,000 corporate middle manager *dropped* to 28 percent for David Rockefeller, Sam Walton and even those with mere million-dollar incomes. The explanation was that the multibillion-dollar revenues gained from putting upper-middle-class taxpayers in a special 33 percent bubble were critical to avoiding a third bracket with a top rate in the mid-thirties that would have applied to genuinely high incomes. Bubbles exist in other parts of the tax code, but the imposition of the highest marginal rate on the upper-middle class, not the rich, had no parallel in any other major nation's late-twentieth-century income tax chart. As progressivity eroded, the income tax was managing to develop a few *regressive* twists.

Meanwhile, the outline of a major new "user fee" emerged in 1988, when Congress and the president enacted a program of health insurance against catastrophic illness for those over sixty-five. Instead of being financed out of general revenues (or even out of Social Security levies on the overall work force), "catastrophic" was to be funded by what was demonstrably a surtax confined to senior citizens, but which politicians preferred to call an "income-based premium." On their regular income tax, the elderly were to pay a 15 percent surcharge, which was capped at $800 per individual and $1,600 per couple in 1989, but rising to $2,100 per couple by 1993. As a percentage of income, the surcharge would have hit hardest those individuals and couples in the $25,000–$45,000 range. In the autumn of 1989, however, senior citizens in the $25,000-and-over range—the "rich" elderly, some reports called them—mobilized in such anger that a trembling Congress repealed the legislation. Despite this retreat under fire, the fiscal philosophy involved remained largely unchanged until 1990.†

By the late 1980s, some senior citizens also faced other marginal

---

*The 1986 bubble and its successor, the slightly different 1991 bubble, will be explained in Chapter 5.

†In 1990, that year's budget agreement raised the true top rate from 28 percent to 31 percent.

rates far above the 28 percent maximum by then applied to the highest incomes. Two cross-effects were involved: first, the 1983 reforms had included a decision to tax Social Security benefits for single persons with incomes above $25,000 and for couples above $32,000; and second, there was a long-standing limitation on *other* income, under which Social Security recipients aged sixty-five to sixty-nine lost $1 in benefits for every $3 of income above roughly $10,000 a year. As pointed out relentlessly in publications for retired persons, the effective tax rate on additional earnings—by the time penalties and federal and state taxes were applied—could reach 80 percent.[12]

Meanwhile, spending responsibilities for programs from Medicaid to transportation were increasingly turned back by Washington to states and localities, often accompanied by proportionately lower federal contributions. This reduced the tax revenues that federal authorities would otherwise have needed, and as we shall see in more detail later, helped make it possible to ease federal taxation of high incomes. However, it also meant much more regressive taxes at lower levels of government: state sales; alcohol, tobacco and gasoline levies; local property taxes; and a host of charges and user fees. Some states and localities did raise their income tax brackets during the 1980s, but the biggest states—New York and California—implemented top-rate reductions paralleling the federal cuts and reflecting Washington's philosophy. In states like Illinois and Massachusetts, among others, incomes were taxed at only one rate. Florida, Connecticut, Texas and seven other jurisdictions didn't even have state income levies.

Like Social Security, state and local levies were generally regressive—and regressive taxes were a fiscal growth area of the 1980s. In 1982 Washington had collected $298 billion in federal income taxes while state and local taxes totaled $266 billion.[13] In 1990 federal income levies produced $493 billion while the state and local tax receipts had jumped to $540 billion, with much of the increment coming from sales and property taxes and user fees.[14] The distributional economics were a far cry from those of the federal income tax—especially the old, pre-Reagan rate structure. Compilations for 1990 showed that combined state and local taxes took 14.8 percent of the annual income of the poor, about 10 percent of that of the middle classes and a much lower 7.6 percent from the top 1 percent.

In 1990 there were even attempts to take back the existing federal day-care tax credit from a large portion of the middle class, prompting Colorado congresswoman Pat Schroeder to complain, "This is not like restricting deductions for a Rolls-Royce or a Mercedes. In many urban areas, you're talking about taking away the benefits for families with two teachers or a fireman and a teacher."[15]

That same year, Congress and the Bush administration increased federal excise taxes on alcohol, tobacco and gasoline, as well as user fees. Some 4.1 million owners of recreational boats were outraged to find they would have to start paying fees of $25 to $100 a year for Coast Guard decals in order to operate in navigable U.S. waters. What had been free to ordinary Americans now, in more and more cases, required access charges. At the state level, the proliferation of user fees and nuisance taxes was even worse, exemplified by Florida's new surtax on speeding tickets and Maryland's fees on burial lots.

Alongside their new emphasis on charging fees for services, some administration strategists proposed to reduce or eliminate middle-class eligibility for federal aid programs by means testing, pursuing earlier hints given when middle-income Social Security pensions were exposed to taxation in 1983. In 1991, federal budget director Richard Darman recommended income-eligibility ceilings for federal agricultural payments, Medicare premium subsidies, college aid and school lunches. The idea of cutting off federal grants to hundreds of thousands of college students with family incomes over $20,000 prompted some educators to complain about hurting the middle and lower-middle classes to help the poor. Darman, however, had even more sweeping transformations in mind, urging Congress and the administration to agree on some income level "higher than $20,000 and lower than $125,000" and then "apply it uniformly across the board" as the cutoff point for "a whole range of mandatory [benefit] programs aside from Social Security."[16] His aim was less to maximize benefits for the poor than to reduce the deficit by curbing middle-class entitlements—even if this meant reducing net income to the middle class—while protecting the reductions in top income tax rates that had been achieved during the 1980s.

Even tax-collection directives were targeted on the middle class instead of the rich. In March 1991 Internal Revenue commissioner Fred Goldberg told the House Ways and Means Oversight Subcommittee about the request he had rejected from the federal Office of Management and Budget. Officials at that agency had wanted to step up tax audits against lower- and middle-income taxpayers, whose wages, receipts and transactions could be easily monitored, and to de-emphasize audits of high-income individuals and businesses, whose financial holdings and maneuvers were much harder to trace.

Taken together, these changes added up to a striking new ideology of favoring the investing class at the expense of the middle class—a considerable turnabout. As we have seen, the new bias also extended to banks, financial markets and corporate mergers. In political terms, though, the future pivot would be whether the policy revolution of the 1980s had quietly decreased the after-tax purchasing power of most families in the mid-section of the U.S. population—and the answer seems to be "yes." Contemporary calculations varied, however, blurred by the tendency of most national organizations to measure only the impact of federal taxes while omitting state and local levies because of the wide variations between jurisdictions.

The effect of federal tax changes alone is spelled out in Tables 3A and 3B, prepared by the conservative Tax Foundation (co-chaired in the early 1990s by former Reagan budget director James C. Miller III). Note that Table 3A showed a 1977–87 *decline* in median family income after adjusting for inflation and changes in direct federal taxes. Within this table, the 1982–87 figures show a gain, but of only 5 percent. For all the 1980s talk about tax cuts, *after-tax* median family income never

Table 3. Changes in Family After-Tax Income, 1977–1990

A) Median Family Income Before and After Direct Federal Taxes and Inflation, 1977–1987

Year	Median Family Income[a]	Income Tax[b]	Social Security	Total	Current Dollars	1987 Dollars[c]
		Direct Federal Taxes			After-tax Income	
1977	15,949	1,466	933	2,399	13,550	25,518
1978	17,318	1,717	1,048	2,765	14,553	25,442
1979	19,048	1,881	1,168	3,049	15,999	25,116
1980	20,586	2,143	1,262	3,405	17,181	23,763
1981	21,462	2,267	1,427	3,694	17,768	22,266
1982	23,036	2,342	1,543	3,885	19,151	22,610
1983	23,943	2,277	1,604	3,881	20,062	22,854
1984	25,415	2,395	1,703	4,098	21,317	23,374
1985	25,992	2,466	1,832	4,298	21,694	23,005
1986[d]	27,144	2,865	1,941	4,806	22,338	23,220
1987[d]	28,230	2,704	2,018	4,722	23,508	23,508

[a]Median income for all families with one earner employed full-time, year-round.
[b]Married couple filing joint return, two dependent children.
[c]Adjusted by Consumer Price Index of the Bureau of Labor Statistics. Assumes 4% inflation in 1987.
[d]Estimated by Tax Foundation.
Sources: U.S. Department of Commerce, Bureau of the Census; U.S. Department of Labor, Bureau of Labor Statistics; Treasury Department, Internal Revenue Service.
Source: *Tax Features,* July/August 1987.

B) Median Family Income Before and After Direct Federal Taxes and Inflation

Year	Two-Earner Median Family Income[a]	Income Tax[b]	Social Security	Total	Current Dollars	1990 Dollars[c]
		Direct Federal Taxes			After-Tax Income	
1980	$29,627	$4,050	$1,816	$5,866	$23,761	$37,902
1981	32,224	4,386	2,143	6,529	25,695	37,155
1982	34,515	4,450	2,313	6,763	27,752	37,800
1983	36,106	4,300	2,419	6,719	29,387	38,781
1984	38,713	4,634	2,710	7,344	31,369	39,684
1985	40,593	4,787	2,862	7,649	32,944	40,243
1986	42,492	5,158	3,038	8,196	34,298	41,130
1987	44,536	5,291	3,184	8,475	36,061	41,724
1988	46,658	5,618	3,504	9,122	37,538	41,705
1989	49,000	6,022	3,687	9,709	39,381	41,744
1990[d]	51,421	6,357	3,934	10,291	41,130	41,130

[a]Median income for household with two earners employed full-time, year round.
[b]Married couple filing joint return, two dependent children.
[c]Adjusted by consumer price index, estimated 6% inflation in 1990.
[d]Estimate.
Source: Tax Foundation; U.S. Department of Commerce, Bureau of the Census; U.S. Department of Labor, Bureau of Labor Statistics; U.S. Treasury Department, Internal Revenue Service.

did recover its late 1970s levels. In 1988, however, the foundation abandoned the official federal yardstick of a median family with one earner to redefine "the median family as two earners working fulltime the year round with two dependents."[17] Such families were doing better. But despite this new formula the 1987–90 data for the average family yielded an after-tax net income *decline*—and even before the 1991–92 data worsened the trend, the overall result for the period from 1977 to 1990 was relative stagnation. Moreover, once state and local tax increases were added, the impact on the average family's after-tax income is even more pronounced, as the state-level details in Chapter 5 show.

In short, for the typical family, the combined tax reforms, rearrangements and user fees of the 1980s, coming on top of inflation, meant no gain in purchasing power. The rich were no longer being soaked, but those in the middle were. Behind the façade of shared prosperity and tax cuts for everyone, the average American family was no longer advancing.

Middle-Class Interests and the Breach of the
Postwar "Social Contract"

Few developments of the 1980s were less expected (or debated) than the breakdown of the broad political consensus, effective from World War II through the 1970s, that government's duty was to the great mass of citizens, not to a small elite. Yet this breakdown was probably inevitable in the 1980s, once heyday capitalism was ready to move beyond its broadly supported first stage of imposing curbs on bureaucracy and regulatory excesses, encouraging entrepreneurial incentive and framing general tax reduction. Successful movements tend to succumb to their own appetites, spurning restraint, and as we have seen, that became a particular pitfall of tax policy in the late 1980s. This chapter will argue that capitalist-conservative theology eventually trespassed on middle-class psychology in several counterproductive ways: (1) by reducing not just unpopular, overbearing bureaucratic usurpations of government but familiar, comforting services and roles; (2) by an intense, overly ideological emphasis on markets and marketplace functions at the expense of some community values and traditions; (3) by "one-world" capitalist approaches to trade and markets that sometimes subordinated national economic interests and sacrificed salvageable industries; (4) by downgrading the principle of shared sacrifice and disproportionate burden-bearing by the rich; and (5) by development of theories of economic efficiency and globalization that either lionized financiers and investors or opposed interference with their interests.

The 1980s, to repeat, began with government fairly in disrepute for its swollen size and record of aggravating rather than solving problems. And for all that conservatism's boldest ambitions failed—such as Britain's poll tax and proposals in the United States to abolish the departments of Energy and Education—the ruling politicians in both countries took advantage of the new climate to achieve much more than simply impugning excessive government and government services. In the United States, for example, programs ranging from revenue-sharing to Urban Development Action Grants were terminated or sharply reduced. By the late 1980s the hostility to government put into overdrive by the rapprochement of neoconservatives and traditional laissez-faire Republicans in the late 1970s had helped achieve a substantial reduction in discretionary nondefense federal spending as a percentage of both outlays and the GNP. Entitlement programs were untouchable, but discretionary domestic spending declined from about 22 percent of federal outlays in 1980 to under 15 percent in 1989.

Moreover, although foreign visitors to the United States might be struck by the decay, the crumbling infrastructure, the "Brazilianization" of old cities like New York, the Reagan and Bush administrations continued to transfer program responsibility back to the states with inadequate financial support. Then, because of the severe recession that began in 1990, state and local governments from New York and Massachusetts to California confronted enormous fiscal deficits that promised to persist well into the decade—and reduced public outlays signaled further "Brazilianization."

Some of the same price was paid in Britain, where the Thatcher government unenthusiastically administered an already aging transportation system, worsening matters by abolishing the Greater London Council with its central planning authority for local buses, underground rail service, roads and traffic. Soon London started seizing up for large parts of the day. Public services in Britain had been so trimmed by the end of the decade that observers despaired at the erosion of public education, British Railways and the once-respected health service. Conditions on London's Underground had deteriorated to such a point that its chief executive described the system as "an appalling shambles."[18] British doctors even talked briefly about organizing a new party to fight the next election on the issue of a better health service.[19]

The changed political economics were the same on both sides of the Atlantic. The rich, with mushrooming after-tax income, were free to buy any service they desired, from helicopters, well-protected townhouses and Harley Street medical specialists to access to Harvard and Eton; it was the middle-class majorities in both countries that needed good publicly provided services—and so they duly reminded officials in opinion polls. In California or New York, Lewisham or Hertfordshire, declining services meant declining quality of life.

As the economic downturn of the early 1990s dragged on, some reductions became painful. In New York, where an $8 billion budget deficit for the 1992 fiscal year obliged the state to make deep spending cuts, suburban communities faced huge reductions in the unrestricted state-aid dollars used to patrol streets, fight fires, shovel snow and maintain parks and libraries.[20] In California the results of cutting services so as to eliminate half of a $14.6 billion state deficit ranged from a crippling effect on the state university system to a sharp reduction in firefighting crews and cuts in food safety and water-quality programs.[21] The next round of cuts in fiscal 1993 raised fears about the end of the California dream: already staggering under the burden of high unemployment, slumping revenues and the Los Angeles riots, the state was forced to slash education, health and welfare and support for city and county governments, as well as raising charges and fees. Moving companies began to report that record numbers of residents were packing and leaving the Golden State.

High-income persons did not suffer, but middle-class voters usually worried when federal and state reductions went too far. They opposed the welfare state in theory and favored rolling it back, but when the Reagan administration made its heaviest assault on middle-class federal programs in 1985, targeting school-lunch assistance, college aid, mass transit, general revenue sharing and others, even GOP voters protested. To the top 1 percent of Americans, government transfer payments were a negligible part of their own income (four tenths of 1 percent in 1988), while the payments Washington made to others merely aggravated federal tax demands. By contrast, citizens in the mid-range 40th to 59th percentiles received almost 10 percent of their total 1988 income from transfer payments, and enjoyed other substantial benefits from government loans, subsidies, aid programs and facilities ranging from national parks to intercoastal waterways. So although no precise data existed, many middle-class families believed themselves net gainers and worried that reduced or privatized services or a new system of means tests, charges and user fees would take money from their pockets. Conservative columnist Warren Brookes complained in 1990 that the broad middle class saw a "bigger stake" in federal spending (being its biggest beneficiary) than in keeping income taxes at their 1990 levels, and polls supported him.[22] As the economic downturn worsened, forcing cutbacks at the state and local levels, voter support for federal-program outlays and activist government grew.

Conservatism's occasional extreme exaltation of economic markets represented another breach with the beliefs that guided America's successful years after 1945. While liberals like to invoke societal and "community" values at the expense of incentive, markets and human acquisitiveness, the failing of the political right—amply indulged in the 1980s and into the 1990s—is to deify "markets" and "incentive" to the detriment of social and community interests. The more extreme mid-1980s examples, such as the Law and Economics movement, verged on self-caricature. One of its leaders, federal appeals court judge Richard A. Posner, proclaimed that the law should emphasize markets, efficiency and "wealth-maximization," not elusive concepts like society or fairness; and in a moment of particular enthusiasm, he even suggested making a market in babies so that it would be easier for couples to adopt.[23] Other market conservatives, such as the editorial writers of the *Wall Street Journal,* thought that "civil rights" should be increasingly defined economically, and President Reagan himself on July 3, 1987, proposed an Economic Bill of Rights in a ceremony at Washington's Jefferson Memorial. In sharp contrast to Franklin D. Roosevelt, who promoted a different Four Freedoms, Reagan invoked *commercial* liberties:

> The freedom to work and pursue a livelihood in one's own way, free from excessive government regulation and subsidized government competition; freedom to enjoy the fruits of one's labor without excessive taxing, spending and borrowing by the government; the freedom to own and control one's own property free from coercive or confiscatory regulation; and freedom to participate in a free market, to contract freely for goods and services and to achieve one's full potential without government limits on opportunity.[24]

Earlier Reagan-era hymns to economic individualism, together with conservatism's seeming abandonment of the egalitarianism of the New Deal and Fair Deal periods, prompted sociologist Robert N. Bellah to complain in mid-decade that rugged self-reliance had become "cancerous," sapping the middle class's sense of community and institutional commitment.[25] In addition to permissiveness toward finance and mergers, the politics of economic individualism, liberals charged, had shortchanged community interests like public schools, public roads, public parks, public health, public transport and public libraries. The supreme American public spaces of the Reagan era were not learning centers but economic arenas—the omnipresent marketplace, from office buildings and suburban malls to gentrified downtown shopping concourses.[26] For Middle America, the new preoccupation with enterprise and markets to the detriment of public services did have a downside: as public outlays on roads, schools and health came under pressure, the predictable results—worsened commuter gridlock, crowded classrooms and shortchanged hospitals and clinics—confronted ordinary families with either accepting lost services or paying new taxes or fees or higher bills, and as Chapter 6 shows, these losses and pressures became an ingredient of the middle-class squeeze.

The international aspect of 1980s worship of markets also broke with the past in a way that affected many average families. Some conservatives became "capitalist one-worlders," scoffing at national boundaries and even the concept of the nation-state. In the words of

The Wall Street Journal, they were "the economists and academics who believe that in a global economy, with goods and especially capital surging across political borders, the economic fortunes of individual countries aren't important anymore. The U.S. trade deficit and other statistics, they argue, are only artificial figures in what has become a multinational corporate economy in which political distinctions matter little. It's all one big market, they contend, so why worry about it?"[27] Workers who lost jobs in embattled U.S. industries were less able to shrug, and federal policymakers' responsiveness to boundaryless economics in the 1980s—including openness to lobbyists who promoted foreign interests—almost certainly abetted the decade's decline in real manufacturing wages. Perhaps America's older manufacturing industries, unimportant to adherents of the global market, truly had been a prop of the broader U.S. postwar affluence, so that their decline pulled America's short-lived blue-collar middle class down with them. Perhaps finance and services could not make up the loss. Views of this sort clashed with prevailing opinion, but we will see in Chapter 8 that previous similar transitions in Holland and Britain had signaled economic polarization and trouble, *not* revival, for the middle class.

Inroads on the principles of egalitarianism and disproportionate burden-bearing by the rich were widespread enough by the end of the 1980s that tax policy was just one ingredient. In the United States, calls for states' rights or "local decision-making" sometimes involved pushing federal programs and activities down to levels of government where the program would be abandoned, where money was unavailable or where funding would be too onerous for those who controlled local policy. While Washington could not openly discriminate against areas with greater needs than resources, pushing burdens back to state and local government often had the same effect. Yet it was striking how few politicians spoke up for the national "commonweal"—the general good or shared prosperity of the community. To America's Founding Fathers of 1776, attention to the commonweal was essential to national well-being. Private property, while important and valuable, was never an end in itself.

In Margaret Thatcher's Britain and Ronald Reagan's United States, however, a contrary philosophic shift became unmistakable. The willingness of America's elite to make economic sacrifice or serve in the military, to cite two conspicuous examples, had begun to erode during the 1960s, and widening urban racial gaps reinforced even liberal doubt about government's usefulness in promoting equality. Lyndon Johnson's ambitious Great Society had been much less successful than

Franklin Roosevelt's New Deal. By the 1980s many public-policy experts openly acknowledged being disheartened by government's failures during the 1960s, and sociologists like Seymour Martin Lipset allowed that increased acceptance of inequality in the West had "even socialist parties . . . acknowledging that for the economy to work you have to have unequal rewards."[28] During the 1980s the economic gap between people at the top and everyone else widened in virtually every arena—from sports and entertainment to business and finance. Inequality began to run amok.

To some extent, America was caught up in a two-part social myth: on the one hand an update of Horatio Alger and the anybody-can-make-it thesis, and on the other what Professor Benjamin DeMott called "the myth of classlessness"—the insistence that there were no classes in America, and that everyone, rich and poor, had common interests.[29] Conservatives were the self-serving propagators, he said, citing George Bush's insistence that class is "for European democracies or something else—it isn't for the United States of America. We are not going to be divided by class."[30] Yet many upper-middle-class cultural liberals shared the conservative desire to suppress any resurgent national discussion of economic class or of the quiet decline of egalitarian culture. Economist Robert Kuttner, a self-confessed populist, stood out from the prevalent elite opinion in being appalled "that the standard line on the declining middle has gone straight from 'It isn't happening' to 'We can't do anything about it.' "[31]

The Emerging Populist Protest

Yet the irony, just as in the 1960s, was that voters were ahead of the nation's opinion-molders in perceiving the failure and self-interest of an elite—this time, one premised on wealth and the glories of the marketplace. Writers and scholars might discuss rising acceptance of inequality and the fashionable admiration of the rich, but polls suggest that the electorate had started to become disenchanted in 1987 and 1988. By early 1990 *The New York Times* noted that Wall Street found an unnerving whiff of populism in the public's anger over junk-bond pioneer Michael Milken's $550-million-a-year salary, coupled with enthusiastic national response to books like *Bonfire of the Vanities* and *Barbarians at the Gates*.[32] Another measurement of popular disenchantment was apparent in the ratings slide of once-hot television glitz operas like *Dallas, Dynasty* and *Falconcrest*.

Then, in the autumn of 1990, when the issues of concentrated wealth and higher taxes for the rich suddenly took center stage in Washington's federal budget debate, public opinion polls in the United States surprised politicians with their populist intensity. Further detail will be set forth in Chapter 3, but *Fortune* magazine's survey right after the November elections found three quarters of respondents indicating that they had supported candidates in the election partly because of promises to spread the tax burden more fairly (from the middle class to the rich). December polling for NBC News and *The Wall Street Journal* found 84 percent of the public backing the Democrats' proposed surtax on millionaires—and that included 80 percent of the Republicans! Then in March 1991 the Roper Poll reported six out of ten Americans calling the federal tax system unfair and emphasizing increased fairness (higher corporate income taxes and a "millionaires' tax"). And an April national survey by the *Los Angeles Times* found a similar resentment of the federal tax system's unfairness, coupled with agreement by three quarters of respondents that "the wealthy should pay a higher tax rate than they do now."[33] There was good reason that by 1992, in what was by then an obvious populist surge, two of the three presidential candidates—Democrat Clinton and independent Perot—favored increasing taxes on the rich.

Nor was resentment of official favoritism to wealth confined to America. As we have seen, surveys were measuring related unhappiness among average voters in Britain, Canada and Japan. In all three countries, voters told polltakers that conservatism or conservative governments favored the rich and paid too little attention to the middle class, although voters had other complaints about the liberal or left alternatives.[34] The belief among some opinion-molders that the public accepted the economic philosophy of the 1980s and opposed raising taxes on the top 1 percent because of belief they themselves would be rich one day simply did not square with the evidence.

Indeed, as the 1992 elections made clear, something vaguely resembling the populist spirit that elected Andrew Jackson and Harry Truman was alive and well in the U.S. political system, and not just in obvious locales like Ohio steel towns and Missouri farm-foreclosure centers but to a significant extent also in raw new subdivisions at the ends of California freeways and on winding lanes in overtaxed suburban Long Island. Clinton's plurality of even the suburban vote should not have been a surprise. Sixty years earlier, under the New Deal, egalitarianism and government economic activism had replaced the conservatism of the 1920s because many in the middle class thought that they, too, might be in jeopardy and people looked to Washington for help. Some of those same concerns and fears were taking shape again in the early 1990s, even though voter doubts about the Democrats lingered, suspicions of government was still strong and the role electoral politics itself could play was unclear: could voters bring about another national watershed from the grass roots, or was Washington, divided for so long between the parties and encrusted with special interests, so paralyzed and self-protective that Americans could no longer expect politics and voting to be a solution?

C H A P T E R 3

The Middle-Class Political Response
of the 1990s: Populism or Stalemate?

The great political upheaval of the 1960s is not that of Senator Eugene
McCarthy's relatively small group of upper-middle-class intellectual supporters, but a populist revolt of the American masses who have been
elevated by prosperity to middle-class status and conservatism. *Their*
revolt is against the caste, policies and taxation of the mandarins of
Establishment liberalism.

—Kevin P. Phillips, *The Emerging Republican Majority,* 1969

Anti-establishment populism has been the most important force in our
politics for the last twenty years. It is neither liberal nor conservative.
Politicians on both sides have used it effectively. American populism has
three important characteristics. It is ideologically ambivalent. And it has
displaced progressivism as the dominant motif of American politics. Elites
tend to be rich and well-educated, hence, economically conservative and
culturally sophisticated. Populism is anti-elitist and therefore just the
reverse—left-wing on economic issues and right-wing on social and cultural issues.

—Political analyst William Schneider, 1986

In 1990 and 1991, as disenchanted Americans started telling pollsters—sometimes by 65 percent and even 75 percent majorities—that
the United States was "seriously off on the wrong track," the anti-
establishment populism so recurrent in U.S. political history roared
once again. As I shall discuss in Chapter 9, angry outsiders like Vermont Socialist Bernard Sanders and Louisiana neo-fascist David Duke
surprised observers by their political success, which foreshadowed the
further populist waves of 1992. Columnist David Broder, a pillar of
establishment thinking, muttered about "populist chic," and to an
extent, his skepticism was appropriate: the capital's political class,
worried about grass-roots anger, began the 1992 presidential election
year weighing appeals to the frustrated middle class. Middle-class
populism became a cliché—until Ross Perot's independent populist

presidential candidacy pulled into a temporary lead in late-spring polls, and fear spread that middle-class frustration might be out of control.

Much of this was predictable. Populism in the United States has been more strident than almost anywhere else.[1] Yet the American style has been not to indulge in dangerous radicalism but over the last two centuries to harness and contain it: recurrent populism has been a periodic restorative of the unique genius of an American political process that, ultimately, has been orderly and centrist.

In contrast to continental Europe, where many capital cities have laid out broad boulevards to let the artillery suppress revolutionary mobs, the United States has achieved its revolutions through the ballot box, changing long-term control of the White House once every generation or so, usually all but expelling the party in power. And because the United States has no hereditary aristocracy to get in the way, these watersheds have also served to reshuffle the nation's elites.

This is what happened in 1800, 1828, 1860, 1932 and, most recently, 1968. After the 1966 elections, my sense that the conservative tide was producing another of these great waves prompted me to undertake my book *The Emerging Republican Majority.* Although very few political scientists agreed with its theses when it was published in 1969, by 1993 the Republicans had held the White House for twenty of the previous twenty-four years, clearly confirming my prediction.

The economics of the 1980s suggested that another tide would soon wash in. In *The Politics of Rich and Poor,* published in 1990, I suggested that many of the prerequisites of such a transition were in place—excessive wealth concentration (the traditional Republican Achilles' heel) and the rising anger of middle-class voters, along with other populist symptoms that ranged from intensifying public frustration with Washington to proliferating ballot initiatives and support for limiting officeholders' terms. The political calendar certainly suggested that another watershed could come in the 1990s, but in *Rich and Poor* I declined to predict that it would take the traditional electoral form.

In Chapters 1 and 2, I have tried to illustrate the rising plight of the middle class since 1973 and how it was made worse by the new economic philosophies of the 1980s. Here, in this chapter, I hope to frame the political importance of that deterioration. On the one hand, the possibility for upheaval could be seen in the economic vulnerability of the Republican middle-class, "populist-conservative" national majority that had been stitched together a quarter century earlier, a vulnerability that was evident in opinion polls revealing fears about future living standards and complaints about the economic unfairness of the 1980s and overtaxation of the middle class alongside inadequate taxation of the rich. Disbelievers, however, pointed to Washington's comfortable and unprecedented division of power between a Republican executive branch and a Democratic legislature, cemented by special interests. Fringe candidates and unexpectedly successful populist presidential contenders might cross the 1991–92 political sky like comets, but a broad national success for outsider politics would not easily be achieved—and even winning the election would only be the beginning. Polls taken for Ohio's Kettering Foundation, which became a touchstone for anti-Washington candidates in 1992, showed voters concerned that Washington had become an iron triangle beyond the reach of effective electoral correction.

The Late-Twentieth-Century Reemergence of U.S. Populism

The populism that had helped conservatives win the White House in 1968 remained wary of government over the next quarter century or so, and these suspicions flamed up again in the early 1990s. The economy had weakened and Washington seemed captive to special interests. Partly because of Watergate but also for other reasons, the Republican dominance of the presidency that had begun in 1968 never became more than a limited Washington beachhead; the Democrats usually controlled Congress, producing a divided government that shared power with a "moderate establishment," bipartisan in its makeup, interest-group in its economics, replacing the prior liberal Democratic one. The result was that populist forces bubbled on the right *and* left, although usually without much serious effect.*

From the standpoint of alienation and institutional disenchantment, however, the electorate of the early 1990s was seething. The average voter's increasing frustration with the domination by special interests of representative government—the constitutional system tailored to the Founding Fathers' insistence that elected legislators and executives make decisions, not voters themselves—had aroused sentiment for popular direct rule or plebiscitary government. By the late 1980s, voters were ready to take matters into their own hands by supporting record numbers of ballot initiatives, drives to limit the number of terms elected officials could serve and crusades to recall governors or oust unpopular judges at the ballot box (as with California chief justice

---

*As an example of the typical marginalization of splinter-party populism, David Duke— later to be the subject of enormous press coverage—ran for president in 1988 on a third-party Populist ticket, receiving only 48,000 votes and almost no media coverage.

Rose Bird), as well as demands that some economic regulators (such as state insurance commissioners) be elected rather than appointed. Disgruntled citizens also reveled in statewide ballot victories that forced legislatures to cut their staffs and budgets (as in California Proposition 140 of 1990) and compelled state officials to detail their contacts with and payments from lobbyists. The support Perot commanded in 1992 for ideas like a national "electronic town hall" and enacting new federal tax changes by nationwide popular referendum drew on this same mood.

Appropriately, it had been during the first populist/progressive reform wave in 1900–1914 that such tools as initiatives, referenda and recalls were first introduced at the state level. Together with nonpartisan or unicameral legislatures and direct popular election of U.S. senators (who had previously been elected by state legislatures), these expedients were a response to the corruption of the Gilded Age, and were advanced by such politicians as Senators Hiram Johnson of California, George Norris of Nebraska and Robert LaFollette of Wisconsin to take power away from elected politicians, who were too easily bought, and give it to the people. California, in particular, inserted the right of popular initiative into the state constitution in 1911 as a specific device for the electorate to diffuse the power of special interests and monopolies.

By the late 1980s, popular concern had regained a similar intensity. As reported by the National Conference of State Legislatures, the number of initiatives on state ballots set records. There were 54 in 1982, then 55 in 1988, 64 in 1990 and finally 75 in 1992.[2] Attempts to limit the number of terms that state legislators and officials could serve also mushroomed from three states in 1990 (California, Colorado and Oklahoma) to 14 in 1992. National polls showed two-to-one majorities in favor of slapping similar limitations on members of Congress.

The Republicans, because they controlled few state legislatures, were particularly active proponents of limitations on terms and prerogatives that they believed would cripple rival Democrats. The American electorate, however, trusted neither party. Mid-1991 polling showed that, by 61 percent to 28 percent, voters thought it better that Congress and the White House be controlled by different parties. The result in early 1992 was still essentially the same: 61 percent to 32 percent.[3] That changed in the summer, to Clinton's benefit, but these suspicions of concentrated power were classic populism: Divide power, let them watch each other. Polls also showed a majority of Americans favoring a third major party.[4]

In the early 1980s, the plebiscitary thrust of U.S. populism had been predominantly conservative, set forth in votes to limit taxes and government and to reject cultural liberalism (the defeat, for example, of state constitutional amendments for equal rights for women, even in ostensibly liberal New York and New Jersey). By the end of the decade, however, some changing economic resentments were apparent in initiatives related to insurance, consumer protection and taxes. In 1991 fully 75 percent of Californians, including a majority of self-identified Republicans, told polltakers they favored increasing the top state income tax rate from 9.3 percent to 11 percent for family incomes over $200,000, in order to restore levels that had existed through 1987. Thus, when Republican governor Pete Wilson reluctantly acquiesced during the state's 1991 budget crisis, a spokesman for the California Tax Reform Association boasted that Wilson gave in because "they knew we were going to the 1992 ballot with an initiative to tax the rich, and they knew we were going to win."[5] A dozen other states also raised top income tax rates in 1991–92.

It was a revealing symptom. As party strategists on both sides turned their attention to the 1992 election, they noted that the U.S. electorate now wanted federal tax fairness and some form of national health insurance. We have seen how polls published in *The Wall Street Journal* and elsewhere showed that 84 percent of Americans favored a surtax on millionaires, 81 percent backed the Democrats' Gore-Downey tax increase on the rich and 67 percent backed a federal health insurance program. A new common wisdom was in the wind.

Less well understood, though, was Americans' gathering anger at the rich and at the speculative practices so widespread in business and finance in the 1980s. In its poll taken right after the 1990 election, *Fortune* magazine found that one out of three Americans felt the United States would be better off without any millionaires at all, up from one out of four a decade earlier, while 55 percent of respondents agreed that "millionaires have gotten where they are by exploiting others."[6] A Democratic party survey by Mellman and Lazarus in 1991 claimed that instead of thinking that the economy improved under Reagan and Bush, more voters believed that "the rich have gotten richer while the middle class got stuck paying the bill."[7] That autumn a Gallup-CNN poll found voters, by two-to-one, tagging the Republicans as the party of "political favoritism and corruption," while three out of four said the GOP favored the wealthy and business.[8] Results like these bespoke a resentment of what had happened in the 1980s, as well as an important mood change: conservative economics and economic elites were beginning to displace liberal social policies and cultural elites as the prime target of populist voters. Seeds that would flower in late 1991 and 1992 were already beginning to germinate.

Corporate America had added to the provocation, as even sympathetic publications like *Business Week* condemned the soaring pay of chief executive officers. Experts told U.S. Senate hearings that in 1990, the average CEO of a major U.S. corporation had received 113 times the compensation of an average worker, up from 29 a decade earlier. Japanese and German CEOs, by contrast, received on average just 20 to 35 times the pay of one of their average workers.[9] The vast size of top-executive salaries and golden parachutes, awarded while so many workers and middle-level managers were being laid off, helped sour even upper-bracket Americans on the workings of heyday capitalism. One early 1992 NBC/Wall Street Journal poll found rank-and-file Republicans just as lopsidedly angry as Democrats at excessive CEO salaries. In 1991 the Roper polling organization showed a startling decline since 1982 in citizens who believed in the worthiness of business profits. The biggest slippage came among the most active and well-informed tenth of the public, some themselves corporate executives. For the first time, favorable statements about the profit motive and profit system drew less than majority support, with 52 percent of "influentials" agreeing that "most [business] profits go to make rich people richer."[10]

Survey-takers were also reporting a broader frustration, in which large majorities of Americans indicated that instead of "going in the right direction," things in the United States had gotten "seriously off on the wrong track." In late 1990, as the recession was deepening and the United States was debating whether to drive Iraq out of Kuwait, Americans had chosen "seriously off on the wrong track" by ratios of over two-to-one. In February and March 1991, as the war ended favorably, optimism flared again for a few weeks. But by summertime pessimism once again led by solid majorities. By 1992 belief that things had gone wrong had returned to the fearful levels of 1979–80.

This wasn't 1894, when Ohio currency reformer and Populist spokesman Jacob Coxey marched his disgruntled "army" on Washington. And it was even less like the 25 percent unemployment of mid-Depression 1933. However, as the 1992 presidential campaign began, the smugness of the 1980s was giving way to that unique mix of populism, frustration and incipient reformism that has been present in most U.S. political upheavals.

Middle-Class Populism and
the Vulnerable Republican Coalition

The extent to which the post-1968 Republican presidential coalition would become restive in the K-Marts and bitter in the subdivisions reflected its origins: as the product of the *previous* wave of middle-class populism—the wave that replaced the old New Deal elites with Nixon's cloth-coat Republicanism—it was particularly sensitive to a redefinition in the 1990s of middle-class priorities. By late 1991, as the recession-trapped U.S. economy weakened again, a national survey by the Times-Mirror Corporation revealed what threatened to become the cleavage line. "The potential for division within the ranks of the Republican party along socioeconomic lines is very strong," Times-Mirror polltakers said, because low-middle- and middle-income Republicans of a populist or "disaffected" stripe were being drawn toward a directional change in Washington in favor of national health insurance, protection of American jobs, higher taxes on the wealthy and more federal government help for the middle class.[11]

The lesson of U.S. history has been that such qualms rarely remain abstract. Nowhere is the populist mode in American politics more pronounced than in its record of inciting once-a-generation national upheavals in which some new regional supremacy, economic ascendancy or demographic majority pushes to the fore, putting a new party in the White House and in the process debunking some existing elite, be it Philadelphia financiers in 1828, slave owners in 1860, economic royalists in 1932 or liberal intelligentsia and bureaucrats in 1968.

Historians date the nation's first watershed from 1800, when Thomas Jefferson, penman of the Declaration of Independence, triumphed over the commercially and financially attuned Federalists of America's coastal strip and went on to build a generation of Jeffersonian presidential dominance. By 1824 this first loose party system had become meaningless and was ready for a new definition. That came in 1828, when Andrew Jackson's presidential victory turned another egalitarian political wave into a watershed for the new Democratic party. The Jacksonian coalition, in turn, lasted until the 1850s, when slavery tore it apart. Then in 1860 the antislavery issue, together with the expansion of the frontier westward, tipped the national power balance and helped elect antislavery Northerner Abraham Lincoln as president. The war followed, and ultimately there arose a new Civil War–based Republican majority, including substantial elements of the old Jacksonian Coalition. *The critical point, to which we will return*

Common man watershed model

shortly, is that in each of these upheavals, the values of the common man were front-and-center.

The next watershed, 1896, worked differently. National politics had been stalemated for twenty years, as neither party was able to win more than a plurality in presidential elections. But in 1896, the industrial and financial captains of the Republican party narrowly beat back the fusion of the Democratic and Populist parties behind William Jennings Bryan of Nebraska. The Bryan movement couldn't reach beyond its agrarian origins to speak for workers in manufacturing—a fatal weakness because, in 1890, manufacturing for the first time represented a larger share of GNP than agriculture. A relatively united Northeast and Great Lakes defeated the fiery Nebraskan, giving industrial Republicanism a second-wave supremacy based in the populous, urbanizing states of the North. The year 1896 was a watershed in which populism defined its common-man constituency too narrowly to succeed.

The political transformation of 1932 produced the more usual egalitarian pattern, as the Depression enabled a new hard-times coalition to fuse the populist South and West with the blue-collar industrial North. This combination included America's decisive new demographic force, urbanization, and what would prove to be the zenith of the immigrant-filled, labor-leaning great cities of the North from Boston, New York and Philadelphia to Cleveland, Detroit and Chicago. Once again, common-man economics had the political muscle.

Which brings us to the next watershed, 1968, and the socioeconomic factors that a quarter century later made the Republican establishment vulnerable to middle-class populism. Before the Nixon coalition came together in 1968, a considerable minority of experts was predicting a progressive or leftish politics, along the lines of what Charles Reich talked about in his 1970 best-seller, *The Greening of America.* Indeed, many political scientists who had grown up under the New Deal concluded that watershed politics in the United States always reflected the interests of the common man, whether the "free soil, free labor" followers of Abraham Lincoln or Franklin D. Roosevelt's "forgotten Americans" of 1932. Any new major change, they said, would have to come from the same direction.

What they missed was that by 1968 the "common man" was driving a two-year-old Pontiac, grumbling about welfare chiselers and pondering a move to suburbia to get away from high crime rates and enroll his children in better schools. Meanwhile the national Democrats were forsaking their old New Deal meat-and-potatoes liberalism to identify with minorities and counterculture forces. This gave Republicans another chance to speak for "average American" interests as the Democrats veered off on parochial tangents. The Republicans had such an opportunity twice before: first in 1860, when Democrats divided over the narrow, unsustainable cause of Southern slave owners and secession, then again in 1896 when that year's Democratic convention, in turning to Bryan, embraced what proved to be parochial images of Farm Belt radicalism and evangelism. It would work again in 1968–72.

In 1968 Richard Nixon and Alabama governor George Wallace, the third-party candidate, together captured 57 percent of the total presidential vote. Without Wallace in 1972, Nixon won by a 61 percent landslide and launched still another of America's "common man" revolutions, this one the most affluent ever. Its swing voters came from what pundit Joseph Kraft called Middle America—the people in the middle whose incomes, relatively traditional culture and flag-waving support of America were generally under siege by civil rights activists, inflation, riots and the worsening mess in Vietnam.[12] Its new bastions were suburbia and the Sun Belt—a combination of lower-middle-class Archie Bunker country at the end of the big-city subway lines, commuter country and small towns almost anywhere, and new look-alike suburbs backhoed and bulldozed out of red Georgia clay, Florida mangrove swamp, East Texas piney woods and the fringe of the California desert.

This fit the common-man watershed model, albeit with lower-middle-class tailoring. Prior to World War II, the much smaller U.S. "middle class"—politically divided by Civil War geography, economically far above the median and culturally closer to establishment values—was split between Northern and Southern regional parties but dominated neither. The New Majority, by contrast, was Northern *and* Southern, conservative *and* populist, middle-class *and* arriviste, an unprecedented and volatile combination to store and handle.

Conservatives confirmed the transition with a new rhetoric. Richard Nixon's outreach was no surprise; his famous 1952 Checkers speech, invoking the Nixon family's less-than-affluent middle-class status and his wife's "good Republican cloth coat"—expensive minks were for "the rich"—resonated in Levittown and Oak Lawn. But the more revealing approach was that of the *other* major standard-bearer of 1964–72 presidential insurgency, Alabama's Wallace. As a boy, Wallace had chopped cotton, and as a World War II enlisted man, he and his wife had lived in a converted New Mexico chicken coop. As a presidential candidate, he aimed his campaign at the "truck driver, the beautician and the barber," and only one broad class appeal was possible. George Wallace was for the "folks"—and in the 1960s, the folks (like the Alabama governor himself) mostly thought of themselves as the "great American middle class."

In short, the Middle America of the Nixon era represented a whole new chapter in political sociology: the self-perceived middle class now took in a vast population whose parents and grandparents had cheered the establishment-baiting insurgencies of Franklin D. Roosevelt, Al Smith, Robert La Follette and William Jennings Bryan. By the end of the 1960s, the typical more or less median-income U.S. voters considered themselves "middle-class," but with enough uncertainties, inelegancies and outsider sentiments to introduce entirely new meaning to the term.

Appropriately enough, 1968 and 1969 saw the emergence of a sweeping new lexicon of politics, producing in two years—just as in 1932 and 1933—the slogans and labels of an electoral revolution. During the 1968 campaign, Richard Nixon talked about the "forgotten middle-class Americans," the "silent center" and the "quiet majority." Then on May 9, 1969, Vice President Spiro Agnew said, "It's time for America's silent majority to stand up for its rights," putting another major phrase in the political dictionary. "Joe Sixpack," beer-drinking symbol of the administration's hoped-for appeal to the blue-collar lower-middle class, made his figurative appearance as the 1970s began.[13] Even middle-of-the-country geography became a repository of implied wisdom when Nixon White House aide John Ehrlichman, resurrecting an old vaudeville cliché, recommended that GOP politics "play in Peoria."

Language like this was profoundly *un*conservative and much disliked by Republicanism's old upper-class elites. The new GOP mindset emphasized the *middle* part of the country in virtually every way—economically, culturally and even geographically—but with enough anti-establishment rhetoric to raise the ghost of William Jennings Bryan. The 1964–72 speeches of Barry Goldwater, Ronald Reagan, George Wallace and Richard Nixon sizzled with caustic references to bankrupt elites, arrogant establishments, "limousine" liberals, Harvard intellectuals, know-it-all judges, Ivy League "pointy-head" experts, the Liberal Establishment and the Eastern Seaboard. Goldwater, the 1964 Republican presidential nominee, had even joked about sawing off the East Coast.

Those were the formative years, because the coalition that elected Ronald Reagan continued to follow most of the same regional, ethnic and religious patterns laid down in 1968–72. Reagan's forty-nine-state landslide of 1984, in which he captured 59 percent of the popular vote, was very similar to Nixon's forty-nine-state and 61 percent popular-vote landslide of 1972, although Reagan was stronger among young voters whereas Nixon had done better among Southerners. However, it was the new circumstances of the late 1980s and George Bush's candidacy in 1988 that revealed the potential instability of a coalition with populist swing voters and elite leaders and forced attention to fall on Middle America's essential schizophrenia: cultural conservatism and traditionalism at loggerheads with decidedly unconservative economic resentments.

The Two Faces of Middle-Class Populism

The populist constituencies of the old New Majority had mixed reactions to the emerging Republican economics of the 1980s. Wall Street Republicanism has never appealed in places like northern Alabama, south Boston and panhandle Idaho. Ronald Reagan, with his innate populist, anti-establishment appeal, could keep this incipient dissent in check, as he did easily in 1984. Not so Bush, the Andover- and Yale-educated scion of a prominent investment banking family. In early summer 1988 polls, in which he trailed several Democratic rivals by 5 to 10 points, GOP strategists perceived that Bush provoked cleavages typical of less happy Republican eras. Voters saw Bush as too friendly to the rich rather than committed to ordinary people. Advisers told him to stay away from his sprawling million-dollar vacation "cottage" in Kennebunkport, Maine, where the aura of old money was as evident as salt spray and lobster pots. Surveys in June and July showed him facing close races even in safe Republican states like Indiana and Nebraska.

Recognizing the coalition's vulnerability, Republican strategists sought to keep anti-elite economic sentiment among swing voters from dominating the election dialogue, so they put forward the New Majority populism's *other* face—cultural, religious, racial and nationalist—another politics with a long history. Its postwar success began in the early 1950s, when reporters shorthanded the key themes of the 1952 Eisenhower presidential campaign as K-1, C-2—"Korea, Communism and Corruption." Then, as we have seen, two successive Nixon campaigns sounded a clarion call against central-city riots, soaring crime rates, permissive judges, antiwar demonstrators and flag burners, campus radicalism, busing for racial balance and racial quotas. One of

1972's most memorable GOP alliterations portrayed Democratic presidential nominee George McGovern as the candidate of "acid, amnesty and abortion."

Resurrecting this demonology proved to be a powerful GOP tactic in 1988. These cutting-edge issues from the social cockpit of the late 1960s and early 1970s had played the same long-term coalition-building role for post-1968 Republicans that slavery, the war between the states and Northern Yankee–versus–Irish Catholic tensions had contributed to the Civil War–based Republican national majority a century earlier. So in 1988, as the Republicans came under criticism for resurgent upper-bracket economics and preferences, it was logical to return to the old symbols—the flags, the battles, the cultural tensions, the disdain for liberal elites and racial fears—around which their coalition had originally gathered so many millions of ordinary people in 1968–72.

Indeed, the Gilded Age provided a direct strategic precedent for the use of cultural themes to suppress economic populism. In the 1870s and 1880s, as Granger, Greenback and Populist splinter candidacies siphoned off Republican voters, especially in the deflation-racked Farm Belt, the GOP countered by "waving the bloody shirt" of Civil War politics. The objective was to make Iowa farmers and Indiana mill workers remember their comrades at Shiloh's Hornet's Nest and Gettysburg's Cemetery Ridge, and forget the railroad owners in Minneapolis and the bankers in New York.

Finally, during the great economic confrontation of 1896 with William Jennings Bryan, the GOP cast presidential nominee William McKinley as the nation's "patriotic leader." In his classic history *The Populist Movement,* Lawrence Goodwyn recalled how the Republican National Committee distributed carloads of flags throughout the country and Mark Hanna "conceived the idea of a public 'flag day' in the nation's leading cities—a day specifically in honor of McKinley. 'Sound Money clubs' of New York and San Francisco were put in charge of enormous flag day spectacles. . . . In the critical Midwestern states, Civil War veterans known as 'Patriotic Heroes' toured with buglers and a cannon mounted on a flatcar."[14]

It worked. On economic issues alone, Bryan might have reduced the GOP coalition fatally, notwithstanding his prairie parochialism. Even with that albatross, he ran a close race in swing states like California, Ohio and Indiana. But with the help of flags and lopsided financial resources, the Republicans won, albeit narrowly. The threat was over, even though Bryan made another reasonably strong (46 percent) race in 1900, when the Republicans introduced still another tactic that would reemerge in the 1990s: parades of U.S. soldiers returning from their overseas victory in the Spanish-American war.

In the 1988 election, campaigners for George Bush not only won but rolled back a large midsummer Democratic lead by waving their own "bloody shirt" and reintroducing the social themes and hostilities of the GOP's 1968–72 crucible years. In 1987 Bush had made a half-hour program for broadcast in Florida describing his Christian experience of being born again; during the election year itself, he paid his famous campaign visit to a New Jersey flag factory. Then there was the campaign's even more famous television commercial attacking Massachusetts' furloughs for convicted killers and featuring Willie Horton, the black escapee who raped a white woman in Maryland. The Horton advertisements renewed America's ongoing racial sensitivities. The Yale-educated Republican nominee even managed to pin the fatal "elitist" label on the Democratic donkey by linking opponent Dukakis to "Harvard boutiques." One Democratic adviser complained to bemused journalists that "They're running a class war against us, saying we're a bunch of Cambridge-Brookline eccentric literature professors. We've got to fight back and say that they're the party of privilege, the party of the rich folks."

But they did not, so what the election showed was that Republicans still understood the two faces of American populism—an enmity toward establishment economics mixed with a distaste for cultural liberalism—far better than the Democrats. Two decades of winning populist constituencies had been instructive. To let capitalist-conservative heyday economics and concentrated wealth become the principal debate could have been fatal. Two years later, as we shall see, the Democrats *did* make economics dominate the 1990 midterm elections, slashing at the Republicans as the "party of the rich" for weeks before a stunned GOP could counterattack. Republican voter identification plummeted, and for the first time since the Reagan era began, the favoritism-to-wealth issue was centrally framed.

As 1991 began, the Republicans knew what they wanted in 1992: an election context in which powerful cultural and patriotic themes suppressed debate over weak economic growth, bias toward the rich and middle-class frustration. And for a few months they had it—thanks to a successful war in the Persian Gulf that sent George Bush's ratings soaring toward 90 percent and whetted party hopes of a 1992 landslide with all-powerful coattails. But by late spring the public had come to believe that Bush stopped the fighting too soon, leaving Saddam Hussein in power, so that voters rated the Gulf war as only a partial

Bush / Rep.
campaign

victory, diluting its political resonance. Even so, knowing that the war was a plus for the president, Republican strategists envisioned a campaign that combined the flags, patriotism and military parades used to combat populism in 1896 with a rekindled attention to the racial and cultural themes of 1968–72. By early summer, pundits were describing the putative strategy as "KCQ"—Kuwait, crime and quotas.

Law-and-order sympathies were exploited by issues like the death penalty and insistence on conservative judges. Racial concerns were touched by a series of White House attacks on racial quotas and on Democratic civil rights legislation for requiring them. The president's attack on "political correctness" invoked yet another genuine tension of the Nixon era—fear of campus radicalism. Flag-burning, too, had angered many Americans two decades earlier, and in 1990 Bush had proposed an anti–flag desecration constitutional amendment. Nevertheless 1992 opened with much of this renewed social-issue strategy in jeopardy. A weak economy was crowding the Persian Gulf war into the background; the administration's civil rights compromise with the Democrats had helped stimulate the rise of two combative Republican presidential primary challengers, David Duke, who quickly faded, and Patrick Buchanan, who, as we shall see in Chapter 9, wound up turning part of the issue of racial tension and quotas back against the Bush administration; and even the anti-crime drumbeat was losing credibility as violence soared in city after city. In the spring of 1992, following the racially triggered riots in Los Angeles, polls showed Bush losing ground for want of domestic-policy credibility despite law-and-order rhetoric. Democrat Clinton gained little for his higher marks for handling racial problems. The big gains after Los Angeles went to the man in the middle—independent Perot. The 1980s schizophrenia of middle-class populism was breaking down.

Hard times also shifted the balance from cultural to economic populism. Economic discontents dominated the opinion polls. With rising anxiety, the 1992 Republican presidential campaign sought to overcome the new anti-Washington and populist economic challenges—from a former Republican-turned-independent as well as a Democrat—with cultural, law-and-order, patriotic and foreign policy themes combined under one description: values. But one after another, these tactics failed, culminating in the disastrous August GOP convention in which "family values" appeared to be increasingly synonymous with the controversial agenda of the Religious Right. Fewer and fewer offsets existed to a politics in which voter unhappiness was increasingly economic.

Uncertain Trumpet: The Democrats
and Economic Populism

From mid-1991 through most of 1992, the Democrats moved toward the presidential election with growing attention to middle-class-squeeze issues and economic populism. However, for most of the 1980s, and again in the first half of 1991, they had been ambivalent, more inclined to work with the Republican architects of the era's conservative economics than to criticize them. That left them with a credibility problem when they rose, belatedly, to the attack.

Not that there was anything unusual in this. In the Gilded Age and then again in the 1920s, large numbers of Democrats were drumbeaters for boom-era capitalism. Grover Cleveland, the conservative Democrat unlucky enough to be president when the Panic of 1893 signaled the beginning of the end of the Gilded Age, was as conservative as Chester Arthur and Benjamin Harrison, the Republicans who had preceded him. And during the 1920s, not only did congressional Democrats collaborate with the GOP on federal income tax changes, but all three Democratic presidential nominees of the decade—James Cox (1920), John W. Davis (1924) and Alfred E. Smith (1928)—wound up by 1936 joining the conservative Liberty League to oppose Franklin D. Roosevelt and the New Deal.

Loyalty to the economics of the common man, not those of the elite, may be the hallmark of history's great Democrats, the Jacksons and Roosevelts, but not of the second-tier Democrats who tend to come to the fore during capitalist-conservative heydays.* These Democrats tend to cooperate with the Republicans in reducing government and cutting taxes, following the broad preference of voters during economic expansions. As a result, party politics in the aftermath of capitalist-conservative heydays and during the subsequent implosion of their debt-and-speculative bubbles has not been a simple story. In the Gilded Age, when Democrats had narrowly elected a president just before the Panic of 1893 hit, they were incumbent *losers,* not out-of-power *beneficiaries* of the embarrassment of conservative economics. Voters were resentful enough in 1894 to give the Republicans an extraordinary 117-seat gain in the House of Representatives. Moreover, fierce 1893–96 economic policy disagreements ripped the hapless Democratic party down the middle, so that when the majority ultimately radicalized to fuse with the Populists and nominate Bryan, many party conservatives bolted, voting for Republican McKinley or backing the

*For a more detailed discussion, see *The Politics of Rich and Poor,* pp. 46–51.

short-lived pro–gold standard National Democratic party. By contrast, had the financial unraveling that followed the Panic of 1893 come with a Republican president in office, a mildly populist Democratic presidential nominee would almost certainly have won in 1896, and the unfolding early-twentieth-century progressive era would have been run by Democrats instead of by its *Republican* White House hero, Theodore Roosevelt.

When the bubble of the 1920s popped in 1929, however, the Democrats were lucky. Republican Herbert Hoover was president, and it hardly mattered that Democrats were, in Arthur Schlesinger's words, "all over the place" philosophically or that their unprophetic 1932 presidential campaign had indicted the GOP for, of all things, excessive federal spending. All that counted electorally was that hapless Republican Hoover was in the White House, getting the blame, as the economy got worse—and worse.

Though "Democrats swooned," according to one pundit, when I laid out in *The Politics of Rich and Poor* the parallels between the 1980s, the 1920s and the Gilded Age, they did not necessarily have cause. The *opportunity* was there; the history of seizing it successfully was something else. Nor was leading a middle-class "populist" reaction something their liberal biases in the years since 1968 had conditioned them for. George Bush in the White House as real estate sagged and marble-halled financial institutions shuddered provided a Democratic advantage, but not a guarantee.

Indeed, during the 1980s economic populism was only an intermittent Democratic tactic. In 1982, when unemployment was about to reach double digits at election time, they could sound populist trumpets. "It's not fair, it's Republican," contended one clever television advertisement. And Democratic strategists attributed their recapture of fourteen Southern U.S. House seats to populist economic themes, so much so that a Populist Caucus was launched in the House of Representatives in February 1983. Populist and economic nationalist rhetoric was also a factor in 1986, when Democrats recaptured the U.S. Senate.

Democratic presidential nominees, however, were less inclined to such approaches. Following Walter Mondale's 41 percent–59 percent loss to Ronald Reagan in 1984, Washington's liberal-funded Economic Policy Institute commissioned a poll by Fingerhut-Granados Opinion Research, which found pro-Reagan "swing" Democrats lopsidedly citing Mondale's green-eyeshade emphasis on deficit reduction and tax increases as one reason they did not vote for him.[15] According to the polltakers, Mondale would have done better with populist positions on themes like Social Security, tax fairness and trade policy because "swing" voters favored them, supporting the Democratic party for its commitment to "working people," "the average person" and "fairness."[16] In those days, though, many marginal voters were also suspicious of "fairness" because they associated the word with redistribution from the middle class to the welfare poor.

Four years later, even harsher criticisms of an insufficient populist approach were directed at Michael Dukakis. We have seen how the Republicans, mindful of popular psychologies, equated Dukakis with Harvard and "boutique liberalism," but, for most of the general election campaign, Dukakis, for his part, rejected economic populist counterthemes. The pre-nomination opportunity had certainly been there. In July 1988 Democratic strategist Robert Beckel brandished a new party poll of 601 "swing" Democrats and explained how the Democrats' ten-point lead over George Bush was largely the product of economic disillusionment: "Ronald Reagan convinced these voters that their interests were with the wealthy. They bought into trickle-down theory." But since then, Beckel added, they have become convinced that "where they are losing out is not to poor people but to wealthy people. They believe that the dollars they have lost have gone up, not down."[17]

What Dukakis preferred to talk about, however, was "competence, not ideology," seeking to claim credit as governor of Massachusetts for a local economic "miracle"—one that was already coming undone. After a brief flirtation with populist language around Labor Day, he returned to it only in late October, when all was almost lost. The irony, as Bush campaign manager Lee Atwater admitted after the election, was that he had been worried in early September because "the way to win a presidential race against the Republicans is to develop the class warfare issue, as Dukakis did at the end. To divide up the haves and have nots and to try to invigorate the New Deal coalition and to attack."[18] Vincent Breglio, director of the Republican presidential campaign's polling division, later disclosed that even Dukakis's half-hearted last-minute populist rhetoric had made Bush survey-takers nervous: "Going into the last week of the campaign, we clearly saw that the populist message of Dukakis was having an impact. It was cutting."[19]

Surveys by Democrats outside the Dukakis campaign showed the same thing. One immediate preelection sampling by the Analysis Group recorded voters giving their "highest priority to a populist agenda: making sure the 'wealthy and big corporations pay their fair share of taxes.' "[20] In addition, pollsters Stanley Greenberg and Celinda Lake pointed out, "had the swing segments of the national electorate focused on the policy agenda, Dukakis would have run much more strongly. These [swing] voters, conventionally seen as conservative, are even more populist than the electorate as a whole. Over 70 percent of Reagan Democrats, moderate conservative Democrats, and undecided [on the eve of election] voters gave fair taxes for the rich and corporations the highest score as a goal for the next president."[21]

The October 1987 stock market crash lingered in voters' minds, but the 1988 economy was reasonably strong. Real disposable income was increasing. By autumn 1990 economic circumstances were much worse, helping Democrats drive home populist issues in the midterm congressional elections, especially after Bush had retracted his promise of "No new taxes." Then the question became *whose* new taxes, and Republicans wriggled with embarrassment for three brutal weeks in October as the media hung on the president's insistence on cutting capital gains rates for the rich along with his refusal to back a new 33 percent top rate or 10 percent surtax on millionaires.

Neo-populism was beginning to find a rhythm. Swing voters moved away from the GOP in droves and, in parts of the country, Republican candidates went into what reporters started calling "free fall." In Iowa not just Democrats but even half the self-identified *Republicans* characterized the GOP as the party of the rich, and populist Tom Harkin became the state's first Democratic U.S. senator to be elected to two full terms. George Bush's own national approval ratings slid from the 70s in September to a low of 48 percent in late-October ABC polls.

It was a brief few weeks of mild populist triumph, though, because public attention soon shifted back to the Persian Gulf—and although the country continued to slide into recession, Democrats, cowed by Bush's success in the Gulf, also found themselves, even for ten to twelve weeks after the war's end in March, holding their tongues on the weak state of the economy. Bush had been calling it "Saddam Hussein's recession," although arbiters from the National Bureau of Economic Research determined that the downturn had begun in July, just *before* Iraq's invasion of Kuwait. The war's end, the president promised, would bring a strong economic resurgence.

For the Democrats the hopes of the prior autumn seemed to have collapsed. By many measures that ranged from the largest collapse of U.S. financial institutions since the 1930s to the record number of Americans drawing public assistance, the U.S. economy was hitting bumps not experienced since the Great Depression, which should have made it easy for Democrats to indict the mistakes of the 1980s. Nevertheless, spring 1991 opinion polls on which party was better able to keep America prosperous found the Democrats falling below the GOP, partly because of the halo Republicans still enjoyed from the Gulf war, but also because Democrats, relentless in attacking prior Republican recessions and their hardships, this time restrained themselves.

However, as the recession lingered into summer and public restiveness resurged, Democratic blood started stirring. Clearly it had not been Saddam's recession, and was probably George Bush's after all. In late June potential presidential candidates were given details from the party poll that, as we have seen, found voters believing that under Reagan and Bush "the rich have gotten richer, while the middle class got stuck paying the bill." The most surprising and intriguing result, though, came from four hypothetical matchups between President Bush and "imaginary Democratic candidate Jones."²² Designed to test different economic populist themes, all four trial heats showed Bush actually *losing* whenever these issues came into play.

By autumn, as the economy slid into the second stage of what was becoming America's longest postwar slump, June's hypothetical matchups had been replaced by actual elections, important ones, in which Bush-supported Republicans lost to populist-sounding outsider candidates in what the press began interpreting as middle-class revolts. On October 19 former Ku Klux Klan leader and ex–American Nazi David Duke, now a Republican state representative from suburban New Orleans but still well beyond the pale of respectability, defeated the sitting GOP governor of Louisiana in an open primary. Four weeks later, he met Democratic former governor Edwin Edwards in a mid-November runoff, winning two fifths of the total vote and getting a surprising 60 percent support from the white middle class.

On November 5, in a special Pennsylvania U.S. Senate election, little-known Democrat Harris Wofford, running on a platform the press capsuled as "middle-class populism," electrified the country by turning an early 44-point Republican lead into a 10-point Democratic victory over Richard Thornburgh, the former Pennsylvania governor and U.S. attorney general who had left Bush's cabinet to make the race. A few days before the election, Wofford campaign strategist James Carville—described as a Svengali by Thornburgh and characterized by *The Wall Street Journal* as "dripping with contempt for Washington"—had said, "This kind of climate is where political tornadoes come from, and maybe we can show the party not to be enthralled with the dominant elite wing of the party and to talk about real economic issues."[23]

After Wofford's landslide, more national Democrats were ready to agree. Back in late summer, when Bush was strong, the Democrats emerging to seek their party's presidential nomination were mostly populists and outsiders—Senator Tom Harkin of Iowa, Senator Bob Kerrey of Nebraska, Governor Bill Clinton of Arkansas, Governor Douglas Wilder of Virginia and ex-governor Jerry Brown of California. Though former senator Paul Tsongas of Massachusetts was a nonpopulist, he was also an outsider. As Bush's ratings fell with the economy in November and December, their decisions to run began to look prescient—and so-called first-tier candidates like House Majority Leader Richard Gephardt and Senator Lloyd Bentsen began to regret their decisions not to run. Clinton, who developed a strong message about 1980s favoritism to the top 1 percent and unfairness to the middle class, quickly became the Democratic front-runner. His ability to blend concern for the middle class with ability to create a biracial coalition increased his strength, although he suffered from alleged sexual scandals, draft avoidance and other questions of personal integrity that followed him from Arkansas.

The most surprising trumpet of anti-Washington outsiderism and economic populism in 1992 came from the emergence of the first billionaire populist in U.S. political history—independent presidential contender Ross Perot of Texas, who had moved ahead of both Bush and Clinton in public opinion polls in June before he withdrew in July. Perot, who openly labeled Bush and Secretary of State James A. Baker III as "country clubbers" and "preppies," came from a moderate Republican background and generally sidestepped the vulnerability of Democratic nominees to charges of social liberalism, which made him more powerful a voice for populist reforms of the federal tax code and what amounted to an outsider revolt against Washington. Perot's July withdrawal made Clinton the only populist in the race, and after a successful acceptance speech to the Democratic convention, he surged to a large and unexpected lead. Perot's reentry in October made Democrats nervous, but on November 3 the Texan drew his 19 percent of the vote about equally from Clinton and Bush in one of the most populist-flavored outcomes in U.S. electoral history.

The Stalemate of American Politics

Political watersheds in the United States depend on the ability to affect institutions as well as grass-roots restiveness. Even as unhappy middle-class voters found themselves cross-pressured between Democratic *economic* populism, Republican *cultural* populism, and a powerful independent with a revolutionary message, national politics circa 1992 also faced unusual, even unprecedented blockages in its circulatory system. The Republican takeover of the presidency that began in 1968, by failing to change Congress as in previous realignments, provided evidence that perhaps politics was no longer fluid enough to produce old-style, top-to-bottom national political upheavals. Two decades later the institutional clogging was even worse. This was part of what made voters so responsive to Perot for several months—the sense that an institutional revolution might be necessary to make the system work again.

Divided government and the interest groups that proliferated around it were at the root of the problem. By the 1980s the pattern of mostly Republican presidents facing Democrats in one or both houses of Congress had a three-decade history reaching back to the Eisenhower years. Indeed, once the Republicans lost their six-year control of the U.S. Senate in 1986, the two parties seemed at times to have partitioned Washington. Capitol Hill and the legislative branch were the Democratic sphere of influence; the broad downtown boulevards, with the White House and executive branch, were Republican. In previous eras, divided power had been a temporary complication; during the Reagan-Bush era it fast became a de facto principle of national governance. At the same time, the effectiveness of government degenerated; economic interest groups fattened on the fragmentation of power and achieved leverage unmatched since the Gilded Age.

From a historical standpoint, what was missing in the U.S. political process was a full-fledged opposition—a party with an outsider's mentality, minimally rooted in Washington and forced back to the grass roots for revitalization by its relative weakness at both ends of Pennsylvania Avenue. For two thirds of the 1932–68 New Deal cycle, the Republicans controlled no elected Washington power base. In the 1960s, as a result, they easily took up an outsidership role. The Democrats, for their part, had been outsiders most of the time from 1896 to 1932. By comparison, what followed after 1968 slowly made split control of government not a fluke but an *assumption*. From 1968 to 1976, congressionally based Democrats schemed to get the White

House back; but the election of Jimmy Carter in 1976 proved so disruptive—politically, even counterproductive—that they were almost relieved when the GOP recaptured the White House in 1980. Loss of the Senate to the Republicans in that same election was a dislocation, but when Democrats recaptured the Senate in 1986, congressional leaders resumed a familiar and comfortable position: control of a co-equal branch of government; partnership (of a sort) in national policymaking.

National political self-renewal processes suffered, and both parties had activists who chafed. However, because the nation's agenda was set more from the electronic bully pulpit of the presidency than by the confusion of Congress, Democrats paid a greater political price. Time after time during the 1980s, they found themselves drawn as collaborators into what were basically *conservative* rescriptings of U.S. economic policy: the tax overhauls of 1981 and 1986, the Social Security tax expansion of 1983, the Gramm-Rudman budget reform, the 1989 Republican-Democratic deal over increased congressional pay (both sides agreed not to attack each other for pay-raise support), the 1990 bipartisan budget (which essentially blocked any anti-cyclical fiscal response to that year's unfolding recession) and so on.

Some collusion was to be expected. During previous GOP conservative-capitalist heydays, as we have seen, leading Democratic politicians had abandoned their "little guy" moorings to join in what were essentially "establishment" economics. However, the institutional cohabitation of a Democratic Congress with two successive Republican presidents in the 1980s was a boom-era first, unseen in previous heydays, and it inhibited Democrats from developing either an opposition mind-set or an effective critique of the 1980s political economy. Belaboring what many of their own senior congressional leaders had joined in shaping wasn't easy.

In the November 1990 congressional elections, when favoritism to the rich became an issue, Republicans drew most of the blame, losing one seat in the Senate and eight in the House. But Democrats paid an unusual penalty for their policy collaboration. Normally, when the party in the White House loses congressional seats in U.S. midterm elections, by way of reaction the other party's incumbents gain on average. Not so in 1990, according to tabulations by Democratic analysts Alan Baron and William Schneider. Granted that Republican incumbents fell further, but on average, Democratic incumbents, many of them prominent participants in bipartisan Washington decision-making, also weakened. Results like these reinforced doubt that the two-party system could still provide a once-a-generation, outsider and reformist broom to sweep out Washington.

What made it worse, ordinary citizens felt, was official Washington's apparent capture by special-interest groups. America's traditional, broad separation of powers set forth in the U.S. Constitution—from the requirement that tax legislation must originate in the House of Representatives to the president's veto power—was a familiar restraint; the mechanics had often been cumbersome in Jefferson's day or Roosevelt's. But interest-group proliferation and Balkanization grew worse during the 1980s, and the talk that lobbies had become a fourth branch of government was less and less facetious.

No other national capital had anything comparable; the District of Columbia was the political equivalent of a coral atoll, with new domestic and foreign special-pleading organisms attaching themselves daily. During the decade following Reagan's inauguration, lobbying firms and consulting groups more than doubled in personnel and billings. The role of lobbyists for foreign interests grew even more rapidly. Worse, as high-tech and multi-media election campaigns grew more expensive, politicians had to pay increased attention to special-interest money, ranging from political action committee donations to the personal contributions of GOP millionaires and the phone banks and in-kind donations of Democratic labor unions. Previous cyclical upheaval had not confronted this kind of entrenchment.

Stymied by such influence, the average person was beginning to conclude that his or her opinion and vote were all but powerless, as the Ohio-based Kettering Foundation discovered in its preelection opinion survey. On the one hand, this perceived institutional unresponsiveness complicated the prospect for an upheaval in Washington, but it simultaneously fed the hopes of an angry public to achieve exactly that—and the extraordinary grass-roots responsiveness to the Draft Perot movement was the most vivid result. "People point their fingers at politicians, at powerful lobbyists and at people in the media," said Kettering president David Mathews, a former U.S. secretary of health, education and welfare. "They see these three groups as a political class, the rulers of an oligarchy that has replaced democracy." Citizens "know that the political system is now designed to respond to interest groups rather than individual citizens and they are hopping mad about it."[24]

That was not unprecedented, especially for those who could recall the corruption of the Gilded Age a century earlier, but the 1990s did raise a new dimension of challenge. Like the fear of middle-class decline, concern over national atrophy and oligarchy also had a ring of plausibility. Pessimists like Professor Mancur Olson in his book *The Rise and Decline of Nations* couched their worry in historical terms, concluding that the United States might be bogging down in the same interest-group paralysis that earlier afflicted previous great empires, including Britain.[25]

In the past, as America had approached its political watersheds, radicalizing and disaffected portions of the electorate had made the system work by, in effect, creating a new political coalition to occupy the political center, which then dealt with the nation's problems. As the 1990s began, the institutional and interest-group barriers to another successful grass-roots revolt and Washington purge seemed enormous. To optimists, Clinton's victory, building on an outsider image of promises to reform Washington and represent the middle class rather than the rich, promised a new common-man loyalty and revitalization of government. Yet Clinton had close ties to party contributors and interest groups, and middle-class radicalization in support of Perot's powerful insurgency was a historical trouble sign, as Chapter 9 will pursue further. Moreover, public dissatisfaction with Washington policy favoritism to the rich and well connected showed little likelihood of subsiding, and the too softly named "middle-class squeeze"—to which we now turn in Part II—was coming into focus as something potentially more ominous.

PART TWO

THE MIDDLE-CLASS SQUEEZE: A PORTRAIT

C H A P T E R 4

Middle America and the "Unfairness" of Conservative-Capitalist Boom Periods

I want to recall our attention to what our economy is really all about: not money, but people. The original Greek word "economy" meant "the management of a household or family." . . . We must let the Greeks remind us that the fundamental purpose of our complicated and technical economy is the well-being of our families. This is why I'm so disturbed about what I see going on on Wall Street these days. Corporations have become chips in a casino game, played for high stakes by people who produce nothing, invent nothing, grow nothing and service nothing. The market is now a game itself.

—House Democratic whip Richard Gephardt, 1987

Unemployment in large cities appears to be far more severe than official government numbers indicate. . . . Employment statistics released recently from the 1990 census show huge differences between the number of people who consider themselves jobless and the numbers reflected in estimated local unemployment rates issued monthly by the Bureau of Labor Statistics.

—The Philadelphia Inquirer, 1992

Despite its widespread currency, the term "squeeze" failed to describe what was overtaking middle-class Americans in the 1990s because the term had arrived in the late 1980s as a quibble with the Reagan boom: that despite the surge of billionaires and the glitter of high finance, ordinary families were under pressure and many were losing ground. But there was no crisis, merely a discomfort. Three or four years later, as the circumstances of the average household worsened and as middle-class populism elbowed its way into 1991–92 politics, angrier terminology was appropriate. The principal provocations of this anger, from corporate job cutbacks, declining public services and unfair taxes to inflationary stresses underestimated by government statisticians, are what these next chapters will examine.

By 1990 the beginning of a debate over wealth and income shifts and their effects on the middle class had become unavoidable. Evidence was falling into place. A decade and a half of upward redistribution, which gave the top 1 percent of the population of Britain and the United States an additional 3 to 6 percentage points of their respective national incomes, had obliged former British prime minister Margaret Thatcher and a number of conservative politicians and pundits in the United States to acknowledge that, yes, the rich had reaped the greatest benefit. Yet for the next several years, through the 1992 elections, conservatives insisted on a politically essential corollary: that while people in the middle had indeed profited less, they had still gained ground, which made the 1980s better than the 1970s, when most people had *lost* purchasing power.

In the coming chapters, we will look at what happened to incomes, taxes and the cost of services middle-class Americans had to buy. It is a discouraging picture. But from the start, another part of the case for 1980s economic policy also rested on a dubious premise. The broadly indicted 1970s had not been uniformly difficult for Middle America. The early stages of inflation often are not. Many Americans who would lose ground in the 1980s had profited during the late 1970s: farmers crowing over high commodity prices, independents and wildcatters in the oil business, a fair proportion of unionized production-line workers whose wages and fringe benefits kept climbing, and even some suburbanites whose fast-inflating home values would soon stall. It was relevant that many who had been angriest about the 1970s— notably, investors whose stocks and bonds took a beating from accelerating stagflation—emerged as the big winners of the eighties, and glorified them accordingly. For many people in the middle, however, the 1980s showed that one relatively stagnant decade was replacing another.

The 1990s also began with doubts, but of a new variety. The 1980s had included a number of boom years, even if their benefits went disproportionately to the rich. The nineties, by contrast, quickly emerged as the era of the hangover after the debt party. For many low-middle- and middle-income Americans, what had been stagnation in the 1980s became economic regression in the early 1990s, and the mistakes of the 1980s began to sink in. Democratic politicians started charging the 1989–92 Bush administration with the weakest economic growth since Herbert Hoover. Claims of economic progress that had been believable in 1987 and 1988 rang increasingly hollow in 1991 and 1992. Perceptions of a "squeeze" darkened into something more.

The crux was how it occurred: that the economic circumstances of many Americans in the 40th to 85th percentiles during the Reagan-Bush years were undercut by deliberate philosophies, even if their eventual results were unsought. Indeed, by emphasizing tax cuts, deregulation, disinflation, finance and the growth of financial assets, all three of America's capitalist heydays have been geared to the investing and capital-forming top 1 percent of the population, benefiting the great economic middle much less and for the most part only indirectly (through achievements in technology and modernization of the overall economy). Capitalism has revitalized itself, but such periods are not easy for the average citizen.

Nor should this have been surprising. From the "survival of the fittest" theories of late-nineteenth-century Social Darwinists led by William Graham Sumner to the "help the poor by cutting the taxes of the rich" claims of supply-side thinkers a century later, conservative heyday philosophy has repeatedly favored the strong and the successful.* As we have seen, theology in such periods regularly abandons the average American for a favored group at the top. The preoccupation with the middle class so characteristic of Jacksonian democracy or the Nixon years fades away in the glorification of wealth. During the late-nineteenth-century Gilded Age and then again in the Roaring Twenties, the top 1 percent of Americans were also the principal beneficiaries of income and wealth, while portions of Middle America lost ground, as in the late-twentieth-century's squeeze. Later in this chapter I will show how these pressures have occurred.

Yet the Reagan-Bush heyday also differed from the previous booms because of confusing and difficult-to-measure circumstances that transformed a nominal 1980–89 improvement of 5 to 10 percent in the average American family's income into a frequent decline in real purchasing power. The various stresses that produced this result are broadly framed in this chapter and then detailed in subsequent ones. They were the undiscussed, even hidden, dark sides of the boom.

One such circumstance was the increasingly dense barrage of federal, state and local taxes that assailed the median American family by 1992. A century earlier, by contrast, comparatively few taxes had affected the typical citizen—they were mostly import duties, property taxes and excise taxes on liquor and certain manufactures. Not so by the early 1990s. Though official statistics on the tax burden and its shifts were piecemeal and never combined federal, state *and* local

*In addition to the shared heyday characteristics profiled in Chapter 2, more detail on the philosophic origins of these periods can be found in Chapter 3 of my 1990 book, *The Politics of Rich and Poor.*

effects, the average family could sense that combined tax pressures were greater than officially acknowledged.

A second source of confusion was ongoing stagflation involving a change of 4 percent or 5 percent a year in the price index. In previous heydays, inflation had been broken or reversed before the boom got under way, so that with prices stable or declining, voters in the 1890s and 1920s didn't have to adjust nominal gains into inflation-adjusted reality. In the Reagan-Bush years, they did.

Then there was the confusion of what was happening to the United States in terms of international indebtedness. *Private* financiers and businessmen a century earlier had borrowed heavily overseas, but the U.S. Treasury itself ran a surplus from 1867 to 1893—and again during the 1920s. In the 1980s, however, Washington pyramided federal budget deficits at an unprecedented rate; and as both private- and public-sector America borrowed around the world, the dollar eventually plummeted, which brought unusual, disconcerting side effects. By the late eighties, well-heeled foreigners could buy U.S. corporations and "trophy" buildings cheaply while middle-class Americans could no longer afford to stay in London, Zurich, Frankfurt or Tokyo. The Japanese were the world's new "rich" tourists. Ordinary U.S. citizens knew something had been lost, but weren't quite sure what.

Moreover, not only did the uneasy middle class of the computer era have to sort out unprecedented complexities, but tricky and unreliable official U.S. statistics added to the problem. Although federal data showed average family incomes up somewhat during the 1980s, even after adjustment for inflation, middle-class families told pollsters that official price-index adjustments underestimated the reduction in their purchasing power. Several new nongovernmental indexes painted the erosion from taxes and inflation in vivid, even shocking colors (see pages 94 and 96). Inadequate and contradictory reports and indexes added to national confusion, as we will also examine.

Yet despite these new complications, it is useful to begin with how the two previous heydays also buffeted Middle America. There is a common thread. And so before I examine such *specific* squeezes as rising taxes, eroding private and government benefits, declining public services and increasingly high-cost private services like schools, banks, insurance and health care, it's appropriate to look at the recurring ideological and historical backdrop—at how previous capitalist-conservative go-go periods affected the ordinary American.

Middle America in the Gilded Age and
the Roaring Twenties

By their nature, heydays tend to bypass the everyday citizen. In January 1928, as the great stock market boom of the 1920s roared toward its speculative mountaintop, the editors of *The Nation* complained of "a pyramiding of wealth beyond all the dreams of Solomon and Croesus" following disclosure by the Internal Revenue Service that the number of Americans with million-dollar-a-year incomes in 1927 "broke all records with 228, while the number of $5,000,000 incomes doubled."[1] But the editors were also indignant that the percentage of Americans with middle-class incomes in the $2,000 to $5,000 range simultaneously fell from 2.17 million in 1926 to 2.09 million in 1927, with "a corresponding decline in the income reported by all these classes." "Prosperity," the magazine complained, "can hardly be called healthy unless well spread out, and these figures would seem to indicate that there is something radically wrong with our distribution system."[2]

The twenties, like the eighties, were, as we have seen, a boom for only a minority of the U.S. population. If no economist or pundit found a "middle-class squeeze" in an era captivated by Wall Street speculators, fast automobiles and short skirts, that, as we have also seen, was partly because the middle class of those days was too small and—at 15 to 20 percent of the population—too elite. The real "squeeze" was on the decade's true "Middle America": farmers, clerical and blue-collar workers. The rural families being pushed off their farms in Minnesota or Kansas had been America's turn-of-the-century yeomanry. The embattled United Mine Workers and railroad brotherhoods, in turn, were the country's biggest unions and their members had been among its best-paid workers, and yet membership was shrinking relentlessly well before the Great Depression.* Textiles, shoes and shipbuilding joined railroads and coal in decline. As many as two hundred thousand workers a year were being replaced by automatic and semiautomatic machinery, giving the dictionary of boom-era economics a new phrase that would recur in the 1980s —"technological unemployment." In 1928, near prosperity's peak, the

---

*Farm families' share of U.S. national income dropped from 15 percent in 1920 to just 9 percent in 1928, and the number of farmers shrank from 31.6 million to 29.6 million. Thirty percent of coal miners were unemployed during the decade, and the United Mine Workers Union saw its membership drop from half a million in 1920 to barely 75,000 in 1928 (Geoffrey Perrett, *America in the Twenties* [New York: Simon and Schuster, 1982], p. 325).

AFL-CIO counted 18 percent of union members out of work, a sharp contrast with more reassuring government estimates.[3] "Forgotten Americans" abounded in ballyhoo years like 1927 and 1928, long before Franklin D. Roosevelt gave them a name in mid-Depression 1932. And in other statistics akin to those of the Reagan era, most of the middle third of Americans seem to have run in place or even lost ground economically during the Great Gatsby period when Charles Lindbergh was soaring across the Atlantic and Radio Corporation of America stock was jumping over the Dow-Jones moon.

Contemporary surveys, in fact, recorded much more erosion of incomes among ordinary Americans of the late 1920s than one would guess from the decade's excited worship of new technology and unchained stock markets. As joblessness cut unexpected swaths, many breadwinners solved their problems—as they would again in the 1970s and 1980s—by sending wives and daughters to work. The official percentage of the work force constituted by women jumped from 20.7 in 1920 to 22.0 in 1930, which probably understates the change. But it did not overcome purchasing-power weakness, even if one is slightly skeptical of the Brookings Institution assertion that the three fifths of American families with late 1920s earnings below $2,000 dollars a year had less than they needed to buy basic necessities. Stuart Chase, the popular economics writer, voiced much the same concern in a prophetic book entitled *Prosperity: Fact or Myth,* published in 1929. Behind the image of new two-lane highways full of automobiles, the first talking movies and the quadrupled ranks of millionairedom, most Americans hadn't really gained during the decade, including many who wore white collars. Here is Chase citing a famous American historian on the frustrations of the upper-middle class:

> For this reason, James Truslow Adams believes that the professional man is worse off than he used to be. His income has not increased as fast as the new demands upon it—leaving a more slender margin than a generation ago, or even than a decade ago. He calls it "prosperity without peace of mind." To bring Mr. Adams into the world cost $100. To bring a baby into the same social stratum today costs $1,500. His family when he was a boy rented a dignified, spacious New York house for $1,200 a year. Today one must pay that sum for a 11 x 14 room with a folding wall-bed and a cooking shelf, in a "good" apartment house. Sunshine, air, quiet, spaciousness, dignity, privacy—where are they to be found in apartment living? One used to get them, together with food, clothing, and all other expenses, for $3,000 a year.[4]

Despite a paucity of government data, analysts have tried to supply specifics about who was hurting. One economist contended that the lower 93 percent of the nonfarm population actually experienced a 4 percent decline in real disposable per capita income between 1923 and 1929![5] Farmers, of course, suffered much steeper declines, but agrarian problems were familiar and widely acknowledged. And looking back in the early 1930s, Marriner Eccles, the New Deal chairman of the Federal Reserve Board, joined in calling 1920s income maldistribution an important reason for prosperity's unsustainability:

> While national income rose to high levels, it was so distributed that the incomes of a majority of families were entirely inadequate and business activity was sustained only by a rapid and unsound increase in the private debt structure, including ever-increasing installment-buying of consumption.[6]

The parallel is hardly perfect, but no one can miss the similarity to the 1980s and early 1990s. Net worths in Roaring Twenties Middle America were affected as well as income, and between 1920 and 1929, years of presumed national prosperity, the U.S. Agriculture Department recorded that the value of farmland fell by 30 to 40 percent in the nation's breadbasket from Indiana to the Dakotas, a little less than the decline registered in the same areas from 1981 to 1987. Farmers' equity also fell sharply.

Things had actually been worse a generation earlier, in the first of the boom-era "squeezes," when the financial backwash of the Gilded Age pounded less at *economic* Middle America—the income midsection of the population—than at *geographic* Middle America, the rural heartland of the nation from the Appalachians west to the Rocky Mountains. In a word, Farm Belt America was devastated. Few late-twentieth-century suburbanites in Ventura County, California, or Rockland County, New York, grumbling about high college tuitions, suburban traffic gridlock or Social Security deductions, could imagine the agonies rural Texans, Missourians or Nebraskans suffered from Washington's restoration of pro-creditor, gold standard policies in the 1870s and the ensuing deflation of the money supply, a shrinkage that reduced commodity prices and farm income while simultaneously tightening farmers' debt and mortgage burdens for a full generation before the 1893 crash. Because 74 percent of Americans lived in rural areas in the 1870s and agriculture constituted the main component of U.S. GNP, huge numbers of livelihoods were ruined, and the Farmers'

Alliance convened massive protest meetings of farm families who stood under giant banners, swatting horseflies in the Texas or Iowa breeze as they heard populist speakers plead for the late-nineteenth-century equivalent of "fairness." But as farm prices collapsed, so did an important early version of the American Dream. Here is William Greider in his history of U.S. monetary policy:

> Millions of humble farm families were forced into deeper poverty. Many were compelled to surrender what they thought was their American birthright—ownership of their own modest plot of land, a tangible asset that meant self-sufficiency and freedom to the hardworking yeomanry. Every growing season, as prices fell, their land and labor became worth less. To begin again at the next planting, they must borrow more at punishing rates to buy seed and supplies, but by harvesttime, prices had fallen further and they were unable to pay off their obligations. To continue farming, they must borrow still more. Eventually, when the debt became overwhelming, they would forfeit the land to their creditors, just as the *rentier* accumulated larger and larger holdings, when the French peasantry failed. The process—liquidation and consolidation—was as old as capitalism.[7]

In sum, all three of America's conservative-capitalist heydays have involved processes of Darwinian renewal and economic redistribution *away* from weak or fading midportions of the population and *toward* the top 1 percent of Americans, along with educationally or technologically advanced portions of the middle and upper-middle classes. The very rich flourish because they have capitalism's all-important lever—capital—and the three heydays have been the country's preeminent periods of expanding millionairedom. As a broad calculus, during these periods of purgation and modernization, some 10 to 20 percent of Americans, mostly those with capital, skills and direction, have made significant, direct gains in real income. On the other side of the ledger, however, and even before the booms ended, another 30 to 50 percent with less capital, skill or education, typically suffered from the harsh effects on humdrum or declining sectors of the economy and on people of average or below-average circumstances. So it was again in the 1980s and early 1990s; cutting-edge portions of the middle class profited along with the top 1 percent, but the general midsection of the population—our hapless median family—once again stagnated or lost economic ground amid circumstances biased toward skilled achievers. In *direct* income effects, at least, ordinary Americans near or below the

50th percentile appear to have been losers during capitalist heydays more often than beneficiaries. And none of the squeezes have been accidents.

Confusing Taxes and Stagflation: The Economic Uniqueness of the Reagan-Bush Heyday

The average family did not get overall tax relief in the 1980s; claims that it did were false. Nor were changes in the cost of living as mild for middle-class Americans as the official data suggested. Indeed, in late 1991, one prominent New York economist, Edward Hyman of the ISI Group, put together a measure of the ferocious interaction of the two trends by combining the rise in taxes, medical payments, Social Security and interest payments as a percentage of personal income and calling it "the New Misery Index." Figure 2 shows how the four categories took 24 percent of personal income in 1960; by 1990 the total had risen to 40 percent—with the largest increase coming during the eighties.

In particular, the gap between the promise of lower tax burdens and the reality of rising ones was new to this boom era. Whatever the problems of the average Middle American breadwinner of the 1880s or 1890s, direct federal taxes were unimportant because Gilded Age Washington raised most of its money in a roundabout way from tariffs and excise levies. Once the temporary Civil War income tax was removed in the 1870s, the federal government did not tax income again until 1913. Even in the 1920s, the income tax affected relatively few Americans. Only 15 percent of U.S. families filed returns in 1927, and for a family of four with $5,000 per year, falling in the economic top 8 percent, the income tax owed was negligible—just $8 a year, according to the U.S. Census Bureau.[8] As for state and local taxes, during the Gilded Age and Roaring Twenties they fell mostly on property, principally farms and other real estate, and when ordinary householders were sorely pressed, commonly farm owners caught between declining incomes and outdated high assessments, they had no problem identifying what was happening.

Income taxes remained a minor burden until World War II, when earnings of many Americans began to rise. A family of four with a median income of $3,000 a year in 1948 paid hardly any income taxes, but in time, more and more households were forced to file returns by the prosperity of the 1950s and the inflationary Vietnam boom of the 1960s. By the 1970s not only had most families started paying signifi-

Figure 2. The New Misery Index?

Taxes + Interest payments + medical + Social Security payments
as a % of personal income

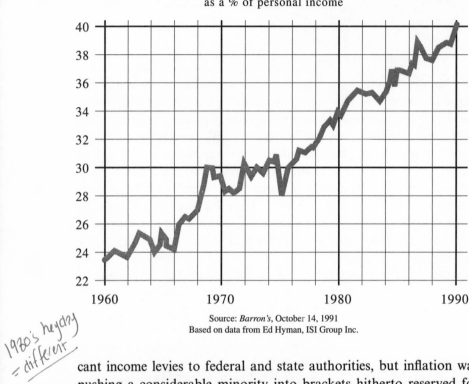

Source: *Barron's*, October 14, 1991
Based on data from Ed Hyman, ISI Group Inc.

[handwritten note: 1980's heyday = different]

cant income levies to federal and state authorities, but inflation was pushing a considerable minority into brackets hitherto reserved for senior executives and professionals. For median families, federal income taxes grew from near irrelevance to obnoxiousness in just one generation. Then in the 1980s, when Washington finally lowered income tax brackets, increases during the decade in all kinds of other taxes—federal excise, federal Social Security, state sales, local property and miscellaneous fees and charges—more than offset the reduction. Ultimately, the reshuffling of the 1980s provided something the 1920s had not: an opportunity for various levels of officialdom to *increase* the total federal, state and local tax burden even while the Reagan administration, in particular, claimed to be *reducing* taxes because of the changes made in federal rates. Rank-and-file voters might not be sure what was happening, but in 1991 the Tax Foundation calculated that Tax Freedom Day, the date when Americans finished paying their yearly federal, state and local tax burden and started working for themselves, had moved ahead to May 8, the latest ever.

Although the Republicans are rarely the proponents of tax increases, the escalation of overall revenue-raising from one GOP heyday to the next was relentless: combined federal, state and local revenues represented only 7 to 8 percent of total U.S. personal income in the 1890s, about 15 percent by 1927 and 42 to 43 percent by 1990. More to the point, during the previous heydays, as noted, the process of reallocating tax burdens had not been a major means of income and wealth redistribution. By the 1980s, however, it had become just that—and the extent to which policymakers significantly restructured the tax burden is part of the discussion in Chapter 5.

Chapter 6, in turn, will examine the unique impact, for a heyday, of steep 1980s inflation in services from health care to college costs and bank fees. By contrast, the 1870s through the mid-1890s had been *deflationary,* because once the paper-money buildup generated by the Civil War ended in the late 1860s, Washington continued to rein in the money supply, dropping prices to lows unseen since Lincoln's election. Price trends in the 1920s were also relatively stable because once the inflation caused by World War I was reversed by the deep recession of 1920–21, the Consumer Price Index stayed within a narrow band.* There was no ongoing deflation as in the late nineteenth century, except in commodity and farmland prices, but overall inflation was not a problem either.

In both heydays, the result favored stock and bond markets because disinflation is good for creditors and financial assets. At the same time, disinflation and especially deflation are painful traps for debtors and commodity producers—and farmers, encouraged to borrow money to buy more land and expand production during flush times, are often both. This was the familiar kind of squeeze, which staggered rural and small-town America during both previous heydays.

What made the 1980s and early 1990s both confusing and different, then, was that they combined the familiar disinflationary boom—surging stocks and bonds as inflation tumbled from 13 percent in 1980 to one third as much three years later—with a lingering inflation that soon stabilized in the 4–5 percent range. Slumping commodity prices put miners, oil producers and farmers through the usual deflationary wringer, at its worst in 1986. However, for the average American, who was neither a crushed farmer nor an exuberant Wall Streeter, a major impact of the Reagan-Bush era was not so much disinflation as ongoing price increases, especially for services, that often seemed to be

*Between 1923 and 1929, it ranged from 51 to 53, based on the year 1967 representing 100.

larger than government yardsticks acknowledged. This time, more of the squeeze would be in understated *inflation,* not *deflation.*

Back in the Roaring Twenties, successful middle-class Americans, such as novelist Sinclair Lewis's stereotypical Midwestern supersalesman George Babbitt, had found themselves trying to keep up with the Joneses in pursuit of luxuries and services that hadn't been available before—autos, radios, toasters, refrigerators, movie tickets and even airplane rides. Undoubtedly this had its frustrations, but the prices of basic goods and services were relatively stable. Movements were small. During the 1980s, by contrast, the middle class was hurt by several offsets to purchasing power that were rising much faster than the ostensibly mild inflation of the Consumer Price Index. The first involved virtually unregulated inflation in the cost of private services—health care, automobile insurance, legal and financial services, bank fees and college tuition. A second reflected how the prices of small, niggling middle-class items from weekly newsmagazines and shoeshines to contact lens solution and per-hour charges at parking garages were soaring at three to four times the CPI rate.* The third represented the onrush of governmental charges ranging from federal taxes, Social Security hikes and state and local taxes to an explosion of miscellaneous governmental fees. The federal government's reassuring calculations of inflation simply did not adequately measure the greater concentrated impact of these costs on people in the middle. The extent of the erosion, detailed in Chapter 6, was critical to whether the middle class was gaining or losing.

While experts generally agreed that the inflationary effects of rising service costs and tax burdens were harder to chart than the inflation of commodity prices during the 1970s, consumers were more blunt, telling pollsters and reporters that federal measurements understated inflation's new burden. In 1991, consumer survey-taker Albert Sindlinger explained that beginning in mid-1990, the three thousand Americans in his monthly sample had reported their perception that the rate of increase in the cost of living (including taxes) had returned to double

---

*The Consumer Price Index gave relatively little weight to miscellaneous items—shoeshines, haircuts, parking and the like—but beginning in 1983 their prices rose sharply. In 1985–86, the Manufacturers Hanover Bank Nuisance Index rose by 15 percent a year, more than four times the CPI rate. Legg Mason's kindred Trivia Index—forty-five items ranging from an ice cream cone to a birthday card—rose three to four times faster than the CPI. In the words of the Manufacturers Hanover chief economist, "Consumers have a gnawing suspicion that there is more inflation out there than is captured in official government statistics—and the skepticism is justified" ("Prices of Small Items, Services, Rise Rapidly," *Wall Street Journal,* April 24, 1987).

digits.* The likelihood that government understated these pressures was important, because recalculating inflation at a level even one or two points above official estimates would force a major reworking of the economic statistics of the late 1980s and early 1990s. Growth estimates would shrivel. Real median-family or average-family income would have been weaker. So would the typical household's purchasing power. And the gap between the huge gains of the rich and the disarray of the middle class would have threatened even more political danger.

Yet, as more and more economists were recognizing, federal statistics *were* becoming unreliable, and sometimes unusable.

The Late-Twentieth-Century Hazard
of U.S. Economic Statistics

By the early 1990s economists, money managers and even journalists had begun to throw up their hands. Horror stories abounded, like the 1991 admission that the Commerce Department had missed $73 billion in U.S. trade accounts or the major revisions later made in 1990 GNP figures. In early 1992 the Commerce and Labor departments released new data revealing that the growth in U.S. manufacturing from 1977 to 1989 was one third below previous estimates. Part of the collective weakness of federal statistics resulted from inadequate government funding, part from conceptual obsolescence and part from simple inaccuracy.

In 1992, after Census Bureau officials held up for four months the release of a study showing that nearly one out of five Americans who worked full time were not paid enough to keep a family of four above the poverty line, critics went further, calling it the third such political manipulation in a year—the first being the refusal by Commerce Secretary Robert Mosbacher to adjust the 1990 Census figures for undercounting, especially of poor people in urban areas, and the second being claims by a Census demographer that her superiors had tried to fire her because she released estimates of Iraqi deaths during the Gulf war that were higher than official calculations and embarrassed the White House.[9] Just before the 1992 presidential election *The Christian Science Monitor* reported widespread suspicion inside and outside the government that the Bush administration had manipulated the government spending process to produce a brighter picture of the U.S. econ-

---

*By December 1991, as official data pegged U.S. annual inflation in the 3–4 percent range and the Federal Reserve pushed short-term interest rates down to that level, Sindlinger reported a much higher estimate of the annual increase in the cost of living—14 percent!

omy in the third-quarter GDP (gross domestic product) statistics released on October 27.

What seems indisputable is that during the 1980s Reagan administration budget cuts forced staff reductions at the various federal agencies that kept statistics while also undercutting the research needed to keep sampling techniques abreast of economic changes. Robert Ortner, the Commerce Department under secretary in charge, later acknowledged that budget pressures had sidetracked an effort to modernize U.S. statistics and make them more comparable to bookkeeping done in other countries.[10]

By the Bush years, disgruntlement over poor data was abundant. One broad charge was that U.S. statistics were out of date because they had been designed to measure the vanished economy of the 1940s and 1950s. Baltimore economist Ben Laden, who studied the statistics problem for the National Association of Business Economists, complained about inadequate attention to regionalism: "Within the past decade, we have had much greater diversity in regional performance than we ever had before, starting with the farm depression and the manufacturing depression in the early 1980s and then the drop in oil prices, which killed Texas. But the federal government is doing very little to track regional differences."[11]

Small sampling bases also contributed to unreliability. "History is being rewritten on a monthly basis," said Allen Sinai, chief economist of the Boston Company. "It makes it very hard for private-sector analysts and public policymakers to come to correct conclusions."[12] Several years into the new decade, Congress and the Bush administration started discussing proposals to increase funding for data collection, stung by reminders like that from James Smith, a former president of the National Association of Business Economists: "The United States spends more money subsidizing the production of honey-bee wax than it does collecting federal statistics. That's a fact."[13]

Specific complaints piled up about the government's unemployment and inflation measurements. In contrast to many European countries, the United States in compiling jobless data excluded persons without employment who had stopped looking for work, while part-time workers who wanted full-time jobs were nevertheless counted as entirely employed. In the spring of 1991, when the official unemployment rate was 6.8 percent, Lawrence Mishel of Washington's liberal-tilting Economic Policy Institute argued that "What you really have is a total unemployment and underemployment rate of 12.4 percent."[14]

Commissioner of Labor Statistics Janet Norwood, after declining reappointment in 1991, began speaking out on the inadequacies of government data. Not only did she acknowledge that the unemployment numbers were misleading, but she said, "I am very worried, extraordinarily concerned, about the polarization I see going on in our country."[15] Shortly thereafter, the California Department of Finance issued an analysis suggesting that in 1991 the federal government had seriously underestimated the effect of the recession in California and some other major states, undercounting job losses nationwide by more than 2 million. The decline in California employment was the worst since the 1930s, and Washington was alleged to have underestimated the plunge by more than 350,000 jobs in that state alone. The department's principal economist, Ted Gibson, said, "To me, it's very obvious that the recession is far, far deeper than the [Labor Department] figures are indicating."[16] In 1992, Labor Department record-keepers all but conceded, admitting that 600,000 more jobs than previously acknowledged had been lost in 1991. For the nation as a whole, roughly a quarter of U.S. families seem to have been affected by 1990–92 unemployment.*

In Philadelphia, where official Labor Department sampling found only 6 percent unemployment in April 1990, the official U.S. Census— conducted that same month with a lot more thoroughness—found 9.7 percent joblessness. Then two years later, with the official rate up to 7.7 percent, *The Philadelphia Inquirer* projected that the city's actual unemployment rate had probably climbed into double digits. The Census counts of unemployment in other cities as of April 1990 were also much higher than the Labor Department's numbers. In Detroit the Labor Department estimated 9.8 percent versus the Census's 19.7 percent; in New York, 5.9 percent versus the Census's 9.0 percent; in Los Angeles, 6.1 percent versus 8.4 percent, and in Chicago, 7.9 percent versus 11.3 percent.[17]

The government's pivotal Consumer Price Index also had critics. First, said some, the CPI had not adequately reflected the 1980s surge in medical and educational costs. Second, the Index understated the effect of inflation on important demographic subgroups like baby boomers, homeowners and the middle class. Moreover, the formula used for the CPI had been updated last in 1987, using 1980 Census data

---

*According to an early 1992 Time/CNN poll, 23 percent of those surveyed said they had been unemployed, not by their own choice, at some time during 1991. In February 1992, New Jersey's Newark Star-Ledger/Eagleton Institute poll reported that more than a third of New Jerseyans said an adult in their household had been out of work and actively seeking a job in 1991.

and consumer spending patterns from 1982–84, and the next update was not scheduled until 1995.[18]

A corporal's guard led by consumer pollster Sindlinger further contended that the CPI greatly understated 1990–91 inflation by its inadequate treatment of taxes. Property, sales and excise levies were included in whole or in part because of their effect on the cost of goods and services, but income taxes, Social Security taxes and many federal, state and local taxes and fees were excluded. "Conceptually, he [Sindlinger] is right," Irwin Kellner, chief economist for Manufacturers Hanover Bank, told *The New York Times,* but "I wouldn't want to be pinned down to his specific number."[19]

Cost-of-living measurements in other nations, however, *did* pay more attention to taxes, especially after the spread of consumption taxes during the 1970s and 1980s obliged governments to incorporate the various new levies into consumer price indexes to increase their accuracy for wage negotiation and other purposes. For example, it was routine in June 1992, when John Dawkins, the treasurer of Australia, announced that increased charges and taxes in Australia's two biggest states would add 0.5 percentage point to the nation's inflation rate in the next fiscal year. Years earlier, U.S. researchers had also toyed with an expanded tax-and-price index, and according to former Labor Department officials involved in the project, combined price *and* tax index inflation averaged 6.9 percent for the period between 1967 and 1985, seven tenths of a point over the 6.2 percent increase actually recorded in the CPI.[20] But official yardsticks were not revised.

Few doubted that important aspects of 1980s and 1990s economic behavior were being poorly measured, not least for categories of Middle America. Blurry statistics might complicate national decision-making, but they also helped confuse—and possibly mislead—voters who otherwise could have been angered.

Misleading Statistics and Political Misperceptions

Those who control definitions and statistics often control policy, a lesson well understood by those who wanted to shape or rebut what Americans thought of 1980s economics. The otherwise confusing multiple series and forms of "government data" were a boon to liberal and conservative economists, activists and commentators who packaged their preferred numbers to serve their partisan purposes. Income trends and tax burdens, in particular, were the favorite clay of ideological sculptors, so for those who would judge the Reagan and Bush eras, a short guide is in order.

Proponents of 1980s economic policies preferred to emphasize gains in real per capita income, which rose from $12,351 in 1980 to $14,387 in 1990, as proof of the administration's success. Yet even before the decline of 1991, the growth in per capita income during the 1980s was deceptive. Some of it reflected gains highly concentrated among America's top earners. Then, as we shall see in more detail in Chapter 6, another substantial part of the 1980s increase, far from representing added productivity, reflected the expansion of the labor force from 58 percent of adults to 63 percent as more women took jobs to keep their households above water. As this happened, family expenses surged, not least child care, but per capita income growth statistics were not adjusted accordingly. So they greatly overstated growth in genuinely disposable real income during the decade.

Across the ideological aisle, liberal foes of GOP economics often strained their argument by uncritical preoccupation with median family income data. True, weaknesses in the broader economy were the principal reason that U.S. median family incomes plateaued after 1973, but as conservatives pointed out, changes in family size also played a role. As the average family shrank from 3.29 persons in 1980 to 3.18 persons in 1990, somewhat less money in constant dollars was needed to sustain its prior living standard. By not making that adjustment, regular Census Bureau data overstated the stagnation.*

A second complaint about median family income data—that by assuming one breadwinner, it misrepresented the "average" family, which by now had *two* earners—prompted some organizations (such as the Tax Foundation) to redefine the "average" family to include two workers and a higher income. These families, however, while more upwardly mobile during the 1980s, were also a minority, and their earnings *overstated* the decade's progress. Yet even their incomes stagnated, as we have seen, once adjusted for changes in the federal tax burden. Definitional hopscotch couldn't dispel the troubling reality.

Liberals, for their part, were correct in emphasizing how hourly manufacturing wages *declined* during the 1980s, yet wrong in insisting

*Conservative detractors of the significance of the median-income trend also contended that the Census Bureau's surveys relied on inaccurate estimates and missed about 10 percent of the earnings assumable from tax returns and W-2 forms. Another complaint was that the median-income calculations involved only *money* income and ignored the growing role of employee benefits and government transfer payments. On the other hand, others counterargued that by the late 1980s and early 1990s, the median income's year-to-year change was being abnormally fattened by a demographic bulge of families in the forty-five- to fifty-four-year-old bracket, where income maximizes. Questions about the exactitude of the year-to-year data, however, don't negate the trend from the mid-1970s to the early 1990s. Relative stagnation is still a fair description.

that the average weekly wage also fell, despite the confirming data published by the Bureau of Labor Statistics. Rival statistics from the Social Security Administration, which showed weekly wages rising, were better because these numbers reflected overall work-force hours and earnings, not just select sampling. The catch, as amplified on pages 157 to 159, was that the principal reason for rising work-force earnings—a sharp increase in men and women working overtime or moonlighting with second jobs—reflected the worries of a *squeezed* work force, not a *contented* one. Household fears were the spur, not economic growth, as conservatives contended.

In short, most of the available income, cost and wage measurements involve some distortion. However, now that some of these biases have been noted, the next two chapters will use the different yardsticks as necessary, while concentrating on the important larger circumstances: inflation's greater-than-acknowledged erosion of middle-class purchasing power and, just as important, the underappreciated burden of federal, state and local tax changes and increases. The tax rearrangements, to which we turn first, were more than simply another economic ingredient in the third and latest squeeze on Middle America. Much like the great deflation visited on the rural United States in the post–Civil War era, they, too, were also a sign that the political establishment of the 1980s was willing to shift fiscal priorities that once favored the broad mass of Americans to serve the interests of a relatively small elite.

C H A P T E R 5

The Great Tax Misrepresentation of the 1980s

> True marginal tax rates in the United States are at their peak for two-earner couples making between $50,000 and $100,000 a year—precisely the middle-income people who would best respond to the incentive of lower rates. America has one of the world's least progressive tax structures . . . the payroll tax wreaks havoc with marginal tax rates. The average proportion of income paid in tax by the poorest 50% of families rose in the 1980s by 6%, while for the richest 10% it fell by 10%.
>
> —*The Economist,* January 20, 1990

> There are many people who believe that the only way we can get this country turned around is to tax the middle class more and punish them more, but the truth is that middle-class Americans are basically the only group of Americans who've been taxed more in the 1980s and during the last 12 years, even though their incomes have gone down. The wealthiest Americans have been taxed much less, even though their incomes have gone up.
>
> —Democratic presidential nominee Bill Clinton, 1992

Compared with the relatively straightforward tax reductions of previous eras, those of the 1980s could be said to represent an era of tax deception, especially where the average American family was concerned. Rhetoric about new efficiency, simplification and fairness in revenue-raising, though often sincere, was misleading. While lower income taxes did become a pleasing reality for billionaires, whose numbers multiplied tenfold as the top rate on unearned income fell from 70 percent in 1981 to 28 percent in 1988 and the stock market soared, *ordinary* households soon found themselves facing their highest overall tax rates in the history of the republic.

In 1992, Thomas Block, president of H&R Block, the tax preparers with seven thousand offices across the nation, explaining that he had commissioned a university research project in response to the growing "perception among middle-income taxpayers that they pay too much tax in relation to high-income earners," announced that was just what his experts had found: between 1977 and 1990, the tax bill for a taxpayer earning $50,000 a year had increased 7.75 percent, while the bill for taxpayers with incomes of $200,000 a year had dropped 27.75 percent. Block allowed that he had hoped President Bush would sign congressional Democrats' middle-class tax cut legislation—which Bush instead vetoed—because boosting the top tax rate on the wealthy "would have gone a long way in restoring equity."[1]

Months earlier, the Washington-based Tax Foundation had determined that for the year 1990, direct and indirect federal, state and local taxes had become an unprecedented weight on the typical U.S. family, taking a record 37.3 cents of every dollar.[2] Data also supported an ironic corollary: that the average wealthy family with a million-dollar income paid a *lower* rate, probably 35 or 36 cents on every dollar—and probably their lowest in sixty years.

Computing the relative burdens was not difficult. The average family, by the Foundation's calculus, would have paid 28 cents of every dollar in all kinds of federal taxes and 9 cents in state and local taxes.* The millionaire's family, using other estimates, would have paid about 28 to 29 cents on every dollar in federal taxes, but probably only about 7 cents in state taxes.† Wealthy households' total dollar payments were much higher than the typical family's, to be sure, yet their relative burden as a percentage of income was lighter, a striking reversal of mid-twentieth-century political and fiscal equity.

In some jurisdictions, moreover, regressive state tax structures made the surprising disparity even larger. In Pennsylvania, for example, the average family would have paid 38 cents on every dollar (28.2 cents in federal taxes, 9.8 cents to states and courthouses) versus approximately 34 cents for the rich; in Texas, the relative combined tax burdens were 37 cents for the middle class, 32 cents for the rich; in Illinois, the ratio was 40 cents per dollar for the average family, 34 cents per dollar for millionaire taxpayers; in Florida, the difference was between 36 cents and 31 cents.[3]

This is hardly what middle-income Americans could have expected from the promises of supply-side economists of the early 1980s or from

*The Tax Foundation, like most other analysts, used a methodology that included both the employee's *and* employer's FICA payments as being attributed to the employee's federal tax burden.

†The estimate of a 28–29 percent effective federal rate for million-dollar incomes is based on Urban Institute and Congressional Budget Office estimates for the top 1 percent, while the estimate of a 7 percent effective state tax rate comes from the 1991 study *A Far Cry from Fair* by Citizens for Tax Justice.

the speeches of administration and congressional tax reform architects circa 1986. The reality, however, was that as Washington lowered federal tax burdens on high incomes, the overall effects of federal fiscal policy wound up boosting other federal, state and local assessments on people in the middle enough to make the nation's collective tax burden of the early 1990s set records as a percentage of peacetime GNP and national income. In Chapters 2 and 4, I described the evolution of this philosophy and how the exactions heaped upon the middle-income family and even the upper-middle-income family came from all directions: federal income tax "bubbles" through which the upper-middle class paid higher marginal rates than millionaires, relentless expansion of Social Security rates and taxable income bases, soaring local property taxes (especially in the Northeast) and state tax increases and fees often targeted on ordinary purchases and breadwinners. Citizens for Tax Justice, a union-funded group, threw its critical spotlight on how Texas, in the late 1980s, raised its sales tax rate from 4.125 percent to 6.25 percent, boosted cigarette taxes by 21.2 cents per pack and increased the gasoline tax by 5 cents. These changes, the group calculated, cost poor Texas families 3.1 percent more of their annual incomes, took 1.6 percent from middle-income earnings and tapped wealthy households for a mere 0.4 percent.[4]

State-level raids on new revenue sources were sometimes comical in their desperation. Wisconsin, for example, in November 1990, began trying to collect sales tax on drinks served on airplanes that were flying over the state until the practice was overturned by the Wisconsin Court of Appeals.[5] But even serious revenue efforts were extending in unusual and provocative directions. New York City, unsatisfied with registering only dogs, decided to charge license fees for cats, too, and began requiring animal-grooming salons to provide names and addresses of pet owners.[6] In 1991 California not only increased the sales tax to 7.25 percent, but became the first state to extend it to snack foods after an angry debate over what was included and what wasn't.* Ritz Crackers were taxed, saltines weren't. On July 16, as the $200-million-a-year snack tax went into effect, the *Los Angeles Times* published what must be one of the more extraordinary charts in the annals of state tax policy.

State Board of Equalization member Brad Sherman, a prominent

---

*A few months later, Pennsylvania applied its sales tax to snack foods and set off a debate about whether bagels were taxable—they were if baked on the store's premises but they were not if prepackaged. In California, however, the debate ended on November 3, 1992, when citizens voted by two to one to repeal the snack tax even though it would cost the state hundreds of millions of dollars in revenue that would have to be made up elsewhere.

Figure 3. Taxing Your Snack

Now Taxed	Remaining Exempt
■ All forms of candy	★ Baking chocolate
■ Rice cakes	★ Baking confections
■ Cupcakes	★ Glazed fruit sold for baking
■ Twinkies	(but not when sold as candy)
■ Granola bars	★ Cereals
■ Screaming Yellow Zonkers	★ Muffins
■ Cracker Jack	★ Doughnuts, pastry sold
■ Fig Newtons	as bakery products
■ Ritz Crackers	★ Slice of pie purchased from a deli
■ Carnation breakfast bars	(but not as prepackaged snack)
■ Pringles chips	★ Saltine crackers
■ Cheese puffs	★ Nuts
■ Doritos	★ Seeds
■ Cheez-It crackers	★ Dried fruit
■ Ding Dongs	

Source: State Board of Equalization

opponent, had complained before enactment that the "definition of snack foods says nothing about caviar or brie. But it does tax cookies, potato chips, corn chips, popcorn and pretzels. In other words, the country club spread or lobbyists' reception menu of brie, caviar and French bread will be untaxed, but the average person's party of chips, cookies and pretzels will be taxed."[7] After enactment, most critics began emphasizing the technical difficulty of distinguishing, as the law required, between foods and snacks. Ding Dongs were foods for federal food stamp purposes but taxable snacks within the boundaries of California. Weeks after the tax went into effect, the Board of Equalization was still debating the revenue status of chocolate chips, marshmallows—and Ninja Turtle Snack Pies!

As the fiscal crises worsened in 1992 the states began enacting more fees and charges in lieu of overt taxes. New York imposed tough new penalties on unpaid parking tickets, where fines and penalties already brought in nearly a half billion dollars a year. In California, where state officials purported to avoid any new taxes, another $530 million a year in fees were imposed on persons who wanted to take college courses, register pleasure boats, enroll children for treatment of leukemia or file lawsuits, while the state also cut $1.3 billion of aid to local governments and special districts, forcing them to raise taxes and utility rates.[7A]

U.S. fiscal history has had its share of revolts against provocative taxes, from the Boston Tea Party and the Whiskey Rebellion of 1794 to California's famous Proposition 13 of 1978. By the early 1990s the provocations were again reaching that level—or worse. The paradox of the 1980s, however, lay in how the tax revolt of the late 1970s, which began as a middle-class or even populist insurgency against rising property taxes in California, was transformed into a dismantling of the progressive income tax and a re-attuning of the federal tax system to concerns about markets and efficiency, not fairness, with the results we have just seen.

To be sure, reforms included in 1986 and 1990 federal tax legislation helped America's poor by cutting millions off the income tax rolls (1986) and by increasing the value of the low-income tax credit (1990). For those at the economic bottom, these modifications mitigated the FICA increases and other regressive changes. But otherwise, as we have seen, the thrust of federal and state tax policy in the 1980s and early 1990s was toward expanding the sort of taxes that took their highest ratios of household income from the poor and middle classes: Social Security, sales, property and excise. Because the average family did not receive new exclusions or credits, the rise of its combined federal, state and local tax burden to record levels by the early 1990s became a central ingredient in the reduction of middle-class real disposable income.

The Downward Redistribution of the Federal Tax Burden

A succinct, one-paragraph history of federal taxation of the ordinary U.S. family since World War II, if penned by angry progressives, might read this way: During these years, the top income tax rate on the richest Americans fell from 91 percent to 31 percent while the burden on the average household soared because of bracket creep, FICA increases and the eroding value of family exemptions. Back in 1948 a family of four earning the median income would have owed little or no federal income tax while paying a mere 1 percent of its income to Social Security. By 1955 that same family would have been laying out 9 percent for Social Security and income tax together, and by 1990, according to tax expert Eugene Steuerle of the Urban Institute, a median-income family faced a combined federal tax rate of almost 25 percent, while other estimates set it at 26 percent to 28 percent.

Traditional families with two or more children were particular losers. Economist Steuerle, who put much of the blame on the declining inflation-adjusted value of family exemptions, emphasized that "taxes on households with dependents have increased at a faster rate than for most other households."[8] Congresswoman Patricia Schroeder of Colorado, chair of the House Select Committee on Children, Youth and Families, said that: "People are just beginning to realize that taxes on families have never been this high in the history of the Republic."[9]

Conservatism's one-paragraph synopsis, by contrast, was cheery, even boastful. Reduction of tax rates on the rich, by stripping economic disincentives from the tax code, culminated in the investment, entrepreneurialism, stock market boom and capitalist bow wave of the Reagan years. As a result, the share of total federal income taxes paid by the flush top 1 percent of Americans kept increasing, especially in the crescendo of the 1980s when it rose from 18 percent to 27 percent. According to supply-side chroniclers, this showed that the U.S. income tax was actually getting *more* progressive—taking more from the rich and gathering less from everyone else.

A foreign visitor asked to arbitrate might assume that one of these analyses had to be false. In fact, *both* sequences of *facts* were correct, which helps explain the debate that arose in the 1990s between partisans of contrary interpretations.

It helps to proceed by laying out basic undisputed circumstances. For a $1-million-a-year earner, the top federal income tax rate fell from 91 percent in 1955 to 70 percent in 1964, 50 percent in 1981, 28 percent in 1988 and 31 percent in 1991. No one suggests otherwise. Meanwhile, for a median-income family of four, it is also beyond debate that the sheltering effect of the federal income tax personal or dependent exemption shrank relentlessly after World War II, whittled by inflation to a fraction of its former value. In 1948, when the exemption was $600 and the median family took in $3,000, a family of four with these earnings, as we have seen, was largely shielded against federal income taxes.* Through the 1950s, the exemption could still minimize median-family federal tax burdens. That ended as rising inflation weakened the benefit of dependent exemptions in the 1960s and shrank them further in the 1970s. By 1990, despite an increase in the exemption to $2,050, the effect was just a shadow of yesteryear's. As Appendix B details, to shelter the same percentage of per capita income as the $600 figure did in 1948 would have required a $7,781 exemption!

Besides doubling exemptions, the federal tax policy of the 1980s cut income tax rates for ordinary families. This, too, was a solid fact. As

---

*The $3,000-a-year family of 1948 would have had a $600 adjusted income after exemptions, to which the lowest rate of 16 percent applied, for an estimated federal income tax of $100.

a result, the effective income tax rate of 11.4 percent paid by the median family in 1981 dropped to 10.5 percent in 1982 and 9.1 percent in 1988.[10] Middle America would have benefited more from rate reductions if they hadn't been partly offset in the late 1980s by the loss of hitherto significant deductions—for state sales taxes, for interest paid on personal loans and credit cards and (in many cases) for individual retirement accounts.

The larger reality, though, was that the shrinkage of dependent exemption benefits from 1950 to 1990 had cost ordinary families many, many more dollars than 1980s bracket reductions could recoup. In addition, Social Security taxes were a fast-rising burden in the Reagan and Bush years, and excise taxes on alcohol, tobacco and gasoline were also climbing. So by the early 1990s, according to Brookings Institution calculations, the median or average family in the $30,000–$50,000 range was laying out a slightly higher percentage of earnings in combined federal income, excise and FICA taxes than it had been at the beginning of the 1980s. Table 4 pairs the 1948–90 decline of the effective federal tax rate on the rich with the rise during the same period of the effective tax rate on the median family.

The Tax Foundation, as noted, also reported that the overall tax burden for the average family set a record in 1990 and that median family income was stagnant, after adjustment for federal taxes. Calculations by the Urban Institute, in turn, show that the median family paid out the following percentages of its earnings in federal income and Social Security taxes: 23.08 percent in 1980, 25.09 percent in 1981, 23.78 percent in 1983, 24.44 percent in 1985, 24.63 percent in 1990.[11] Excise taxes, not included in the institute's calculation, further increased the weight. Overall, expanding tax pressures were part of a declining purchasing power. As we have seen, the Congressional Budget Office calculated that in constant 1990 dollars, a typical middle-income family's earnings after federal income tax dropped from $30,900 in 1980 to $29,500 in 1992.

Net federal tax reduction for the 1980s, then, was largely an illusion. Despite politicians' contrary pretenses, federal revenue needs made it impossible to let the middle class off the fiscal hook. The decision in 1983 to boost Social Security taxes even as income tax rates were coming down had been a bellwether. What Washington gave $40,000 households with its income tax hand it largely took back with its FICA hand. Appendix B shows the relentless 1980s rise of the FICA tax rate and the even more sweeping enlargement of the earnings base to which that taxation applied.

The fairness complaint was that while the overall tax changes of the

Table 4. The Great Tax-Rate Turnaround, 1948–90
Median Families versus Millionaires or the Top 1 Percent

	Median Family's Effective Federal Tax Rate (Income and FICA)*	Millionaire or Top 1% Family's Effective Federal Tax Rate (Income and FICA)†
1948	5.30%	76.9%
1955	9.06	85.5
1960	12.35	85.5
1965	11.55	66.9
1970	16.06	68.6
1975	20.03	
1977		35.5
1980	23.68	31.7
1981	25.09	
1982	24.46	
1983	23.78	
1984	24.25	
1985	24.44	24.9
1986	24.77	
1987	23.21	
1988	24.30	26.9
1989	24.37	26.7
1990	24.63	

*The data in this column originates as follows: the 1948 figure comes from *The Statistical History of the United States, 1976;* the figures for 1955 to 1983 come from Alan Lerman of the U.S. Department of the Treasury Office of Tax Analysis. The calculations after 1983 come from Eugene Steuerle and Jon Bakija, *Right Ways and Wrong Ways to Reform Social Security* (Washington, D.C.: Urban Institute Press, 1993).

†The figures for 1948 to 1970 represent the effective tax rates for those earning $1 million a year and come from U.S. Treasury Department unpublished data set forth on p. 1112 of *The Statistical History of the United States, 1976.* FICA is not included, but the rates would not even be affected by a percentage point. The rates from 1977 onward are for the top 1% of families as computed by the Congressional Budget Office tax simulation model and include all federal taxes. Source: the 1992 Green Book of the House Ways and Means Committee, p. 1510. The effective rate on millionaires would be close to the rate on the top 1 percent.

1980s slightly raised rather than reduced the total federal tax burdens of the average or median family, these same revisions did reduce—*significantly*—the tax burdens of the richest Americans, continuing a pattern of relief that began in the mid-1950s. Back in 1948 or 1955, when the average American family was paying only 1 to 2 percent of its income for Social Security and little or no federal income tax, a senior corporate executive making $200,000 in yearly salary, admittedly rare in those days, would have paid 65 to 75 percent or so. One profile of Charles Wilson, the chairman of General Motors, estimated that he would have kept only $164,000 from a 1950 salary of $626,-000.[12] Wealthy salaried people generally paid high federal income taxes during the Truman and early Eisenhower years, although oilmen had lucrative depletion allowances and other shelters and entrepreneurs enjoyed the advantage of low capital gains taxes. The pyramiding deductions, credits and gimmicks of the 1960s and 1970s, which President Jimmy Carter would call a disgrace, were still largely a gleam in the eye of Washington lobbyists and congressional tax-writers.

Meanwhile, over the next three decades, the broad funding strategies on which Washington depended to support federal expenditures slowly shifted away from a reliance on taxes that burdened the upper brackets (the personal and corporate income taxes, along with estate taxes) toward borrowing and levies that fell elsewhere. In the 1950s, as Table 5 shows, the personal income tax, corporate income tax and estate tax provided over three quarters of all funds. By the 1980s that had fallen to roughly half. As the burden on those at the top fell, a greater proportion of money was raised by taxing those in the middle or borrowing against future living standards.

By its late-1980s zenith, the philosophic reversal involved had far-reaching practical effects. In the early 1950s, when $600,000-a-year salaried executives faced an effective tax rate that official estimates placed near 75 percent, a median-family breadwinner, as we have seen, virtually escaped the Internal Revenue Service with an effective income tax rate of just 5 percent. Federal income tax tables back then applied twenty-three successive brackets eventually reaching 91 percent. This made tax progressivity obvious on its face. Thirty-five years later, an extraordinary convergence was taking place: the effective combined rate of federal taxes (income, excise and FICA) on median or average families had climbed to the 25–28 percent range, depending on the calculation, while the rate on households with $500,000 incomes had

Table 5. Source of Funds for Federal Spending
(Average Annual Shares)

Decade	Personal Income Tax	Corporate Income Tax	Payroll Tax	Excise/ Estate	Borrowing
1950s	42.0%	26.9%	11.5%	17.2%	2.5%
1960s	42.0%	20.4%	18.4%	14.9%	4.4%
1970s	40.3%	13.3%	27.7%	11.3%	11.1%
1980s	38.0%	7.7%	29.2%	8.2%	17.7%

Source: Robert J. Shapiro, "Paying for Progress," Progressive Policy Institute, February 1991. Calculations derived by the author from *Budget of the United States Government,* fiscal year 1991, "Historical Tables," Tables 1.1 and 2.2.

declined to roughly 28 percent. There, in a sentence, was the fiscal revolution.

We have already examined the philosophic transition that supported the tax changes of the sixties, the seventies and (especially) the eighties and how they reduced the bite on the rich and increased it on the average family. In less than a generation, the average American went from being a political icon to being a fiscal milch cow. As Chapter 8 will show, historically this has been a dangerous transformation for great nations. Yet the contrary insistences marshaled by conservatives require some further clarification: After all, the share of federal income taxes paid by the top 1 percent did rise sharply from 1980 to the end of the decade. Wasn't this proof that everyone else actually got off more easily, paying a *shrinking* share of the federal tax burden?

Not really. During the 1980s the portion of overall federal income tax revenues that were collected from the richest 1 percent increased by about 50 percent (from 18 percent to 27 percent) because that group's share of national income grew by roughly that same ratio—from about 8 percent to 12–13 percent. Actually, because the tax rates of the rich were significantly higher than those of others during most of the decade, their share of taxes paid should have increased even more sharply than their share of income, but that is where the rate cuts came in.

The role of tax policy in upper-bracket gains was both direct and indirect. The indirect role, all too often ignored, was the more important. From 1979 to 1982, as the maximum tax rate on capital gains fell from 49 percent to 20 percent while the maximum income tax rate on unearned income dropped from 70 percent to 50 percent, the effect on the financial markets—once they were also reassured by disinflation—was to fuel a massive boom. In a nutshell, the lower tax rates raised the return on and thus the value of financial assets like stocks and bonds, just as many supply-siders had predicted. Economist Robert Shapiro of the Progressive Policy Institute later summarized how the 90 percent growth in incomes for the top 1 percent of Americans during the 1980s came about because "the top 1 percent own vast capital assets, the value of which increased when tax incentives artificially raised their rate of return."[13] As the Dow-Jones Industrial Average soared during the 1980s, so did its ability to turn new stock issues and financial deals into wealth for affluent Americans. From 1978 to 1988 the number of persons with million-dollar annual incomes skyrocketed from 2,041 to 65,303. Even allowing for inflation, that was an eightfold increase.[14]

Moreover, when the owners of financial assets—the top 1 percent

Figure 4. The Comparative Benefits of the Tax Reform Act of 1986

Income Bracket	Size of Tax Cut	Average 1989 Tax Savings per Return
Up to $10,000	11%	$37
$10,000–$20,000	6%	$69
$20,000–$30,000	11%	$300
$30,000–$40,000	11%	$467
$40,000–$50,000	16%	$1,000
$50,000–$75,000	16%	$1,523
$75,000–$100,000	18%	$3,034
$100,000–$200,000	22%	$7,203
$200,000–$500,000	27%	$24,603
$500,000–$1,000,000	34%	$86,084
$1,000,000 or more	31%	$281,033

Source: Internal Revenue Service, *Philadelphia Inquirer*, October 21, 1991

Fewer people pay the minimum tax . . . And they pay less

Income bracket	Taxpayers 1n 1986	Taxpayers in 1989	**down**	Income bracket	Avg. tax paid in 1986	Avg. tax paid in 1989	**down**
$100,000–$200,000	126,127	29,195	**77%**	$100,000–$200,000	$10,295	$4,561	**56%**
$200,00–$500,000	46,874	14,112	**70%**	$200,000–$500,000	$23,237	$9,037	**61%**
$500,000–$1,000,000	10,428	4,176	**60%**	$500,000–$1,000,000	$45,218	$20,694	**54%**
$1,000,000 or more	15,259	2,361	**85%**	$1,000,000 or more	$116,395	$54,758	**53%**

Source: Internal Revenue Service, *Philadelphia Inquirer*, October 21, 1991

owned half of the privately owned corporate stock in the United States—received their dividends, rents or interests, those, too, were taxed at new low levels. As noted earlier, the top tax rate on unearned income dropped from 70 percent in 1980 to 50 percent in 1982 and 28 percent in 1988—the biggest decline since the 1920s. Changes in the alternative minimum tax also quietly reduced its effect on America's richest individuals, and as Figure 4 shows, by 1989 the top 1 percent of Americans had collected large and lopsided benefits from the supposedly reformist Tax Reform Act of 1986. Thus, while it was the *indirect* effect of the several tax cuts that produced the explosion of pretax income as the rich took profits from the stock market, there was also a smaller *direct* effect felt in the greater amount of income that was left after income and capital gains taxes were paid. Before the Reagan cuts, the collective rich had kept their effective rates in the 33–40 percent range through tax shelters. After the rate cuts, some new income came as money was taken out of shelters, although a much larger amount came from rising business and stock market profits. As the income of the top 1 percent soared, so did the share of total income tax receipts they paid.

As for the percentage of federal taxes paid by the huge block of Americans in the anonymous and often stagnating middle, that went down because their share of national income dropped. They were running in place as those at the top soared. The burden of their taxation increased, however, because the effective federal tax rate—the portion of their income taken by FICA, excise and income taxes combined—*rose* for median- and average-income families during the 1980s. The top 1 percent and (to a lesser extent) the top 5 percent were the only groups for whom the effective federal rate *fell* significantly. The details of these shifts can be found in Appendix B.

Federal tax trends poignantly illustrate how, in three or four decades, the mid-century fiscal tilt to the middle class was reversed. During the buoyant 1950s, increased middle-class taxes were largely a product of prosperity, growing as the average family's real income grew. By 1960 the annual income tax of $700 for a family of four at the median income just under $6,000 was not oppressive.[15] But then came inflation. The 1970s hit the middle class hard, as stagflation eroded real median-family income while bracket creep pushed taxes up anyway. Then in the 1980s, the realignment of federal, state and local taxes became more ideological and complex.

In short, as America's mid-century hegemony faded, the average middle-class or working-class family stopped being the economic favorite of federal policymakers, yielding that place to a much smaller group of top-bracket investors and wealth creators, for whom all sorts of vital roles were proclaimed. Until late 1990, when the rich became a target again, the top 1 percent of Americans of the 1980s had reassumed the place they had held in the 1880s and 1920s in a restored conservative fiscal theology. Meanwhile, at the state and local level, to which we now turn, regressivity was even more pronounced—and so were the effects of tax changes on the typical household.

State and Local Taxes—The Rising Weight of Regressivity

From the 1870s to the early 1940s, save for the years of World War I, state and local revenues—the resource for building roads and running schools—*exceeded* those of the federal government. Governments closer to the people raised and spent most of the money. Then the cost of World War II quickly centralized fiscal power in Washington, and over the next half century, federal taxation, led by the income tax, remained substantially larger than state and local levies, thereby dominating the attention of lobbyists, economists and reformers.

However, as the return of program responsibility from Washington to the states accelerated in the 1980s, the increase produced in state and local taxes became an essential component in the broad rearrangement of the national tax burden that worked to squeeze the middle class. By 1991 state and local taxes had risen to 44 percent of the national tax revenue total (exclusive of FICA), up from 32 percent in 1960, according to the New York–based Center for the Study of the States.[16] Not only was the progressive income tax being weakened as a linchpin of the U.S. revenue system; the state and local levies moving to the fore were often regressive.

For American families in the median- or average-income range, we have already seen how rising FICA and excise taxes ate up most or all of the 1980s reduction in federal income taxes. State and local levies and charges, which also fell most heavily on low and middle incomes, were climbing as fast as FICA. Between 1980 and 1989, per capita state taxes almost doubled, growing from $658 to $1,150.[17] To supply yet another measure, as of 1990 state and local revenues had climbed to 22.1 percent of U.S. personal income, up from 20.5 percent in 1982 and 16.5 percent in 1967, while federal revenues oscillated in a steady band from 23 percent to 26 percent. Yet because state and local levies varied from jurisdiction to jurisdiction, computations of trends in disposable income generally sidestepped their impact, thereby missing a growing source of damage to the average household.

For 1990, as already noted, the Tax Foundation showed that the average family with $46,000 a year, two earners and two children, suffered a direct and indirect federal tax bite totaling 28.2 percent of income. State and local taxes took another 9.1 percent.[18] Citizens for Tax Justice, in its own exhaustive survey, set the 1990 figure for the state and local tax burden on the average family slightly higher at 10.0 percent, and simultaneously detailed the wide range between the *lowest* state and local combined burden (Alaska at 2.9 percent) and the *highest* (Michigan, with 13.1 percent).[19]

As a matter of course, state and local governments varied in how much they had enlarged their activities and outlays during the go-go years. Some jurisdictions had recklessly expanded programs, personnel and pay, and by the late 1980s needed new revenues accordingly.

However, another important reason for the new upward pressure on
state taxes lay in how Washington had reduced federal aid to states and
localities, specifically eliminating federal revenue-sharing with local
governments launched a decade earlier by Richard Nixon, while Congress and the executive branch also required state and local authorities
to absorb significantly more of the total cost of Medicaid, transportation, housing and education. The result, computed in constant dollars,
was that federal aid to states and cities *dropped* by an eighth from 1978
to 1989, according to the Advisory Council on Intergovernmental
Relations, and by the end of the decade, Washington provided just 17
percent of state and municipal budgets.[20] To add to local troubles,
legislative and executive branch officials in Washington frequently
compensated for their own difficulty in funding new domestic programs by mandating specific instructions and duties upon the states as
a condition of getting the federal aid that still flowed.* All of these
factors put states in the same painful situation: needing to raise more
revenues.

Municipal, county and local governments also found themselves
grasping for revenues, all the more so after the 1990–91 downturn
thrust many states into their greatest fiscal crises since the 1930s. New
York governor Mario Cuomo voiced the complaint of the hard-
pressed urban Northeast: "In effect, the middle class and the working
poor of our cities have been called upon to pay for the huge income tax
cuts at the federal level. Prosperity never trickled down in the 1980s,
only the tax burden did. And no one noticed it."[21]

The same governors and state legislators quick to protest how "shift
and shaft" federalism had passed the fiscal buck stateward during the
1980s were, in turn, often just as ready to cut assistance to lesser units
of local government, forcing *them* to consider tax increases. By 1991
Hal Hovey, editor of *State Policy Reports,* indicated that cuts in state
aid to counties, cities and towns were being discussed in half of the fifty
states.[22] Meanwhile, counties and municipalities were also being dog-
ged by federal cuts, and the U.S. Conference of Mayors released a
study saying that Washington's contribution to U.S. cities dropped 64

*Over one quarter of all the federal acts preempting state and local laws in favor of federal
standards and mandates since 1789 were passed between 1981 and 1989, most of them
dealing with health, safety and education—and representing a growing load on the states.
Even against the background of recession, *The New York Times* reported in 1992 that federal
authorities continued to create or expand domestic spending programs with little or no
review of the financial burdens then placed on state and local government ("U.S. Adds
Programs with Little Review of Local Burdens," *New York Times,* March 24, 1992).

percent between 1980 and 1990.[23] As both higher-level funding sources dried up, cities and villages in New York State began the 1990s with only 25 percent of their budgets from federal and state aid, down from 40 percent a decade earlier.[24] Fiscal weakness was aggravating fiscal weakness. The dominoes were falling.

Cuomo and others were correct in that one reason taxes were going up in Hempstead, Riverside and Bangor was that they had gone down on Washington's Form 1040. Some of the cost of the federal income tax reductions, federally mandated programs and other federal responsibilities shifted to the states would be billed through thousands of legislatures, county councils, city halls, town assessors' offices and special tax districts from Maine to California. In 1991, the *Chicago Tribune*'s Jon Margolis offered a wry summation:

> So if your property taxes have gone up, if there are too many other kids in your child's class, if it takes two minutes for the "911" dispatcher to answer, if you're waiting longer for the bus and if the nearby lake is getting dirtier, please understand that this is the cost of cutting [federal] taxes, somebody's if not yours. You are paying for the tax cut that had to go to that guy in the Lincoln Town Car who just zoomed by taking his kid from their privately guarded subdivision to a private school.[25]

Moreover, even though the burden would increase more rapidly in the 1990s, the rise in state and local taxes during the 1980s had *already* affected Middle America, adding a further offset to nominal income gains. Table 6 illustrates how combined state and local taxes constituted a rising burden on an average family of four during the 1980s:

Besides the obvious problem—that fast-rising state and local taxes

Table 6. The Rising State and Local Tax Burden, 1980–1991
Percentage of Average Families' Incomes Spent on State and Local Taxes, 1985–90

	1985	1990
Lowest 20%	12.6%	13.8%
Second 20%	10.0	10.9
Middle 20%	9.1	10.0
Fourth 20%	8.6	9.5
Next 15%	8.4	9.2
Next 4%	8.2	8.7
Top 1%	7.1	7.6
Average Family	9.1	10.0

Source: *A Far Cry from Fair*, Citizens for Tax Justice, April 1991, p. 18.

weighed heaviest on low and middle incomes—the effects of this changing tax load on consumer purchasing power and inflation were difficult to calculate. Some state and local taxes are included in federal inflation (CPI) measurements, so that part of their escalation found its way into CPI as an offset to family purchasing power, but part of it went unmeasured. From federal bailouts to local taxes and fees, the cost of government was soaring, which should have found its way into the cost of living, but by and large did not.

Many important increases in state taxes occurred unannounced following the 1986 federal tax revisions, when the large majority of states using the federal definition of adjusted gross income took advantage of Washington's elimination of some federal credits and deductions. These automatically increased the taxable income of middle- and upper-bracket taxpayers, thus enlarging state revenue bases. However, in circumstances where states passed legislation for new taxes, they usually opted for regressive-type levies. For example, after tabulating 22 separate increases in state sales-tax rates between 1985 and 1990, 92 separate increases in state motor-fuels taxes, and 62 separate increases in state cigarette taxes, Citizens for Tax Justice, a labor-oriented group, said the impact would be hardest on the little guy. Middle-income families paid on average 4.2 percent of their incomes in sales and excise taxes while those in the top 1 percent paid just 1.3 percent.[26] The new increases would follow a similar distribution.

Federal levies on alcohol, tobacco and gasoline also rose in 1990. They, too, were regressive. The combined results of federal and state excise taxes, especially the gasoline tax, were particularly painful to rural areas.[27]

State levies were also becoming increasingly ingenious. California had its snack tax, and the list of new taxes passed by New York in 1990, to cite an egregious example, included a new container tax of 2 cents on soda, a 5 percent surcharge on hotel rooms costing over $100 a night, a 5 percent surcharge on car rentals, a 4 percent tax on cleaning and security services and parking garages and a 4 percent sales tax on telephone services using 800 and 900 numbers.[28] And as we have seen with Florida's taxes on speeding tickets and Wisconsin's attempt to tax drinks on airplanes, innovation was a 1991–92 byword in state taxation—and often concentrating its maximum impact on the middle class.

Fees and penalties began substituting for visible additional taxes. Those for auto licenses, mortgage filings and park visits were familiar. But in some jurisdictions, particularly California, fees were becoming a major preoccupation of state fiscal authorities. Back in 1953 California had started levying penalty assessments or surcharges on motorists' fines. As budget problems worsened in the 1980s and early 1990s, the surcharges soared, so that 1991's basic assessment for the state was $17 for every $10 of fine—enough to turn a $100 infraction into a $270 violation and earn $480 million a year for the state treasury.[29] "The basic problem here is that the state is in financial trouble," said Richard Stanford, presiding judge of the Orange County Municipal Court. "They're looking to the courts as a revenue source. And that's not what the courts are meant to be."[30]

In California, after the passage of Proposition 13 in 1978 curbed property taxes, other kinds of fees also soared. Business license fees, for example, increased by 229 percent from 1979 to 1990.[31] New York State imposed a broad range of new "fees"—including such items as a "laundromat inspection fee," based on a state employee visiting a laundromat, counting the washers and dryers, multiplying the total by $12 and presenting the owner with a bill in that amount.[32] In Dallas, Texas, where property taxes had risen by 67.8 percent in five years, the City Council decided to avoid a tax increase in 1991, opting instead to approve higher charges for water, gas, electricity, garbage pickup and the 911 emergency telephone system.[33] In a trend closely linked to the rise of user fees, utility charges, especially water bills, were increasing sharply in many jurisdictions, not least Boston, where water and sewer rates for the sixty cities and towns served by the Massachusetts Water Resources Authority rose 420 percent between 1985 and 1992, and were expected to double again by 1995, putting the average annual bill for a family of four at more than $1,000.[34] In New York's Long Island, rates soared so much that some senior citizens complained about paying more for water than for heat.

Local property taxes, curbed in many other states besides California after Proposition 13, were themselves again on the rise. In 1982 property taxes had averaged $3.26 for every $100 of personal income, *down* from the 1970s. But by 1988 the average was back up to $3.51 for each $100 of income.[35] Upward pressure was greatest in the Northeast, which had four of the nation's five highest-property-tax states, and where many suburban townships (and even a few counties) taxed homeowners steeply enough that a family of four with an average income and a midsized house paid $2,500 to $5,000 a year in real estate taxes. Appendix B shows the ten counties charging the highest per capita property taxes in the nation. It also shows how property taxes in New Jersey, a cockpit of voter revolt, expanded during the 1980s at a rate far exceeding the Consumer Price Index.

In February 1991, *The New York Times* profiled Angelo Verduci, a seventy-four-year-old retiree in the fast-growing suburb of Edison, New Jersey, whose income was $13,000 a year and who was paying $2,654 a year in property taxes on a small cement house that he built himself thirty years earlier when the Raritan Valley was still rural.[36] Each tax increase, he said, cut into his budget for food, clothing and medical care. Lower-middle-class families in Long Island, New York, and retirees in the Washington suburbs with $28,000-a-year pensions made the same complaint: local property taxes, not income taxes, had become their greatest fiscal burden.

In Maryland and Virginia, counties, not cities, provided most municipal services and set countywide burdens on homeowners. But the usual pattern elsewhere was for taxes to vary from town to town, which also involved inequities. In Illinois's Cook County (metropolitan Chicago), countywide averages camouflaged a wide variation. Suburbs blessed with crowded shopping malls, corporate plants and office buildings billed homeowners only about one third as much as poor jurisdictions without these lucrative revenue sources. In north suburban Niles, police officers got new Oldsmobile 88s each year and residents enjoyed free bus service, yet owners paid taxes of only $1,500 or so a year on houses worth $150,000. By contrast, in south suburban Harvey, $1,400 a year represented the taxes on a mere $50,000 house, and the cash-starved city of 36,000 left abandoned cars on the streets for months and removed snow mostly by letting it melt.[37]

In some areas, the collapsed real estate boom of the early 1990s made property taxes politically incendiary. Jurisdictions happily feeding on higher tax revenues from inflated real estate values went into fiscal shock as the boom went bust: as values plummeted, angry ratepayers demanded that their own assessments be marked down to reflect how 1989's $300,000 home had become 1991's $220,000 white elephant, and then the problems began. Local authorities sometimes had to wait (Connecticut towns, for example, could revalue only once every ten years). Yet even where revisions were feasible, reduced *assessments* often simply forced jurisdictions to raise *rates* to maintain revenues. Many cities and suburbs faced a glum prospect: rising property taxes *and* declining services in the years ahead.

In some jurisdictions, fees on builders had become a device for sidestepping property tax increases. Beginning in the 1980s, revenue-strained local governments had started requiring developers of residential subdivisions, shopping malls or office parks to agree to absorb many of the expenses hitherto financed by tax dollars. Municipal politicians liked levying "impact fees" to reduce upward pressure on

homeowner taxes because their constituents felt the fees only indirectly, through higher home prices and rents. One pioneering county,
Anne Arundel, in Maryland, collected—up front—$2,629 for roads
and schools and $3,000 for sewers for each new home, and in 1990 fully
thirty-nine states allowed their municipalities to tax builders in this
way.[38]

The effect on housing prices was inflationary enough to help launch
a federal Advisory Commission on Regulatory Barriers to Affordable
Housing, whose chairman pointed to an unnamed builder whose costs
had jumped 126 percent in six years because of fees and deplored how
Southern California home buyers paid $20,000 extra for houses.[39]
However, if the fees hadn't been levied, real estate taxes necessarily
would have been somewhat higher, although as a trade-off the initial
price tag of new homes would have been somewhat lower.

Some areas divided their property levies, tailoring them to particular
community services and needs through a multitude of special-purpose
taxing districts—sewer, flood control, elementary school, high school,
even library. Duplicative and confusing it might be, but ratepayers did
have more sense of exactly where their money was going. Of the fifty
states, Illinois led with the most taxing bodies in the nation, an extraordinary 6,500.[40]

User fees and special taxes, like real estate impact fees, also mushroomed during the late 1980s as states, counties and municipalities
became increasingly desperate to charge citizens for services previously
funded by federal aid or broad-based taxes. Here, too, some efforts
were innovative. In 1990, Fort Collins, Colorado, on the historic Over-
land Trail, tried to redefine its local streets as public utilities so that
revenues for repairs could be raised by charging residents fees for road
use.[41] To pay for a beach park in Port Hueneme, California, city
fathers levied an unprecedented "view tax" on residents based on how
much of the Pacific Ocean could be seen from each home.[42]

In November 1990 the nearly bankrupt city of Philadelphia agreed
to levy a special higher real estate tax requested by—and, indeed, to be
paid solely by—property owners in an eighty-block downtown area.
Special guards and private street cleaners were to be hired to obtain
levels of security and sanitation not provided to other neighborhoods.
Kindred customized arrangements were also worked out in parts of
New York, Denver and New Orleans. John J. DiIulio, director of
Princeton University's Center of Domestic Policy Studies, saw Philadelphia's arrangement as an ominous trend: "We're moving away
from a system that monitors a concern for general equity in the distri-

bution of government services, toward a market where citizens are treated very differently within the same jurisdiction based on their ability to pay special-purpose taxes."[43]

The rise in state and local taxes at record rates, even as services declined, underscored the economic polarization taking hold in the eighties. For the upper-middle class, the over-$100,000-a-year families in the top 5 percent but not in the top 1 percent or 2 percent, the increase in state and local taxes was annoying, but affordable. Inadequate services could be paid for privately, albeit with grumbling. To average-income families, however, the accelerating state and local taxes, as well as the escalating user fees and special charges—frequently imposed, as Chapter 6 will discuss, to pay for access and services that had been free back in 1955 or 1962—contributed to a fading real purchasing power. America's return to localism added new fiscal pressures to the middle-class squeeze.

The Gathering Threat to the Upper-Middle Class

The upper-middle-class family with an income of $100,000 or $150,000 finished the decade with significant advantages over the $45,000-a-year average family. Its bracket cuts during the 1980s had been bigger, and a fair part of its earnings still escaped rising FICA taxes. Yet it's also fair to say that by the 1990s those edges were beginning to erode. Partly to keep rates low at the very top, federal and state policymakers were nibbling more and more at the upper middle: those families who were in the top 10 percent (over $80,000 a year) but below the $250,000-a-year households of the top 1 percent. Although Bill Clinton had pledged in 1992 that his plans to increase the rates paid by the rich would not affect families with annual incomes under $200,000, for many reasons these strata were beginning to look like the next revenue target of government at most levels.

As we have seen, one of the most striking changes in federal tax treatment of the upper-middle class during the Reagan era was that even though their income tax rates declined, their gains were less than those of the rich, so that the two groups wound up paying roughly the same effective overall federal tax rate (25 to 28 percent). This was an enormous change from, say, 1928, when upper-middle-class taxpayers just inside the top 3 percent of incomes had paid an effective rate of 1 percent, less than a twentieth of the rate that applied to millionaires. Even in the mid-1950s, a taxpayer just inside the top 3 percent would have paid about a third of the rate that applied to million-dollar-a-year earners.

After the 1986 tax revisions, however, not only did the effective rates converge, but as we saw in Chapter 2, federal tax-writers came up with an unusual income tax device—the "bubble," in which a 33 percent marginal rate applied to households in the $70,000–$170,000 bracket, thereafter falling to 28 percent for those with higher earnings. There is no great mystery about its origins. Attempts to shrink the bracket structure down to just two rates—15 percent and then 28 percent (which kicked in at more or less the average family income)—didn't raise quite enough money in the computer projections. To meet their needs, policymakers seemingly had three choices: to lower the income threshold at which the 28 percent rate began, or to keep just two rates but raise the 28 percent bracket to something like 29 percent, or to create a third bracket of 33 percent kicking in at roughly $200,000. Legislators in both parties, led by Oregon Republican Bob Packwood, opposed a third rate that would single out the top 1 percent and chose instead to raise the needed several billion by a complicated bubble-cum-surcharge that would take the same money principally from the upper-middle class, giving *them* a higher marginal rate (33 percent) than a billionaire.

In the 1950s or 1960s, such a proposal would have been shouted down. In the 1980s, however, it was enacted, and a large bipartisan group of politicians and tax experts thereafter insisted that the bubble didn't undercut progressivity because millionaires wound up paying a slightly higher *effective* rate on their overall incomes even though the upper-middle class paid a higher *marginal* rate on their highest earnings. Never mind that the bubble manifestly did undercut progressivity because its revenues were used to avoid a higher rate on the richest Americans. What was striking was how drastically former values had been transformed. A Mellon or Rockefeller or Milken probably paid a slightly higher effective rate than a Los Angeles police captain, but hardly anyone cited the vivid contrast with 1929, 1950 or even 1960 to make an indisputable historical point: *that the progressivity of the U.S. income tax system had been largely lost.*

In 1990, because of what tax expert Emil Sunley of the accounting firm Deloitte & Touche called George Bush's "passion for subterfuge," a new bubble was created.[44] Bush refused to accept a new third rate any higher than 31 percent, which by itself would not bring in enough new revenue to match the billions being collected from the 2 million upper-middle-class taxpayers in the existing bubble or surcharge zone. As a result, the new 31 percent rate was teamed with a *second* bubble-cum-surcharge arrangement, prompting one former Treasury economist to tell a Washington tax conference that "Like a bad nightmare, the bubble is back, only in a more insidious form."⁴⁵ This time, the distortion involved a phaseout of family exemptions and a rising offset against itemized deductions that combined to create a surcharge for incomes above $150,000 but less than $275,000.

While this second bubble affected fewer people, critics pointed out that it introduced a new bias: unfair treatment of large families. That was because as households in the $150,000–$275,000 range saw their individual family-member exemptions phased out, the de facto surcharge was greatest on the largest households. John G. Wilkins of Coopers & Lybrand explained that the effective marginal rate for 1991 in that bracket varied from 33 percent for a married couple with no children to 37.3 percent for a family with eight children. For incomes above $275,000, the marginal rate dropped back to 31 percent. Figure 5 shows the structure and marginal-rate effects of both the "old" (1988–90) and "new" (post-1991) bubbles.

Figure 5. The New Tax Rate Bubble

Figures are based on average gross income for a family of six under the old and new tax laws

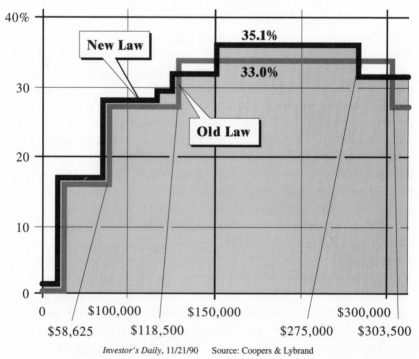

Investor's Daily, 11/21/90   Source: Coopers & Lybrand

There was also a broader basis to the rising burden of the upper-middle class. Former deputy assistant treasury secretary Steven Entin pointed out that "Federal marginal rates of 33 percent to 34 percent put taxpayers who face state and local income taxes and payroll taxes on earned income in fairly high tax brackets easily exceeding 35 percent to 45 percent."[46] He had in mind the additional effect of state and local income tax, but the 1990 budget act also expanded the reach of the 1.45 percent Medicare component of the Social Security tax, increasing the taxable income base to which it applied in 1991 from $53,400 to $125,000. Self-employed doctors, lawyers and others would also have to pay the employer's share, for a total tax of 2.9 percent on the more-than-doubled income base.

Worse still, from the upper-middle-class standpoint, the income base to which the Social Security portion of the FICA tax applied was predicted by some to climb toward $100,000. No serious moves were made in the 1992 election year, but forecasts of subsequent increases were commonplace. Movement toward taxing $100,000 or $125,000 families at 7.65 percent for Social Security and Medicare would push their *effective,* and not just *marginal,* rates of income-type taxation well above those of million-dollar earners.

In the meantime, tax experts also foresaw a threat to the federal deductions for state and local income taxes, as well as for property taxes and mortgage interest paid on homes. Indeed, following a provision in the 1990 budget act, a taxpayer's itemized deductions were reduced in 1991 by $300 for every $10,000 of adjusted gross income above $100,000. That meant that a $150,000-a-year family would lose $1,500 in deductions and, based on their new 31 percent rate, pay an additional $465 a year. In its first year, only a small, prosperous portion of the middle class was affected, and not very burdensomely. Skeptics, however, pointed out that during the 1990 debate, legislators from New York and other high-tax states had predicted that deduction limits, once established, would expand and possibly lead to no further deductibility for state and local income taxes.[47]

A second federal tax change was also bearing down on middle-class Americans—subjecting employee fringe benefits, now largely untaxed, to the federal income tax. Health and Human Services Secretary Louis Sullivan announced in 1991 that the Bush administration was considering that beyond a certain "cap" level, employees would have to pay taxes on employer-provided health benefits. If a cap were set at $1,200, for example, then a worker whose employer paid $2,000 in health insurance premiums would be taxed on the additional $800.[48]

A third gleam in the eye of federal fiscal policymakers involved eliminating or reducing middle-class—and especially *upper-middle-class*—eligibility for federal income tax credits and federal program benefits. Millionaires would not care, but $75,000 or $125,000 families were angry at being called "rich." There was also interest in restricting the federal day-care credit, still claimable on April 15 tax returns by prosperous families (despite being capped for them at $480 a year for each child), to stop affluent households from qualifying.

State governments, too, were intensifying the pressure. In 1990, 1991 and 1992, enormous projected budget deficits obliged many states to reverse the tides of the 1980s and start raising top income tax brackets again, almost always hitting the upper-middle class as well as the rich. The changes in 1990 had been minor; those enacted in 1991 were much more significant. In California the top rate was raised from 9.3 percent to 10 percent on incomes over $200,000, and 11 percent on incomes over $400,000, restoring the old top rate that had been in place through 1987. In New York, Governor Mario Cuomo opposed a rate increase but gave in on a computation change that increased the take from New Yorkers with six-figure incomes. Vermont, which had previously claimed 28 percent of federal income taxes owed as its state tax, hiked that assessment to 34 percent of federal taxes over $13,100, raising the effective top rate to 11.56 percent, from 9.52 percent, of taxable income. Minnesota established a new top rate of 8.5 percent, up from 8 percent, for families with taxable incomes exceeding $173,000. In Maine, GOP governor John McKernan proposed raising the top rate from 8.5 percent to 10 percent for couples with incomes of more than $75,000.[49] North Carolina raised its top rate from 7 percent to 8 percent, but only for joint returns with income of at least $100,000. Steven Gold, director of the New York–based Center for the Study of the States, suggested that the pattern was following the projection in *The Politics of Rich and Poor*: "Concern about 'fairness' is in, and tax rates on the wealthy are more likely to rise than fall."[50]

State taxes on services and service professions also gained momentum in 1991 and 1992, despite prior embarrassments in Florida and Massachusetts (two states that found themselves repealing service taxes only months after they had been enacted). What made such levies inevitable, supporters argued, was the economy's slow shift from manufacturing to services, which obliged revenue-raising methodologies to follow suit. And they pointed to New York's quiet success with a piecemeal strategy of minimizing powerful opposition by targeting just a few additional services at a time—in 1990, for example, adding taxes on cleaning and security services to previous existing taxes on auto repairs and appliance installation. In 1992, Connecticut legislators targeted groups ranging from podiatrists to fur breeders, while Ohio raised registration fees on such professionals as licensed nursing home administrators to asbestos hazard evaluation specialists.[51] "They [the states] are going to go after groups one by one instead," predicted Fred Ferguson, director of state tax policy at Price Waterhouse. "They'll start with landscape gardeners, architects, people who don't have much political pull. Then they'll gradually expand it to everyone else."[52]

Finally, as the 1990s unfolded, state and local politicians showed a growing disposition not just to tax upper-middle-class services and professions, but to target items principally consumed by moderately affluent households. Evanston, Illinois, seat of Northwestern University, seriously considered slapping an 0.5 percent tuition tax on Northwestern's 10,500 students, as well as others at three smaller local colleges.[53] By 1991 almost fifty cities in California had enacted local taxes on cable television, and, on a national basis, travelers began to notice more and more taxes on airline flights, car rentals and hotel rooms. In 1991, airline ticket taxes and user fees rose by $2.5 billion. Some eighty airports hit renters with a 5–10 percent "off-airport car-rental fee." And local taxes on hotel rooms, many well into double digits—21 percent in New York City, 15 percent in Houston, 12 percent in Chicago—expanded by $500 million over three years.[54]

If the 1980s were the decade in which the average $45,000-a-year household was stuck between a rock and a hard place, the 1990s began with a similar prospect—worsened by accelerating white-collar-job cutbacks—for many of the $85,000-, $115,000- and $150,000-a-year Americans whose earnings put them within the top 6, 4 or even 2 percent on the national charts. To think of them as wealthy was an illusion.

Deceptive Discussions of Taxing the Wealthy

One significant contrast between the 1980s and previous conservative-capitalist heydays of U.S. history resulted from inflation's role in nurturing deceptive notions of who was rich, setting the scene for an unappreciated favoritism to those whose level of wealth was beyond the ken of even most college graduates. For the typical American forty-five, fifty or sixty years old who had grown up in the 1940s, 1950s or early 1960s thinking that a millionaire was really rich and that $50,000 a year was a high income, the impressions of childhood lingered. Debate after debate in Congress took place as unrich politicians, who knew *they* could not keep homes in two cities on $125,000 a year, nevertheless orated about burdening the "rich" by phasing out itemized deductions for families in the over-$100,000 bracket or curbing federal Medicare subsidies at the $125,000 level.

That kind of income had fallen short of truly "rich" even in the early years of the century, although ordinary Americans getting by on $2,000 a year could plausibly miss the distinction. Then the enormous inflation since World War II gave a well-off professional of the early 1990s a nominal $150,000-a-year income, which seemed more affluent than it was—in after-tax purchasing power, it was no greater than the earnings of a $10,000-a-year lawyer of 1927 or the $6,000-a-year man of 1900. These bourgeois worthies of the McKinley and Coolidge eras had been prosperous, yes, but nobody would have taken seriously the idea that revenue measures aimed at them were hitting the rich. In 1990 or 1992, however, people *were* fooled that way about $150,000-a-year professionals, and those with truly large incomes took shelter in the confusion.

Actual "riches" in the 1990s began much higher—maybe at $1 million a year and $8 million to $10 million in assets. The number of billionaires had increased tenfold during the 1980s from six to sixty; investment banker Michael Milken took home $550 million in 1987 alone; for baseball shortstops and second-echelon rock stars, $2 million a year was common; and portraits of corporate chief executives paid hundreds of times as much as their average worker typically cited $8 million or $18 million compensation packages. Yet the who-was-really-rich implications of these new numbers lagged so much that ostensibly serious journalists, economists and public servants talked about taxing "wealthy" retirees with $50,000, targeting the itemized deductions and fringe benefits of "rich" $150,000-a-year households and fulfilling "progressivity" with a federal income tax bubble that imposed higher marginal rates on $165,000-a-year orthodontists than on multimillionaires. Misperception was rife, and the upper-middle class was starting to pay the price.

For all these reasons, from new philosophic values to statistical numbness, tax policy in the 1980s rode a wave of deception. The ultimate fiscal truth of the early 1990s was that for America's two or three hundred thousand somewhat rich or genuinely rich families, combined taxes as a share of income were probably at their lowest point in more than sixty years, whereas for middle-class families, combined federal, state and local taxes took a higher portion of income than ever before and were rising steadily.

C H A P T E R 6

Services, Quality of Life and the Middle-Class Squeeze

If you're a typical American, the car you'll drive to work tomorrow and the road you'll take to get there will be older and shoddier than the ones you were using one decade ago or even two. Your children's school will have more pupils per teacher; your paycheck precious few more dollars per hour.

—*The Boston Globe*, 1992

To appreciate the magnitude of the economy's deterioration in the last two decades, imagine what the living standards of the typical middle-class family would be like if it had as many wage earners (just one)—and as many children—as its parents had and also was responsible for subsidizing its parents' retirement, including medical bills.

—David Vogel, editor, *California Management Review*, 1987

Government and the market, joined with Points of Light, will overwhelm our social problems.

—President George Bush, June 12, 1991

Middle classes do not rise or fall on tax burdens alone. For many U.S. families in the 1980s and early 1990s, a broader range of economic circumstances was also worsening. Public services were declining in quality and availability across much of the nation, especially in the big cities. Private services vital to the middle class like health care, higher education and insurance were becoming less affordable. Employee benefits and retirement options were beginning to erode. So was family leisure time. And middle-class net worth was starting to slip—especially for younger Americans unlikely to achieve the wealth of the previous generation.

These fears, along with the unprecedented tax bite, were what made the middle-class squeeze of the 1980s and 1990s unique. The foreclosure notices tacked by sheriff's deputies to the doors of late-nineteenth-century Nebraska and Texas farmhouses had been harsher, but the broad middle class was not eroding back then—it was growing. Nor is there much parallel to the consumer complaints of the 1920s. Local gentry, with their diminishing fortunes scaled to the prior century's economy, might complain that $3,000 or $4,000 a year no longer provided much if any social status, while the new middle class— George Babbitt and his confreres—might grouse that they didn't have enough money for all the new household gadgetry available. Yet the cost of basic, vital middle-class services like education and health care was not climbing out of sight. Public services were improving rather than failing. Suburbia was not apprehensive even amid prosperity, as in 1987–88. There was nothing remotely equivalent to a $4 trillion national debt. Foreign visitors to Henry Cabot Lodge's Boston or Babe Ruth's New York City did not pen sorrowful commentaries on incipient "Brazilianization."

In short, previous cyclical troughs for the U.S. middle class had been mere hiccups in the historical expansion that reached a late-twentieth-century zenith at some point in the 1960s or 1970s when 50 to 55 percent of Americans belonged to an economic middle class without any foreign or historical equivalent and another 10 to 15 percent loosely felt that they did. The potentially critical change by the 1980s and 1990s was that the middle class was no longer expanding but declining—even in intervals of economic recovery like the mid-eighties—under the ongoing pressures of global economic realignment, polarization and income stratification.

Defenders of the Reagan and Bush years had a partially plausible rebuttal: that an important part of the middle-class shrinkage reflected that millions of people were climbing toward *higher* economic status, witness the expansion of Americans with constant-dollar incomes over $50,000 a year from 24.8 percent in 1980 to 30.5 percent in 1990. This *was* happening. But as we shall see, the middle-class pressures described in this chapter justify skepticism, suggesting that many such income gains took on a phantom quality after further adjustment for taxes and fees, declining public services, increasingly unaffordable private services, shrinking employee benefits and retirement prospects, lost leisure time and quality of life, and even declining net worth. If much of the gain for those climbing over $50,000 (or in some areas, over $100,000) was an illusion, how much more important were the difficulties of the millions simultaneously falling from the vulnerable portions of the middle class—the downwardly mobile victims of the collapsing blue-collar wage structure of Fort Wayne, Indiana, or the nervous members of the Roswell, Georgia, country club that began offering unemployed executives seminars on joblessness.

Declining Public Services

As the 1980s boom ended, the public sector, far from being a counter-cyclical safety cushion as in the New Deal years, was more like a domino. Many federal outlays were contracting, but the most visible cutbacks would be at the local level. "All the way across the country, the fabric of local government is being shredded," the president of the National Association of Counties said as the recession unfolded in early 1991. The message from the federal government in the 1980s had been "You locals, you need to have the federal government off your back. But what it really meant was 'fend for yourself.' "¹

If a potential state and local financial crisis had been gathering on the horizon, the early 1990s downturn brought it to a head. Henry Aaron, director of economic studies at Washington's Brookings Institution, said gloomily, "I think you would have to go back to the Great Depression to find similar anguish, in terms of the number of states that are facing an unprecedented cutback in services or significant increases in taxes," and from New England to California the cold surgery of budget-cutting knives bore him out.² Mayors, managers and town supervisors up and down New York State found themselves stunned by Governor Mario Cuomo's 1991–92 proposed budget reductions of 50 percent in the unrestricted aid used by their localities to police streets, remove snow and keep parks and libraries operating, of 60 percent or more in state money for road and highway maintenance, and of an average of 10 percent in state aid to local school districts.³ Final cuts were lower, but in Suffolk County, where suburbs thrown up nearly overnight in Long Island potato fields had been a symbol of the post–World War II housing boom, the county government began furloughing most of its twelve thousand employees every Friday, reducing public services.* Next door, Nassau County's vaunted Republican machine had ruled for three quarters of a century and employed the highest ratio of park workers of any major U.S. suburban jurisdiction, with amenities ranging from public beaches, pools and golf courses to free concerts at the Eisenhower Park bandshell. Budget pressures brought these good times to an end in 1992.⁴

In California, where two dozen school districts were flirting with bankruptcy, one district superintendent said he had cut as much as he could: "There's not much more I can do here without closing the doors, handing over the keys to the state, and saying 'You guys run

*In September 1992, local authorities announced that for the first time in memory, the assessed value of property on Long Island was going down—meaning that tax revenues would erode without rate increases, adding to the pressure to reduce public services.

it.' "⁵ By 1992 Los Angeles could not afford to fill vacancies opening up in the police department, and across Massachusetts, small towns were fighting big-city problems with shrinking police forces. Especially on both coasts, state and local government was starting to deliver less.

In spring 1992, as the National Association of State Budget officers released its annual *Fiscal Survey of the States,* executive director Brian Roherty predicted that as those states badly hit by the recession emerged from its shadow after several more years, there would be less assistance to the middle class and poor alike: "What we will see are downsized state governments with smaller work forces, new ways of doing business and new priorities. There isn't enough money any more, so states will have to find long-term solutions and make some grim choices."⁶ Raymond C. Scheppach, executive director of the National Governors' Association, predicted a permanent reduction in state government that would force attention to restructuring major state services such as education, welfare and health."⁷

This gathering constriction of public services, more severe than recession statistics alone would have suggested, was also worsened by several 1980s public-policy legacies. Many state and local governments had expanded their payrolls and ambitions with thinly disguised recklessness, while Washington had reduced and transformed the nature of its own important financial help. Federal matching grants to the states did roughly double for a group of burdensome entitlement programs over which the states had no control and where enlarged assistance was an ill omen—Medicaid, for one, and also Aid to Families with Dependent Children. On the helpful side of the ledger, however, the flexible federal grants hitherto popular for giving states money to meet local needs—revenue-sharing was the prime example—fell by more than half.⁸ In the late 1970s, Washington had provided 25 percent of state and local budgets; by 1990, as we have seen, that had dipped to 17 percent.

The federal government's own resources were strained, to be sure, both by the money lost in income tax reduction and even more by the galloping 1980s expansion of Social Security, Medicare, defense outlays and interest payments on the national debt. So it was the category of Washington assistance called "discretionary" that had to shrivel. So-called domestic discretionary outlays fell from 22.6 percent of federal outlays to 14.7 percent in 1987 and stabilized at less than 15 percent through 1991. Revenue-sharing and other state and local aid programs were prominent among the losers. As federal support was withdrawn from states and localities, one trigger of the early 1990s public-services crisis was already being cocked.

Too many states had overexpanded during the 1980s, naively assuming that revenues would keep rising. Not only did state and local government employment expand by 15 percent during the decade, but wages outpaced inflation by increasing 82 percent during the ten years ending in June 1991.[9] That was faster than the wage growth of private-sector workers. So as prosperity wound down in New England in 1989 and then across much of the rest of the country in 1990–91, what should have been a merely painful readjustment verged on fiscal calamity, raising a choice between large-scale cuts in services, payroll reductions and increases in state and local taxes—or, as it turned out, all three.

Not that public services slumped overnight. Diminishing commitment in Washington harked back a decade to the Reagan administration's new emphasis on privatization and the marketplace. But the early 1990s downturn brought the budget issue front and center—and on a painfully broad front.

The "three R's" were especially quick to suffer. Public libraries, which got 81 percent of their financing from local government, began cutting back hours and even closing across much of the country, in some hard-pressed communities because lending books could not compete with maintaining police and fire protection. In rural West Virginia, in small towns like Poca, Eleanor and Buffalo, 1991 revenue pressures shut one-room libraries that served as community centers and classroom auxiliaries. One third of the libraries in Massachusetts reported reduced hours, and in New Bedford, all but one of the branch libraries closed in July to save money for the rest of the fiscal year.[10] Demonstrators in Brooklyn, New York, draped library doors with black cloth to protest layoffs and service cuts.

When librarians and their supporters from around the United States converged on Washington in July 1991 to demonstrate for more financial help, officials of the American Library Association drew a surprising contrast: The plight of public libraries, they said, was worse than during the Great Depression. Back then, government authorities had placed great emphasis on keeping the libraries open. In the early 1990s, priorities were different. The Bush administration's fiscal 1992 budget recommended a 73 percent *decline* in the annual federal allotment for public libraries—to just $35 million.[11]

Public education, a traditional middle-class preoccupation, was in fiscal trouble from primary and secondary levels right up to community colleges and state universities. Even in prosperous 1987, spending by all levels of government on public and private education had totaled just 5.1 percent of the U.S. Gross National Product, putting the United

States a weak tenth among fifteen advanced nations, far behind leaders like Denmark (7.6 percent), Sweden (7.2 percent), Canada (7.1 percent) and the Netherlands (6.8 percent), albeit on a rough par with Japan and Britain (5.0 percent).[12] Then the pressures of the new decade forced states and localities to apply their budget scalpels, and spring 1991 saw cash-strapped school districts, especially in Massachusetts, New York, Florida and California, send dismissal notices to tens of thousands of teachers, a grim ritual signaling the worst school layoffs in a decade. No national records were kept, but thousands of teachers were eventually discharged that year, notwithstanding burgeoning school attendance in states like Florida and California, where teacher-pupil ratios worsened.[13] Nineteen ninety-two brought more of the same. For many states, ongoing weak revenues meant an ongoing crisis in financing local public education.

In many hard-pressed school districts, where two or three years of cumulating cuts had undercut teacher-pupil ratios and curriculum enrichment, more and more middle-class parents scrimped to afford private schools. At the end of 1991 the National Association of Independent Schools announced that at elementary- and secondary-school levels, private school applications were up as much as 33 percent from 1990, despite tuitions averaging $6,400 a year, because parents wanted to avoid the overcrowded classes, violence and drugs that plagued so many public schools. Thirty-six percent of these parents sent children to private schools on incomes of less than $50,000 a year.[14] But in a growing percentage of districts, government-provided primary and secondary education was becoming a bare-bones service, unacceptable to those who could somehow afford something better.

The squeeze on the middle class took slightly different form at the higher-education level, where state colleges and universities were chalking up some of the nation's steepest price hikes—tuition increases that the American Council on Education calculated at an average 10 to 12 percent in 1991.[15] Despite the rise, a simultaneous decline in education budgets in many states still required staff to be slashed, class sizes to be increased and courses to be consolidated. In California's state university system, about one thousand full-time instructors were laid off and another two thousand part-time lecturers were not replaced before classes opened for the 1991–92 school year.[16] In many places, particularly California and the Northeastern states, the 1992–93 school year brought further glum tuition and layoff notices, but in several others, tuition increases eased because of declining inflation and voter anger. The chairman of the California Assembly's higher education policy committee estimated that with student fees having increased 65 percent in the past two years in the University of California system, 60 percent in the California State University system and 100 percent at community colleges, 200,000 students could be pushed out of higher education. Peter Magrath, president of the National Association of State Universities and Land Grant Colleges, summed up what was happening: "All public four-year universities, with some limited exceptions, like Utah and Alaska, are under the worst fiscal stress since the Great Depression."[16A]

The burden of rising tuition, observers agreed, would fall on middle-class parents, including many whose deteriorating financial condition made it impossible to keep children in expensive private colleges and universities. Applications at many of the better public institutions were up by 15 percent, because although the cost of tuition, room and board at the average four-year institution rose to $4,970 for in-state students in 1990, it remained well below the $13,544 price tag at the average private institution.[17] Nevertheless, between 1980 and 1987, the average tuition at public four-year universities increased from 3.8 percent to 4.8 percent of median family income.[18] By the early 1990s it was over 5 percent.

Until they bowed to political pressure in 1992, Bush administration officials were surprisingly unsympathetic. In pursuit of its blueprint for curbing federal aid to middle-class and working-class families, the White House announced in May 1991 that it would ask Congress to slash federal tuition grants to college students whose families had incomes above the poverty level, disqualifying some four hundred thousand.* Across the country, at little-known schools serving humdrum communities, local officials told the press that the plan could devastate student aid and further tighten the squeeze on middle-income and working-class students, obliging more of them to take out loans, use up a bigger chunk of family savings, find jobs, go to college only part time or simply drop out.[19] Other governmental and private student aid was already shrinking.

In some places, student reaction to the state-level cutbacks in public education had turned violent. State university students in New York joined in a demonstration in which thousands of irate protesters smashed the glass doors outside the governor's office. In September 1991 thousands of incensed Texas high schoolers laid siege to school

*In 1992, as the elections got under way, the Bush administration partly reversed itself and helped arrange a new loan program.

administration headquarters in Dallas, throwing bottles and rocks and facing police in riot gear to protest the layoffs of some three hundred teachers and cutbacks that put as many as seventy-two students in classrooms designed for thirty-five.[20]

Class differences colored Washington perceptions. In response to the Bush administration's proposal to cut college loans for the middle class, Democratic U.S. senator Bill Bradley called for *expanding* loan assistance to the middle class and funding it with a 10 percent income tax surcharge on million-dollar-a-year incomes.[21] Meanwhile, neoconservative James Q. Wilson, with a blithe indifference to middle-class economic frustration, proposed a program of federal assistance to "enable families in underclass neighborhoods to enroll their children, at an early age, in boarding schools" for uplift.[22] It was the sort of cavalier sociology that conservatives a generation earlier had attributed to liberals.

Public hospitals across the country, admittedly more important to lower-income groups than to the middle class, were also failing or running unsustainable operating deficits. In their 1991 annual report, New York City's Hospital Visiting Committee described municipal hospital care as the worst "in recent memory."[23] The same was true from Boston to Los Angeles. In Illinois, the *Chicago Tribune* worried over the incipient breakdown of the state's mental health system.[24] The unfortunate overlap of declining services with rising charges and costs also came to the fore in another important sector: transportation in general and urban/suburban mass transit in particular. In the early 1980s, an ideological lack of interest in public mass transit, whetted by a desire to shift transportation ownership and finance into private hands, had been almost as pervasive in Ronald Reagan's Washington as in Margaret Thatcher's Britain.

For politicians, the repair and finance of the U.S. transportation infrastructure posed an extraordinary post-1981 challenge. The nation's aging roads and bridges, railroad systems, mass transit facilities, airports, waterways and water treatment systems were deteriorating—in some places, massively. Back in 1952, even before the launching of the interstate highway system, 6.9 percent of the nonmilitary portion of the federal budget went to "infrastructure"; by 1990 that had fallen to 1.2 percent.[25] The result was poor maintenance and cumulative structural neglect. State and local governments, of course, had to concentrate a much higher ratio of their revenues on these priorities, yet even so, whereas back in 1960 public works had accounted for 19 percent of combined government spending at all levels, by 1984 it represented only 7 percent.[26] Too many needs were competing for too few dollars. Motorists and travelers found potholed highways, trembling bridges, crime-ridden subway stations and overcrowded airports, especially in the Northeast, which had the highest ratio of worn-out and unsafe facilities. More than just annoyance was involved; Pat Choate, author of *America in Ruins,* estimated that nationally, wear and tear from poor road surfaces increased the costs of car ownership, on average, by about 30 percent.[27]

Inadequate "infrastructure"—could technocrats ever have chosen a less appealing label?—gained recognition as a full-fledged crisis in the 1980s, but the financial alarms sounded by the nation's inventory of crumbling concrete and sagging steel came at an almost impossible time for federal policymakers committed to a new philosophy of reducing taxes, cutting domestic spending and privatizing government functions. Rebuilding was incompatible with economizing and privatizing. Within a few years, a Republican-run Transportation Department estimated that it would cost about $50 billion to replace or repair the nation's 240,000 deficient bridges and another $315 billion to maintain highways through the year 2000 in the condition they were in in 1983.[28] And that was just a down payment, because by the end of the eighties, officials were estimating the nation's overall infrastructural needs at as much as $3 trillion.

Deficit-conscious Washington could not even contemplate this kind of investment. The Reagan administration's contrary leanings, unfolded during the 1980s, were to deregulate the bus industry, sell off the government-run railroad systems (Amtrak and Conrail), propose elimination of federal mass transit subsidies and decline to release the $17 billion sitting in the federal highway and airport trust funds (because spending the money on hand would have made the federal budget deficit look worse). Privatization, deregulation and localization would be the Republican answer to any crisis. As federal support ebbed, TRIP (The Railroad Information Program), a Washington transportation research group, calculated that as federal support ebbed, the share of highway-improvement costs borne by state and local governments had risen to 77.6 percent of the total in 1988, up from 74 percent in 1980.[29] So after the Bush administration's announcement in 1990 of a national transportation policy, which proposed a further proportional rise in the burden borne by the states, TRIP prepared and released its data to document that such a shift had *already* taken place.

Shrinking transportation services were becoming commonplace in different parts of America. As the forces of the market took over from politics and government regulation, many small cities lost airline service, railroad service, bus service—or some combination. Riders of urban mass transit systems also suffered as the federal share of operating expenses slid from 28 percent in 1981 to 17 percent in 1991.[30] Shrinking federal support and the recession's impact on state and local revenues brought cutbacks in local public transit services and fare hikes. "What we've been seeing is a spate of fare increases over the past six months or so," a spokesman for the American Public Transit Association said in 1991. "Many systems have found themselves with no choice."[31]

Meanwhile, for the average breadwinner in the suburbs, with their new majority of the nation's population, the mounting inadequacy of the U.S. transportation system was felt most in traffic gridlock, the ten-mile-long snails of steel, glass and rubber that crawled through most major U.S. metropolitan areas twice a day. In California, which had the most cars and the worst gridlock, the state Chamber of Commerce indicated that delays in 1988 cost each motorist $135 in lost time and $97 in fuel and maintenance, and later official estimates were far higher.[32] The Texas Transportation Institute had calculated in 1986 that the state's per capita traffic congestion cost was $400, while the Federal Highway Administration estimated the national cost of traffic congestion that same year at $9 billion and about 750 million worker hours.[33]

Congestion had worsened by 1991, when California officials estimated the cost to each state motorist at $1,200 a year, including 1.2 billion hours per year sitting in traffic, or 10.5 workdays per driver.[34] Sky-high housing costs in Los Angeles and San Francisco had been forcing more and more median-income families out to affordable but distant new suburbs—places like Moreno Valley, Simi Valley and Santa Clarita, with three- or three-and-a-half-hour round-trips to the office. Commuters from these hinterlands spent 15 to 20 percent of their waking hours in cars. Statewide, the average driver might face only 6 to 7 hours a month of congestion and gridlock; commuters on the San Bernardino and Riverside expressways, however, could match that in a bad week. Time spent in traffic was a rapidly emerging nonmonetary tax on leisure time and quality of life.

Around Los Angeles, moreover, gridlock was moving off the freeways and spreading into backup roads and residential neighborhoods. The average ten-mile commute in 1990 took thirty to forty minutes, ten to fifteen minutes longer than it had two years earlier.[35] Commuters eagerly awaited new handbooks detailing shortcuts from community to community that avoided main routes. "I can regularly count 100 cars lined up down a shortcut that two years ago was completely vacant," said Neele Mayer, a Sherman Oaks resident who used six different routes to get to work. "It's a real nightmare."[36]

Tightened budget pressures, however, were only one reason that government was delivering poorer services by the early 1990s. The inefficient public sector, as conservatives complained, was characterized by entrenched bureaucracies, obsolescent programs and greedy public-employee unions. The proof could be stark. In 1986, to deal with the working-class municipality of Ecorse, Michigan, which was some $6 million in debt and in violation of a court order to balance its budget, a tough-minded local judge decided to put the city into receivership under a municipal-bond expert whose solution was to "privatize just about everything, holding the line on taxes, slashing the municipal work force almost by half and signing up private firms to provide most services."[37] This ice-bath worked where politics as usual would have failed; Ecorse learned how to operate within a reasonable budget. The crunch on state and local finances in the early 1990s, the worst since the 1930s, had some of the same effect nationally. Bankruptcies, receiverships and privatization became chilling but often effective solutions for bloated municipal pay scales and labor contracts, all frequent by-products of Democratic politics or union alliances.

Consolidating or sharing services also made sense. Nyack, New York, dissolved its police force in 1991, paying to be patrolled by officers from nearby Orangetown and Clarktown. In northern New Jersey, two neighboring school boards agreed to negotiate a joint arrangement with a private food company, saving $40,000 annually. Civic leaders of Westchester County, New York, began debating a report called *Government at the Crossroads,* which, besides proposing a central school board to oversee the existing fifty-six districts, went so far as to suggest that some of the country's smaller towns and villages be combined.[38] New York State listed some ten thousand governmental entities, from counties down to sewer districts, and as revenue pressures tightened, voters began to wonder: Just how many of their tax dollars went to support four or five partially duplicative layers of local authority? Declining assistance from larger jurisdictions was only part of the cash squeeze on state and local services; an important part also came from excess bureaucracy and top-heavy payrolls relative to the changing 1990s revenue base.*

But conservative enthusiasm for reducing federal support for many

---

*Pressures to reduce the size and staffing of state and local government had a mixed impact on the middle-class squeeze. On the one hand, they did limit tax increases, but on the other hand, widespread public-employee discharges also undercut the middle class.

public services, in the name of localism and privatization, often had less admirable motives than increasing competition and improving efficiency. As we have seen, fiscal burdens were also redistributed by localizing government services and shifting their funding from Washington back to cash-strapped grass roots. As federal aid to states and localities and federal income tax rates both shrank in the 1980s, the increasing demands on local revenue to support local services required not just higher taxes but also higher tolls on New York bridges and steeper state university and community college tuition in California. Services once virtually free for average-income families were now increasingly expensive. Users, not taxpayers, should bear more charges, conservative philosophers argued. "From each according to his degree of use" was to replace the mid-century credo of "From each according to his ability to pay." Then there were the situations, like central Philadelphia's special police protection, where a service formerly free to the general public became available only to a limited group for an extra fee. So, too, with high-priced private tollroads that let affluent commuters buy their way out of the traffic jams of a public transportation infrastructure inadequately maintained out of general revenues.

Similarly, where public schools became underfunded, prosperous middle-class families didn't always shift their children to private schools; some raised private money to turn their local schools into public-private hybrids. In Los Angeles, where most public schools were choking in a budget noose, relatively affluent parents, principally Westside residents, developed a subsidy system of carnivals, bake sales, raffles and booster clubs to raise the tens (or hundreds) of thousands of dollars for what local school authorities had once routinely provided—music teachers, art instructors and supplies, librarians and physical education instructors. "As bad as it is, and it is bad, it is going to get worse," Los Angeles School Board president Jackie Goldberg said in 1991. "I don't want to see people trying to make up the losses of hundreds of millions of dollars with fundraisers . . . but I do think this is going to be the wave of the future."[39]

Crime prevention and personal security, meanwhile, offered the most striking metropolitan-area example of the same phenomenon. It was only during the nineteenth century that large-scale publicly supported police forces took over urban security functions, but by the 1980s and 1990s there were signs that this public role was declining. Safety, too, was being privatized. After the city of Philadelphia and downtown businessmen negotiated their 1990 arrangement whereby special taxes would buy special police services, a survey by The Phila-

delphia Inquirer came to a sweeping national conclusion: "Americans who can afford it have stopped relying on the government to protect them from crime. They are hiring their own police."[40]

There were about 1.5 million private security personnel by 1990, in fact—from security guards to armored-car drivers and private investigators. As late as 1975, combined federal, state and local government spending on police protection, approximately $30 billion, had been roughly twice the money spent on *private* security. By 1980, however, private security outlays had gone ahead, and by the early 1990s, they had roughly doubled the expenditures for public police protection, while private security payrolls were twice as large. James K. Stewart, former head of the National Institute of Justice, the federal Justice Department's think tank, summed up the metamorphosis: "Something has really changed in this country. I'd say we are moving from a system of justice to a system where people are purchasing security, which is different from justice, because justice is a value that benefits all of society. Private security partitions off security to just a few."[41] Lawrence W. Sherman, president of Washington's Crime Control Institute, agreed that special taxes like Philadelphia's (and other special-purpose levies in New York, Michigan and Kansas City) could warp the system: "The logical place for this to wind up is that every crime will have its own tax, except for the unpopular offenses that involve the poor or are not important to middle-class voters."[42]

Families with merely average income, though, rarely profited from such arrangements. This embattled tier of the middle class could not afford the expensive apartment buildings, exclusive neighborhoods or walled-in clusters of golf villas with state-of-the-art private security and guards. For those with ordinary earnings in major metropolitan areas, danger was just a street or a staircase away. Buy-it-yourself police protection was beginning to make personal security in parts of the United States into an Anglicized, high-tech version of Italy or Brazil: generally reliable, even cushioned, for the top 1 to 5 percent of the population, increasingly thin not just for the poor but for significant layers of the middle class.

With even less debate than in the reorientation of tax policy, many public services in the United States were slowly undergoing a gradual transformation in their availability and financing, reflecting a polarizing, stratifying nation in which people in the middle were slowly losing not just services but the solicitude of government that their forebears of 1948 and 1962 had taken for granted. For more and more Americans, lost or reduced public services in schools, universities, parks, libraries, transportation and family safety meant increased household outlays, which subtracted from what officialdom called real disposable income and represented a de facto tax levied by the inadequacy of government in the early 1990s relative to the regimes of twenty to thirty years earlier.

The In-Between Sector—Charitable Services

Charity—which provides services coming between the public and private sectors—also became a burden that fell disproportionately on the average American during the 1980s. If liberals have been overenthusiastic about the services of the welfare state, U.S. conservatives have been naive about how charitable or nonprofit organizations can partially replace the role of the state. Back in the 1920s, Herbert Hoover's emphasis on the role of voluntary organizations—charitable and business—in lieu of government regulation foreshadowed what would emerge again in the 1980s.*

Ronald Reagan had crystallized the new mood in October 1981 with a speech to the National Alliance of Business proclaiming volunteerism "an essential part of our plan to give government back to the people" and calling for $100 billion a year in individual, foundation and corporate contributions. The hopeful theory was that charity would take over welfare functions from government, while Reaganomics would give middle-class and rich potential donors more surplus income to contribute to organizations assisting the truly needy, who alone would require and receive help.[43]

This view of government, carried into the 1990s in more moderate form through George Bush's Thousand Points of Light program, included the belief that services should not be provided to the middle class, which was prosperous enough to take care of itself. There was a catch, however—in fact, several catches: first, this philosophy fur-

*In 1931, as the Great Depression deepened, Hoover renewed his emphasis on voluntarism by recruiting Walter S. Gifford, president of the American Telephone and Telegraph Company, to head the President's Organization on Unemployment Relief. Hoover theorized that traditional American altruism would feed the hungry in place of a government role that was to be avoided. Gifford promised that " 'America will feel the thrill of a great spiritual experience,' but he and his colleagues could only raise $100 million of a hoped-for $175 million budget, and in any event, the task was far too great" (Milton Goldin, "Sweet Charity," *History Today,* September 1991, p. 10). Fund-raising consultant Goldin pointed out that "given these developments, philanthropy's critics during the 1930s and 1940s considered private-sector giving not only a bankrupt tradition but a contemptible device used by the rich to escape taxes."

thered conservative plans to reduce or end middle-class eligibility for federal aid programs; second, the middle class did *not,* as we have seen, make notable economic progress; and third, funding assistance to low-income Americans through charity and volunteerism turned out to be yet another surprising chapter in the burdening of the middle class and the working poor.

Throughout history, Americans have always dug deeper into their pockets to help redress hard times, and they did so in 1981–82, then again in the mid-1980s when the regional recession rolled across the commodity states, and then once again in the downturn of the early 1990s. Ironically, however, the people who dug deeper were mostly poor and average-income individuals and families—people who could see the hardship around them. A survey by the Gallup Organization and Independent Sector found that in 1990 contributors with incomes under $10,000 gave away 5.5 percent to charity, more than any other group.[44] And Internal Revenue Service data indicated that among taxpayers itemizing deductions, those who had adjusted gross incomes of $25,000 to $30,000—median-income families, in short—raised their average donations by 62 percent between 1980 and 1988 ((from $665 to $1,075) despite tax changes that made giving more costly.[45]

Conversely, as the top bracket shrank from 70 percent in 1980 to just 28 percent in 1988, taxpayers with incomes over $1 million slashed their charitable donations from $207,089 to $72,784, while taxpayers in the $500,000–$1 million group cut their average charitable outlays from $47,432 to $16,602.[46] "We're seeing a new spirit of giving and caring across the nation," Brian O'Connell, the president of Independent Sector, said in 1991, "but the sad thing is that most of the truly wealthy are proving to be downright stingy."[47] In short, the extent to which charitable services filled growing gaps left by declining government services became a charge to ordinary Americans, not to those at the top whose incomes were soaring.

By the end of the 1980s, just as the weight of the tax system had been shifted to fall on Middle America, so had the weight of giving for charitable services.

The High Cost of Private Services

If deflation on the farm and in the oil patch kept the prices of commodities under control after 1981, thereby reducing the overall national inflation rate, that was not true of services, where costs rose in the early 1990s just as they had in the 1980s, even while, in many everyday services, quality continued to deteriorate. In 1987, at the peak of the hurry-up, go-go mood of the Reagan years, *Time* magazine captured a powerful frustration bothering Americans in a cover story on the collapse of personal service in the U.S. marketplace, whether by flight attendants, repairmen, bank clerks, salespeople or hospital assistants.[48] The heyday of personal services, historians said, had probably come in the postwar era, when labor was reasonably paid and prices fairly stable. Businesses could afford to lavish service on customers—for example, music stores provided record players for those who wanted to listen to disks before buying them, and drugstores offered free delivery. That changed in the 1970s and 1980s, when inflation forced businesses to slash services to cut costs and deregulation fostered price wars and further cutbacks in service.[49]

By the end of the 1980s, real service with a genuine smile was mostly a memory. The movie *Back to the Future* entertained audiences with the scene in which the time-traveler played by Michael J. Fox walked past a 1950s-style filling station and was stunned to see four cheery, neat attendants run up to a car that had just pulled in in order to fill its gas tank, check the oil, wipe the chrome and do the windows. In late-1980s Japan, by contrast, service station attendants not only still did that, but they also doffed their hats, shouted their thanks and they stopped traffic so the customer could drive away.[50]

Yet annoying as the change in quality of service was, price changes were even more painful during the 1980s, especially for services important to the middle class. When the Conference Board, a business-sponsored research group, sampled the consumer satisfaction of seven thousand families in early 1990, they identified a number of services that were perceived to give the poorest value: hospital and health costs, auto insurance, bank service charges, college tuition, lawyers' fees, cable television and admission to sports events.[51]

Not only did costs for these services outpace inflation during the 1980s, but they consumed an oversized chunk of the average middle-class family's outlays. The rich and most of the poor were proportionately less affected. Economists disagreed whether these kinds of fast-climbing service costs were fully reflected in the overall national Consumer Price Index. However, had there been a CPI specifically for middle-class consumption patterns, it was indisputable that these categories of increases would have been more heavily weighted.

Regulation—or often its lack—was a recurrent culprit. High bank charges and soaring cable television rates followed 1980s deregulation. Insurance and health care, in turn, were important unfolding regulatory challenges of the 1990s. Indeed, many of the fastest-rising costs for private services owed part of their momentum to nonregulation. Government, it was starting to appear, could be inflationary not simply through excessive bureaucracies, extravagance, overregulation and wage settlements, but also through permissiveness toward professions and industries.

If tuition at public universities and colleges outpaced inflation during the 1980s, as we have seen, the increase at private colleges and universities was even steeper. From 1980 to 1988, incomes in the United States rose only 53 percent, compared with a 68 percent increase in the cost of public colleges and a doubling of costs at private ones.[52] Appendix C shows the change. Ivy League schools were greening themselves the most rapidly. The result, said Williams College economist Morton Schapiro, was a loss of middle-class enrollment. The costlier private colleges and public universities alike lost a disproportion of students from families in the badly squeezed $40,000- to $60,000-a-year range; some transferred to lower-cost private schools; others left for community colleges, where tuition was comparatively cheap.[53] Meanwhile, the proportion of low-income students at the more expensive schools remained stable because of financial aid, and the spaces opened by the middle-class exodus were generally filled by higher-income students whose families could afford the tuition.*

The percentage of freshmen who chose colleges because of low tuition or financial aid or because they could live near home and save money reached an all-time high in 1991, according to the Higher Education Research Institute at the University of California at Los Angeles.[54] At a number of the country's most prestigious private universities, financial pressures were so bad that administrators began to talk about prospective annual deficits akin to those of major suburban counties—$40 million to $50 million at schools like Stanford, Columbia and Yale—unless major cutbacks could be made in faculty and administrative costs.[55] Not only fewer middle-class Americans but also fewer Americans of any kind would be able to attend these schools because more top schools were stepping up pursuit of affluent foreign students. At the University of Pennsylvania, for example, international students made up 11 percent of the entering class in autumn 1991, up from just 2 percent ten years earlier. Only 8 percent of the foreigners at Penn required financial assistance versus 45 percent of the overall student body.[56]

Entertainment was another area where the middle class was paying

*In 1991 the Bush administration negotiated a consent decree under which the seven Ivy League universities agreed not to collude in setting tuition, salaries and financial aid—as they by and large had since 1986.

much more. In July 1991 the federal General Accounting Office released a study showing that in the four years following deregulation of cable television in 1986, the cost of basic service had risen 56 percent—twice the rate of inflation—while the more expensive "second tier" service (channels like CNN, TBS and TNT) rose 61 percent.[57] In Los Angeles the increase was much worse—107 percent in four and a half years.[58] Many companies also began charging for what had previously been free, such as converter boxes. To keep costs under control, squeezed subscribers dumped expensive premium channels and pay-per-view services. Economists unsympathetic to the cable companies charged that subscribers were being forced to underwrite the huge buyout costs that the larger surviving cable firms found themselves left with after absorbing smaller rivals, although industry officials blamed rate increases on skyrocketing program costs, especially in sports and entertainment.

That prices for concerts and sports events were going skyward was also obvious to consumers. In 1991 the *Los Angeles Times* showed how the laissez-faire economics of ticket sales had been running amok in Southern California, supporting so many promoters and middlemen that "tickets to many events can no longer be purchased anywhere at face value."[59] The price of a $17.50 concert ticket, for example, would, in reality, be anywhere from $19.50 to $26.05—$19.50, if bought at the box office, which added a $2.00 "facility fee"; $22.75, if bought through a neighborhood Ticketmaster outlet, which added a $3.25 "convenience" charge to the $2.00 facility fee; and $26.05 when a single ticket was bought by telephone (the $2.00 facility fee, plus a $5.00 phone convenience fee and a $1.55 processing fee). Admittedly, the high basic charges principally reflected the enormous compensation paid to both sports figures and entertainers—$10 million a year to heavyweight boxing champions and $2 million to right fielders, for example, and the forty highest-paid entertainers listed by *Forbes* magazine in 1991 all made at least $18 million over a two-year period.[60] But packagers and promoters further swelled the ticket price to consumers.

Complaints about Ticketmaster's various charges had already convinced New York's State Consumer Protection Board that it should ask the legislature for a 10 percent cap on service fees: "I have serious concerns about the excessively high level of service fees that ticket agencies like Ticketmaster sometimes charge," said executive director Richard Kessel in 1991. "And now, due to the proposed merger of Ticketmaster and Ticketron, there will be less competition in the field, which in turn could lead to even higher service fees."[61] Some state regulators and legislators asked the Bush administration to disapprove the merger, but it declined.

Legal fees also surged during the 1980s, at a cost to consumers but also to the broader economy. In the process, the average earnings of a law-firm partner ballooned from $74,000 a year in 1979 to just under $150,000 a year in 1990. By 1989–90 some state and federal judges, themselves among the lower-paid U.S. lawyers, became so outraged at swollen legal fees that they started to disallow the charges that came before them. In scaling back one bloated billing, Chief Judge Donald D. Alsop of the U.S. District Court in Minnesota observed that "it is no wonder that the average business person or citizen can no longer afford to resort to the courts and engage in litigation to resolve private disputes."[62] The press even found itself starting to pay attention to HALT—Help Abolish Legal Tyranny, a consumer rights watchdog founded in 1978 by two Rhodes scholars—despite the naive, even utopian cast to HALT's proposed remedies: that lawyers, like auto mechanics and other service providers, would have to give prospective clients written estimates, would have to give clients refunds for over-charging or incompetence, and would have to let non-lawyers share in handling out-of-court legal matters.[63]

Beyond its up-front charges to consumers, however, the American legal system—lawyers in general and trial lawyers in particular, as well as many plaintiffs, some judges and many jurors—was imposing an even greater burden on the American economy through what foes cataloged as unprecedented litigiousness, overexpansion of rights and liabilities, extremism in jury awards and clogged courts.* Critics also deplored the negative impact of excess legalism on the international competitiveness of U.S. business, on new-product development, and (as this chapter will pursue) on the rocketing costs of health care and insurance, especially automobile insurance.

As for banks, many trembling on the precipice of insolvency in the early 1990s, the surge in their charges, like the rise in cable television fees, was partly a consequence of deregulation. The permissiveness of the early 1980s had helped lure commercial banks and savings and loan institutions into unsound speculative practices that eventually left sur-

---

*In 1991, Vice President Dan Quayle, in his role as chairman of the President's Council on Competitiveness, pointedly asked the annual convention of the American Bar Association, "Does America really need 70% of the world's lawyers? Is it healthy for our economy to have 18 million new lawsuits coursing through the system annually? Is it right that people with disputes come up against staggering expense and delay?" (*Time,* "Do We Have Too Many Lawyers?" August 26, 1991, p. 54).

vivors grasping for every possible way to increase income. To many large banks small customers were an inconvenience, given the broader vistas of deregulation, so in 1990 and thereafter, once defaulting real estate loans and rising federal deposit insurance premiums started biting, institutions began to announce a wide range of additional requirements, minimum balances, charges and service fees. By spring 1991 a few bold institutions were informing depositors that a special fee was being levied to cover the rising federal deposit insurance costs on commercial checking accounts. Most banks, however, recognized the explosiveness of levying a specific charge whereby *consumers* would be billed for the higher insurance fees the Federal Deposit Insurance Corporation started charging following the speculative failures, so instead they wound up taking the money indirectly: by raising service charges, levying new fees and posting high personal loan and credit-card rates while giving unprecedentedly lower interest rates on customers' deposits.[64]

Thus, while Federal Reserve Board chairman Alan Greenspan was lowering interest rates in late 1990 and throughout 1991, *banks,* not *consumers,* were the principal beneficiaries. Although the rates banks *paid* on savings accounts, money market accounts and certificates of deposit might be plummeting into the 4.5 to 6 percent range, the interest they *charged* on unsecured personal loans and on bank credit cards was simultaneously rising to 17.4 percent and 18.9 percent.[65] Appendix C shows how this extraordinary disparity developed and widened in the 1980s. As charted by Bank Rate Monitor, the "spread" between the (low) average yield on one-year bank CDs and the (high) charge on bank credit cards widened from 8.5 percentage points in April 1989 to an extraordinary 12 percentage points in April 1991. By early 1992 the gap was a stunning 14 to 15 percentage points. By sanctioning this unprecedented disparity, federal authorities facilitated a shift of billions of dollars from the pockets of consumers to the profit ledgers of banks and other financial institutions (and to their shareholders). There *was* a larger public-policy rationale: transfusions like these, along with funds strategically deposited by the Federal Reserve, may have kept banks from failing in dangerous numbers. Troubled financial institutions used the time and funds to rebuild and rearrange themselves, and by 1992 many were reporting large profits again. Nevertheless, it was a levy on the citizenry, not least the proverbial middle-class widow in Florida receiving two thirds of her $30,000-a-year income from bank CDs. Lowell Bryan, head of the banking group at McKinsey and Company, the management consultants, acknowledged the economic reality: "Consumers and smaller businesses, which do not have much alternative to banks if they want to borrow, are going to have to pay for banks' bad lending decisions in the past."[66]

Charges by insurance companies were also rising. By 1990–91 bad investments in junk bonds and losses in commercial real estate were a factor, but for automobile insurers—whose rates were particularly controversial—the basic problem of the 1980s had been the soaring costs of litigation, medical care and car repairs, which collectively consumed 86 percent of every premium dollar. As Appendix C shows, the cost of automobile insurance premiums ballooned by nearly 150 percent between 1980 and 1990, far ahead of the inflation rate, yet most companies were making little or no money from auto insurance because claims paid out were rising even faster. There were, of course, horror stories that seemed to document excess: annual auto insurance bills of $3,000 or $4,000 for families in suburban California or Long Island with two cars and two young male drivers under twenty-five. Yet for the most part, while the middle-class squeeze effect of insurance was indisputable, much of its increased cost, in turn, reflected the painful medico-legal vise on the industry.

Which brings us to one of the most critical pressures of the early 1990s: soaring medical-care and health-insurance costs, which in each year after 1980 outpaced the Consumer Price Index. For the entire decade of the 1980s, they were up 118 percent compared with inflation's 71 percent, boosting health care's share of the GNP to 12 percent from 9 percent in 1980 and less than 5 percent in 1947. None of the other major Western economies experienced this kind of medical inflation or explosion, and their health-cost shares of GNP remained much lower—somewhat over 8 percent in Canada and Germany, 6 percent in Britain.

By 1989 and 1990 unhappy Americans were telling pollsters they favored a national health program to bring costs under control. Moreover, because foreign polls also showed citizens of Canada and Germany, in particular, much happier with their systems, these two approaches gained widespread attention as possibilities for the United States to imitate. Americans feared that the U.S. system was failing—not, of course, in its splendid technology but in its expense, its cumbersome uncontrollability, and in how 33 to 39 million Americans, many of them employed and well above poverty levels, had no health insurance in 1991, because their employer didn't offer it or because they couldn't afford it. Millions of others accepted inadequate policies, while others paid almost unbearable costs for comprehensive coverage.

heahh care

Ultimately the election-year politics of 1992 complicated deliberations over what polls suggested two thirds of Americans wanted: a *national* response to the gathering crisis. Because the federal government wasn't moving, the states, too, began to feel pressure from middle-income voters losing access to health care, from small businesses unable to buy insurance for employees, and from hospitals and other health providers stuck with uncompensated care. Yet few states produced broad blueprints; only the federal government could afford to confront such an expensive nationwide challenge.

Republicans hostile to any national program pointed to survey data showing that the groups most concerned about health care were Democratic: blacks, Hispanics, the poor, the uninsured. Yet aspects of health care were also a middle-class headache. Two thirds of the roughly 35 million Americans uninsured in the early 1990s were employed or from a family in which someone worked. But for the four fifths of Americans with insurance, the problem lay in reduced benefits and rising personal outlays. According to one survey, the percentage of health benefit costs picked up by employers declined from 80 percent in 1980 to 69 percent by the end of the decade, thereby increasing the employee share.[67] The result was to inflate costs for the average employee and family. Hay/Higgins and Company, the benefits consultants, estimated that the typical corporate employee with family coverage was paying more than $1,300 a year from his or her pocket for health insurance, up from $150 in 1980.[68]

For nervous Middle Americans, mostly insured but worried about high premiums and uncovered illnesses, the objective was comprehensive coverage at the lower prices available elsewhere, which required reducing some of the U.S. health-care costs already at 12 percent of GNP and projected to reach 15 percent in 2000. Experts looking for a federal-level solution could point out several contributing U.S. costs that were better managed elsewhere. One was high pay for doctors, whose average earnings had climbed by 79 percent from $89,900 in 1981 to $155,800 in 1989, well above either inflation or the income gain of the average family.[69] By contrast, physicians' fees in Canada, capped by the government, brought them incomes about one-third lower than those in the United States—an average of roughly $100,000 in 1990, according to unofficial estimates.[70] As for Germany, since 1986 total spending for office-based physicians had not been permitted to rise faster than the average wage, German doctors also made less than their U.S. counterparts in 1989—$107,200 a year versus $155,800. This was about four times the average German wage, down from a six-to-one ratio in 1986, whereas doctors in the United States made 6.7 times the average U.S. wage in 1988, according to the American Medical Association.[71]

A second inflationary factor was the American legal system's liability explosion, which obliged doctors to pay large sums ($20,000 or $25,000 a year) for malpractice insurance and simultaneously encouraged them to provide expensive or possibly unnecessary treatments, which, after all, could be billed to insurers. North of the border, medical lawsuits were rare because Canadian lawyers had to work for a fee rather than a share in malpractice awards and patients could not sue for punitive damages.[72] Malpractice premiums were very low in Germany by U.S. standards because Germans very rarely sue.[73]

Over the years the Canadian and German national health care approaches, while different, had both evolved much simpler, more efficient administrative systems, which gave little incentive for medical excess, whereas in the United States, payment and responsibility were so diffused—among patient, doctor, hospital, insurer, employer and often several layers of government—that spending decisions were made by people with little reason to economize. And, of course, this fragmentation and massive staffing of U.S. health administration was also expensive in itself, a bureaucrat's dream. The U.S. General Accounting Office estimated in 1991 that a government-sponsored health plan following the Canadian model would save Americans some $67 billion a year, principally by ending insurance overhead and reducing the procedural costs of reimbursing U.S. hospitals and doctors by America's crazy quilt of public agencies and private insurers. In Germany the country's eleven hundred Sick Funds (insurers) were all financed by the same government-run payroll tax and all supplied with the same government-mandated forms, so that only 5 percent of total health-care costs was consumed by administration versus almost 25 percent for the United States.[74]

Factor number five was the vast U.S. lead in—and voracious consumer appetite for—the most advanced medical technology. "We are to medical-care technologies what the French are to wines," observed Robert Blendon, chairman of Harvard's health policy department.[75] Namely, the greatest experts, the biggest exporters and the proudest consumers. This, too, worked to build inflation into the system, although the Germans, almost equally technology-oriented, managed to control that aspect as well. Canada stinted on technology.

The cost of drugs was also much higher in the United States than in almost any other country. Appendix C charts the surprising international comparison. Americans paid an average of 54 percent more than Europeans for twenty-five commonly prescribed drugs, according to one study, and some individual prices were worse: a month's supply of Eldepryl, the Parkinson's disease medication, cost $240 in the United States and just $28 in Italy.[76] One cause of the disparity, economists said, was that European governments typically used their mass purchasing power to bargain drug prices with pharmaceutical firms, letting them recover their manufacturing and distribution costs but very little of their overall research outlay. The U.S. government, however, was allowing foreign and domestic drug companies to set their own prices in the American market, enabling them to recover a disproportionate share of their *worldwide* research at the expense of American consumers.

In late 1991 the U.S. Senate's Special Committee on Aging noted that even while U.S. health-care costs were growing at two to three times the inflation rate, prescription drug costs were rising 10 to 15 percent faster than health-care costs.* So favored, the drug industry was America's most profitable, earning 13.6 percent on industrywide revenues in 1990 while Fortune 500 companies averaged 4.1 percent.[77] The special committee's chairman, Senator David Pryor of Arkansas, unmistakably angered by the findings, raised the prospect most worrisome to the drug industry: substantial new price regulation.

Taken together, these various health-cost inflators were part of a U.S. system better for those adequately insured than any other in the world—and better also for its component doctors, manufacturers and administrators. Yet for many median- or average-income American families, the unavoidable corollary was a growing financial fear of doctors, hospitals, health insurance and prescriptions.

For the 1980s as a whole the cost of these seven private services, about which Americans particularly complained to the Conference Board, more than doubled, while general inflation went up by two thirds, although only a few of the seven had reliable indexes. What's more, it seems beyond debate that the broad Consumer Price Index fell far short of reflecting the cumulative, converging weight of these soaring charges on middle-income families making $40,000 to $75,000 a year, especially in expensive large metropolitan areas. For many, their disposable income after subtracting these costs was shrinking, not growing. Besides, even household incomes that stayed just ahead of

*A follow-up report in 1992 by the Families USA Foundation, endorsed by the U.S. Senate special committee, found that prices of the twenty most popular prescription drugs jumped 80 percent on average between 1985 and 1991, about three times the inflation rate.

inflation could be squeezed well below it by the sudden cost of a teenager's auto insurance, a sick relative's medicine, a moderate legal bill or a child at a university with mushrooming tuition. Back in the 1950s or 1960s, middle-class incomes and purchasing power had not been so much at risk for these same services.

The politics of whom to blame was raised only indirectly, even as the 1992 debate over the middle-class squeeze heated up. Democratic administrations from Johnson to Carter had been more responsible for the underlying inflation that began to roll in the 1960s and 1970s, yet in many ways, the inflation of the 1980s and early 1990s was a new variety. *Commodity* prices were not rising very much; it was *service* costs that were. Back in the 1970s, conservatives had come up with a perceptive analysis that identified the expanding size and regulatory role of government—the so-called inflationary state—as a major cause of rising prices. By the early 1990s questions were starting to take shape about the inflationary role of the "deregulatory state" or the "non-regulatory state."

Deregulation in most industries had some favorable effect on consumer prices, but there was not much doubt about its inflationary impact on bank and cable television charges. With respect to banks, polls taken in 1991 and 1992 showed the public favoring *more* regulation. Likewise for cable television. And in the entertainment area, state consumer officials were beginning to call for regulation of the fees charged by ticket services. As for colleges, collusive Ivy League "price-fixing" helped double tuition during the 1980s until the government secured a consent decree in 1991. Lawyers, too, effectively doubled their rates, although large corporations began to follow angry judges in rejecting attorneys' billings and forcing reductions, and by the decade's end, legislators in Washington and the states were pursuing ways to crack down on trial lawyers, outrageous verdicts and the broad problem of the "litigation explosion." As for the soaring costs of insurance, worsened in some instances by some insurance companies' speculative or business practices, these were at least abetted by regulatory gaps—insurers were regulated only at the state level, and there often weakly. In 1991 the House of Representatives held hearings on establishing some partial federal regulatory role.

Soaring health costs, however, were probably the area of the greatest regulatory vacuum during the 1980s—and the greatest target of regulatory discussion during the 1990s. Doctor's fees, already regulated in almost every other major nation, moved further in that direction in 1991, when federal authorities rewrote what doctors could charge and be reimbursed for under Medicare, increasing allowable fees for family physicians but curbing them for some specialists. In 1992 the American College of Physicians broke with most other doctors' organizations and endorsed a national cap on health-care spending, including limits on doctor and hospital fees. The biggest change, that of assembling some sort of national health program, was merely debated during the presidential election campaign; enactment remained in the future. Yet even private groups like Blue Cross and Blue Shield were talking about the inevitability of an increased federal regulatory role.* Calls for greater regulation of the galloping prices of prescription drugs mounted following the critical 1991 report of the U.S. Senate Special Committee.

Government regulation had begun the 1980s in disrepute for spurring inflation, but by the early nineties the rising service-cost ingredients of the middle-class squeeze were laying the framework for another shift. In a variety of situations, some economic regulation by some level of the government was starting to look like the best way—or even the only way—for Middle America to squeeze back.

Imperiled Benefits, Pensions and Retirement

If wage and salary gains for earners in the $20,000–$40,000 range lagged during the 1970s and early 1980s, as they clearly did, one reason was the simultaneous increase in employee benefits. During the 1980s, in fact, nominal benefits, unadjusted for inflation, grew faster than wages and salaries, as the table below shows:

To an extent, it was deceptive. Much of the surge in benefits represented the exploding payments made by employers for employee health insurance. That was important coverage; without insurance, unexpected health costs could be a disaster for an employee. At the same time, however, the increasing expenses companies had to bear for health insurance payments minimized employee wage gains, on an overall basis keeping them at or below inflation. Then, by the end of the eighties, it was clear that companies, unwilling to let their profits

*In 1992 a survey by *The New York Times* reported that a growing number of states, convinced that the free-market model of unchecked competition was failing to curb the growth of health costs, were adopting new laws and regulations to control the construction of hospitals and nursing homes and the purchase of costly medical equipment. Many also started convening groups of doctors, consumers, hospital executives, insurers and employers to negotiate the allocation of health-care resources ("States Are Moving to Re-regulation on Health Costs," *New York Times*, May 11, 1992).

Table 7. Comparative Increases During the 1980s:
Anemic Paychecks, Healthy Benefits

Year	Benefits	Wages and Salaries
1981	12.1%	8.8%
1982	7.2	6.3
1983	7.4	4.9
1984	6.5	4.2
1985	3.5	4.1
1986	3.4	3.2
1987	3.4	3.3
1988	6.9	4.1
1989	6.1	4.1
1990	6.6	4.0
1991	6.2	3.7

Source: Bureau of Labor Statistics, Employment Cost Index (Scott Burns, *Dallas News,* April 29, 1990), with a BLS update for 1991.

suffer, were reducing employee benefits and shrinking their rosters of full-time employees. The benefits tide of the 1970s had reversed and started to ebb. International Survey Research, a Chicago consulting company, after measurements of employees at twenty-eight companies, found sharply fewer willing to rate their employer's benefits as either good or very good. Overall satisfaction with company tuition-refund plans dropped from 87 percent in 1982–83 to 32 percent in 1989–90. For life insurance the satisfaction decline was from 92 percent to 36 percent, for dental plans from 83 percent to 38 percent, for medical plans from 87 percent to 45 percent, for pension plans from 75 percent to 37 percent, and for disability insurance from 86 percent to 47 percent.[78]

Part of the disquiet, as we have seen, was that employers were asking employees to pay a higher and higher share of their benefits, especially health coverage, which added yet another untabulated offset to nominal income. The second blow to Middle America came as more companies reduced their full-time core work force in order to reduce long-term liability for benefits like health insurance, profit sharing and pensions. "The whole idea of reducing your core work force has developed in parallel with the growth of employee benefit costs," said Frank Cassell, professor of management at Northwestern University. "You sort your labor market into two parts. One gets good benefits and has continuity of employment. The secondary work force . . . get no pensions and no benefits."[79] In California, Robert McDonough, chairman of Remedy Temp, a thriving new personnel agency, posited a new business creed for the 1990s: the company with the fewest permanent workers would win.[80]

As the relatively benefit-less "contingent work force" grew in the 1980s, the number of part-timers grew by 19 percent, from 16.4 million persons to 20 million. In 1990, over 4 million of these indicated that they would rather have full-time jobs; by early 1992, 6 million were saying so. The number of self-employed grew almost as quickly, rising by 18 percent to more than 10 million in 1990, many of them thinly disguised part-timers. Still another telling indicator lay in the 1.4 million persons working for "temp" firms—"personnel supply services," in the stilted language of the Bureau of Labor Statistics. Between 1980 and 1990, their numbers had soared by 151 percent.[81] Each of these categories had significant percentages of unemployment or underemployment, but, for purposes of federal data, none of the individuals counted as unemployed.

Most part-time workers were ineligible for unemployment insurance, poorly paid (with a 1987 median hourly wage of $4.42 versus a full-timer's median of $7.43) and unlikely to get health insurance or pension coverage. According to one calculus, only 22 percent of part-time workers received health insurance and only 26 percent had employer-supplied pension coverage.[82] During the early-1990s recession, the number of part-timers saying they would prefer full-time work rose rapidly. For many, part-time work was becoming subemployment—often at real expense to living standards.

Unemployment benefits themselves shrank as a safety net during the 1980s. Federal legislation encouraged states to tighten eligibility for benefits, which they did. Consequently, as the recession began, the percentage of workers receiving benefits fell dramatically below the levels of previous downturns. According to one study, less than 38 percent of U.S. unemployed workers received benefits in 1990 as compared with 75 percent in the 1974–75 recession.[83]

Other benefits were being reduced, too. As we have seen, in 1991 the Bush administration proposed to cut federal aid benefits to the middle class, not merely by increasing Medicare premium charges to those retirees with six-figure incomes but also by cutting school-lunch subsidies and by eliminating the eligibility of students from median-income families for federal college tuition aid.

Private retirement benefits were also weakening. As the 1990s began, firms across the United States were reducing benefits, terminating pension plans and failing to start new ones either because of financial pressures or because federal rules governing retirement programs were becoming increasingly expensive and complex to interpret. In 1989, according to the Association for Private Pension and Welfare Plans, about 15,856 defined-benefit pension plans were shut down, up 37 percent from 1988, while only 5,461 plans were created, a 67 percent drop. "Retiring with pension is becoming the exception, not the rule," a Kemper Financial Services publication indicated, citing Census Bureau figures that showed a significant decline in the percentage of workers covered by pension plans—from 55.7 percent in 1979 to 49 percent in 1990.[84] In previous decades since World War II, that coverage had been rising, so the decline was striking. Appendix C details these changes, including the sharp 1975–88 ebb in the percentage of U.S. workers with pensions that were federally insured. Keith Kilty, an Ohio State University professor researching retirement planning, went so far as to predict that "by the year 2000, people probably won't be able to retire at all," given the strains on the system. He predicted a steady increase in the age at which people retire, beginning in the early 1990s.[85]

Many employees still sure of a private pension had reason to doubt that health insurance coverage would come with it. Personal finance columnist Jane Bryant Quinn told her readers that "when you retire, your blanket (health) plan may be buried wherever the boss's promises go to die." Although some 25 million workers and spouses forty and up enjoyed lifetime company-paid health insurance, or believed they did, the odds were that many companies would be forced by future cost and profit pressures to alter or drop these promises, which had no legal backstop.[86]

In short, still another part of the American dream was at risk. Back in the 1970s, while median family income stagnated, and in the early 1980s, while hourly wages failed to keep up with inflation, employee benefits were a growth sector, even if runaway health costs gobbled up much of the increase. By the early 1990s, however, employee and retirement benefits, now diminishing, were no longer an exception to the tightening noose; they were shrinking, too.

Changing Households, Rising Life-style Pressures and Declining Leisure

In addition to the other aspects of the middle-class squeeze visible by the early 1990s, many counted the erosion of family life and the increasing costs imposed on the new "average" two-earner household with a working wife as well as husband. Families getting their extra income through a second earner paid for that help with added strains in dollars, emotional stress and lost leisure, little or none of it included as an offset to real income—and women lost the most.

The wage pressure was real enough. Husbands' inflation-adjusted salaries declined in 80 percent of married-couple households between 1979 and 1986, according to one estimate, and only a dramatic (18 percent) increase in the number of hours worked by wives kept a majority of these household incomes from falling behind the cost of living.[87] Many fell behind anyway. Traditional families, with just the husband working, on average lost even more ground.

In reality, though, the traditional U.S. family of the suburban white picket fence and mother-at-home 1950s stereotype wasn't really traditional at all—most eighteenth- and nineteenth-century wives had worked, albeit often at onerous household or farm chores rather than as part of the outside work force, so that America's mid-century families were a brief aberration. "After the war, all of our competitor nations were devastated," explained Martha Farnsworth Riche, an editor at *American Demographics* magazine. "Up until the 1960s, we had an unnatural competitive advantage and were making, in terms of real earnings, much more than we should have been. For the one and only time in our history, an ordinary guy with a high school degree could afford to have a non-working wife."[88] The 1970s, and still more the 1980s, were the painful economic transition that brought the aberration to an end.

The result was a slow reshaping of middle-class culture. More than before, families shattered in divorce, children returned home after graduating from college without jobs or unable to maintain a household of their own; and unrelated individuals grouped to share housing they could not otherwise afford. Divorce often dropped wives out of the middle class, and young people from solid suburban families found it hard to maintain middle-class status once they were on their own. Downward mobility was everywhere. Working divorced women with children could often keep their middle-class status and purchasing power only by moonlighting at a second job. The Bureau of Labor Statistics found in a late 1980s sampling that the number of women with two or more jobs had soared from 2.2 percent of 28.9 million working women in 1970 to 5.9 percent of the 52.8 million at work in May 1989.[89]

Even the two-earner family that held on to its middle-class status paid a stiff price, which is the concern of this subchapter. Princeton

University's Rebecca Blank, who studied two-income couples, noted that for many wives, going to work or returning to it could be a difficult decision "taking into consideration both what she will have to pay for child care and the increased expense the family is likely to incur for such things as more meals eaten out, assistance in the home or yard maintenance."[90] For a wife who might earn $18,000 a year, those costs—plus additional travel expenses, clothes and the like—might reach $6,000 to $8,000, yet government per capita and family income statistics would gather in the full $18,000, grossly overstating economic reality. According to one study cited by the Joint Economic Committee of Congress, the additional expenditures and taxes offset between one third and one half of the additional earnings of a second earner.[91]

Arranging child care was the largest of the nontax costs. It hit the poor hardest, with some families paying 15 to 25 percent of their income for care, but middle-class families paid about 6 percent.[92] Moreover, child-care expenses were rising faster than inflation, reaching an average of $49 per week in mid-1987, up 17 percent in thirty-two months relative to a CPI increase of just 10 percent.[93] By 1990 costs were higher still, especially in cities like Boston, where care averaged $5,664 a year; New York ($4,956); and Washington, D.C. ($4,548). Ogden, Utah, turned in the lowest figure—$1,992 a year.[94] In the major metropolitan areas, the maximum allowable child-care tax credit available to the middle class—$480 per child—constituted negligible relief. Many working women considered such a small credit insulting compared with the businessman's deductible lunches and hotel rooms.

Meanwhile, fewer could afford a home. In late 1989 Ira Gribin, president of the National Association of Realtors, summed up the new residential economics:

> There has been a definite trend over the past eight years. What is beginning to happen is that only the wealthiest families can afford housing. People with low incomes are being forced to move farther and farther from work and are having to drive one to two hours. This has begun to cause problems in families.[95]

In 1989 a Harvard University study suggested that the plummeting ratio of homeownership for households in the twenty-five- to twenty-nine-year-old group threatened "to produce a permanent underclass of disadvantaged renters and to jeopardize the long-term financial security of future generations."[96] The Census Bureau's own publication *Home Ownership Trends in the 1980s* reported that just 63.9 percent of households owned their own home in 1989, down from 65.6 percent in 1980.[97] Then in a 1991 report entitled *Who Can Afford to Buy a House?* the Census Bureau provided the unhappy answer: 57 percent of all households couldn't afford a median-priced house in their market with a conventional thirty-year fixed mortgage, and 48 percent couldn't swing even a modestly priced home (defined as one cheaper than 75 percent of the homes in that market)—including, of course, many lucky enough to already occupy a median or modest dwelling. Young families were particularly unable to buy, but even 37 percent of married couples could not afford a median home.[98]

California prices, in particular, were so high relative to incomes that by 1990 households of two or more unmarried individuals accounted for 12 percent of all statewide home sales, twice the rate of 1986. "The surge in the number of nontraditional households buying homes over the past five years was sparked by the state's continuing affordability crisis," said the president of the California Association of Realtors. "Affordability pressure has forced some unmarried individuals to form nontraditional households to make homeownership possible."[99] In and around New York City, a similar pressure could be seen; many of the middle class could not afford houses; working-class families could not afford apartments. Nationally, housing economist Michael Sumichrast complained that "it requires two members of families to buy a typical house, but even then it's sometimes impossible. We are approaching more European-type income-price house relationships, which is terrible, absolutely terrible."[100]

In parts of the nation the decline in housing prices starting at the end of the 1980s and continuing in the early 1990s eased this predicament—as did lower mortgage interest rates. But lower-middle- and middle-income Americans, in general, were still broadly priced out of the single-family home market, and not just by the price of housing itself. Legal, financial and government fees had grown so much that whereas back in 1952, it took a factory worker just one day to pay the closing costs on a new house in Levittown, then costing $10,000, the 1989 closing costs, broadly construed, on that same Levittown home, by then selling at roughly $100,000, would have required a number of weeks of work.[101]

In New England, although per capita income soared during the 1980s, housing costs rose even faster. In 1989, 40 percent of all renters were paying rents that were at least 30 percent or more of their household incomes. "People's incomes were consumed by the basics of shelter, which led to a deterioration in overall spendable income," according to Gary Ciminero, chief economist of Rhode Island's Fleet Financial Group.[101A]

Besides two-earner family expenses and the cost of housing, an increasing number of families was also burdened by the cost of providing for elderly parents—to say nothing of fears that health care and pension trends could increase this parental dependency. By 1991 Census Bureau analysts were suggesting that over the next three decades the number of dependent *elders*—aging relatives who need intermittent or even constant care—could wind up surpassing the number of dependent *children*.[102] Indeed, an internal survey by IBM found that the proportion of its employees with elderly dependents had doubled from 8 percent in 1986 to 16 percent in 1991.[103]

The toll on families was high. Pollyannas could burble about the enjoyment and benefits of new technology and products ranging from personal computers to videocassettes and microwavable "gourmet" meals, but for households below the top tier, these were often overshadowed by more pressing basic situations like unaffordable housing, escalating taxes, deteriorating services, undereducated children, declining leisure and eroding purchasing power. Not only was a record percentage of Americans working by the early 1990s, but they were working longer hours. Between 1979 and 1987, the average U.S. worker put in 95 more hours a year to make up for the decline in real wages, with the result that he or she was working 5.9 percent more hours at an hourly wage 3.3 percent less than in 1979.[104] By 1987 manufacturing workers in the United States spent more hours on the job each year than did their peers in Germany, France or Britain.

Though men were conscious of losing ground—of staying ahead of inflation only because of their wives' earnings—the larger leisure-time burden fell on women. Harvard economist Juliet Schor, attempting to calculate the impact of work both at home and at the job, estimated that, between 1973 and 1985, hours spent working rose from 40.6 to 48.8 while leisure time dropped from 26.2 hours to 17.7.[105] The decline in leisure particularly affected women, whose tasks at home did not ease much even after they took jobs, although cooking-time was reduced by new easily prepared foods and by eating out.

By the early 1990s, as companies thinned their ranks of employees, they were also starting to curb vacations and personal leave, and to demand more hours of work from those who remained. Vacations became use-them-or-lose-them propositions year to year, company picnics were disappearing, frequent-flier miles were becoming company property, personal days were shrinking and so were company outlays for conferences, staff training and personal development. Some companies were quietly extending workweeks for little or no extra pay, asking traveling employees to spend weekends away from home to get cheaper airline fares by staying over a Saturday, and requiring employees to accept one or two connecting flights instead of nonstop travel where that saved money.[106] Just before Labor Day, 1991, the *Chicago Tribune* reported that the length of an average American vacation had peaked in the mid-1980s and was shrinking fast, having fallen by almost one third.[107] Appendix C charts the decline.

In 1990 surveys began recording unprecedented frustration, especially among women. That year, Yankelovich, Clancy and Shulman, a market research firm, reported 80 percent saying they would quit their jobs or reduce their workload if they didn't need the money, a massive increase from just 39 percent a year earlier.[108] In Los Angeles and Orange counties, California, local survey-takers found 40 percent of fathers and 80 percent of mothers haunted by anxiety about spending too little time with their children and wishing they could quit their jobs.[109] Then in 1991 a study by the Americans' Use of Time Project at the University of Maryland determined that 61 percent of Americans, regardless of marital status, education or geographic location, were willing to sacrifice one or even two days' pay each week to have those days off. "We are at a point in history where, to most Americans, the value of time is reaching parity with the value of money," said project director John Robinson.[110]

As the quality of life seemed to deteriorate, more and more frustrated middle-class Americans were saying they wanted to get off the merry-go-round. For most, however, there was no getting off.

By the early 1990s, then, middle-class Americans found themselves beset on all sides. Government services were costing more in taxes and delivering less, forcing new outlays. Private services, in turn, usually involved soaring costs, rarely or reluctantly regulated by politicians loyal to the marketplace and to upper-bracket contributors. Employee benefits were eroding, and voters worried that future pensions were in greater jeopardy than corporate or government officialdom would admit.

As we saw in Chapter 5, rising taxes had turned nominal Middle American income gains into stagnation. The effect on households of unavoidable costs and fees surging far beyond the increase in the Consumer Price Index, conjoined with declining employee benefits, made that stagnation into something worse. Much of the great American middle class was losing ground—and knew it. For the median family of 1990, to send a child to a four-year private college cost 43 percent of annual income versus 30 percent back in 1970. To buy an average new car took 47 percent of that income in 1990, up from 35 percent in 1979.[111] In 1989 the mortgage payment on a median-priced family home required 33 percent of the median income of entry-level buyers in the twenty-five to twenty-nine age group, up from 21 percent back in 1969. To more and more Americans, the assurances of the 1980s seemed to have been betrayed.

Survey after survey showed that people were starting to sense that the so-called middle-class squeeze was really much more: a sign of America's declining position in the global economy, posing a real threat to their own futures and their children's. How they would respond—and whom they would blame—were also becoming important. As we will now explore in Part Three, fears of declining net worth and future economic jeopardy were in the air. Middle-class radicalization and the politics of frustration were gathering force.

THE POLITICS OF
ECONOMIC
FRUSTRATION

Economic Polarization, Shrinking Assets and the Implications of Middle-Class Decline

The 1973 period marked the beginning of the decline of the American standard of living. The Reagan years interrupted that trend by borrowing and spending, which led to the retrenchment that has deepened the current slump.

—Allen Sinai, chief economist of the Boston Company, 1992

And in the '80s a funny thing happened to the middle class, meaning, roughly, those who inhabit the middle of the income-distribution curve. If a middle-class life-style is defined by home ownership, vacations in Orlando and college for the kids, then a middle-size income was shrinking to the level of an inadequate pittance. While the price of housing and tuition went shooting through the roof, the median household income remained stuck where it has been ever since the late '70s, at about $30,000 a year. The curious result being that if you want to be middle class in the old-fashioned suburban sense, you need to be pretty near rich.

—Barbara Ehrenreich, author, 1992

. . . an imbalance between rich and poor is the oldest and most fatal ailment of republics.

—Plutarch, first century A.D.

A major deterioration in any nation's middle class is a profound cultural and political event—and by the early 1990s, as we have seen, the economic and psychological pressures building on Middle America were beginning to produce not only restiveness but occasional radical election results. Defenders of the policies of the 1980s insisted that middle-class decline was a myth, that, at worst, prosperity was simply changing gears, and that the silicon-chip economy of the twenty-first century would lead its American pioneers to unprecedented affluence. Yet the economic erosion of 1990 and 1991 provided an unsettling counterpoint—household net worth in the United States suffered its sharpest loss since the 1930s, while even in high-tech citadels from Massachusetts to California businessmen feared that America's entrepreneurial zenith had passed, that middle-class decline might be secular and long-term, not brief and cyclical.

As we will see in this chapter, such worries went beyond either the immediate job losses of the recession or the tax- and inflation-linked inroads on purchasing power discussed in Part Two. There was an equally unnerving erosion of assets, especially home values, and Americans also worried about their provisions for the future—pensions, annuities and insurance policies. If too many streets were no longer safe, neither were hard-won levels of home equity, the wherewithal to retire or even middle-class status itself. In Part Two, we looked at inroads on disposable and after-tax incomes; in Part Three, we will look at the larger threat to the middle class of economic polarization, weakening safety nets, endangered assets and fears that the next generation might not live as well as their parents—and then weigh the political and cultural effects and implications.

These fears have always been the stuff of political upheaval, especially when the rich get richer while the average person loses ground without quite understanding why—and also when the nation involved has just experienced its zenith of broad-based success. The more exhilarating the peak, the more alarming the valley. After the middle-class triumph of Holland's golden seventeenth century, the social stratification and economic decay of the eighteenth century eventually led to revolution. Similarly, after Britain's transformation from the mid-nineteenth-century middle-class workshop of the world to the extravagance of the Edwardian era, rising class politics produced the Labour party.

More recently, when such countries as Argentina, Uruguay, Australia and New Zealand lost the great agricultural export prosperity that had put them among the world's richest nations from 1900 to 1929 ("rich as an Argentine" was a cliché in London and Paris), frustrated voters grasped at social welfare schemes—often promoted with populist rhetoric—to maintain their living standards. In the 1930s the German middle and lower-middle classes, devastated by defeat in World War I and then by the inflation of the 1920s, turned to the populist far right under Nazism.

Closer to home for most Americans, Canadian voters reacted to the 1990–92 recession and their own middle-class squeeze by embracing the socialist New Democratic party in provincial elections from Ontario to Saskatchewan and British Columbia. Pundits started wondering whether the rise of the new populist conservative Reform party based in oil-rich Alberta might even mean the end of Canada's governing Conservative party. Though the politics of economic frustration varies from nation to nation, a pattern recurs where a middle-class standard of living is under pressure. In Chapter 9, I will look at how this started to happen in the United States as the 1990s began.

No comparable squeeze on the middle class could have taken place in the postwar quarter century when the interests of Middle America dominated the political agenda and the lessons of the 1920s and 1930s were still remembered. *De-polarization* had been the postwar vogue: as the middle grew stronger, those farther down could begin to rise, although the difficulty of achieving these hopes became increasingly apparent in the late 1960s. By the late 1970s or early 1980s, income and wealth began to polarize in the United States and most other major financial powers for the reasons we have seen in earlier chapters: a rightward shift in politics, accompanying upheavals in technology, and industrial and financial deregulation that favored people with capital, skills and education. Billionaires and centimillionaires flourished and multiplied under Reagan, as did cutting-edge portions of the middle class, especially those in finance, the professions, high technology and communications. At the opposite pole, as we have also seen, many of the working poor and substantial segments of the middle class were losing ground, especially those on overpaid Midwest production lines or overinflated corporate staffs, or otherwise propped up by the last fading artificial advantages that had favored the postwar U.S. economy for more than a generation after 1945. Fearful voters were beginning to wonder where it would end.

The Downscaling of Middle America?

The critical political question, rarely confronted by elected officials, was whether America was really in economic decline in the 1990s—and how much? Some of the evidence could be dismissed as merely short-term. Bankruptcies multiplied in the best-manicured areas of New York, New Jersey and Connecticut. Companies that made stretch limousines—the quintessential 1980s ego symbol—began to go out of business in 1990, and the New York Debutante Cotillion presented only half as many young women in December 1990 as in December 1989.[1] Such symptoms often reflect no more than the business cycle, and the *Forbes* and *Fortune* lists of America's richest men and women continued to show that most of the great fortunes were increasing.

Below the median income, however, Darwinian economic effects had already convinced some dispassionate marketing strategists to give some of their business and retail clients blunt new advice: *Go downscale.* The extremes, panhandlers and the homeless, might lack purchasing power, but "downscale" America—households with unskilled breadwinners and incomes circa 1991 below $25,000 a year—was a large market predicted to get larger despite upturns in the business cycle. Management Horizons, a retail consulting firm, projected that the number of households with annual incomes of $15,000 or less, as calculated in 1984 dollars (some $22,000 in 1991 dollars), would expand to 36 percent of the U.S. total in the year 2000, up from 31.2 percent in 1970 and about 34 percent in 1991.[2] Retail chains like Lerner's and catalog merchants like Fingerhut were already building high sales from nonaffluent consumers, and in late 1990 food retailers followed suit, as chains like McDonald's, Hardee's and Red Lobster posted new bargain meals. Harris Rusitzky, president of the National Restaurant Association, acknowledged "considerable evidence that customers now want a more casual, less structured, less expensive dining-out experience. To a great extent, casualization will be manifest in the down-scaling of existing restaurants."[3] He meant that eating out would be getting cheaper.

Whether in rural areas, manufacturing centers or service-industry suburbs, the downward pressure on the ordinary family's purchasing power was a fact of the early 1990s. All too frequently, job opportunities and incomes were shrinking. By 1988, well before the downturn, the U.S. General Accounting Office was even reporting a resurgence of small sweatshops—shops and factories that employed workers at low wages for long hours under poor conditions.[4] By January 1991, as the recession bit, 11 percent of Illinoisans, right in the heart of Middle America, were receiving some form of state assistance, and welfare recipients reached their highest number since the Great Depression.[5] Official national measurements of work-force unemployment remained in the neighborhood of 7 percent, but when underemployment was added, the total exceeded 12 percent.

Many of those affected were—or *had been*—in the middle class. When the Illinois Department of Revenue published data on the distribution of income for 1989 and appended similar statistics for 1980, the *Chicago Tribune* and First National Bank of Chicago published rough inflation-adjusted comparisons, and the polarization was stunning. Even before the recession of the early 1990s, the decline in well-paid manufacturing jobs had devastated middle-range incomes, while a surge in unearned income and sharp growth in highly paid professional and financial-services jobs bolstered gains at the top. "There was real growth in per-return dollars in the 1980s, but those figures lie," explained Diane Swonk, regional economist for the First National Bank of Chicago. "You didn't get growth in the bulk of the population. The bulk of people were getting poorer, while the rich were getting richer."6 The number of million-dollar-a-year households in Illinois rose sixfold, from 920 to 5,860. However, the proportion of reportable earnings going to "middle Illinois" plummeted.

The shock was the erosion of the group making $50,000 to $100,000 in constant 1989 dollars. Back in 1980 those in the comparable income range ($32,876 to $65,750) had been 17.2 percent of the total; by 1989 that had fallen to 13.7 percent. The small upper tier, by contrast, boomed. The 4.2 percent of Illinoisans with adjusted gross incomes over $50,000 had mustered 19 percent of the state's reported income in 1980, but by 1989 the smaller 3.4 percent of all taxpayers making over $100,000 controlled a startling 29.9 percent of all reported Illinois income. Because a $50,000 income in 1980 equaled roughly $80,000 in 1989, the two groups were reasonably comparable in scope, yet the top 3.4 percent enjoyed a much larger share of state income than the top 4.2 percent had just nine years earlier.

This was polarization with a vengeance—the widening split between the 1 percent or 2 percent of increasingly wealthy haves and a growing bottom third of have-nots, as the great in-between postwar middle class quietly eroded. Mid–Corn Belt Illinois was no center of financial, social or communications glitterati; it was the Land of Lincoln, proudly so proclaimed by its own license plates, the site of cities like Peoria, America's colloquial synonym for middle-class culture, and of Chicago, Carl Sandburg's blue-collar "hog butcher" to the world. If polarization could drain the middle class there, it could do so anywhere. The downscaling of Middle America was real.

Polarization and the Upper-Middle Class:
A Metaphor for America?

Yet Peoria, with its old-line economy, was not necessarily the right yardstick. Conservatives insisted that any significant decline in the middle class really reflected the number of middle-class earners crossing the $100,000-a-year line, where true affluence supposedly began. Magazine publisher Malcolm Forbes, Jr., excited by Census data showing that one American family in twenty-five had a 1990 income over $100,000, predicted that by the late 1990s, as the high-technology economy grew, one family in ten could rise to a comparable income. That, he thought, would make them allies of the Forbes 400: "Karl Marx would be proven right about the political power of the rich, but in a way he never would have believed possible—because there will be so many of them."[7] Most of those who anticipated this upward mobility expected it to relieve popular economic frustration. But some took a contrary perspective.

Social thinker Charles Murray hypothesized a nation in which the most prosperous 10 percent (or more) of Americans would cluster in privileged enclaves, leaving the public-service world of inadequate schools, unsafe streets, uncollected garbage and gridlocked transportation to the lower and middle classes—and taking their tax dollars with them. "The Left has been complaining for years that the rich have too much power," said Murray. "They ain't seen nothing yet."[8] Others who agreed that the top 10 percent of Americans would continue to gain while average families were forced downscale were more hopeful that mobility and new values could keep the economy and society vibrant. Yet there was something wrong with these glib assumptions about a pampered top tenth or fortunate fifth: decay and declining opportunity were even beginning to lap at the top 4 percent of families already making over $100,000.

In California's Silicon Valley, a survey in late 1991 by the *Los Angeles Times* found a pervasive worry, transcending the immediate recession. The big electronics firms weren't growing much, and many midsize companies were faltering; middle managers had few prospects for dramatic advancement, while intense competition was making successful start-up companies rare. As a result, "it is now clear to all but the most blindly ambitious that the vision of entrepreneurial riches is mostly myth."[9] Between April 1989 and April 1992 Silicon Valley lost about 6 percent of its electronics jobs—although that was a relatively minor loss compared with the steeper decline in electronics jobs in the Boston and Dallas areas.

Following the 1990 census, a study by the California governor's office of planning and research found that the "most remarkable" change was that rich "counties like San Mateo [adjacent to Silicon Valley] and Marin, and cities like Beverly Hills, Rancho Palos Verdes and San Marino, showed no gain and even population loss during the decade," mostly because potential residents could not afford these locations; that was true even of suburban children who had grown up there.[10] Instead, population was increasing in cheap, distant, end-of-the-freeway tract homes and in poor urban neighborhoods, where "much of the growth comes from immigrants doubling up or more in existing dwellings." Thousands of families, the report found, were housed, often illegally, in what had been residential garages.

Twenty-five hundred miles to the east in East Brunswick, New Jersey, at the crossroads of America's great pharmaceutical and medical-equipment corporations, the twelfth annual conference of the New Jersey Data Center agreed that the boom had ended. Houses would be less grand. "The upscale outer-suburb life style will fade," said Rutgers University demographer James Hughes. "The 80s consumer would pay anything to save time. Now people will drive to outlet stores to save money."[11]

The new high-technology economy was not proving to be an immediate boon to the ordinary householder any more than capitalism's previous breakthrough periods—the nineteenth-century Industrial Revolution and the great expansion of commerce in the sixteenth century following the Renaissance—had been.* Part of the problem was that the United States, even as it invented and launched the silicon chip, was also the seat of huge automobile, steel, machinery, textile and electronics industries, all of which had declined rapidly following the overseas spread of computer technology, robotics and other innovations that helped many nations with low wage scales develop advanced production facilities and outsell American producers. This globalization, in turn, obliged American firms to squeeze their workers, first blue-collar, then white-collar. Rising productivity no longer brought employees wage increases. By 1991–92, after serious corporate layoffs and the unsuccessful United Autoworkers' strike against Caterpillar, labor relations experts like Harley Shaiken at the University of California suggested that competitive pressures were striking at long-held American assumptions:

We've always seen aggressive managements in many industries. What's different now is that a number of companies who for most of the

*Both the period of the Renaissance and the rise of capitalism and the period of the Industrial Revolution were eras in which those who had capital, skills and education gained, often greatly, but ordinary people generally lost ground. The great economic historian Fernand Braudel has noted that during the two centuries of capitalist excitement from 1450 to 1650, the "progress made by the upper reaches of the economy and the increase in economic potential were paid for by the hardship of the mass of the people whose numbers were increasing as fast or faster than production" (Fernand Braudel, *The Perspective of the World, Civilization & Capitalism 15th–18th Century*, p. 87). And moving ahead to the earlier years of the Industrial Revolution in Britain, Braudel concluded: "I am inclined to agree with the earliest historians who studied the question, that there was indeed a deterioration in the well-being of the British masses, a decline in real wages, for farm labourers as well as for workers in factories or transport" (Braudel, op. cit., p. 614).

last 40 years operated on the basis of a certain social contract are rede-
fining the terms of that contract. It isn't just a back-alley machine shop
with 200 workers going after its union. It's AT&T violating seniority
rules. It's Caterpillar threatening to replace its work force. . . . Public
companies that would have shunned these tactics a decade ago are now
using them.[12]

If European peasants, artisans and small farmers in the mid-six-
teenth century and British manufacturing workers of 1825 saw that no
matter how hard they worked, they could not live as well as their
fathers, the same fear was overtaking tens of millions of young Americans of the 1990s, for whom yesteryear's high-paying factory and, to
a lesser extent, corporate white-collar jobs were just a memory. Employment in the new high-tech industries, by contrast, depended more
on education and therefore helped polarize wages and rewards.

educ.

Inadequate U.S. education was part of the threat. In 1990, 31 percent of men between the ages of thirty-four and forty-five had completed four years of college; in the younger twenty-five- to thirty-
our-year-old group, only 25 percent had done so, as college was
becoming less affordable.[13] Meanwhile, only 20 percent or so of Americans, according to Harvard's Robert Reich, had the training and skills
to compete in the tougher international economy of the postindustrial
era. Trade rivals like Japan and Germany, by contrast, were providing
35 to 40 percent of their populations with competitive technical and
educational skills. America's less well-equipped work force might not
be able to support a strong enough economy to maintain an economic
elite of 10 percent high-earners.* The elite might be much smaller.

Few debates went more to the heart of the economic future. One
prominent study prepared by the Hudson Institute for the U.S. Labor
Department assured policymakers that the new computer-chip economy would generate a dramatic "upskilling" of available jobs, thereby
increasing highly paid positions. The liberal Economic Policy Institute
replied that upskilling and occupational changes would come even
more slowly in the 1990s than in the 1980s.[14] In 1992 the Census
Bureau released a survey, supporting the Hudson Institute findings,
that argued that nearly three fifths of the 6 million jobs created between 1987 and 1989 were in high-paying, not low-paying, industries.
The deception, critics insisted, was that many of the jobs created in
"high-paying" industries like finance were actually low-paying back-
office positions. Skeptics also questioned the future contribution of

---

*Rising U.S. illiteracy was also a broader harbinger of a class society, but it was not usually
a middle-class problem. Inadequate education, however, often was.

U.S. exports, cautioning that while some were sophisticated—airplanes, entertainment products, drugs and medical technology—others were merely commodities that might as easily have been shipped from a low-wage Third World nation: soybeans, wheat, coal and unprocessed timber.

By late 1991 and 1992, corporations were being forced to break their "social contract" with upper-level as well as lower-level employees. As I discussed in the previous chapter, more and more managers saw their jobs and benefits at risk as company after company reduced its permanent work force in order to cut benefit costs with more part-timers or to "outsource" production and jobs to low-wage Mexico or Taiwan. Corporate chiefs, many of whom enjoyed record compensation, declared that their U.S.-based employees had to make do with less. "Wages overseas will come up, but one way or another, the gap will have to close," said Robert E. Mercer, chairman of the Goodyear Tire and Rubber Company. And the chief economist at General Electric, Walter Joelson, added: "Let's talk about the differences in living standards rather than wages. What in the Bible says we should have a better living standard than others? We have to give a bit of it back."[15]

If the top 1 percent was not much at risk, substantial parts of the upper-middle class were. Record numbers of stunned advertising managers, accountants and aerospace engineers found themselves on unemployment lines. Silicon chips would have to create a lot of new, highly paid jobs to make up for the millions of low, middle and even upper managerial positions eliminated as General Motors, Du Pont and 3M and multitudes of lesser firms reduced large and expensive staffs.

There was another problem, for even if new economic forces did increase the end-of-the-century ratio of American households with incomes over $100,000 in constant 1990 dollars from 4 percent to 10 percent, other circumstances were eroding that supposed income's real economic meaning—and had been doing so throughout the 1980s. Many ostensibly prosperous persons and families crossing the $100,000 line were on a treadmill, not an elevator.

Consider the hypothetical Jones family of Riverside, California, or Oceanside, New York. In 1980 Mr. Jones earned $40,000 a year while his wife had a half-time job that paid $10,000. By 1990, his salary had climbed to $65,000 while she drew $35,000 for going back to work full time. That put the Joneses into the magic $100,000-a-year category. Although inflation came to 60 to 70 percent for the decade, this left at least a $15,000 real gain, or it appeared to.

The real world of the middle class, however, made the actual result very different. The Joneses' federal income tax would have climbed from roughly $5,500 to about $9,000. Their combined FICA, or Social Security, burden would have risen from about $2,100 to about $6,000. Their state and local taxes—income, sales and property—probably doubled from $5,000 to $10,000. However, parts of the sales and property tax increases were also in the CPI (and would be factored into yearly inflation adjustments), so the remaining state and local tax increase can be set at $3,500. By this calculus, then, increased taxes would have eaten up roughly $10,000 of the after-inflation gain. In addition, Mrs. Jones's added expenses for going back to work full time drained off another $2,000 or so. Then there's the higher cost of child care or college expenses, neither of which had much weight in the CPI inflation calculus. If we assume that the Jones family had either small children or collegians, then because tuition roughly doubled during the 1980s and day-care costs were not far behind, either burden could easily have increased by over $2,500 during the decade.

So much for the nominal gain. Already, $14,500 is gone, with nothing to show for it—and no adjustment has yet been made for health care; automobile insurance; lawyers' fees; water bills; federal, state and local government fees; cable television charges; prescription drug costs; and other important areas where the burden on middle-class families far outran the CPI. For many families like the Joneses, it's possible that the whole $15,000 to $20,000 of after-inflation extra income disappeared without any notable gain in living standard.

Yet it was individuals or families like these, doubling incomes from $50,000 in 1980 to $100,000 in 1990 or from $55,000 to $110,000, who pushed 4 percent of all households above the Census Bureau's $100,000 frontier versus a little over 1 percent a decade earlier. But if most of these gains were unreal, then the significance of $100,000-a-year households expanding from 1 percent to 4 percent of the population was also largely illusory. One angry California taxpayer expressed the frustration: "Earning $100,000 doesn't make you wealthy in Southern California. I have a lot of friends in the same tax bracket, and they'll tell you that they are barely getting by. The last thing we need is to get hit with a rich man's tax."[16] The average-income family, of course, was worse off, because as income brackets dropped toward the median, nominal gains got smaller. Slackening public services aggravated the problem, and as later sections of this chapter will show, a parallel decline in assets and net worth provided an even more disquieting signal.

By the early 1990s, social scientists and pollsters perceived a related change: that so many years of stagnant incomes had begun to affect the middle-class psyche. Earlier psychologies rooted in unprecedented U.S. affluence—in which homeownership, upward mobility and high levels of consumer spending were assumed to be American birthrights—were breaking down in favor of a new one. Young householders, in particular, while still pursuing the good life, were beginning to pick their purchases to simulate affluence, not to achieve it.[17] A suburban home with two reasonably new cars in the garage might be unachievable—as it had not been for their fathers and mothers in 1954 or 1963—yet a chic alternative (and more akin to the tastes of stratified urban Europe) could be achieved by concentrating money on stylish clothing, compact disc players and sophisticated wine and food.

Economically, then, even large portions of the upper-middle class were not secure. To call them new rich was silly. Only two and a half million people in America's top 1 percent of households, with annual incomes ranging upward from $250,000 and net worth typically well above a million dollars, were clearly on the winning side of economic polarization. The clearest winners of all were those ranging from 100,000 decamillionaires to billion-dollar households to which ordinary bills were no great bother. Yet for seemingly prosperous Americans in the top tenth of the population but short of the top 1 percent, the nineties brought surprising economic uncertainty. White-collar suburbs and high-tech centers seemed almost as nervous as Peoria.

Debt, Eroding Home Prices and Declining Middle-Class Net Worth

The record buildup of debt and speculation during the Reagan years, combined with the wicked rise and fall in home prices, provided an ominous accompaniment to the polarization of income. By 1992, things were just as bad or worse on the net-worth side of the ledger. We have seen how between 1983 and 1989 the top 1 percent of Americans increased their share of the nation's total wealth from 31 percent to 37 percent, a level unmatched since the 1920s. For many middle-income families, however, the economic changes of the Reagan years wound up depressing their net worth.

Household debt soared during the 1980s, mirroring the devil-may-care attitudes of Washington and Wall Street. For investors, debt became "leverage," and often worked to enlarge wealth. Many middle-income households, however, borrowed not to invest but to pay for a house or college or simply to stay afloat, and the debt they took on during the 1980s became a major offset to nominal gains in income and assets.

According to the Federal Reserve Board, American households as a whole increased their combined home mortgage and consumer debt almost threefold during the 1980s—from $1.3 trillion in late 1980 to just under $3.4 trillion at the end of 1990.[18] This was about 50 percent faster than the rate at which consumers' income grew. In 1991, the average household owed about $35,000 and paid interest of about $3,500 per year, almost 18 percent of its disposable income.[19]

But economists disagreed over what the new indebtedness meant—for families and for the nation as a whole. Optimists said that households could easily service higher payments because assets had increased even faster than debt. Worriers said that federal statistics based on averages camouflaged critical differences between the rich, the middle-class and the poor. The rich—the familiar top 1 percent of Americans—had borrowed enormous sums to invest and speculate with, but for the most part (real estate developers and builders were a troubled exception), their net worths, fattening with the stock market, had expanded far more than their debt. They could pay their notes.

For the bottom 80 percent of the population, though, debt ratios appear to have risen sharply even while incomes and assets were relatively stagnant, suggesting that a lot of their borrowing was to make up for declines in wages or purchasing power. Prominent proponents of this interpretation, such as Robert Pollin, author of a study entitled *Deeper in Debt,* were often sharp critics of Reaganism.[20] Nevertheless, considerable evidence supported their arguments. Even during the ostensible prosperity of the late 1980s, the nation's savings rate had fallen, partly because so many families had no margin to save. Then during the 1990–91 recession, foreclosures and bankruptcies increased, reaching an all-time record of nearly one million in 1991. Federal bankruptcy courts expanded and bankruptcy law became a growth industry. Tens of millions of Americans, many in the middle class, obviously had been borrowing to stay afloat.

Broad government data don't show how much more of its disposable income the typical middle- or upper-middle-class family was spending on debt service in 1990 or 1991 relative to 1980 or 1981. One credible private estimate was that in 1990 *overall* U.S. household debt service consumed 14 percent of disposable income, up only a little from 13 percent at the start of the 1980s, when interest rates were sky-high, but well above the 11.5 percent of 1987.[21] As for a typical two-earner family with an income that rose from $30,000 in 1980 to $50,000 in 1990, it's possible that the cost of debt service climbed from 15 to 16 percent of disposable income to 18 percent. As we have seen, the share of U.S. personal income spent on a combination of debt service, taxes, Social Security and health insurance soared—up from 33 percent in 1980 to 40 percent in 1990 (see the chart on page 94). For the average family, debt service was one of the Four Horsemen of slowly declining purchasing power.

Debt's impact on net worth, however, was even more damaging. According to the Census Bureau, the typical household's net worth, which had been $37,000 in 1984, actually *fell* slightly over the next four years, based on a national sample of twenty-four thousand households, which the bureau acknowledged involved very few wealthy families.[22] The latter had done much better. The Forbes 400 richest Americans almost doubled their net worth from $125 billion to $220 billion during these same four years.[23]

This divergence of net worth between the top 1 percent and the stagnant middle worsened as the overstretched economy slid into the 1990–92 recession. Depressed by soaring bankruptcies and plummeting home values, real household net worth—assets minus liabilities—sank by 5.8 percent in 1990, the biggest decline since the Federal Reserve Board started keeping records in the early 1950s.[24] As we shall see, much of the slide hit ordinary families, especially in the value of their homes. The circumstances of the rich varied. Yet three quarters of those in the Forbes 400 continued to gain from 1990 to 1991, with their combined net worth rising another $15 billion.[25]

In troubled New England one survey for local banks found that among a sample of one thousand regional professional and managerial households in the thirty-five- to fifty-four-year-old age bracket and with an average income of $55,000, fully 53 percent were at or near a negative-equity position in 1992. After a buying binge in the 1980s, the cash liquidation value of their assets, including real estate, was near or below their total outstanding debt. Nationally, the "nebbies"—negative-equity baby boomers—were estimated to constitute 20 to 30 percent of their age bracket.[25A]

The wealth that different groups added during the 1980s depended on the types of assets they held. The rich, from billionaires down to the approximately 100,000 decamillionaires, derived most of their wealth from business ownership and financial investments. If we start with the Forbes 400, add some 1,200 to 1,500 other Americans with net worths of over $100 million, and then add the decamillionaires, whose members ballooned from 30,000 in 1982 to 100,000 by the end of the 1980s, this entire group may well have increased its net worth by $1.5 to $2.5 trillion. The remainder of top 1 percent America—another 900,000 families—probably added an average of $800,000 per household, for a total of $700 billion. Overall, one can plausibly conclude that the top 1 percent might have garnered some $3 trillion of the $7 trillion of new net worth added by households during the 1980s. This overall $7 trillion increment, it should be underscored, was in *nominal* dollars; using inflation-adjusted 1982 dollars, the expansion of U.S. household net worth was only $3 trillion—up from $10 trillion in 1982 to $13 trillion in 1989. Furthermore, it's entirely plausible to assume that the top 1 percent got some 40 to 50 percent of the increase in household net worth because these families already had roughly 31 percent of the existing wealth, and, more specifically, they held about half of the individually owned corporate stock, two thirds of the bonds, an even higher percentage of the municipal bonds, and roughly 45 percent of the nonresidential real estate!* What was going up during the 1980s was mostly what they owned.

Ordinary Americans, by contrast, had most of their assets in less-favored real estate—in their houses, farms or small commercial properties. According to the Census Bureau, 43 percent of collective U.S. net worth in 1988 came from homeowners' equity.[26] Right up to the 95th percentile, the solid middle class was home-dependent because only the top 1 percent or 2 percent of U.S. households had most of their net worth in financial assets like stocks and bonds. Even for taxpayers with net worths of $100,000 to $200,000, most of whose incomes would have been in the top fifth, homes were all-important. ✱ The consequence was that the disinflationary 1980s worked *for* the wealthiest households that held financial assets and *against* the net worth of the middle and upper-middle classes that was so dependent on personal residences. In 1982, when Washington responded to inflation with higher interest rates, Murray Weidenbaum, chairman of the President's Council of Economic Advisers, predicted that disinflation would bring "a major redistribution of wealth," at the expense of the American homeowner.[27] Which is exactly what happened. Home prices soared in a few locales during the 1980s—Hawaii, California, New England and the New York–Washington megalopolis (regions where demand was bolstered by large concentrations of financial and profes-

---

*Indeed, the Federal Reserve Board estimate, released in 1992, that the top 1 percent of Americans increased their share of the nation's wealth from 31 percent in 1983 to 37 percent in 1989 suggests that they must have collected at least 50 percent of the new wealth created during this period.

sional workers). Nationally, though, the Census Bureau later estimated that the median value of owner-occupied homes rose only modestly from $47,200 in 1980 to $79,100 in 1990, about 5 percent after inflation—and the true increase for *preexisting* homes was even less, possibly a decline, because the nation's housing stock was enlarged and improved during the 1980s by many high-priced new houses with central air conditioning and other amenities.[28] In the 1970s, by contrast, the median value of the owner-occupied housing had increased 39 percent even after adjustment for inflation.

In the hardest-hit places—Oil Patch cities like Houston or Baton Rouge or Farm Belt centers like Omaha—home prices were virtually the same in 1990 as they had been back in 1980, which meant huge after-inflation declines for the owners. In constant dollars, local net worths sank. Yet even in more typical metropolitan areas like Cincinnati, Milwaukee and St. Louis the fact that housing prices added 20 percent or 30 percent in nominal dollars faded to real 25 percent to 30 percent losses for homeowners after inflation. In Milwaukee, where television producers had set the location of *Happy Days,* the nostalgia-for-the-1950s television show, the *Milwaukee Journal* sorted data from the 1990 federal housing census into a vivid front-page portrait of "a punishing decade" for Wisconsin homeowners. Expressed in real 1991 dollars, the 1980 statewide median home value had been $87,000 and fell to $65,900 by 1990, a decline of 25 percent. In metropolitan Milwaukee, the decline was slightly higher.[29] Nothing of this sort had happened since the 1930s. Roughly half of America's major metropolitan areas chalked up at least 15 percent inflation-adjusted drops in home values.*

Nor were principal residences the only personal real estate losing ground. According to the business-backed Conference Board, the total value of farmland in the United States fell from $712 billion in 1980 to $392 billion in 1986, although part of that loss was recovered later in the decade.[30] In mid-1991, the U.S. vacation-home market was so weak that in Nantucket, Massachusetts, where 82 percent of the island's homes were vacation residences, prices had fallen 35 percent in 1989, slipped 11 percent further in 1990 and were continuing to drop in 1991. In the overbuilt resort of Hilton Head, South Carolina, the price of two-bedroom condominiums dropped from $90,000 in 1986 to $40,000 in 1991.[31]

Increased debt not only drained the average family income but

---

*Moreover, even in areas where housing prices nominally doubled, the increase after inflation was only 30 percent. In a sale by someone who had bought in 1980, capital gains taxes, fees and real estate broker commissions would eat up most of that.

reduced equity in the family home. Even as the inflation-adjusted value of homes declined—which during the mid-1980s happened mainly in the oil and farm states and Rust Belt but then from 1989 to 1992 concentrated in California, Florida and the Northeast—expanding mortgages and home-equity loans also reduced net worth. From the mid-eighties to 1990, home values in the United States rose by roughly $1 trillion, but because home-mortgage debt (including home-equity loans) increased even faster, homeowner equity actually *declined.* The Census Bureau reported that the average homeowner had $43,070 of equity in 1988, down from $46,106 in 1984.[32] In 1989 and 1990, the mortgage-debt surge further accelerated, as the hard-pressed middle class channeled its borrowing through second mortgages and home-equity loans, which were among the few loans on which interest payments still qualified for federal tax deductibility in the 1990s.

For the average family's net worth, the declining home values, combined with stepped-up use of second mortgages and home-equity loans, often meant a significant write-down. For 1990, alone, the Mortgage Bankers Association reported a stunning 15.7 percent drop in the equity that Americans held in their homes, the sharpest one-year decline since record-keeping began in 1945.[33] Mortgage debt as a percentage of total home value jumped to 57.6 percent in 1990, up from 50.5 percent in 1990 and just 36.7 percent in 1980.

Automobile values, another major component of net worth for median- and average-income families, also sagged. By early 1992, as the devastation of the U.S. automobile industry became clear, industry analysts explained that one of the reasons was the excessive debt on existing cars:

> All of a sudden, 60% of the cars that have been financed over the last few years were under water (they actually had negative equity in them). So when people walked into a dealership thinking they had a car to trade in, in fact they still owed several thousand dollars on the car that was sitting outside. They were unable to buy the car because they had a balance sheet problem. They didn't have the values and assets they thought they did.[34]

Facing this kind of undertow, real household net worth declined sharply in 1990 and then stabilized in 1991. And fears of what else might be involved were also real. The average family's deposits in the thousands of savings and loan associations that fell into insolvency during the 1980s had been protected, but the commercial bank failures of the 1990s raised new questions about the adequacy of federal deposit insurance. In some midsize failures, like New York's Freedom National Bank, accounts over $100,000 were not fully covered. Credit unions were another potential problem; in 1991, more than 150,000 Rhode Islanders had their savings immobilized in a credit union collapse.

Collapses and bankruptcies of insurance firms were also a worry, although they remained on a small scale. As a rule, when an insurance company failed, policyholders were covered for the losses up to $100,000 for policy values and up to $300,000 for death benefits by the individual state-operated funds of the National Organization of Life and Health Guaranty Associations.[35] In the early 1990s, however, as failure overtook major insurance companies like Mutual Benefit Life and Executive Life, skeptics noted that one or two major collapses could wipe out the thinly financed state guaranty associations. In Louisiana, where forty-seven insurance firms, mostly small, collapsed between 1986 and 1991, tens of thousands of people lost annuities or found themselves with unpayable claims. The New Orleans *Times-Picayune* worried that the state's private insurance system might collapse.[36]

While the shambles in Louisiana was unique, experts identified three other acknowledged vulnerabilities in the insurance safety net. The first affected the 3 to 4 million Americans who, willingly or by employer arrangement, drew their retirement benefits in the form of annuities from insurance companies. Howard Weizmann, executive director of the Association of Private Pension and Welfare Plans, called retirement annuities "the Achilles heel of the private retirement system" because, unlike defined benefit pensions, they were not covered by the federal Pension Benefit Guarantee Corporation.[37] A second problem area, insurers agreed, lay with title insurance—the virtually unregulated segment of the industry that provided protection to U.S. real estate owners by guaranteeing their titles to the property. As claims soared in the early 1990s, both Wall Street analysts and the Federal National Mortgage Association became concerned about the adequacy of the title insurers' reserves.[38] With the failure of a major title company, worriers argued, millions of homeowners and lenders would be vulnerable until they found another title insurer, and the real estate industry could be snarled. A third weakness lay in health insurance coverage. When Blue Cross and Blue Shield of West Virginia failed in October 1990, it left fifty thousand policyholders with $42 million in unpaid medical bills.

Retirement pensions, in turn, were another "asset" that voters worried about. As we have seen in Chapter 6, steadily fewer Americans were covered by the private pension system, and many of those who thought they were covered had reason for concern. During the 1980s, scores of major corporate pension funds had been tapped—most of the time legally—by corporate raiders or by a nervous management in need of money. In other instances, financially troubled corporations had simply stopped making payments to their pension funds, knowing that the Pension Benefit Guarantee Corporation, the Washington-based federal safety net, was obliged to pay defined-benefit pensions to retirees after their companies or plans had failed. By 1991, PBGC had taken over payment of 125,000 individual pensions, up from 28,000 in 1980. In November of that year, however, nervous PBGC officials announced that the nation's fifty largest underfunded corporate pension plans alone had a potential shortfall of $21.5 billion, up 50 percent from the year before.[39] Because the PBGC was already in the red, executive director James Lockhart worried that "unless we find a way to stop the growth of our deficit, the specter of ever-increasing premiums and ultimately an S&L-type bail-out looms over our future."[40] "People are already losing benefits," Lockhart said in 1992. "We see some sad stories" of retirees whose pension checks are halved after the PBGC takes over and can offer only a maximum annual pension of about $28,000.[40A]

Public-employee pensions also stirred some concern. Experts testifying before a joint hearing of the House Select Committee on Aging and the Joint Economic Committee in late 1991 warned that millions of Americans might never collect the pensions owed them because economically strapped state and local governments were raiding public-employee pension funds. In California that year, the governor and legislature sought to take $1.6 billion from the state workers' pension fund to apply to the huge budget deficit, and in Illinois $21 million was transferred out of the state pension fund to help meet the deficit despite the state comptroller's insistence that state pension funds were underfunded by $10 billion. One expert told the hearings that six major pension funds—teachers' plans in West Virginia, Oklahoma, Maine and Washington, and state employee plans in Maine and Massachusetts—were "in such bad shape that assets were insufficient to meet benefit payments for current retirees."[41]

Despite the FICA tax increases of the 1980s, many workers doubted the future solvency of the federal Social Security system. In late 1991 Dorcas Hardy, Social Security commissioner during the Reagan era, published a book entitled *Social Insecurity,* in which she called the system "a ticking time bomb. In the next century the United States will face a potentially devastating crisis: the retirement checks that should be sent to benefit millions of Americans will not be there." Her concern echoed that of Daniel P. Moynihan and other U.S. senators. "The Treasury," Hardy said, "siphons the money off to pay for current operations, and in exchange it gives Social Security an IOU. When the IOU comes due, there will be no money in the Treasury to pay it off, so one way or another, at that point Congress will have to raise revenue" from taxes or bonds.[42] Other former senior Social Security officials criticized Hardy for making unnecessarily alarming statements, but she was voicing fears widely shared by the public. The nation's pension system, like the single-family home, showed signs of becoming a weak link in the American Dream.

In the 1930s homes and other assets lost 30 to 45 percent of their value across much of the United States and household net worth plunged.* Many families had no safety net, and New Deal programs and agencies like Social Security, the Federal Deposit Insurance Corporation and federally insured mortgages were established to create one. The early 1990s stirred some new concerns. But there were also differences. In the early 1930s, Hoover's hands-off Republican administration did not decide which groups would be protected and which would not as the economy unraveled. Sixty years later, the Bush administration would manage the implosion in behalf of America's financial assets holders.

The Imploding Debt-and-Speculative Bubble of 1989–92 and Its Effects on Polarization and Wealth Distribution

The Reagan administration's controversial budget director, David Stockman, gone from Washington to Wall Street before the debt-and-speculative bubble finally popped in the late 1980s, later described it as "a once-in-50-year flood-type of cycle that happened because a generation that had learned all the lessons from the last great correction finally left the financial system. That's about where we were in the 80s. We were due for a final era of excess."[43]

After the great collapses of 1893 and 1929, conservative presidents Cleveland and Hoover let the speculative breakdowns play themselves

---

*One landmark study by Robert Williams, a UCLA professor, showed Los Angeles home prices declining steadily from 1925 to 1940, slipping from a median $7,660 to $4,200 ("Unlike Stocks, Home Prices Rarely Collapse," *Los Angeles Times,* August 28, 1988).

out. So many financial institutions failed in 1893 that U.S. bank deposits shrank by almost one third. There were enormous losses in the stock market and in speculative railroad bonds. Almost forty years later, Republican Secretary of the Treasury Andrew Mellon made his famous but impolitic remark about letting weak companies, financial institutions, farmers and investors go under and be replaced by strong ones. In neither downturn was federal deposit insurance available to prevent panics and protect depositors. As for the Federal Reserve Board, it did not yet exist in the 1890s, and although it did exist during the crisis of 1930–33, its governors declined to assume a countercyclical role.

The late 1980s and 1990s were different. After the 508-point stock market crash of October 1987 the Reagan and then the Bush administrations, along with the Republican-controlled Federal Reserve Board, sought to head off a major economic downturn and control the limited implosion that slowly developed. With the help of the ill-fated Federal Savings and Loan Insurance Corporation (FSLIC) and the Federal Deposit Insurance Corporation (FDIC), the economy did not collapse as it had in the earlier downturns, despite the S&L debacle and the sharp drop in real estate prices. But what was also unusual was that the post-1987 financial implosion was generally managed in behalf of the same classes and economic strata that had enjoyed and profited from the pre-1987 boom.

One reason, beyond general party loyalties, was that many powerful executive branch officials, including Bush and his close friend James Baker were Texans from a financial culture where bank failures, real estate collapses and bankruptcies were not abstract but involved familiar faces—friends, relatives, political allies and campaign contributors. From leveraged-buyout architect Henry Kravis to real estate developer Trammell Crow, many leading 1980s speculators were also allies and campaign contributors. The chairman of the Federal Reserve Board, Alan Greenspan, was not just an economist but a New York money manager and consultant who had written a testimonial letter for Charles Keating, who was later to be convicted in the S&L scandal. Greenspan said that Lincoln Savings and Loan, Keating's flagship, was as sound as seventeen other "thriving" thrifts, sixteen of which wound up bankrupt.[44] Unlike Andrew Mellon, none of these high officials believed in letting the overextended speculators and developers go under in the name of a cleansing, rehabilitating financial Darwinism.

Consequently, as events unfolded after 1987, from the October

Crash through the 1988–89 S&L debacle to the 1990–92 crisis of junk bonds, real estate, banking and insurance, key Washington decisions were made with great concern for financial markets, banks, speculators and highly leveraged transactions, having the taxpaying middle class pay to bail these interests out. The results upheld the redistribution of the 1980s.

The most blatant example was the mammoth cost of sorting out the large portion of the savings and loan industry that had taken advantage of deregulation to speculate in everything from real estate to art and junk bonds, leading to numerous failures, sometimes through what amounted to open looting by owners. The initial stage of Washington's negligence—the excesses of deregulation, inept supervision and political protectiveness toward wrongdoers—was essentially bipartisan. It was the next stage, the costly financial mismanagement of the bailout, largely by the executive branch, that had a profound impact on the distribution of U.S. wealth and income.

In 1988, as the magnitude of the breakdown was becoming obvious to those directly involved, the Reagan administration's first approach was further privatization: groups of almost insolvent or insolvent S&Ls were assembled for sale to private buyers (corporate and individual) at low prices made even more attractive by huge tax breaks and subsidies. Thus the government's books didn't show a payout from the FSLIC insurance fund. The General Accounting Office later estimated that these hastily given tax breaks cost the government $8.5 billion (federal regulators ultimately sought the return of some of the money and commitments given in several of the major late-1988 deals).[45] This, however, was a prelude. A much larger burden fell on the public when the Bush administration, wanting to minimize immediate costs and afraid to alarm voters, decided to finance the bailout with federal bonds, issued off-budget by a quasi-governmental corporation, to be paid off over thirty years. Experts set the ultimate cost to taxpayers at between $300 billion and $500 billion—$1,200 to $2,000 for each American alive in 1990—and economists from Stanford University contended that over those forty years, total outlays might reach $1.3 trillion, with $900 billion representing interest payments alone.[46]

The overall U.S. economy also suffered, although estimates varied widely. The Congressional Budget Office, using a computer model designed to simulate the effects on the national income of the capital resources lost in the bailout, figured the overall loss for the years between 1980 and 2000 at about $484 billion, with the highest annual impact in the early 1990s—about $40 billion a year. As of early 1992, according to *The New York Times,* that was roughly equivalent to the output lost up to that point in the 1990–92 recession![47]

Ralph Nader's Public Citizen group argued that instead of issuing bonds several hundred billion dollars' worth of taxes should be levied over the next five to ten years on those who had been participants in the 1980s speculative bubble. Public Citizen praised a proposal that included an additional 7.5 percent tax on unearned income—interest, dividends and capital gains.[48] Other critics generally urged surcharges on individual and corporate income. Publisher William Randolph Hearst called for a 25 percent surtax on the profits of every bank or S&L that sold junk bonds or made bad loans until taxpayers were repaid for the cost of the bailout.[49] Self-styled populist Jim Hightower, chairman of the Financial Democracy Campaign, proposed surcharges on incomes above $540,000 a year and taxes on large currency trades. "The wealthy folks, those who had the party and made the mess in the 1980s, should pay for it in the 1990s," said Hightower, characterizing the administration's program as a "class transfer" of wealth from the middle class to the rich.[50] At the very least, the bailout spared investors who had moved deals and funds through high-flying S&Ls during the 1980s from paying for the costs of the breakdown. The generality of taxpayers would pay instead.

Then in 1991 it became clear that commercial banks also needed to be rescued—and with kindred considerations at stake: would investors and financial elites pay, or would taxpayers as a whole? That spring, Treasury Secretary Nicholas Brady had asked Congress for a package of $70 billion in taxpayer-backed loans to the Federal Deposit Insurance Corporation, denying that another bailout was under way because the bankers had pledged to repay the money when they were healthy again. Others thought the cost would be much higher. Congress reluctantly voted the funds, although skeptics suggested that instead of opening up yet another line of public credit, it would be cheaper to let some of the big banks fail and have the government reimburse depositors only up to $100,000 for each account. That, however, would have involved major losses by banks' stockholders, bondholders, creditors and large depositors.

Meanwhile the federal government was abetting a second, less obvious rescue of financial institutions, with the result that their profits— except in a few incurable cases—rose substantially.* Chairman Greenspan moved Federal Reserve Board deposits to needy institu-

*The prices of bank stocks also soared in 1991, rewarding shareholders.

tions, including Lincoln Savings and Loan. As identified by conservative financial columnist Warren Brookes, the Fed made huge "overnight" loans reaching nearly $100 million to Lincoln, just as it was about to fail, keeping the wolf away from the door for four months "to allow all those depositors with accounts of more than $100,000 to get out 'whole' from the Lincoln mess without losing a dime."[51] Otherwise, large deposits / made in search of high rates would not have been covered because federal deposit insurance stopped at $100,000.

In Chapter 6 we saw how banks imposed new charges and fees on depositors and checking-account holders without objection from regulators, permitting them to charge customers indirectly for the sharply rising cost of federal deposit insurance, in effect billing the cost of their earlier speculative practices to the public. Next, and far more significant, as the Federal Reserve Board relentlessly cut interest rates, letting banks reduce what they paid depositors and holders of checking accounts, regulators allowed the banks, many of them hard-pressed, to keep charging borrowers sky-high rates for credit-card interest and personal loans. Appendix C shows what dropped and what didn't. The spread was one of the largest and most profitable on record; commercial banks that ended 1991 paying depositors 4½ percent on their short-term money were charging ordinary borrowers three to four times as much.

Angered by the gap, Democrats on the House Banking Committee introduced legislation to require the nation's credit-card issuers, including banks, to "share the wealth" with borrowers by reducing their charges.[52] In late 1991 the Senate actually passed legislation to cap credit-card interest-rate charges, but then backed off when the stock market appeared to tremble. There were other implications for wealth distribution that went far beyond bank profits. As Chairman Greenspan eased interest rates, helping speculators and banks as well as small businessmen and would-be home buyers, a few economists, such as John Williams of American Business Econometrics, calculated a net drag on the economy as huge numbers of Americans, especially middle-class retirees, would suffer as interest payments tumbled. At the beginning of 1990, interest had represented 15 percent of U.S. personal income. In the next two years that percentage took its biggest slide since World War II.[53] Williams calculated that the four-point decline in short-term interest rates between autumn 1989 and autumn 1991 had caused a $34-billion-a-year drop in household interest income—a dangerous contraction—while interest payments by households fell by only $4 billion a year.[54] A significant chunk of the $30 billion net household loss was going from the pockets of Florida widows and retired Iowa farmers to financial institutions.*

As a result, there was little change in the distribution of wealth and income during the 1990s, despite the weakness of the economy and the financial and real estate crises. In 1991 the largest number of Americans since the Great Depression were receiving public assistance, average-family net worth was sliding and troubled state and local governments were raising taxes on everything from homes to potato chips to speeding tickets. Yet in 1992 the stock market was setting new highs, federal tax rates on the rich remained close to their post-1932 lows and bank stocks were climbing again, a sharp contrast with 1893–96 and 1929–33. Those crises, however, had not been managed by an activist government in behalf of the same financial elites that had created the bubble.

The Decline of Young America and the Trend to Wealth by Inheritance

For young Americans, those under thirty or thirty-five, two decades of polarization had brought a special, though widely unappreciated, irony: not only were they (and those younger) in danger of being the first generation of Americans to suffer a lower standard of living than their parents, but they would be the first generation to receive—or not receive—much of their economic opportunity from family inheritance, not personal achievement.

By the early 1990s it had become a cottage industry for journalists to show how young Americans were losing ground. Hardly any could buy a home. Many could not even afford to marry. Young men with only a high school education, who could have gone into steel plants or auto factories—and earned blue-collar middle-class wages—back when postwar America enjoyed the economic hegemony won at Bastogne and Iwo Jima, now faced what Brookings Institution economist Gary Burtless called "a future of lousy jobs." Only the skilled 25 percent, the college-educated, had middle-class opportunities. Huge numbers of others found themselves caught up in what some called the K-Mart Economy—low-paid employment in retail stores, discount centers, back offices and fast-food emporia.

---

*When the Federal Reserve Board's interest-rate reductions finally brought serious declines in mortgage interest rates in late 1991 and early 1992, the benefit to ordinary households increased, but Williams and some other economists contended that the near-term effects on overall household income were still negative.

Some of the statistics were extraordinary. Back in 1950 the average thirty-year-old man would have added 58 percent more pay by the time he reached forty, and in 1960 his successor would have added 44 percent more over those same ten years. By contrast, the thirty-year-old of 1977 had gained only 21 percent more by 1987.[55] In terms of real purchasing power, the earnings of a typical thirty-year-old high school graduate of 1991 bought about 20 percent less than the earnings of his counterpart of 1973, when the great postwar expansion came to an end. Research by the Children's Defense Fund and the Center for Labor Market Studies at Northeastern University developed an even more stark analysis. The average earnings, in 1986 dollars, of families headed by someone under thirty dropped from $19,243 in 1973 to $13,607 in 1987, a decline of nearly 30 percent. The drop was even larger—36 percent—for young families with children; and young families headed by high school dropouts lost nearly 52 percent. During the early years of the Great Depression, by comparison, the loss of purchasing power by Americans was roughly 27 percent.[56]

Meanwhile, persons between the ages of forty-five and seventy-five controlled the overwhelming bulk of America's household net worth, the proceeds of both the postwar era and the 1980s heyday. Future opportunities were expected to be thinner. Frank Levy and Richard C. Michel, in their book *The Economic Future of American Families,* projected that the baby-boom generation at middle age would have only half of the real net worth their parents had at that same stage.[57] With the American economy losing its power, their younger brothers and sisters would fall even further behind.

But not uniformly. For those who were twenty, thirty and thirty-five years old in the 1990s, achievement and inheritance were beginning to reverse their traditional economic roles. Some $8 trillion to $10 trillion in net worth was in the hands of Americans over fifty, and as it began to pass to the next generation—largely baby boomers—in the 1990s, the pattern of opportunity and success in the United States would be transformed. Economist Robert Avery of Cornell University, a leading student of the phenomenon, predicted that "we will soon be seeing the largest transfer of income in the history of the world. The passing of the extraordinary wealth created in America in the past five decades will speed up in the 1990s, as those alive and working during those years reach their 70s and 80s."[58]

Inheritance, then, was about to become a critical component of the younger generation's future, something America had never before experienced. Edward Wolff, a New York economist studying the pattern, contended that "if it weren't for gifts and inheritances, most baby boomers would never be able to accumulate any real wealth." Indeed, the process had already begun. In 1973, 56 percent of the total wealth held by persons aged thirty-five to thirty-nine was given them by their parents. By 1986 the figure for thirty-five- to thirty-nine-year-old baby boomers had risen to 86 percent.[59] Higher ratios were still to come, and according to economists, inheritances would peak between 1997 and 2011, with each year's volume equaling roughly 6 percent of GNP.[60]

If these predictions came true, baby boomers would be the most polarized and stratified generation in U.S. history. Economist Wolff projected that if inheritance followed the approximate lines of U.S. wealth concentration in the 1990s, then the wealth going to the top 1 percent would average $3 million, that going to the richest 5 percent (the 95th to 99th percentiles) would average $900,000. Thereafter, the 90th to 94th percentiles would average about $400,000, the 85th to 89th percentiles $200,000, and the 80th to 84th percentiles $100,000. Those in the middle fifth (40th to 59th percentiles) would receive $49,000. For those further down, inheritances would be negligible.[61] Among the upper few percentages, inheritance taxes would take a significant chunk, but the overall pattern would be unmistakable: inherited wealth would create a hereditary caste; class lines would harden.

For all these reasons—from the downscaling of Middle America to the declining net worth of the average family and the chances of hereditary stratification—economic polarization was becoming a reality in the 1990s. So doubts about the economic future and its fairness grew, and politics began to seethe. But as concern among ordinary families rose, history offered some disturbing precedents: the United States wasn't unique; other great economic powers had been there before—and the lessons they taught were disturbing.

C H A P T E R · 8

The Late-Twentieth-Century United States and the Historical Symptoms of Middle-Class Decline

The cities [Greek city-states] that were formerly great, have most of them become insignificant; and such as are at present powerful, were weak in olden time. I shall therefore discourse equally of both, convinced that human happiness never continues long in one state.

—Herodotus, fifth century B.C.

A number of influential Japanese writers and commentators were exchange students in the U.S. in 1950s. Many were greatly impressed by this high-point of American power. Many, too, have been appalled by America's social and sexual revolutions of the 1960s, its war-torn and oil-shocked 1970s, and its economic excesses during the 1980s. They see American decline, as Edward Gibbon viewed Roman decline, as a long process of unhappy change. Americans may not see it.

—*Japan Times*, 1992

I think America is at a crossroads and Americans know it. I think that Americans know we are winning the Cold War and losing the competitive war. I think they know that we are defeating the Soviet empire, but that we are losing the domestic struggle against the drugs, crime, ignorance and welfare. They know we are losing the world market to Germany, Japan and Korea. They know we are losing faith in our constitutional system, that they do not see it working. They do not see their leaders being effective. They do not see the structures their Founding Fathers gave them producing results. And so they are almost in agony.

—U.S. House Republican whip Newt Gingrich, 1992

While many ordinary Americans found their eroding circumstances economically painful and politically frustrating, they were hardly unique. Nor was the larger decline overtaking the United States unique. Holland and Britain had also fallen from their middle-class zeniths when manufacturing, trade, nationalism and bourgeois spirit gave way to "financialization"—the cumulating influence of finance, government debt, unearned income, *rentiers,* overseas investment, domestic economic polarization and social stratification.

Excessive preoccupation with finance and tolerance of debt are apparently typical of great economic powers in their late stages. They foreshadow economic decline, but often accompany new heights of cultural sophistication, in part because the hurly-burly expansion of the middle class and its values are receding. Yet these slow transitions involve real economic cost to the average person or family, and political restiveness reflects that.

This chapter will consider what happened to the middle classes and ordinary folk in three nations that succeeded one another as the dominant economic powers of modern Europe: the Britain of Queen Victoria and King Edward VII, Holland of the seventeenth and early eighteenth centuries, and imperial Spain of the sixteenth and early seventeenth centuries. Spain's precedents are less direct, but still worth some attention. All three provide a context in which to contemplate the United States at the end of the twentieth century.

The warning to Americans is pointed. Holland and Britain experienced a crisis of values and circumstances similar to what seems to be happening again in the United States. Just as the rise of the Dutch and British middle classes was inseparable from their countries' emergence as great powers, the onset of polarization and declining purchasing power for ordinary families in each country signaled a broad national decline.

To be sure, more was involved than the wider distribution of prosperity that accompanied manufacturing and was slowly lost by a shift to finance. Burdensome taxation was another frequent sign of decline. So was cosmopolitanism, and the way in which prolonged free-trade doctrine and retention of a costly global military role—so-called imperial overstretch—have also seemed to accompany the ebb of great powers' broadest prosperity. At early stages these trends had been helpful, but at late stages they have hurt the average citizen and family. In Chapter 10, we will look at how the United States might best learn from these lessons of the past, but first let us see what happened to the Dutch and British middle classes as their national economies rose and fell.

The Crucial Role of Manufacturing, Commerce and "the Middling Sort"

Some American economists of the 1980s and 1990s felt that the United States no longer needed some of its old manufacturing industries—steel, textiles, even consumer electronics—any more than it needed new ships to rebuild the almost vanished American merchant marine. These were the productive assets of another era. If other countries could produce such things better and more cheaply, then let them, the argument went. National boundaries were losing economic meaning. The United States, for its part, would thrive on finance, services and high-value-added manufactures. Besides, although the American economy was in transition, manufacturing circa 1990 still accounted for about the same share (23 percent) of the Gross National Product that it had ten to fifteen years earlier. Talk about the de-industrialization of America was misleading; large elements of manufacturing—pharmaceuticals, for example—had never been more profitable for shareholders.

What manufacturing in the United States no longer held out, however, was the opportunity for blue-collar workers to achieve middle-class status that had been so important from the 1940s to the mid-1970s. Not only did the average hourly wage in manufacturing fall during the 1980s, from $8.49 to $8.14 in constant 1982 dollars, but from Pittsburgh and Buffalo west to Missouri and Wisconsin, huge chunks of industrial America—a region quickly nicknamed the Rust Belt—had become graveyards of vocational mobility. Between 1985 and 1990, Flint, Michigan, whose dying automobile industry sparked a popular movie lampooning General Motors chairman Roger Smith, lost 30 percent of its automotive jobs and 20 percent of its manufacturing jobs.[1] In metropolitan Pittsburgh, the largest employer was health services, with over 100,000 workers by 1991, who earned far less than steelworkers, of whom only 25,000 remained. Local wits called Pittsburgh the Incredible Shrinking City because of its 12.8 percent population drop in the 1980s.[2] The longer-term decline was worse; between 1950 and 1990, 306,926 residents had departed, leaving only 369,879 behind. As we shall see, what happened to Flint, Pittsburgh and other American industrial cities resembled the fate of Enkhuizen, Leiden and the Zaan when Holland's fishing, textile and shipbuilding industries slumped in the eighteenth century, and then the woes of Teesmouth, Lancashire, South Wales and Clydeside as British steel, textiles, coal and shipbuilding declined after World War I.

Yet the overall story of how U.S. manufacturing was losing its earlier ability to support a blue-collar middle class was more complex. Jobs lost to foreign competition in heavily unionized, highly paid industries like steel, autos and machinery were not being replaced simply by low-wage service jobs at McDonald's and K-Mart. Sometimes they were, but not *necessarily*. Between 1980 and 1990, manufacturing employment in the United States dropped by only 6 percent—from 20.3 million to 19.1 million. More to the point, manufacturing work was shifting from unionized heavy industry to nonunionized light industry, and many of the new manufacturing jobs—in computerboard assembly, beverage bottling or grocery manufacturing, for example—didn't pay as well as the old ones. Often that wage reduction was the difference between middle-class status and ex-middle-class status. The worst-paying jobs of all were in the sweatshops that reappeared during the 1980s, many employing the growing number of legal and illegal immigrants entering the United States and willing to take positions shunned by even laid-off native workers. The wages of the unskilled, in particular, eroded as immigration boosted the foreign-born share of the U.S. work force from 6.9 percent in 1980 to 9.3 percent in 1988.[3]

The net effect on one relatively successful Middle American city can be seen in Fort Wayne, Indiana.[4] After 28,000 jobs vanished in the early 1980s, one third of them because a large International Harvester plant closed, the Fort Wayne area rallied to add 57,000 new positions later in the decade, winning a place on *Inc.* magazine's 1989 list of places where job and economic growth was highest. Insurance and other services were part of the resurgence, but so were new poorly paid manufacturing jobs, because once Harvester shut down, there was nothing left to keep a floor under manufacturing wages. Declining wages, in other words, fueled local recovery. Thomas Guthrie, director of Purdue University's Community Research Institute, acknowledged that "in part, we've traded high-paying union jobs in and around Fort Wayne for relatively low-paying non-union jobs farther out" in surrounding rural areas.[5] Lower wages made such companies competitive internationally, but millions of Americans dropped out of middle-class ranks. This was the slippage so vivid in the 1980–89 Illinois income and tax data examined on pages 170–71.

More than income was lost with high-value-added manufacturing. Historically, national populations tend to be at their most spirited as they shape the industries that briefly move their countries ahead of the rest of the world—the revolutionary Dutch of the early seventeenth century, expelling Spanish overlords while gathering world trade into Amsterdam; the British of the mid-nineteenth century, already leading the Industrial Revolution, amazing the world with the technology on display at the famous 1851 Crystal Palace Exhibition; and mid-twentieth-century Americans, building the world's largest and richest middle class on their massive post–World War II manufacturing supremacy. Finance cannot nurture a comparable class, because only a small elite portion of any national population—Dutch, British or American—can share in the profits of bourse, merchant bank and countinghouse. Manufacturing, transportation and trade supremacies, by contrast, provide a broader national prosperity in which the ordinary person can man the production lines, mines, mills, wheels, mainsails and nets. Once this stage of economic development yields to the next, with its sharper divisions from capital, skills and education, great middle-class societies lose something vital and unique, just what worriers believed was happening again to the United States in the late twentieth century.

History's lessons are instructive, even the lesson of great-power Spain, with its limited manufacturing and its small middle class, that such a prosperity is not sustainable. When Spain began receiving growing quantities of gold from the New World after 1492, textiles and ceramics, the iron of Vizcaya, the blades of Toledo, were all examples of Spanish manufacturing success, albeit limited. Visitors to such cities in northern Spain as Burgos and Medina del Campo described them in the early 1500s as dominated by merchants, artisans and financiers.[6] A bourgeoisie was in the making.

Yet by the mid-1550s, the effect of ever-growing supplies of gold, the disdain for trade on the part of Spain's military and aristocratic *hidalgo* tradition, and the anti-individualist Counter-Reformation attack on Protestantism all came together to squelch industry, the bourgeois spirit and the incipient middle class. Laws overtly stigmatized pursuit of trade and manufacturing: why stoop to manufacture when Holland, London, Milan and Flanders were willing to do so for Spanish gold? Guilds were disbanded, the incipient industrial and mercantile centers lost half or more of their populations by the century's end. By the early 1600s, as it became clear that Spain's lassitude and polarization between rich and poor would soon leave her vulnerable when the gold and silver of Mexico and Peru ran out, the economic wise men of the *arbitrista* movement identified the danger brought on by the lack of a manufacturing economy and a bourgeoisie: Spain "has come to be an extreme contrast of rich and poor, and there is no means of adjusting them to one another. Our condition is one in which we have rich who look at ease, or poor who beg, and we lack people of the middling sort, whom neither wealth nor poverty prevents from pursuing the rightful kind of business enjoined by natural law."[7]

The emergent country that proved what mercantile spirits could achieve was Holland circa 1600, even then in the process of winning its independence from Spain. In contrast to aristocratic Spain, puritan Holland was dominated by artisans and merchants—the brede middenstand—with a strong sense of its own destiny as a class and nation:

> They stamped indelibly the persona of their class on Dutch society. Their cautious, prudent, self-satisfied, unostentatious faces stare out of the canvases of Rembrandt or Hals, giving little away of their unconscious drives, but speaking eloquently of the sobriety and dedication of their lives. The comely facades of their great houses along the Keizersgracht and Heerengracht of Amsterdam, dignified, restrained, so unemphatic in their elegance, bespeak the integrity of generations of bourgeois endeavour—that amalgam of hard work, calculated risk, guarded self-indulgence, all without panache or ostentation or flamboyance, which became the hallmarks of the Dutch character.[8]

Until 1620 or so, the Dutch thrived mostly on seafaring and the booming commerce of Amsterdam. By mid-century, however, they had used their technical sophistication and control of vital raw commodities to build successful industries ranging from textiles to tobacco, sugar, distilling, Delftware, diamonds and shipbuilding. Supported by Holland's bourgeois virtues, trading preeminence and credit, Dutch manufactures soon dominated a number of European markets. Visitors to Holland circa 1680 were struck by Dutch innovations, ranging from multiple-blade timber saws to Leeuwenhoek's microscope and grinding machines for processing coffee, chocolate, mustard and liqueurs.[9] Yet by some point in the early to mid-eighteenth century— Dutch historians disagree just when—Holland had lost its cultural, industrial and technological momentum.

We have no need of a compendium, but by roughly 1750, although Holland still had its sea trade, the country's high-value-added exports had shriveled: Leiden's textiles slumped, so did Gouda's pipe industry, and Delftware was swept from the drawing rooms of Europe.[10] The Dutch industrialists and technicians, who were to the seventeenth century what Scots engineers would be to the nineteenth, faded from prominence.

Finance, as we shall see, rose in its place, bringing economic and social polarization—the erosion of the *brede middenstand* and prudent, unostentatious Calvinism. Historians call the mid-eighteenth century Holland's Periwig Era because of its stratifying wealth and rising social pretensions. French clothes, paintings, wines and culture had become fashionable in the late seventeenth century, and historian Fernand Braudel interpreted the spread of the French language as another way for the emerging elites to stand aloof from the common people.[11] By 1764, James Boswell could write from Utrecht that: "Most of their principal towns are sadly decayed, and instead of finding every mortal employed, you meet with multitudes of poor creatures who are starving in idleness. Utrecht is remarkably ruined. There are whole lanes of wretches who have no other subsistence than potatoes, gin and stuff which they call tea and coffee; and what is worst of all, I believe they are so habituated to this life that they would not take work if it should be offered to them . . . you see, then, that things are very different here from what most people in England imagine. Were Sir William Temple to revisit these Provinces, he would scarcely believe the amazing alteration which they have undergone." Fourteen years later, the Dutch newspaper *De Borger* ventured an analysis of Holland much like those of the Spanish *arbitristas* one hundred seventy-five years earlier: "the body of the Commonwealth would shortly consist of little more than rentiers and beggars—the two kinds of people who are the least useful to the country."[12] In both Spain and Holland, the ordinary people were left with nothing from their country's zenith.

Britain, too, achieved its peak of worldwide supremacy and comparative affluence on a wave of middle-class economic and political emergence conjoined with manufacturing and the Industrial Revolution. Middle-class political consciousness, which dated back to the late 1700s, finally triumphed in the 1830s and 1840s with the democratization of parliamentary constituencies and the repeal of the corn laws, which protected the agricultural interests of the British aristocracy.[13] The term "middle class" came into actual use around 1812, quickly developing larger implications—both in the narrow sense as a shorthand for the emerging commercial and manufacturing classes and in the far grander context of the middle class as the emerging repository of Britain's new liberal individualism and commercial spirit. Thomas Macaulay, the principal historian of the age, described it as "that brave, honest and stout-hearted class, which is as anxious for the maintenance of order and the security of property, as it is hostile to corruption and oppression."[14]

The extent to which such florid language dripped with politics is important, because by the 1850s and 1860s the British middle class was the sort of touchstone that Middle America would become a century later. Though aristocrats still dominated the cabinets of Liberal and Conservative prime ministers alike, the rise of the middle class was the true measure of Britain's greatness, and elements of the Liberal party were already beginning to theorize about rule by a democratic majority.[15] In short, the Britain that became the "workshop of the world" in the 1840s and 1850s—and by 1860 controlled 40 to 45 percent of the world's industry, two fifths of its trade in manufactures and one third of its merchant ships—was a nation in which a rising middle class was bursting its old bonds, just as the burghers of Holland had been some two centuries earlier and the citizens of the postwar United States would be a century later.

It was reasonably clear that British national self-confidence and Britain's share of world manufactures probably peaked more or less together around 1870. The pattern of later decline was not so neat; great supremacies are not lost quickly. Concern about foreign competition began to gnaw at national optimism in the 1870s, especially after the downturn of 1873, but the average Briton's standard of living continued to improve. Gains were still occurring in the 1890s, even after fifteen years in which British industrial production grew by an average of only 1.5 percent annually, much less than that of the United States (which now led Britain in manufacturing) or Germany (which was catching up). Nevertheless, the 1890s were the decade in which some deterioration came into the open as Britons began to see their great industries—steel, coal, even machine tools and engineering—losing ground to American and German competition, and by the mid-1890s, popular writers in Britain were tapping growing popular anxieties with books entitled *Made in Germany* and *The American Invaders.*[16] If it all sounds familiar to Americans of the 1990s, it should.

As the twentieth century dawned the dilemma had become clearer: British finance and overseas investment had never been so strong, with implications we will pursue later in this chapter, but British manufacturing was flagging. Joseph Chamberlain, the prophetic colonial secretary, warned in 1903 that "in the course of another generation, this will be much less an industrial country inhabited by a race of skillful artisans than a distributive country with a smaller population consisting of rich consumers on the one hand and people engaged in the work of distribution."[17] The gap between the rich and the ordinary folk was growing, which Chamberlain thought inauspicious, because the living standards of the average family had finally started to decline even as the dividends, interest income and life-styles of the rich continued to expand.

For the Victorian equivalent of the median-income family, historians seem to agree that erosion began around the turn of the century, when manufacturing began to slide. G.D.H. Cole, in his famous chronicle of *The British Common People, 1746–1946,* concludes:

> There can be no doubt that the standard was falling. Between the later 'nineties, when the cost of living began to rise, and about 1910, when the great labour unrest set in, home consumption of wheat per head of population remained stationary, and home consumption of both meat and sugar declined. There was a great fall in the consumption of both beer and spirits; but it does not appear that this was offset by a rise in the consumption of food. According to Mr. G.H. Wood's calculations, average real wage-rates were 4 per cent lower in 1910 than they had been in 1896; and even in 1914 the purchasing power of 1896 had not been regained. Between 1899 and 1913 real wages had actually declined by about 10 per cent. Wages were reckoned as having constituted in 1880 about 41 or 42 per cent of the national income: in 1913 they were only 35 or 36 per cent. Doubtless, some part of this decrease was due to the increased numbers of salary-earners and professionals; but even so there is a large fall left unaccounted for.[18]

Sampling in London revealed a fall of 6 percent in real wages between 1900–1901 and 1911–12, while other surveys confirmed this deterioration.[19] As manufacturing declined, British industrial workers, whose wages in 1860 or 1870 had exceeded those on the Continent, were slipping for reasons similar to those confronting U.S. manufacturing employees in the Rust Belt of the 1980s: increasing competition from overseas competitors whose workers were paid less and whose plants were newer. Moreover, the die seems to have been cast. British manufacturing boomed again during World War I, boosting worker incomes and living standards, but then more ground was lost from 1920 to 1924–25 as postwar economic reality sent British heavy industry into another retreat.

For a generation, ordinary working-class Britons experienced the decline earlier visited upon the Spanish and Dutch. On the other hand, the middle classes, which, by including clerks and shopkeepers, accounted for some 25 to 30 percent of the population of Britain just before World War I, continued to gain in the 1900–1914 era. The upper-middle class fared very well, and the lower-middle class held its own, although economists began to take note of what would squeeze Middle America three generations later—the unique burden of middle-class expenditure, with its relatively heavy outlays for insurance, schools, health care, home purchase and the like.[20] The middle class did not come under severe pressure until the end of the 1930s and the war years, when Britain, having fought one draining conflict and now embroiled in another, neared the end of its financial resources.

Nevertheless, in an irony we shall revisit in Chapter 10's look ahead at America's possible pathways, the rich-poor divisions of the Edwardian era radicalized British politics, making the socialist Labour party the official opposition, and then later in the 1920s, Labour became the government. Social welfare expenditures climbed, as did taxes and a mild redistribution of income, and from the mid-1920s on, the working class found its living standards improving, especially in the 1930s as consumer prices declined, wages more or less held even and the welfare state began to take firm hold. Prosperous Britons, conversely, found *their* income tax burdens climbing to help the bottom two thirds of the population. Between 1913 and 1937 the total effect of income redistribution by government was to raise the incomes of the working classes by 8 to 14 percent and *reduce* those of the upper and middle classes by 10 to 15 percent.[21] Parenthetically, social historians differentiate between the lower-middle and middle classes, who did better or held steady in the between-the-war years because of both relatively low taxes and continued availability of domestic servants, and the upper- and upper-middle-income groups, who were losing ground.[22] Britain's decline was catching up with them.

For Jaguar- and Daimler-driving Britons, moreover, worse was still to come. Taxes rose in the late 1930s as the United Kingdom rearmed against Hitler and the welfare state bit even deeper. Then, as World War II cut British global economic clout and investment income to the bone, the real, pretax income of the wealthiest 100,000 plunged by 64 percent between 1938 and 1949 while real pretax income for the largely upper-middle-class top 500,000 Britons fell by 37 percent.[23] And that was *pretax*; the Treasury's higher levies aggravated the relative decline.

To upper-bracket Americans of the 1990s these precedents were only partially relevant, because mid-century socialism in Britain and elsewhere was on a rare historic roll. By the late 1940s, indeed, welfarism, socialism and redistribution of income had partially reversed the polarization of the Edwardian years even though heavy manufacturing would never recover its old prosperity. As we have seen, British workers were better off, with higher incomes; elements of the lower-middle class were, too. But for the upper-middle class, the 2 percent or 3 percent of British families in the professional and managerial classes who had lived so well in 1910 on £1,500 or £2,000 a year, when such families generally had a cook, a parlor maid and one or two other servants, when meals were a groaning board of joints and roasts, and holidays were excursions to Nice, Tuscany or Montreux, the economic circumstances of 1945–49 were an extraordinary comedown. British finances had been shattered by the war; senior officials hung on details of the latest dollar loan from Washington. Facing punitive taxes, some dukes and earls held on to their family castles by personally conducting guided tours for gawking coveys of tourists from Paducah and Burbank, but for the average London solicitor, Edinburgh bank manager or Coventry works director, the late 1940s were unpleasant in a way that went far beyond crimped income.

Few Britons care to remember, but although World War II ended in August 1945, food rationing for British families didn't end until 1954. Worse still, in peacetime 1948, food allowances had fallen *below* the wartime average.[24] The average adult male's weekly allowance was 13 ounces of meat, 1½ ounces of cheese, 6 ounces of butter and margarine, 1 ounce of cooking fat, 8 ounces of sugar, 2 pints of milk and 1 egg. Doctors reported that poor diets were lowering resistance to infection, especially among older citizens. In pursuit of new and cheap protein sources, the government brought in huge quantities of *snoek,* a tasteless fish no one wanted to eat, from the waters off South Africa. *Vogue* magazine published recipes for cauliflower soup and stuffed marrows. Going out, even to the Savoy Grill, was no solution, as one contemporary chronicle recalls:

> In restaurants, bread was made one of the maximum number of three dishes allowed at any one meal. Served as bread and cheese, or as the ground floor of Welsh rarebit or sardines on toast, it didn't count as a separate dish. But any customer who now demanded bread with his soup would find, by the end of the meal, that he had forfeited his right to a pudding.[25]

The lavish tables at which Edwardians stuffed themselves were only a memory. Fresh fruit was a luxury often unavailable in the nation that just forty years earlier had been Europe's best provisioned. Air Vice Marshal "Pathfinder" Bennett, a war hero, won new fame by flying in peaches from France. Even the royal family was constrained—when Princess Elizabeth got married, it was announced she would be given

100 ration coupons for her wedding, but rationing would apply. British tourists, yesteryear's "milords," traveled abroad in no style worth mentioning—if they traveled at all—because only a small amount of money could be taken out of the country, which needed every shilling for foreign exchange. The decline of upper- and upper-middle-class Britain in the long generation between 1914 and the late 1940s was a painful and extraordinary one. Even in the late 1980s, when Britain had a boom of sorts under Margaret Thatcher, British per capita incomes had fallen behind Italy's, whereas in 1910, the average Briton had been roughly twice as well off as the average Italian. As things turned out, the ebb of manufacturing and of ordinary British living standards that was shrugged off during the 1900–1914 period had been a signal to heed.

Debt, Rentiers and the Pitfalls of Financialization

A significant part of what overtook each of these nations was the emergence of finance, debt and an investor or rentier class within their respective societies, as the bourgeois emphasis on manufacturing and trade diminished. In many respects, of course, sharp finance is an asset. Highly developed financial services have been a strategic advantage to major powers, as well as a useful national economic cushion when manufacturing industries began to decline. Yet the drawback lay in how investment, speculation and brokerage, at a certain point, worked to polarize incomes and wealth at the expense of what had been—at least in Holland and Britain—aggressive societies of entrepreneurs, tinkerers and engineers. Because a similar pattern of booming finance while old manufacturing industries declined was apparent in the United States of the 1980s and 1990s, it's useful to review the process of "financialization" and its effect on the ebb of the former great economic powers—even atypical Spain.

In a sense, Spain was the ultimate hollowed-out economy—a financial shell once the flood of New World gold and silver in the sixteenth century undercut any manufacturing potential. The leader of Spain's *arbitrista* economic critics, González de Cellorigo, looked back from the next century with a regretful perception that Spain's gold had not been "true wealth" because it increased only its stock of precious metals, not its productive agricultural or industrial capacity. "Money is not true wealth," de Cellorigo said, and Spain's was being unproductively invested—"dissipated on thin air—on papers, contracts, *censos* and letters of exchange, on cash, and silver and gold instead of being expended on things that yield profits and attract riches from outside to augment the riches within."[26]

More specifically, the huge wealth brought by the treasure fleets was fatal for embryonic Spanish industry; it eroded belief in hard work and manual labor while also forcing up prices, making local labor and goods expensive. Cheap foreign products poured in, convincing Spaniards that so long as the gold lasted, other nations would produce their needs. In addition, the willingness of European bankers to lend money against the arrival of the galleons at Seville made Spain's already wasteful Hapsburg rulers even more so. The result, by the 1540s, was that Charles V had borrowed from the bankers of Genoa, Germany and Antwerp by mortgaging large chunks of *future* Spanish revenues. Innovative debt instruments proliferated, another poor augury. The Crown also began to raise money by selling, on a mammoth scale, bonds or annuities called *juros,* which paid about 7 percent a year. Financial practices like these, besides demanding huge shares of the national revenues and diverting money that might have been invested in more solid enterprise, also created an influential and apparently pernicious creditor class:

> Juros were bought by foreign and native bankers, by merchants and nobles, and by anyone with a little money to spare. The result was the growth of a powerful rentier class in Castile, investing its money not in trade or industry but in profitable Government bonds, and living contentedly on its annuities. If ever a suggestion was made, as it was in 1552, that the Government should undertake a gradual redemption of the juros, there was an immediate outcry from all holders of juros, who saw no safe alternative for their investments except in the purchase of land, the price of which would rise sharply if the juros were redeemed.[27]

To put the perils of debt financing in perspective, at the death of King Philip II in 1598, interest payments on the government's debt took two thirds of Spain's yearly revenues. Spanish elites had come to look to investment in juros and place-holding in the bureaucracies of the Catholic Church, the Royal Court and the government to secure the incomes they haughtily disdained to earn from commerce. Together with the hunger for titles of nobility (which included exemption from most taxes), these attitudes led the bourgeoisie to throw in with the unproductive upper class. Narrow monetary wealth, irresponsible finance and an indolent rentier class were important in the decline that was taking hold in Spain one hundred to one hundred fifty years after Columbus's voyages.

The extraordinary thing was that Calvinist Holland, through a different evolution, reached a somewhat similar stage within two centuries. The ability of the thrifty, puritanical Dutch to save large sums of money and lend them at low interest rates had been central to the country's rapid emergence as the seventeenth-century center of world commerce. By the end of that century, however, after two or three generations of prosperity, finance was taking on a different social role. Traders were complaining that whereas the town regents had previously been active merchants, they were no longer active, "but derived their income from houses, lands and money at interest."[28] Rentier influence steadily intensified, and by the mid-eighteenth century, when Dutch manufacturing, fishing and engineering were losing headway, Dutch banking, finance and the Amsterdam stock market were booming, aggravating social and economic polarization. "Seventy years ago," wrote one foreign observer in 1771, "the wealthiest businessmen [in Amsterdam] did not have gardens or country houses comparable to those their brokers own today. The worst thing is not the building and immense expense of maintaining these fairy-tale palaces, or rather bottomless pits, it is that the distraction and negligence occasioned by this luxury often causes prejudice to business and trade."[29] Moreover, not only was Dutch capital forsaking industry and commerce, switching to government finance, stocks and credit operations, but it was increasingly looking to overseas rather than domestic investments.

No other eighteenth-century nation matched the Dutch as international lenders. British authorities estimated that in 1737 Dutch investors held about 22.7 percent of the British public debt, and a 1762 estimate put the proportion at 25 percent. Meanwhile, Hollanders were estimated to hold about a third of the stock in both the Bank of England and the East India Company.[30] This huge foreign investment sparked controversy, however, because critics were outraged at how so much money was being invested abroad rather than at home to relieve Holland's decay and unemployment. True, the interest and dividends that flowed back to Holland were large, but they went mostly to the rich and increased economic polarization. Fernand Braudel, criticizing the "perversion of capital," noted that Holland's small financial elite had so much to invest, even as ordinary Dutchmen starved, that by the late eighteenth century they were drawn into increasingly risky loans, producing bubbles and panics. The money men themselves recognized how they had drawn apart from the rest of Holland. Finally, after sporadic tax and food riots, Holland faced the angry but unsuccessful Batavian Revolution of 1780, when mobs decried *les richards* in a foretaste of the French Revolution a decade later.[31]

Britain, too, saw the emergence of a substantial rentier class as it reached its global trade and manufacturing zenith in the 1870s. The sums put Dutch finance in the shade. Since the end of the Napoleonic wars in 1815, Britain's annual foreign investment had ballooned from £6 million to £75 million, for a grand total of £700 million in 1875, and the resultant annual flow of dividends and interest back into Britain exceeded £50 million, also a huge sum for those days. According to one chronicle, "by 1871 Britain contained 170,000 'persons of rank and property' without visible occupation—almost all of them women, or rather 'ladies'; a surprising number of them unmarried ladies. Stocks and shares, including shares in family firms formed into 'private companies' for this purpose, were a convenient way of providing for widows, daughters and other relatives who could not—and no longer needed to—be associated with the management of property and enterprise."[32]

Even more to the point, banks and investment firms had prospered and multiplied, with additional stock exchanges to supplement London's having been organized in Liverpool, Manchester and Glasgow during the 1840s. Through the 1890s, the rise of finance was not generally criticized as being at the expense of other parts of the British economy. But then, as the new century opened, such worries found increasing voice.

In a split that would foreshadow the late-twentieth-century United States, ordinary families dependent on manufacturing employment were seeing their purchasing power decline, while Britain's turn-of-the-century rich enjoyed a surge in income from business profits and interest—up 55 percent between 1899 and 1913, according to income tax authorities.[33] Revealingly, while "accumulation of capital out of profits became swift beyond all precedent," according to historian G.D.H. Cole, relatively little of that flowed into *British* industry. Instead, in the manner of the Dutch, most was invested in overseas portions of the empire or in foreign countries where interest rates were higher or where greater profits could be realized by taking advantage of cheaper labor. What fattened finance, however, often had the simultaneous effect of helping countries that competed with British industry. From a total of £700 million in 1875, British overseas investments soared to £1 billion in 1900, £3 billion in 1907 and £4 billion by 1914.[34] By 1913 overseas holdings were bringing the British investing classes a net annual return of about £200 million a year—a huge sum, which exceeded the annual budget of the British government, and which was only minimally taxed.

Despite the limitations of early-twentieth-century economic statistics, a small minority of British economists and politicians sensed a dangerous imbalance. Even back in 1865, Matthew Arnold had suggested what must have seemed farfetched at the time—"an imminent danger of England losing immeasureably in all ways, declining into a sort of greater Holland."[35] Colonial Secretary Joseph Chamberlain, in words that now seem prophetic, warned that Britain could not survive as merely "a hoarder of invested securities" if it was not also the "creator of new wealth." In 1904, to a meeting of bankers in the City of London, he said that "granted you are the clearing house of the world," but

> are you entirely beyond anxiety as to the permanence of your great position. . . . Banking is not the creator of our prosperity, but is the creation of it. It is not the cause of our wealth, but it is the consequence of our wealth; and if the industrial energy and development which has been going on for so many years in this country were to be hindered or relaxed, then finance, and all that finance means, will follow trade to the countries which are more successful than ourselves.[36]

Financialization, however, also meant that—from their own perspective—bankers, insurers and financiers had good reason to fear that protection of declining home manufacturing industries could bring foreign retaliation against Britain's profitable shipping, investments and financial services. And they *were* profitable. Even after the economic blows of the 1914–18 war, while British heavy industry sank further during the 1920s, the City of London managed to hold its place as the center of world finance. What's more, British international investments actually earned more than ever before, as did financial and insurance services, which seemed to disprove Chamberlain's fears. Then, however, the devastating economic effects of World War II tragically confirmed the forecast that finance would be a thin reed. The £175 million Britain had earned from overseas investments in 1938 slumped to £73 million in 1940. The postwar annual figures nominally returned to prewar levels, but adjusted for inflation they were much lower—and Britain also staggered under the weight of $13 billion of new external liabilities. Financial supremacy followed economic and manufacturing supremacy to the United States, and we have seen how hard times caught up with middle- and upper-middle-class Britons, although the City of London—like Amsterdam—still maintained an important world role.

The purpose of these quick summaries is to illustrate, particularly with reference to Holland and Britain, a progression all too visible in the United States of the 1990s. The later-stage financialization of the world's leading economic powers has generally accompanied the decline of domestic industry and led to the growth of a rentier class, the erosion of economic patriotism, the rise of rich-poor polarization and the economic stagnation (or worse) of the average citizen or family. If the examples I have given in this chapter seem repetitive, they are meant to underscore that the problem is repetitive—and the extent to which the same trends and circumstances were recurring in the United States in the 1980s and 1990s makes the Dutch and British lessons especially cautionary.

We have seen that, much as in turn-of-the-century Britain, heavy industry in the United States has receded significantly, eliminating jobs that provided high wages for many ordinary breadwinners. Simultaneously, burgeoning U.S. financial services—the business of insurance companies, credit managers, stockbrokers, shipping agents and investment bankers—sold well enough in global markets to offset a fair portion of the U.S. trade deficit in manufactured goods. The service and investment sectors were king, even though by 1990 foreigners took almost as much from the United States in interest and dividends as Americans earned overseas. A decade earlier, the U.S. earnings edge had been lopsided.

By some calculations, the rising percentage of U.S. investments directed overseas cost many American jobs. Economists Norman Glickman of Rutgers University and Douglas Woodward of the University of South Carolina estimated the loss at 2.7 million positions in the United States between 1977 and 1986.[37] By reducing domestic employment, these overseas investments also worsened economic polarization in the United States—and according to a National Bureau of Economic Research study, the increase in the trade deficit during the 1980s brought the same effect.

Whatever was happening to manufacturing workers, the earnings of American financiers had never been higher. At their peak in the late 1980s, the highest-earning individuals in the U.S. financial community, as cataloged each year by *Financial World* magazine, counted levels of income and wealth far exceeding those of the Dutch financiers of the Periwig period and Britain's Edwardian moneymen.* These riches were further confirmation of rising economic polarization. The same

---

*The financial community's fees, incomes and wealth during this period are discussed at some length in Chapter 6 of *The Politics of Rich and Poor.*

mergers, leveraged buyouts and other restructurings of American industry, devastating for so many blue- and white-collar workers, were manna for Wall Street and its attendant law firms, proxy solicitors and accountants. And like Spain, Holland and Britain, each in turn, the United States of the early 1990s was home to a disproportionate financial and rentier class. Between the mid-1970s and the late 1980s, the percentage of U.S. national income categorizable as unearned—interest, dividends and rents, rather than wages and salaries—grew from 14 percent to 20 percent. New financial and debt instruments proliferated by the hundreds, producing zoological acronyms like LIONS (Lehman Investment Opportunity Notes), CATS (Certificates of Accrual on Treasury Certificates), OPPOSSMS (Options to Purchase or Sell Specified Mortgage-backed Securities) and LYNX (Liquid Yield Note Exchanges).* In a controversial statement to the Japanese Diet, Prime Minister Kiichi Miyazawa, while admitting that Japan shared the problem of excessive financialization, argued that during the 1980s the United States had become so caught up in Wall Street speculation and easy money that it neglected manufacturing and stopped producing engineers.†

Rising indebtedness was another troubling sign. As with previous great powers, economic complexity, debt and speculation fed on each other in the United States of the 1980s. Conservatives replaced liberals as the principal excuse-makers for federal debt and deficits. In 1992 the Bush administration acknowledged that federal deficits of $200 billion to $400 billion a year were inevitable at least through 1997; meanwhile, government debt had expanded so much that net federal interest payments came to $195 billion a year, swallowing 15 percent of the total budget—up from just $17 billion and 7 percent in 1973.

That 15 percent was well under the two thirds of the yearly budget that Spanish debt service required by the 1590s, but, like Spanish 7

---

*The prize for the new financing instrument with the most amusing acronym, however, went to sale-and-leaseback obligations—SLOBs.

†Miyazawa's statement, distorted in some reports, was actually quite reasonable: "Over the last 10 years," he said, "it seems that America has reached the point that the mindset to produce things and create value has loosened sharply. Many people getting out of college have gone to Wall Street for very high salaries, with the result that the number of engineers who produce goods has gone down quickly." Miyazawa then criticized the "money market" because of its junk bonds, leveraged buyouts and large loans that require big interest payments. "These things, which nobody thought could last long, have gone on for 10 years," Miyazawa continued. "And I have thought for a long time that the work ethic is lacking as far as that area is concerned" ("Miyazawa: Work Ethic Flags in U.S.," *Washington Post,* February 4, 1992).

percent juros, Washington's huge interest outlays represented a transfer to rentiers of money that could have been used for investment in industry and infrastructure. By 1989–90, interest payments to Americans alone had grown so large—about 15 percent of personal income—that when short-term interest rates plummeted, the decline in household income caused by slumping interest payments significantly affected U.S. purchasing power. At the same time, observers made the point that besides draining industry and abetting private indebtedness, the federal government's huge outlays for servicing U.S. long-term debt at high interest rates represented a thinly hidden transfer of wealth.[38] George Will, the conservative columnist, stated the case with particular flair:

> To pay the interest component of the 1988 budget will require a sum ($210 billion) equal to approximately half of all the personal income-tax receipts. This represents, as Sen. Pat Moynihan has said, a transfer of wealth from labor to capital unprecedented in American history.
>
> Tax revenues are being collected from average Americans (the median income of a family of four is slightly under $30,000) and given to the buyers of U.S. government bonds—buyers in Beverly Hills, Lake Forest, Shaker Heights and Grosse Pointe, and Tokyo and Riyadh.[39]

This, of course, is another way in which great-power "financialization" has been a burden on ordinary families. History, alas, suggests that the whole process, while destructive, also has an air of inevitability.

Taxes and Middle-Class Decline

If high public debt and interest payments to a rentier class have often been a signal of great-power decline, unfair or oppressive taxes are another signal. When taxes are high in emerging great powers, reasonable balance and fairness usually have been observed. The United States, for example, had imposed high taxes on the rich in the decade before World War II and during the two golden decades after 1945. Holland, during its emergence as a great power, required Europe's highest taxes to finance its revolution against Spain. The tax policy of a declining power, however, often displays characteristics different from those of the policy of happier periods. Some of the tax trends in the United States of the 1980s and early 1990s, such as California's sales levy on snack foods rather than on luxuries, burgeoning state and local fees and charges, and the layers of federal taxation that wound up making middle-class marginal rates higher than those of the rich, were omens, although mild next to earlier European excesses.

Hapsburg Spain levied a tax called the *servicio,* imposed by local authorities on a list of taxpayers or ratepayers from which the *hidalgos,* or noblemen, were exempted. This kind of charge put the burden of paying for government on the peasantry and what there was of a middle class, inducing wealthy businessmen to abandon their enterprise and buy "hidalgo" status in order to escape taxation.[40] The declining Holland of the mid-eighteenth century imposed Europe's highest taxes, mostly consumption taxes that fell disproportionately on the poor and sat lightly on the rich, whose growing wealth was provocative. One historian noted that Dutch resentment of "patrician opulence . . . gathered momentum through the mid-18th Century and kindled an increasing number of [tax] riots and disturbances."[41]

By contrast, the British were lightly taxed as their nation's relative decline began in the 1880s and 1890s, so taxes were not an obvious culprit. But taxes rose sharply later, so that for an upper-middle-class family with £10,000 a year, the share taken by income tax escalated from 8 percent in 1913–14 to 39 percent in 1937–38.[42] Then from 1938 to 1949, as we have seen, the tax burdens of upper-class and upper-middle-class Britons escalated again, not just because of Britain's growing debt burden, but also because the income tax became a vehicle for deliberate downward redistribution of income. Taxes clearly made Britain's postwar decline worse.

Taxes in the early-1990s United States were in between: lower than those of most other major nations, but of greater overall weight than those of Britain circa 1925. More to the point, for ordinary Americans taxes were starting to show some resemblance to the Spanish and Dutch precedents. The danger sign, however, lay less in the total U.S. tax burden than in the inequities of its arrangement and distribution.

Free Trade, Immigration, Cosmopolitan Culture and "Imperial Overstretch" Military Policy

The eras in which great economic powers have been dominated by assertive middle classes have been provincial rather than sophisticated. Cosmopolitan internationalism has come at a later stage when economic vitality is past its peak.

The golden eras of Holland, Britain and the United States were marked by bourgeois patriotism and provincialism, whereas their decline as manufacturing and ordinary-family income stagnated seems to have been characterized by recurrent attitudes: a diminishing concern for fading national industries, rising transnational values, support for minimal restraint on immigration, willingness to sell critical technology overseas and an eagerness of domestic capital to invest in rival foreign economies. "Cosmopolitanism" is as good a collective label as any. Yet another variety of globalism typical of such eras is what Paul Kennedy called "imperial overstretch"—the tendency of great-power elites to cling to an expensive international military or peacekeeping role that a weakening economy can no longer afford.

Far from being abstractions, these great-power circumstances affect average families as well as nations. Take great-power commitment to some variety of free trade and adherence to the theory that in the optimal world economy, restraints on trade should be avoided so that each nation might do what it does best. For great powers at the crest of the world economy, the rationale is simple: free trade is commercial self-interest. Restraints on imports into Spain circa 1550, Holland circa 1650 and Britain circa 1870 were relatively few, because in trade terms, these nations saw the world as their commercial oyster. One cocky Spaniard of the sixteenth century even wrote:

> Let London manufacture those fine fabrics of hers to her heart's content; Holland her chambrays; Florence her cloth; the Indies their beaver and vicuna; Milan her brocades; Italy and Flanders their linens . . . so long as our capital can enjoy them: the only thing it proves is that all nations train journeymen for Madrid and that Madrid is the queen of parliaments, for all the world serves her and she serves nobody.[43]

At roughly the same point in Britain's heyday, economist William Jevons expressed a similar enthusiasm, naming "Chicago and Odessa our granaries, Canada and the Baltic our timber forests . . . Spain and France our vineyards."[44] In turn, much of the world bought British manufactures. We can be sure that a seventeenth-century Dutchman or two wrote enthusiastically about how their vessels carried the tar and pitch of Sweden, the beaver pelts of New Amsterdam and the coffee of Java, just as Americans of the 1950s and 1960s gloried in a world at their beck and call.

Within a generation or two of these enthusiasms, however, each of these great powers saw its manufacturing competitiveness weaken as factories began to age, technologies lagged and aggressive protectionist or mercantilist practices by commercial rivals took their toll. Moreover, capital needed for domestic industry was diverted because the nation's financial or rentier sector preferred more profitable overseas investments. Nor could mature great economic powers enact or implement plans for national manufacturing renewal, because they could not mobilize divided interest groups. As many domestic manufacturing industries lose their earlier advantage, free trade and national self-interest diverge.

Spain's manufacturing industry, as we have seen, was sacrificed early, so that foreign imports became a necessity. Holland, however, illustrates the usual evolution. Sometime in the early 1700s, Dutch manufacturing and technology began to slip, in part because of Dutch investors' moving their capital elsewhere, but also because of rising European protectionism. Textiles—the greatest of Dutch industries—"were at the heart of mercantile policy in all countries," save free-trading Holland. England and France first imposed heavy duties on Dutch cloths in the late 1600s, followed by Russia, Prussia, Denmark, Norway and Spain in the early 1700s, ensuring the decline of Holland's textile industry.[45] Yet increased Dutch dependence on international shipping and finance ruled out serious countermeasures to protect embattled manufactures. Holland had no alternative to maintaining free markets, yet by a certain point that commitment was partly a trap.

Britain's experience is also relevant. Exports had started to slip in the 1870s, and in 1885 the Conservative government of Lord Salisbury appointed a commission to report on the "Depression of Trade and Industry," because of concern over losing domestic and overseas markets, especially to German competition.[46] In fact, apprehension was overdue, because continental Europe's brief mid-century flirtation with free trade had ended. France raised tariffs in 1872 and 1882, Germany in 1879 and Russia in 1883 and 1887. In the burgeoning United States, steep duties were pushed higher in the 1890s.[47] In addition, by the turn of the century, the former "workshop of the world" had lost much of its earlier lead in science and technology to Germany and the United States. Moreover, some of what Britain sold to maintain high export volume was partly counterproductive. Much export growth was in coal, which was not just raw material but a commodity critical to foreign industry. Two other major exports—ships and machinery—also helped nurture rivals in trade and manufacturing.

By 1903 Conservative prime minister Arthur J. Balfour was worried enough to propose a mild agenda of protection and imperial preference.* He told the House of Commons that the free-trade circumstances of the 1850s no longer existed: "We have seen, to begin with, a tariff wall steadily raised against us in every one of the great countries with whom we desire to deal. We have seen . . . an enormous growth of the trust system working behind tariffs."[48] The result, he claimed, allowed foreign producers to dump goods in Britain, reducing the profits of British industry and crippling its ability to undertake needed modernization. His solution—which Americans would also find themselves debating in the 1980s and 1990s—was to establish a framework for imposing retaliatory tariffs on countries that erected protective walls against British goods.

But Balfour failed, and his government lost the next general election in 1906. Many economists and rival politicians simply rejected his analyses, preferring to take comfort in free-trade theory, in Britain's past commercial glories and in claims that since the economy was continuing to grow, it was not in trouble. However, a central constraint, as in Holland two centuries earlier, was that shipping and financial services had become so important to Britain's international earnings that these sectors opposed risking foreign retaliation by protecting aging manufacturing industries. So no action was taken. For Britain, too, free trade had gone from being a strength to being something of a trap.

In the late twentieth century the United States was following suit. Old heavy industries were in decline in the Rust Belt and elsewhere. Handicapped by inferior scientific and mathematical education (as late-nineteenth-century Britain was weak relative to Germany), the United States was losing ground to Japan in technology. Neomercantilism, industrial strategies and export subsidies were routine practices on the part of U.S. trade rivals—continental European as well as Asian. Yet the Reagan and Bush administrations, which leaned toward free trade, generally opposed efforts to wield conditional access to the U.S. market as a retaliatory club against foreign neomercantilism.

As had earlier happened in Britain, free traders insisted that U.S. weaknesses had been exaggerated, citing the high U.S. exports of 1988–91.† Nor was there any real willingness to protect old-line manu-

---

*These paragraphs draw heavily on Aaron Friedman's excellent book *The Weary Titan: Britain and the Experience of Relative Decline, 1895–1905*.

†In another perverse coincidence, just as Britain enlarged its early-twentieth-century exports by shipping huge quantities of coal, the United States of the 1980s and 1990s achieved high export levels partly through shipments of coal, wheat, soybeans, timber and paper pulp. Neither pattern promoted long-term high-value-added industry growth.

facturing industry—automobiles, textiles or machine tools—on the part of internationally minded trade, insurance and financial sectors, on which the United States, like prior maturing powers, had come to depend for strong worldwide earnings and profits. Protectionism was implausible, given this dependence, but significant chunks of blue-collar Middle America paid the price as old-line industry eroded.

There are other ways in which internationalism can mean neglect of parochial interests. Each of the great nations at which we have been looking experienced rapid internationalization of its outlook during its zenith and thereafter. Besides opening up much of America, sixteenth-century Spain was also ruling a Hapsburg empire that extended beyond the Iberian Peninsula to Flanders, Germany, Austria and Italy. Increasingly, Madrid came to look to the worldly financiers of Genoa, Augsburg and Antwerp; Spain's upper classes bought large quantities of foreign goods, and by the mid-seventeenth century even Spain's once-Castilian army had become largely one of mercenaries.

The Dutch republic provides a more apt example. At first militantly puritan and nationalistic, shaped by its bitter religious, commercial and political revolution against Spain, early-seventeenth-century Holland scorned French wines and luxury goods. The increasingly polarized and sophisticated Holland of a century later cherished them. French art and the French language, as we have seen, became fashionable. The Dutch traded all over the world, and, in turn, people from almost everywhere came to make their fortunes in Amsterdam. Some were poor—like the soldiers and sailors drawn from virtually everywhere in Europe, and the low-wage German workers known as the *Hollandgänger*—but many were more prosperous or even rich: the French Protestant Huguenots, who came after the revocation of the Edict of Nantes in 1685, Flemish refugees from Hapsburg Antwerp, Sephardic Jews from Spain and Portugal. Braudel notes that by 1650 no less than one third of Amsterdam's population was foreign-born or of foreign extraction. So it was not surprising, during the 1700s, as Dutch investors and financiers sent their ships to Surinam and Java, invested in huge chunks of British government debt, and wooed borrowers—from the Prince of Mecklenburg-Strelitz to the Empress of all the Russias—that the monied classes were in no hurry to rebuild the decaying towns and industries described so vividly by Boswell. Grand international exposures do not whet concern for the low and middle order of one's own nation.

Britain's traditional antipathy to France also faded in the late nineteenth century, as the entente cordiale took shape, and then the Edwardian era acquired an increasingly cosmopolitan taste for things French—not least richly sauced food and the balmy winter temperatures of Nice or Menton. One chronicler, noting the conspicuous consumption of the Edwardian period, pointed out that these were the years when international luxury hotels redrew the profiles of Biarritz, Cannes, Monte Carlo and Marienbad.[49] The Edwardians certainly had the cash. By 1914 Britain's investments overseas represented 43 percent of the *world* total, an unprecedented share, so that investment firms like Rothschilds, Barings and Hambros were not just merchant bankers but global powers. Middle-class investors from Tiptree to Tooting thrilled to the profits of Argentine railroads, Canadian gold mines, and Ceylonese tea plantations. Like the mobile or migratory rich who had flocked to Amsterdam two centuries earlier, foreign millionaires found themselves purchasing British estates or London town houses. Like mid-eighteenth-century Holland, Edwardian England was for the wealthy, not a country in which opinion molders worried about the declining purchasing power or prospects of the ordinary British family.

The same was true of the United States of the 1980s. Under Ronald Reagan, the nation attracted many categories of foreigners: political refugees from Latin America and Asia; poor people looking for jobs, mostly from below the border; investors looking for high interest rates; and an upper-bracket minority who partied from the Hamptons to Palm Springs and bought expensive luxury goods and homes in Hawaii and California, Florida and New York. As we have seen, the global chic of market economics, low taxes and deregulation turned conservatives into the most enthusiastic internationalists. In general, free-trade advocates also applauded easy immigration, both legal and illegal, which furnished cheap labor for America's harvests and factories, Irish nannies for Boston, Hispanic and Asian restaurant and household workers for almost every major metropolitan area. For job-seeking Americans with median skills, they might be competitors who depressed wages. For prosperous landowners, factory owners and householders, cheap immigrant labor was a godsend.

A further measure of immigration's interaction with U.S. cosmopolitan capitalism was that in 1990 Congress and the president agreed to extraordinary legislation establishing a yearly allotment of permanent residence visas for the families of those who would invest at least $1 million in enterprises that create ten or more new jobs. International investment from nonresidents was also a source of wealth to Americans. Foreigners' purchases of homes and commercial property in

California, New York and elsewhere tended to boost real estate prices in the late 1980s while paying major commission dollars to U.S. brokers. Moreover, so much money was involved in selling small and large corporations to foreign investors that one newsmagazine observed in 1987 that "the buying of America has virtually turned into an industry of its own."⁵⁰ And Japanese investors were also a mainstay of the U.S. bond market.

Downsides abounded. In Hawaii Japanese purchasers pushed the price of houses so high that local residents could no longer afford them. In Washington, D.C., three dozen of the fifty largest foreign multinational corporations had established some form of corporate office by 1991, often because they had bought or established U.S. subsidiaries, and the accelerating influence of foreign lobbyists in the U.S. political process became an issue in Congress and especially in the 1992 presidential race. American multinational corporations also looked overseas, setting up scores of offices in London, Tokyo, Paris, Geneva and Brussels; many were caught up in a transnationalism that de-emphasized commitment to U.S. employees and reduced dependence on the U.S. market for earnings. Prior to the opening of the 1992 World's Fair in Seville, Spain, the U.S. commissioner, Frederick Bush, acknowledged that U.S. companies didn't want to participate and identify themselves as "American." Firms like Time-Warner, CNN and Du Pont, he said, "considered themselves global and transnational and didn't want to be pegged as an American company."⁵¹ Meanwhile, in the automobile industry, production of models and parts was so dispersed around the world that even U.S. government agencies could not agree between themselves on which models were domestic and which were foreign. In 1991–92 the purchase by U.S. investors of *foreign* rather than American stocks and bonds set record after record. As had earlier been the case in Holland and Britain, this cosmopolitanism was no asset to the ordinary American family, which often saw consumer prices rise, public policies shift, manufacturing plants relocate and job opportunities shrivel with a relentlessness that produced a sense of helplessness and frustration.

The third variety of international involvement, a burden on Spain, Holland, Britain and, by the late twentieth century, the United States, was the inevitable overcommitment of declining great economic powers to the sort of military might they could truly afford only at earlier, wealthier stages. In each case, more important national needs were sacrificed.

Spain's military overextension was almost a caricature. Even with gold from the Americas, the wars of the 1540s and 1550s forced the

Spanish Crown to declare itself bankrupt in 1557, and a little less than a century later, as the gold shipments slackened, Spain finally bled to death economically from financing its campaigns in the Thirty Years War that raged across Europe. Paul Kennedy's vivid descriptions in *The Rise and Fall of the Great Powers* hardly require repetition here: Spain spent far beyond its means, even as those means were drying up.

However, even the initially pragmatic Dutch, after less than a century of independence, indulged imperial overstretch in the War of the Spanish Succession (1689–1713) by undertaking a disproportionate military commitment in Flanders and the Iberian Peninsula. The strain broke Holland as a naval power and forced Dutch interest rates up to 9 percent, the highest since independence. The Dutch national debt, just 30 million guilders in 1688, had quintupled to 148 million by 1713, at the end of the war.[52]

The British, in turn, began their tour in the global sun with restraint. Just as their taxes were low in the mid-nineteenth century, so were their military outlays, representing some 2 to 3 percent of GNP. The Crimean War of 1854 had not been widely popular; London kept out of the wars and confrontations on the European continent; and the Liberal governments of the period often displayed anti-imperial tendencies. Britain's national debt fell almost steadily from the finish of the Crimean War to the 1890s. But by the end of the nineteenth century, imperialist sentiment, military outlays and Conservative governments flourished together, culminating in the Boer War of 1899–1902, which increased Britain's debt by 25 percent and precipitated a financial crisis—the first of three, each worse than its predecessor, that would follow Britain's twentieth-century conflicts.

As in Spain, the debt by which Britain ruined itself was largely war-related. World War I saw Britain's national debt expand tenfold, forcing the British to liquidate one fifth to one quarter of their overseas investments, while borrowing £1 billion from the United States and exchanging the status of global creditor for that of debtor. Yet London could not give up its empire, on which the sun still did not set and in which British troops paraded from Bermuda to Bombay while the Royal Navy steamed from Scapa Flow to Singapore.

Then as World War II loomed on Britain's global horizon, the share of GNP spent on defense rose from 5.5 percent in 1937 to 12.5 percent in 1939 and then took over the wartime economy.[53] Once again, national debt rose, more overseas assets were liquidated, and, as we have seen, British economic prowess was reduced to a shadow of yesteryear's.

The historical moral is simple: Excessive global pride or peacekeeping is fiscally self-destructive. Those great economic powers whom the gods would humble, they first line up on the parade grounds of imperial overstretch, although the process seems as much inevitable as voluntary. Great powers do have international responsibilities. And if trade follows the flag, so does ego. Moreover, even when economic resources start running too low to support previous military and policing commitments, fading great powers invariably find themselves involved in military-diplomatic commitments to uphold cherished roles—be they in India, Egypt, Korea or the North Atlantic Treaty Organization.

When the United States was defeated in Vietnam, some historians drew a parallel to Britain's turn-of-the-century embarrassment in the Boer War. But in retrospect, the U.S. disarray after Vietnam was much worse in terms of lost prestige, public frustration, increased debt and inflation. The last quickly caused the oil-producing nations to decide that *they* needed a price increase, making inflation worse. In this sense, the end of the post-1945 era and the stagnation of the 1970s began in the rice paddies of Indochina. What came out of the velds of the Transvaal was minor by comparison.

Yet imperial overstretch is partly psychological, and because Americans were uncomfortable with the lowered world respect that followed U.S. defeat in Vietnam, they rallied to Ronald Reagan's promise in 1980 to rebuild American military strength and prestige. They applauded the series of successful invasions and punitive actions against Third World dictators launched by the Reagan and Bush administrations: Grenada (1983), Tripoli (1986), Panama (1989) and the Persian Gulf (1990–91). Each expedition was followed by 70 to 85 percent support in opinion polls, boosting presidential ratings and diverting attention from less popular domestic and economic policies. But by the early 1990s the huge U.S. federal budget deficit suggested that the military buildup of the 1980s had done serious fiscal damage—though it also contributed to the devastation of the rival Soviet Union, which came undone in 1990–92 partly because its leadership had devoted an even more crippling level of resources to the military.

Reagan entered the White House in 1981 with a federal budget deficit of $74 billion and a total national debt of $1 trillion. By 1992 the budget deficit had quadrupled to roughly $300 billion a year and the total national debt had quadrupled to nearly $4 trillion. Formerly the world's leading creditor, the United States had borrowed enough money overseas—shades of 1914–45 Britain—to become the world's leading debtor, although careful computations suggested that talk of a $700 billion or $800 billion indebtedness was exaggerated. Because of these pressures, as the Bush administration moved closer to war in the Persian Gulf, it responded to congressional demands that other military allies—in particular the kings, emirs and sheikhs of the Gulf, plus the rich Germans and Japanese—share the financial burden. They did, but while fighting in the Gulf the Bush administration neglected the recession at home, and the public's persisting conclusion that the United States was still militarily overextended became an important political complaint in 1991–92. Commitments and expenditures abroad were needed at home, not abroad. Candidates in the primaries of both parties used a battle cry that had not been heard since 1940: Stop dissipating our resources elsewhere; take care of "America first."

Unfortunately, even this concern has its historical counterparts. American defense strategists of the 1990s can usefully recall that in the 1620s Castile, well past its peak, saw that it could no longer afford to bear the principal burden of financing Spain's soldiery—the crack troops whose "Castilian steel" remains a cliché for strength—and the king's chief minister asked the separate parliaments of Aragón, Valencia and Catalonia to share the burden of men and money in a Union of Arms. Aragón and Valencia partially complied; Catalonia scoffed.[54]

British attempts at military burden-sharing began in 1897, when it was suggested that the colonies—principally Canada, Australia and New Zealand—might contribute more to the navy. But by 1902, after the financial stress of the Boer War, the British government called representatives of the colonies and dominions to London to discuss formal naval burden-sharing arrangements, greeting them with charts showing how the average British taxpayer paid 15 shillings a year to support the Royal Navy, the average Australian or New Zealander just a few shillings, and the average Canadian absolutely nothing.[55] Australia, in particular, increased its contribution, but Canada opted for its own small navy. Like Madrid three hundred years earlier (and Washington ninety years later), London wanted to divide the economic burden, but not the strategic control. Unwillingness to divide decision-making is an important reason that imperial overstretch— and its pressure on declining nations and their populations—prevents financial solutions until it is too late.

By the late twentieth century, U.S. opinion-molders had embraced internationalism and cosmopolitanism, and sophisticated Americans had become enthusiastic internationalists. For the economic top 10 percent, that orientation clearly paid off. But as the end of the century drew near, polls showed that the average American believed that "internationalism" was one reason that for them the American Dream was fading.

. . .

In this chapter I have tried to show that within a broad framework, repetition of certain national transitions and failures has marked the decline of great economic powers—and reduced the prospects for ordinary families. In Chapter 10 I shall come back, briefly, to what these historical precedents suggest the United States should do in the 1990s and beyond. But, first, it is appropriate to return to politics—to the signals of economic frustration that were building as the 1990s got under way.

C H A P T E R   9

The Politics of Middle-Class Frustration

Historically, the idea of a broad middle class living in relative comfort—with meat on the table, a car, money in the bank—was a wild fantasy. For most Americans, it did not become reality until the end of the Second World War triggered the swiftest, broadest rise in living standards any society has ever known. But what happens if the fears of more and more of us turn out to be true? What if the middle class discovers it cannot pass a good life on to its children? . . . That kind of realization, I think, can throw our political stability into real jeopardy.

—Columnist Jeff Greenfield, 1991

For the first decade since before World War II, middle-class Americans worked harder, spent less time with their children and spent more on health care, education, housing and taxes. We saw the absolute destruction of the middle class and an explosion in poverty. Only the very wealthy did better in a decade in which Americans literally thought their country was coming apart.

—Democratic presidential nominee Bill Clinton, 1992

The problem is a government and mainstream political parties that don't address the legitimate grievances of the middle class. Until these grievances are addressed, these white working-class and middle-class voters will turn to demogogues who offer simple explanations and simple solutions.

—Lance Hill, executive director of the Louisiana Coalition Against Nazism and Racism, 1991

There was nothing surprising about the spasms of middle-class political radicalism that occurred in 1990–92 as the United States slid into the economic slump that followed the debt-and-speculative orgy of the 1980s. Populism, as we have seen, is never far from the surface of U.S. politics, and signals that had been largely ignored in the elections of November 1990—from the success of independent Socialist Bernard Sanders in his bid for Congress from Vermont to the upset U.S. Senate victory of radical Paul Wellstone in Minnesota—were followed by even more striking results in 1991. Democrat Harris Wofford stunned observers of that year's special Senate election in Pennsylvania by molding issues like national health insurance, fairer taxes, protection for U.S. industries and disdain for Washington into a so-called middle-class populism and achieving that rarest of political successes—an upset *landslide*. The Philadelphia Inquirer, with its daily circulation of a million, had helped shape local restiveness with a preelection series of eight front-page articles describing how the middle class was being hurt by Washington policies that favored the rich. The other big shock came in Louisiana, where former American Nazi David Duke beat the incumbent Republican governor in an open primary, then went on to win two fifths of the statewide total and a surprising 60 percent of the white-middle-class vote, following a campaign in which he presented himself as their political hope. Together, the two results made the political establishment fearful that 1992 was about to bring another of America's periodic rounds of frustration politics—and it was, culminating in Clinton's victory and the 62 percent of the vote cast for populist candidates and change in Washington.

In the United States and Europe alike, popular fear of downward mobility has been one of history's proven sources of political radicalism, both cultural and economic. As we have seen, polarization and anger among ordinary citizens of previous great economic powers who saw themselves losing ground led to food and tax riots and finally revolution in eighteenth-century Holland, and then, in early-twentieth-century Britain, to rapid gains for the Labour party, with its blueprints for class warfare, socialism and the expansion of the welfare state. In both of America's earlier capitalist-conservative boom periods, the Gilded Age and the Roaring Twenties, mild forms of the politics of economic frustration arose even during the optimistic years, and then stronger versions emerged once the debt-and-speculative bubble burst. Partial radicalization of the middle class played a role in both post-boom reactions.

While it is to these frustration politics that we now turn, a second lesson of American history is that corrective mechanisms have worked; the political mainstream *has* adjusted, sometimes unhappily. In 1992, of course, the pressure on the major parties to cope with popular alienation was particularly intensified by the independent challenge of Ross Perot. Yet, over the years, one critical key to the success of the U.S. political system has been its ability—except during the unique Civil War of 1861–65—to control radicalism by absorbing it and/or defusing it in the great watershed realignments we have already discussed in Chapter 3. In these pivotal elections, change-minded or reformist politicians absorbed the messages of splinter candidacies and public discontent, captured the presidency and gave their successive parties a new generation of White House control. In most of the upheavals, specifically in 1824–28, 1892–96, 1932–36 and 1968–72, spasms of radicalism briefly unnerved political moderates, but each time moderate change prevailed, although sometimes it was a close thing.

Against this backdrop, fears expressed before and after the 1992 election that U.S. political stability might break down were also nothing new. Similar predictions had been made in the mid-1890s, early 1930s and late 1960s, always wrongly. True, several of the warnings offered in 1991 came from men to whom the 1930s were a personal memory. William L. Shirer, whose Berlin diaries recorded Adolf Hitler's rise to power, called the politics represented by David Duke in Louisiana a "serious threat to our society," analogizing his appeal to Hitler's.[1] Columnist Max Lerner suggested that, like Weimar Germany, "America today has social and cultural vulnerabilities open for exploiting. Where we hurt most is in the fears, anxieties and rages of our middle class. It has been collecting injustices and letting them fester inwardly since the 1960s. The 90s may prove to be the decade when the explosive angers break out openly and play havoc with party loyalties."[2] As we will see, other serious observers saw fascist and anti-Semitic overtones not just in Duke but in Patrick Buchanan's strong primary challenge to Bush. The brief Democratic primary success of Jerry Brown, with his vitriolic attacks on the corruption of the U.S. political system, followed by Perot's stunning spring emergence and unexpected November strength, held up yet another mirror. And Perot, too, was charged with fascism and authoritarianism. No sooner had one practitioner of frustration or outsider politics subsided than another took his place. If Clinton sounded more radical in 1992 than Franklin D. Roosevelt had in 1932, it was no coincidence.

Prior U.S. Capitalist Heydays
and Middle American Frustration Politics

Indeed, the political response of the frustrated middle class in the 1990s recalled previous Middle American responses to earlier boom-and-bust cycles. As we have seen, even before the financial crashes of 1893 and 1929, huge numbers of Americans were being squeezed from farms or jobs by upheavals in technology and shifts in the global economy, which accelerate during boom times.* Then the financial crashes brought much wider pain, and each time this pain produced angry politics.

The excesses of the Gilded Age coincided with a slow and relentless deflation that brutally shrank the agricultural sector after farmers had borrowed to expand during the Civil War decade. We have seen how after 1873, as agricultural income declined and as farms were foreclosed or turned back to prairie, the financial system recycled the credit withdrawn from tillers of the soil to expand railroads and manufacturing, creating huge new wealth for their owners—larger fortunes, indeed, than any the world had ever seen before.

For farmers and dependent small-town merchants and professional men, it was an unbearable policy, a moral outrage. They came to hate the bankers in Wall Street and London, the "robber baron" operators of the great whiskey, leather, beef and tobacco trusts, the railroad owners in Minneapolis, Chicago and Kansas City who charged such high rates for their freight and the politicians who represented these various interests in Washington and state capitals. Because much of this anger was justified, the Granger and Greenback movements of the 1870s and 1880s and the great Populist protest of the 1890s have received a generally sympathetic nod from history. Not coincidentally, many of the measures the Populists proposed—from the progressive income tax to direct election of U.S. senators and popular initiative and referendum at the state level—became law in the progressive reform years from 1900 to 1914.

But Populist frustration involved more than a courageous yeomanry gathering at church suppers and giant open-air rallies to fight for economic justice. When the interests of so many ordinary people are trampled and their entreaties ignored, they turn angry, bitter—and radical. Genealogists seeking the ancestry of political alienation in the early 1990s will find forebears in the late nineteenth century.

The original Populist economics were radical enough that the party's 1892 platform proclaimed that "a vast conspiracy against mankind has been organized on two continents," and William Jennings Bryan's platform in 1896 attacked international moneylenders. A few Populist leaders like Mary Ellen Lease attacked the influence of Jewish bankers and British gold, although Seymour Martin Lipset in his book *The Politics of Unreason* allows that most major Populist leaders made no anti-Semitic references.[3] Part of the reason, however, was that

*See Chapter 4.

anti-Catholicism and concern about immigration were the more typical and familiar response of the largely Protestant population to hard times. As job fears intensified after the Panic of 1893, the American Protective Association, which claimed 2.5 million members, repeatedly raised allegations that Catholics were taking over politics and getting unfair preference in civil service exams. This was a forerunner of the concern over racial quotas and job and college preferences for blacks that would throb in the first years of the 1990s. Even absurd claims that Pope Leo XIII had instructed American Catholics to kill all heretics were taken seriously, and in September 1893 the mayor of Toledo, Ohio, kept the national guard on duty for a week to protect local Protestants against a Catholic murder plot.[4] The American Protective Association was by no means beyond the respectable pale; powerful in California and the Midwest, it was closely connected with the Republican party in the 1894 election. Two years later, however, the GOP was looking for Eastern industrial-state Catholic votes against Bryan and avoided the group.

Most middle-class voters had distrusted Bryan, but once his defeat in 1896 calmed their fears of hayseeds, anarchists and backwoods economists, many well-established Americans felt freer to develop their own parallel indictment of the Gilded Age, laissez-faire and the growth of the great trusts. Historian Richard Hofstadter described the new mood: "The great capitalist entrepreneur, hitherto heroic, lost much of his glamour. He was condemned as an exploiter of labor and an extorter from the consumer, pilloried as an unfair competitor and exposed as a corrupter of political life."[5]

By the first decade of the new century the movement had a name: *Progressivism.* And as one of its leaders, Kansas journalist William Allen White, admitted, he and his allies had originally looked down on the Populists and other "agrarian movements [that] too often appealed to the ne'er-do-wells, the misfits—farmers who had failed, lawyers and doctors who were not orthodox, teachers who could not make the grade, and neurotics full of hates and ebullient, evanescent enthusiasms."[6] Within a few years, however, White would admit that Progressives "caught the Populists in swimming and stole all their clothing except the frayed underdrawers of free silver." And in 1912, when he surveyed the ranks of those who supported Theodore Roosevelt's Progressive third-party bid for the presidency, he described the reformist constituency as "in the main and in its heart of hearts *petit bourgeois*: a movement of little businessmen, professional men, well-to-do farmers, skilled artisans from the upper-brackets of organized labor . . . the successful middle-class country-town citizens, the farmer whose barn was painted, the well-paid railroad engineer and the country editor."[7]

The result, according to Hofstadter, was that after 1900 "populism and progressivism merge." In partially absorbing radicalism, the middle class subdued it—and with far-reaching legislative success, even though Roosevelt lost his 1912 bid to establish progressivism as a political force that would displace or capture the Republican party. From trust-busting to popular election of U.S. senators, much of the old Populist platform found its way into the statute books.

To better understand middle-class frustration in the 1990s, it is fair to recall early-twentieth-century progressivism as the middle-class response to the kindred excesses of the first Gilded Age. Delayed and separately channeled by middle-class cultural incompatibility with rustic Bryanism, progressivism was nevertheless a related response to the disruptions of Darwinian economics, unbridled capitalism and the gaudy conspicuous consumption of nouveaux riches whose colossal fortunes overshadowed and aroused the gentry and professional classes, all phenomena that repeated themselves in the 1980s. Hofstadter and other historians described progressivism circa 1910 as partly the response of a "displaced elite"—the anger of the old Northern Protestant middle and upper-middle classes, from shopkeeper to gentry, at the upheaval that had diminished their influence in favor of robber barons, Wall Street speculators, labor leaders and Catholic big-city machine bosses with their immigrant flocks. As we shall see, this is what the politics of middle-class frustration have often involved: a mixture of cultural conservatism, apprehension about economic status, nativism and anger at the new rich.

The capitalist-conservative heyday of the 1920s, in turn, also produced a backlash even during the boom itself. As early as 1924, maverick GOP senator Robert La Follette of Wisconsin ran for president on a third-party ticket, claiming that 1920s prosperity excluded groups ranging from Midwest dairy farmers to Pacific lumber-mill workers and national railway workers' unions. Beyond broad boom-era support in some areas for the Ku Klux Klan, which was then less controversial than it would soon become, the electorate's flirtation with political extremism did not become serious until well *after* the 1929 Crash—not until 1934 and 1935, after two years of the Roosevelt administration had still not cured the worst economic slump anyone could remember.

With the Depression still unfolding, the election of 1932 had been reasonably sedate, although the Communist and Socialist vote tripled to nearly one million. Some observers suggested that voters were still numb. Not so by 1934, when socialist Upton Sinclair got 38 percent of the vote running as the Democratic nominee for governor of California, and partly socialist factions or third parties dominated state politics in Washington, North Dakota, Wisconsin and Minnesota. While William Dudley Pelley's Silver Shirts were a small Nazi-like group, as was the Black Legion, which a grand jury in Michigan refused to indict for fascist conspiracy because its leaders were so unintelligent, the largest radical movements of the time combined components of left *and* right, as well as elements of both populism and middle-class radicalism.[8] These were the Share-the-Wealth movement of Louisiana U.S. senator Huey Long and the National Union for Social Justice, organized and run by Father Charles Coughlin, the Michigan-based Catholic radio priest, both of which somewhat foreshadowed Duke and Buchanan in 1991–92.

Both traded on the deepening frustration with the moderate politics of Franklin D. Roosevelt as the Depression continued, and because Long and Coughlin together had the political support of millions heading toward the 1936 elections, Roosevelt shifted his tax and economic policies leftward in 1935 to head them off, but that is getting ahead of our story. Long, who had risen during the 1920s to become Louisiana's governor, thereafter moving to the U.S. Senate in 1932, was a fierce populist who rejected that label and lineage because of its leftover bumpkin implications. As governor he had an extraordinary record—if one overlooked his dictatorial manner and open corruption—of giving children free textbooks, building roads and schools, and restructuring state taxes so that corporations and utilities had to pay. One way or another, his whole career foreshadowed what he finally proposed in 1934 and 1935: his revolutionary scheme for sharing the nation's wealth through a minimum wage of $2,500 a year, an end to unemployment, a gift of $4,000 for every family from the confiscation of millionaires' wealth and college educations at federal expense for every boy who had the abilities.

Huey Long had begun his career in Washington as a supporter of FDR, but he had changed his mind by 1933, calling the new president an enemy of the poor. By 1934 he had launched his Share-the-Wealth organization, started a regular national weekly radio program and established a newspaper, the *American Progress,* through which he attacked Wall Street and its power, harangued against how much the rich spent on yachts and even discussed plots by Standard Oil to kill him. His enemies were characterized as "high-brow Brain Trusters, low-brow eastern politicians, top-hatted . . . cigar-smoking Wall Streeters" allied in their commitment to bilking the common man.[9] When asked if he intended to be a candidate against Roosevelt in 1936, he said, "If events appear to be what they are now and circumstances are what they appear to be, it's almost certain that I will be a candidate."[10]

White House strategists were more than worried. In February 1935 Long claimed to have more than 27,000 Share-the-Wealth clubs, plus the names of almost 8 million members on file. When the Democratic National Committee commissioned a private opinion poll to measure his appeal as a potential third-party candidate, it found that he might draw 3 or 4 million votes, 7 to 9 percent of the total, and, in the words of party chairman James A. Farley, "might have the balance of power in the 1936 election."[11]

Father Coughlin, much less important, was another 1932 Roosevelt supporter who had turned against the administration as the Depression persisted and he saw the president courting establishment interests. In the autumn of 1934 he founded the National Union for Social Justice to press for a guaranteed annual wage and government ownership and control of U.S. banks. Although Coughlin, like Long, shunned the populist label, his speeches had an unmistakable populist flavoring. One chronicler notes that he denounced rich and well-educated Easterners, "the luxury of Park Avenue and Westchester" against "widows, orphans and inarticulate farmers," and "Wall Street attorneys, the erudition of Harvard, of Yale, of Princeton, of Columbia," directed against servant girls, laborers, farmers.[12] Coughlin claimed 5 million members for the National Union, and a Gallup Poll suggested that 7 percent would vote for a Coughlin-favored candidate in the 1936 presidential election.

Franklin Delano Roosevelt didn't wait to find out. His close adviser Raymond Moley later recalled that the president began discussing ways of trying to steal "Long's thunder" by making a "counteroffer" to the voters. This he did in June 1935 by asking Congress to pass the Wealth Tax Act, with its soak-the-rich income levies, new inheritance tax, increased estate- and gift-tax levies and new graduated tax on corporate incomes. In his message to Congress, Roosevelt stole some of Long's thunder and declared, "Our revenue laws have operated in many ways to the unfair advantage of the few, and they have done little to prevent an unjust concentration of wealth and economic power."[13] Along with other legislation like the Social Security Act, the Public

Utility Holding Company Act and the Farm Mortgage Moratorium Act, the Wealth Tax Act was the centerpiece of the Second New Deal—Roosevelt's shift to the left in preparation for a 1936 election in which he would be opposed by Long on a third-party ticket, attacking Roosevelt as the lapdog of the Mellons and Morgans.

It never happened, because in September 1935, only months after the Second New Deal was completed, Long was assassinated in the state capitol in Baton Rouge. His followers were devastated. As one half-admiring journalist wrote years later of his funeral, "one hundred thousand people trekked to Baton Rouge to pay their respects. Funeral trains left New Orleans every half hour, and cars backed up for miles waiting to cross the Mississippi River by ferry."[14] Without Long, and with Roosevelt having turned to the left, Father Coughlin and other, lesser figures turned increasingly shrill and anti-Semitic, falling from the heights of their broader 1934–35 appeal.

Even so, Roosevelt took no chances. In his 1936 annual message to Congress he welcomed "the hatred of entrenched greed," later telling a campaign rally, "I should like to have it said of my first Administration that in it the forces of selfishness and of lust for power met their match. I should like to have it said of my second Administration that in it, these forces met their master."[15] Some of Roosevelt's rallies turned these sentiments into something uncommon in U.S. politics— open class warfare:

As the 1936 campaign got underway, the note of class conflict sometimes reached a high pitch. At an excited night meeting at Forbes Field in Pittsburgh, a stern-faced Danton, State Senator Warren Roberts, spat out the names of the Republican oligarchs: Mellon, Grundy, Pew, Rockefeller. The crowd greeted each name with a resounding "boo." "You could almost hear the swish of the guillotine blade," wrote one reporter afterwards. Then came Governor George Earle, their handsome Mirabeau, and he too churned up the crowd against the enemies of their class. "There are the Mellons, who have grown fabulously wealthy from the toil of men of iron and steel . . . Grundy, whose sweatshop operators have been the shame and disgrace of Pennsylvania for a generation; Pew, who strives to build a political and economic empire with himself as dictator; the duPonts, whose dollars were earned with the blood of American soldiers; Morgan, financier of war." As he sounded each name, the crowd interrupted him with a chorus of jeers against the business leaders. Then the gates opened at a far corner of the park; a motor-cycle convoy put-putted its way into the field, followed by an open car in which rode

Franklin Delano Roosevelt, grinning and waving his hat, and the crowd, whipped to a frenzy, roared its welcome to their champion.[16]

The 1936 elections were a great Democratic success and cemented realignment. Roosevelt had absorbed the vital part of Long's message. Coughlin's presidential candidate, North Dakota congressman William Lemke, running as an independent, could manage only 2 percent of the total vote. Coughlin's radio programs continued, but the possibility of a major national radical movement ended in 1935.

Just as the 1991–92 rhetoric of Buchanan and Duke would mix an anti-elite and populist message in a confusing package that also included nationalism, anti-immigrant sentiment and economic appeals to the middle class, historians disagree on what Long and Coughlin represented—lower-class populism, fascism or a blurred middle-class radical response to economic upheaval. Arthur Schlesinger, Jr., identified the adherents of Long and Coughlin as coming "mostly . . . from the old lower-middle classes, now in an unprecedented stage of frustration and fear."[17] Seymour Martin Lipset and Earl Raab, while pointing out the basically populist antecedents of Long's low-income Louisiana electorate, argued that both men enjoyed a considerable middle-class following as their national movement swelled during the peak years of discontent in 1934–35.[18] Periods of economic frustration commonly produce this kind of ideological confusion; indeed, it's to be counted on.

Perhaps the best analysis of the hybrid forces involved was Alan Brinkley's in his 1982 book, *Voices of Protest.* Long and Coughlin, he pointed out, declined to call themselves populists, despite their similar depiction of foes as scheming financiers or sybaritic plutocrats, first because they preferred to avoid a linkage with past electoral failure, but also because they preferred to shun some of Populism's economic radicalisms so as to enlarge their middle-class appeal. Whereas the Populists had often criticized local merchants and bankers, Long and Coughlin often romanticized them, upholding their role against the threat of giant corporations, militant labor unions, remote bureaucrats and international bankers. Duke and Buchanan would read from somewhat similar scripts sixty years later. In 1935 *The New Republic* had been surprised, Brinkley points out, that Long and Coughlin seemed to be rallying the "lower middle class," "small businessmen and professionals," in a "militant and honorable protest."[19] Because of its relevance again almost sixty years later, his explanation is worth quoting in full:

The term "middle class" is a vague one, to be sure; and if the conventional, popular image of the American bourgeoisie were to be the standard, few Long and Coughlin supporters would qualify. They were not usually men and women who lived in neat suburban bungalows or who worked at comfortable, white-collar jobs. More often they lived precariously and somewhat shabbily. Their membership in the middle class was less a result of their level of material comfort than of a certain social outlook. They were, they believed, people who had risen above the lowest levels of society, who had acquired a stake, however modest, in their community, who were protecting hard-won badges of status and carefully guarded, if modest, financial achievements. Others may have suffered more in absolute terms from the 1930s economy, but those on the fringes of the middle class confronted an especially agonizing form of loss. Having gained a foothold in the world of bourgeois respectability, they stood in danger of being plunged back into what they viewed as an abyss of powerlessness and dependence. It was that fear that made the middle class, even more than those who were truly rootless and indigent, a politically volatile group.[20]

The New Deal and World War II rescued these worried Americans, so that they or their children would march in the broad, triumphant middle-class parade of the 1950s and 1960s. But the next decade brought back kindred concerns, making the hybrid radicalism of the early to mid-1930s—what some academicians have called "extremism of the center"—a psychological and political precedent for the anger that flared again in Middle America at intervals of economic stress from the mid-1970s down to the 1990s.

The New Wave of Middle American Radicalism, 1973–1981

The Republican presidential majority that was created in the 1968–72 period, stealing the third-party thunder of George Wallace much as FDR had stolen that of Huey Long, once again affirmed the success of the system. As in previous U.S. political realignments, the "center" had radicalized, shifted, and was settling. But within two years, the OPEC oil shock of 1973 and Nixon's resignation over Watergate would leave the direction of U.S. politics and economics in doubt once more. George Wallace's political insurgency of 1964–72 had drawn largely on national (and especially Southern) racial and cultural frustration. From 1973 on, a third factor became increasingly important— economics had now joined culture and race.

Not surprisingly, the first forced resignation of a president of the United States in 1974 and the stagflation of 1973–74 sent the American political fever chart rising. George Wallace, until he was shot in 1972, had warned about a radicalization of the middle class. By late 1974, in the trough of that year's recession, polls gave new weight to that prospect. Back in the mid-1970s, I briefly collaborated with Patrick Caddell—who had been George McGovern's pollster in 1972 and would be Jimmy Carter's in 1976 and 1980—on some research into middle-class radicalism. Caddell believed that America was caught up in a new wave of frustration politics, and in late 1974, with Watergate a fresh scar on the nation's psyche and unemployment climbing toward a post-Depression high, he conducted a survey based on two-and-a-half-hour, in-depth interviews designed to drag to the surface political beliefs and pathologies overlooked by more superficial samplings.

The results were fascinating. Back in 1972 Caddell had found 18 percent of those queried willing to back George Wallace for president—9 percent really wanted him in the Oval Office and the other 9 percent were willing to cast a protest vote. By late 1974, however, Caddell found fully 18 percent eager to put Wallace in the White House, while another 17 percent were willing to cast a protest vote for him. That came to 35 percent, twice Wallace's 1972 strength and nearly triple his actual 1968 third-party presidential vote. Voter ideology was churning, the Democratic polltaker pointed out, as a growing number of people simultaneously favored radical socialist economic positions while backing a hard-line, even authoritarian position on social issues. "The people smack in the middle—the people who are the least ideological—are the most volatile," he said. Forty-one percent agreed that "the true American way of life is disappearing so fast we may have to use force to save it." He concluded that "the middle class is coming unhinged. 'Center extremism' is correct" as a description.[21]

That was at the low point of the recession. But another analyst, University of Michigan sociologist Donald Warren, argued more broadly that the convulsions of the 1960s and early 1970s had turned 20 to 30 percent of the electorate into what he called "Middle American radicals"—men and women whose ideology fitted neither liberal nor conservative prescriptions but mixed economic apprehension with indignant social conservatism and suspicion of rich and poor alike:

For many white Americans, the rejection of the blacks and poor is only one part of a larger rejection of the government and the rich. Preliminary data from a national cross-section probability sampling of 1690 white Americans indicate that 30 percent of the population thought that the blacks had too much political power; 63 percent said that about the rich. Approximately 30 percent said that poor blacks were getting more than their fair share of government aid; 56 percent said the same thing about the rich. Eighteen percent said that blacks have a better chance than whites to get fair treatment from courts, while 42 percent said that about the rich. In other words, hostility toward the rich is extensive; it may equal, or even exceed, hostility toward blacks.[22]

By this analysis, racial tensions were partly fueled by a larger frustration. What Caddell and Warren were talking about in the 1970s, besides its continuity with elements of the Long and Coughlin movements of the 1930s, also foreshadowed dynamics that would operate again in the early 1990s. Indeed, David Duke's roots in the American Nazi movement, although he disavowed them in 1991 and 1992, suggest a further perspective: The "center extremist" analysis of a radicalized Middle America had also described—in much more inflammatory circumstances—the surprising support base of Adolf Hitler's National Socialist German Workers' party. According to the sociologist Harold Lasswell in the 1930s and Seymour Martin Lipset in the 1960s and 1970s, the core of national socialism was a frustrated and radicalized lower-middle and middle class. The Nazi party arose not out of the traditional political right but out of the breakdown of what had in the 1920s been the middle-class parties of the political *center*.[23] Nazism, from this perspective, was middle-class radicalization at its extreme.

In the less provocative context of the United States, the trauma of 1973–75 had left enough disillusionment that by 1980, as the Carter administration was overtaken by further embarrassments ranging from double-digit inflation to Iran's seizure of the U.S. embassy staff as hostages, confidence in government slumped and another round of radicalism stirred on the periphery of Middle American politics. Harold Covington, leader of the U.S. Nazi party, got over 40 percent of the vote in the May 1980 Republican primary for attorney general of North Carolina; Thomas Metzger, leader of the state Ku Klux Klan, won the Democratic nomination for Congress in the June primary in the suburban 43rd Congressional District of California; and former Nazi party member Gerald Carlson, who quit to found the National Christian Democratic Union, won the Republican primary in the suburban 15th District of Michigan, and then scored heavily in the general election as well. In both California and Michigan, party officials expressed concern that the radical votes were cast deliberately, and that the more publicity Metzger and Carlson got, the more support they would get.[24]

It turned out not to matter, though, because in a sense the most important "radical" success in 1980 came at the White House level: the election of an "outsider conservative" Republican president—Ronald Reagan—whose appeal reinvigorated the basic coalition that had put Richard Nixon in office twelve years earlier by promising a new prosperity, a new patriotism and a new U.S. global eminence. Middle American radicalism thereupon waited to see if the promise would be fulfilled.

David Duke, Patrick Buchanan, Jerry Brown, Ross Perot and the Return of Middle American Radicalism in the 1990s

By the early 1990s the acid eating into America's confidence measured how much those hopes were fading. There had been some disturbing evidence in 1988; by 1991–92 there was much more. Senior Japanese officials were publicly scoffing at the United States, and opinion polls found that a 63 percent majority of Americans described the United States as in decline. The American Dream was collapsing in a cross fire of shrunken home values, eroding real family incomes and shaky pensions. And so politics, the inescapable mirror, began producing another round of Middle American radicalism. Autumn 1990 brought several unexpected election results, and then in 1991, when Duke surprised in Louisiana and liberal Democrat Wofford won Pennsylvania's Senate race on a platform of middle-class populism, Democratic strategist Robert Beckel identified the feelings to which they had successfully appealed: frustration and fear.[25]

It was Wofford's success, ironically, that persuaded right-wing populist commentator Buchanan to oppose Bush in the 1992 Republican primaries. Then Duke quickly followed suit. Middle American radicalism would have a national forum. Buchanan's Irish Catholic father had listened to Father Coughlin back in the 1930s, and some journalists perceived a recurring isolationist and anti-Semitic thread: the Louisiana neo-fascist and the feisty Irish rightist were tapping into old currents.*

---

*Democratic Senator Tom Harkin of Iowa, whose Irish father also listened to Coughlin, was, despite his liberalism, the other 1992 presidential candidate who joined the conservative Buchanan in populism, class warfare, trade protectionism, neo-isolationism and likening Bush to Britain's King George III.

Indeed, one can identify common ingredients that reach from Buchanan and Duke back through the 1930s and in some cases to the 1890s: middle-class economic apprehensions and status fears, concern that other groups are getting unfair job preferences, overtones of anti-Semitism and nativism, opposition to excessive immigration, economic nationalism and distrust of foreign bankers and diplomats, explicit isolationist or America First psychologies, hostility to various groups—Wall Street, Washington, big labor or big business—and the intensifying of the desire of voters for more "direct democracy" in order to bypass entrenched interest groups. Brown and Perot also voiced some of these viewpoints while avoiding the pitfalls of anti-Semitism, nativism, racism or isolationism. Candidates drawing heavily—rather than marginally—on such themes have generated significant political bow waves only in periods of high economic fear, notably the busts following the three booms that this book has been examining.

Yet despite this continuity with previous periods of fear for the American Dream, the malaise of the 1990s also involved important differences. In sharp contrast with its situation in the 1890s and 1930s, the United States was past its global economic peak, losing ground in ways that threatened purchasing power and standards of living for many Americans. These threats produced an international focus largely missing in the 1930s or 1890s, specifically fear of Japan and the emergence of the Japanese as 1992 political bogeymen for Americans, although concern that U.S. manufacturing jobs were moving to Mexico was also a factor. Still another difference lay in the greater importance of racial fears, which had been a part of the post-1968 Republican presidential coalition. Duke and then, more prominently, Buchanan spoke to both racial and international apprehensions; Brown and Perot confined themselves to the economic concerns about Japan and Mexico.

Let us stipulate: ethnic, racial and religious tensions in the United States have typically accompanied hard times as individuals and groups worry about lost jobs, declining incomes and competition for scarce rewards. So the rise of racial quotas as an issue among white votes in the early 1990s in several ways echoed the 1890s. On one hand, it bore some resemblance to the fear among Northern Protestants in the mid-1890s of job preferences going to Catholics with the help of big-city political machines. In the South, however, the intergroup tension in the 1890s was racial, and at the state level, conservatives often used race to defeat populist challenges, sometimes by mobilizing blocks of subservient black voters to defeat white populists, but sometimes by using racial animosities to break up tentative black-white populist coalitions.

Some analysts believed that national frustration would produce similar effects in the 1990s—that economic progressivism or populism would fail because conservatives would employ racial politics to suppress it. According to this argument, the Republicans, after building their presidential coalition around racial tensions, would continue to inflame them, helped by Democratic insensitivity to middle-class concerns on taxes, crime and the welfare system. There was some basis for these assumptions because the 1968–72 realignment had left the Democrats with 90 to 95 percent of the black vote and a liberal social philosophy disliked by parts of Middle America for seeming to "pander" to blacks at the expense of white interests. After 1968, presidential voting across much of the South had indeed polarized along racial lines. Moreover, the 1988 Bush campaign had sought to tap racial tensions with its emphasis on Willie Horton, the black murderer who raped a white woman while he was on furlough from prison, and then again in its 1991 attempt to elevate racial quotas into a major national issue.

Despite these tactics, the racial basis of voting was frequently exaggerated, as shown by Democrat Clinton's ability to subordinate old tensions in a 1992 victory that combined a majority of the black vote with a close division of the white vote. Many critics of the GOP did not fully understand how earlier Democratic loyalties in the South and Northern ethnic areas had broken down over two generations for a wide range of reasons, far beyond race. When the Democrats had a winning message again, racial tensions would not stop them. In 1969, in *The Emerging Republican Majority,* I laid out the history of the forces combining to pull the South and border states into the Republican presidential coalition. The first momentum came in 1952, when most of the segregationist Dixiecrats who had voted for Strom Thurmond's States Rights presidential ticket in 1948 realigned to support Republican Dwight Eisenhower. Parenthetically, Eisenhower didn't give them any racial concessions; on the contrary, he lost some support in the Deep South in 1956 after he sent federal troops into Little Rock, Arkansas, to uphold the school desegregation mandated in 1953 by the U.S. Supreme Court. However, Dixiecrat voting, highest in the plantation South and affluent suburbs, was motivated by economics as well as by race, so that once historic ties to the Democratic party of the Confederacy had been broken, these constituencies had broad socioeconomic reasons to vote Republican. Southerners followed suit again in 1956—despite Eisenhower's enforcement of desegregation—so that the GOP incumbent, besides carrying Texas, Tennessee, Florida and Virginia, also won Louisiana and came surprisingly close in Arkansas and North Carolina.

By the 1960s, then, Southern white Democratic presidential loyalties had been fading for over a decade and were all but gone in high- and upper-middle-income areas. Yet, with the civil rights revolution at its peak, some Republicans foolishly gambled in 1964 that they could hasten Southern realignment by opposing civil rights—the basis of the disastrous presidential campaign of Arizona senator Barry Goldwater, who lost every state in the nation except for the Deep South tier of South Carolina, Georgia, Alabama, Mississippi and Louisiana. Four years later, with Alabama governor Wallace bolting the Democratic party to run as a pro-segregation independent, the Republicans under Richard Nixon had wisely fallen back to a pro–civil rights posture waiting for regional third-party activity to exhaust itself so that disillusioned white Democrats would be drawn to the GOP by a broad range of cultural issues. This meant that in 1968 Nixon carried essentially the states of the Outer South; the rest would wait.

I discussed these pro-Republican forces in detail in my 1969 book, and as they converged so massively in Richard Nixon's 1972 Southern sweep, they included not just race but also small-town and rural values, patriotism, doubts about welfare, religious traditionalism and a hostility toward bureaucrats, judges, intellectuals and the news media.* No one doubted, for example, that the South was the most hawkish part of the United States in supporting the war in Vietnam—on the day George Wallace was shot in Maryland in 1972, he had been attacking liberals for starting the war and then not letting America win. Moreover, in the early 1970s several books were published on the rapid emergence of white fundamentalist and evangelical Protestants, many of them Southerners, as a key swing vote that threatened the Democratic party's future.[26] Race was a catalyst of Dixie realignment, but by no means its only one, there were many others.

What *The Emerging Republican Majority* had shown, in a nutshell, was that the Democratic presidential coalition was collapsing because it reflected obsolescent and unsustainable Civil War loyalties. Back in 1960, counties in the fifteen or so Southern and border states still voted

---

*Published in 1969, *The Emerging Republican Majority* predicted that the South would turn into a mainstay of a Republican presidential cycle and explained the dynamics involved. *Newsweek* described the book as "the political bible of the Nixon Era," and it had a substantial effect on GOP strategy.

largely as they had fought in 1861–65, an allegiance that made decreasing sense as the presidential Democratic party turned away from its old values and became the party of Harvard, Harlem and Hollywood. Cultural upheaval in the United States of the 1960s was simply too intense to permit a national party committed to left-liberal elites and their values to retain small-town, rural and suburban presidential voters of moderate to conservative outlook who were Democrats largely because a century earlier their families had worn Confederate gray. For this reason, I predicted that the Republicans would first win the relatively moderate Outer South and then would win the racially tense Deep South or Contingent South once these states acquiesced in the civil rights revolution and stopped supporting sectional third-party protest candidates.

That is what happened by 1972, but power shifts invariably breed controversy, and some liberal critics of the Republican party found malevolent depths in the Southern realignment, calling it racist. The irony was that Richard Nixon, while opposing busing for racial balance, permissive jurisprudence and weak handling of crime and riots, was a Quaker with a strong civil rights record. As president, he proposed—somewhat naively—a family-assistance (guaranteed-income) plan for the poor, successfully launched the federal food stamp program and submitted an early version, refused in Congress, of a national health insurance program. He even endorsed affirmative action proposals—the so-called Philadelphia plan—that paved the way for racial hiring quotas. To other critics, not just the GOP but the U.S. electorate as a whole was "racist." Historically, though, the old Civil War Democratic presidential coalition was simply unsustainable by the mid-1960s. Its collapse empowered a cultural and economic conservatism that benefited from some obvious racial cleavages, but categorically racial interpretations were unwarranted, at least at the time.

In the 1980s, however, the politics of maintaining the Republican coalition became more strident. Back in 1970, not only did Richard Nixon remember his Quaker upbringing and the 20 to 30 percent of the black vote he received in the 1960 presidential election, but the memory of the 1964 Goldwater debacle was still strong and cautionary while an egalitarian commitment remained a powerful force in U.S. culture. After Ronald Reagan's inauguration, as we have seen, a new climate began to unfold. Goldwater's defeat in 1964 had been avenged by the election in 1980 of a GOP president almost as conservative; once avenged, Goldwater's loss was no longer a chastening memory. Egalitarian thinking was also in retreat; survival-of-the-fittest economic conservatism and use-your-own-bootstraps antiwelfarist ideology were first cousins. As the apparent boom of the eighties got under way, Republicans believed themselves to be building a realignment and new national majority in which blacks didn't matter much save for a small but growing minority of conservative black businessmen and entrepreneurs. Voters also reflected the new ideology and restated it bluntly enough to inquiring pollsters: the Democrats were too soft on crime, welfare and racial quotas and paid too much attention to blacks. GOP political postures were reinforced accordingly.

Yet too little attention was being paid to important countercurrents. Despite the racial tensions and polarization apparent in the Deep South and in many big cities, national opinion polls showed Americans distinctly more liberal on racial issues than they had been twenty or twenty-five years earlier. By 1989, when David Dinkins became New York City's first black mayor, most of the other big U.S. cities had already broken this barrier. That year also saw the victory of the nation's first elected black governor—Douglas Wilder of Virginia. Then in 1990, Harvey Gantt, a black former mayor of Charlotte, drew 47 percent in North Carolina's Senate race against conservative Republican stalwart Jesse Helms. Incumbent Helms ran TV commercials unfairly linking Gantt to racial quotas, but Gantt *had,* in fact, participated in a broadcasting license application involving a minority preference. Also to the point, had Gantt opposed Helms back in 1972, he would have been lucky to get 36 percent or 38 percent of the vote. In 1990, however, the onetime Charlotte mayor ran well enough in some normally Republican-leaning suburbs to help the Democrats *gain* seats in the North Carolina House of Representatives, and when that House met in January 1991, it elected its first black Speaker. These events hardly symbolized a powerful new backlash against blacks.

Such perceptions were widespread, though, and partially in response, the Bush administration decided to attack the so-called Civil Rights Act of 1991 as a Democratic attempt to enact a system of racial quotas. Bush himself made this charge on several occasions. Aware of how much voters disliked quotas, some commentators proclaimed that Bush had found a way to override Democratic attempts to dabble in class warfare or economic populism. The middle class, they said, would vote according to racial, not economic, resentments. But there were complications even within the Republican coalition. Suburban and upper-income moderate voters, unhappy with the president's racial tactics, were pressuring him to stop, while critics on Bush's right, such as Duke and Buchanan, charged him with appeasement of racial disorder and insincerity in his anti-quota position. Conservative cohesion was crumbling.

Then in late 1991, after Duke's defeat of Republican governor Roemer in Louisiana's open primary, pundits and civil rights leaders unleashed a new criticism. The Bush administration, they charged, had helped create the harsh atmosphere in which an ex-Nazi could succeed. Some moderate Republicans agreed. Bush thereupon quickly agreed to a civil rights bill very much like the one he had earlier opposed, rejecting conservative complaints that the bipartisan compromise still accepted racial quotas.

His decision was a two-edged sword. Blacks were minimally reassured, but both Buchanan and Duke accused the president of betraying low- and middle-income whites. Indeed, following his surprising February GOP primary showing in New Hampshire, Buchanan made a powerful speech to the national Conservative Political Action Conference: upper-class Republicans couldn't be trusted, he said, because they were willing to let ordinary families bear the brunt of minority preferences. It was the "sons of Middle America," in the factories, front offices and fire departments, who were being betrayed on racial quotas by the "Exeter-Yale GOP club . . . the scions of Yale and Harvard . . . the Walker's Point GOP." Such bitter, class-based attacks from the populist right struck at the core of what some described as a White House strategy of administering racial preferences while publicly deploring them and dabbling in covert racial incitement to distract less affluent white voters from economic dissatisfactions. That kind of straddle was unworkable against a serious opposition on the right that demanded anti-quota actions, not just words, even while liberals belabored Bush's inconsistency from the other direction.

Exactly this, however, was part of what Buchanan and Duke briefly represented: significant right-wing insurgency against a Republican president and ruling GOP establishment for the first time since the 1970s. By spring, independent presidential candidate Perot, a former Republican, attacked from yet another direction, this one centrist and critical of Bush's inattention to the cities and lack of a domestic policy as well as his reliance on racial tactics like the Willie Horton ad. Middle American radicalism was back, but in a new role. *Frustrated voters were now ready to question the tactics, loyalties and failures of establishment conservatism, and thus begin fragmenting the right.* Populist dissatisfaction with elite conservative performance would make some cultural and racial issues *divisive* instead of *expansive* for the aging

Republican coalition. Several Rupublicans complained that Bush was hobbled on the quotas issue; the Democrats would only need to quote Pat Buchanan. Moreover, populist voters—not least George Wallace supporters and their heirs, who had been pulled into the Republican coalition by Nixon and then Reagan—were starting to demand government activism, which they doubted could ever come from establishment Republicanism. Voter dissatisfaction with the weak economy and seeming White House inattention to domestic policy was pervasive. Thus, when Los Angeles burst into flames in late April, White House strategists were stunned: instead of profiting from rising racial tension, George Bush lost support for appearing indecisive and trying to blame the chaos on the programs of a Democratic administration that had left office in 1969!

Simply put, liberalism circa 1992 had been out of power too long to be an effective straw man and conservatives had been in power too long to shift responsibility. Voters were anxious over economic and social problems—including unemployment and urban breakdown—that had worsened during three successive Republican presidencies after 1980. Liberals might share blame—indeed, most Americans thought they did—but voter opposition to the status quo necessarily created problems for the party with twelve years in the White House. Moreover, whether in 1860, the 1890s, 1932 or 1968, voters blamed the party in the White House when the national social fabric was torn by riots and other expressions of discontent, and they did again in 1992. Assumptions by Bush strategists that racial tensions and family "values" would still rescue them on Election Day staggered under three separate challenges—from right-wing populists who charged them with deceiving Middle America on behalf of the Exeter-Yale GOP Club, from centrists who said the nation could not afford a domestic policy premised on negativism, and from Democrat Clinton, who took advantage of the failure of both conservative economics and liberal social theory to start building a biracial coalition around a new centrist politics.

The Democratic nominee himself used reasonably strong populist language about taking the country back for middle-class and working-class Americans, words and images that helped him win a large percentage of the disillusioned and outsider electorate. However, the full-fledged frustration candidates had played a pivotal role—and also an extraordinary role because there were so many of them. In different ways and degrees, Duke, Buchanan, Brown and Perot were successive heirs in 1991–92 to what Caddell and Warren had called center extremism and Middle American radicalism. In the end, Duke faded with little lasting effect save to help embarrass Bush into abandoning the racial-quotas issue. Buchanan and Brown both played important catalytic roles, and the 37 percent that Buchanan drew against Bush in the New Hampshire primary *did* turn out to forecast the president's November defeat. No elected Republican president since William Howard Taft—not even Herbert Hoover—had been forced to spend almost a month actively campaigning against a challenger for renomination, and many of the 30 to 35 percent of GOP voters who supported Buchanan in February and March primaries hardened their further opposition to Bush. Buchanan's pollster, in fact, soon turned up taking surveys for Ross Perot.

The Texas billionaire, of course, was the most powerful voice of 1992 frustration politics, attacking Washington's scandals, foreign lobbyists and special interests, exhorting citizens to preserve their children's future and demanding that the United States take care of American interests and American jobs and worry less about the rest of the world. His was a more centrist and less ideological message than that of the others—several pundits likened Perot to a national Roto-Rooter-man —and it proved so powerful that in May and June national surveys showed him pulling ahead of both Bush and Clinton, the strongest independent showing ever recorded. When he dropped out of the race in July—following sharp personal attacks orchestrated by the Bush White House—the fight between the Republicans and Democrats for Perot supporters, as we shall see, became the key to the election, with Clinton the principal beneficiary. Although Perot reentered the race in October to promote his economic message and institutionalize his support for some future purpose, his most important effect on the 1992 political outcome was to damage Bush and divert a large chunk of the Republican coalition, something Clinton had been too weak to achieve during the April, May, and June period when Perot was at his peak. More than any other aroused voices of 1991–92, Perot enlarged the "frustration electorate" to the detriment of the crumbling Republican coalition.

And so in large measure, history appeared to repeat itself. Once again, the forces of Middle American radicalism, unable to carry the day in their own right, were obliged to imprint the valid portions of their agendas, platforms and demand for change on mainstream politics. This was what had happened during the Progressive and New Deal eras, and Democrats assumed that the new Clinton administration, elected on the rhetoric of populism and progressivism, would be similarly energized. But although 1992 appeared to follow this familiar pattern, there were potentially significant differences.

C H A P T E R 1 0

The Election of 1992 and the Prospect of Middle-Class Renewal

A Democratic candidate then (in 1992) must link the idea of America's larger role in the post-cold-war world with the U.S. economic crisis, which must be considered as the crisis of the middle class. These crises—of the U.S. economy and the middle class—must be seen as one and the same. Any drift in the message away from this central linkage will almost certainly prove to be self-defeating. The indispensable element for national action remains a strong purposeful, energetic presidency.

—*The New Republic,* 1990

For some time, it has been clear that U.S. national security interests must include the development of policies that will increase our economic strength and domestic stability. Now, I believe a new definition of national security that recalls the vision of 1947—and augments it with more forceful economic and domestic policy components—is urgently needed. Indeed, I suspect that no foreign challenge of the 1990s will affect America's security as much as what we do, or fail to do, at home on a range of economic and social issues.

—Peter G. Peterson, chairman of the Council on Foreign Relations, 1991

If there is not a substantial reversal of this [federal budget deficit] trend, you will see a third party in 1996, and it will be a broadly based third party.

—Republican U.S. senator Warren Rudman, October 1992

November 3, 1992, was a sunny day in Washington, bright with optimism, and long before it was over, the capital was caught up in reports of a huge Election Day turnout and a Democratic landslide in the making.

By the next morning, Democrats were speaking of a political watershed, but without saying exactly what this watershed would be. However, in the last weeks of the campaign, it had become clear what any watershed would have to involve: nothing less than the economic renewal of the United States and its worried middle class. As the race ended, George Bush and Bill Clinton were each promising middle-class

Americans not to raise their taxes or cut their entitlement programs while warning that the other candidate could not be trusted. Never before were such commitments so central to a presidential campaign. In the watershed election of 1968 the promises of the winning Republicans were largely cultural—to curb crime, restore order and uphold patriotism; in 1992, however, the critical pledges were economic: *that the federal government would not further jeopardize the already endangered middle-class standard of living by taking more money from ordinary Americans' wallets.* National politics, in short, was parading onto a new battlefield.

Clinton had helped draw the lines in the late October presidential debates. Pressed on his tax intentions, he reiterated that he planned "to raise marginal income (tax rates) on family incomes above $200,000 from 31 to 36 percent," but added a new commitment: that "if the money does not come in there to pay for these [spending] programs, we will cut other government spending or we will slow down the phase-in of the programs. I am not going to raise taxes on the middle class to pay for these programs." Then on *Meet the Press* on October 25, the moderator pressured Clinton campaign chairman Mickey Kantor: "Yesterday, the campaign spokesman for your campaign defined the middle class as $50,000. Bill Clinton had said previously that he wouldn't raise taxes on anyone making less than $200,000—any family. Can we expect that people making between $50,000 and $200,000 are eligible for taxation?" Kantor took the bait: "He is only going to raise taxes marginally on those folks making $200,000 a year or more. . . . There will be no taxes on the middle class."[1]

These were not promises to be taken lightly. Bush's widely criticized breach of his own 1988 promise of "Read my lips—no new taxes" had established a new guideline for the 1990s: breaking a tax pledge to the embattled middle class could be dangerous, even fatal. Failing to restore middle-class economic health and confidence could be just as dangerous. The new challenge of American politics was in place.

A Democratic Middle-Class Watershed?

The Democratic strategists who crowded the microphones on the day after the election had reason to be pleased: The 1992 results could be interpreted as a Democratic watershed. Turnout had surged from 50 percent in 1988 to 55 percent, significant because increases in voter participation have frequently characterized turning points in U.S. electoral history. Furthermore, the 1968–88 Republican presidential coalition had collapsed in 1992, just as the earlier GOP coalition had in 1932 after the Roaring Twenties slid into the depressed thirties. The parallel economic circumstances that marked the 1980s, the 1920s and the Gilded Age, which I outlined in *The Politics of Rich and Poor,* yielded another political shift. Though George Bush tried to deny even a partial resemblance between the early 1990s and the early 1930s, the electorate did not.

One comparison is particularly apt. Each of the three major presidential realignments of the Republican-Democratic rivalry since the 1850s started with an electoral "big bang" in which the party in power lost 16 to 18 percentage points of voter support, the extreme magnitude of rejection. Between 1856 and 1860, the ruling Democrats plummeted from 45 percent of the total vote to 29 percent, and the Civil War Republican coalition took its place. Then between 1928 and 1932, support for the ruling Republicans collapsed from 58 percent to 40 percent, putting the New Deal Democratic coalition in office. Then between 1964 and 1968 the Democrats dropped from 61 percent of the total presidential vote to just 43 percent, and the Nixon-Reagan GOP coalition controlled the White House for twenty of the next twenty-four years.* By this yardstick, the 16-point drop in Republican support between Bush's 54 percent in 1988 and his 38 percent debacle in 1992 also qualified as a "big bang." The important geographical differences from previous presidential voting patterns visible in 1992 supported the same conclusion.

The erosion of GOP ideological appeal in the late 1980s and early 1990s also suggested a change whose causes went far beyond the personal weaknesses of George Bush. Breakdowns could be seen in all three of the major issue sectors—foreign affairs, economics and domestic policy—that had promoted GOP presidential success in 1968 to 1988. The Cold War had underscored competencies in dealing with the Soviet Union, keeping America strong and protecting national security, and the GOP was the beneficiary. The collapse of Russia, however, dropped foreign policy so far down the list that fewer than 10 percent of voters gave it major priority. For the average American, Washington's new international emphasis was to safeguard U.S. jobs and industries. The most important foreign policy priority was to have less of it. Returning the national focus to domestic affairs was a shift that favored Democrats.

*The only other comparable loss of support for the party in the White House came in the three-way Wilson–Taft–Theodore Roosevelt race of 1912. The unusual 1896 watershed did not involve this kind of change.

The reversal in economics was devastating. Economic policy hadn't been a critical GOP issue in 1968–72, but by the mid-1980s Reagan made taxes, prosperity and economic management work for the GOP, hiding the party's traditional vulnerability on these issues in a boom financed by debt. By 1992, however, after the financial bailouts and the speculative implosion, the long downturn and tax policy controversies, the old Republican albatross was back. In domestic affairs, we have seen how much of the critical GOP momentum in the Nixon and Reagan years had come from social issues: rising crime, judicial permissiveness, the death penalty, riots and racial tension, welfare, pornography, campus radicalism, busing, quotas, patriotism, parades and support for the flag. Religious themes and appeals were closely related. Not only did these points, too, lose importance next to 1992 dislocations in the economy, but a new set of domestic and cultural issues were emerging for the 1990s: health care, education, urban problems, the environment, economic fairness, abortion and what could be called a "women's" array of concerns, including day care, parental leave, equal pay, the feminization of poverty, the glass ceiling in employment, women's political empowerment and sexual harassment. Issues like these favored the Democrats, affirming that electoral watersheds usually overlap with new domestic-policy agendas.

Another such sign came from the 1988–92 breakdown of presidential GOP voting in suburbia. The greater the local distress, the greater the loss. From Long Island to Los Angeles, through metropolitan Philadelphia and the "collar counties" of Chicago, postelection analysis confirmed a stark new reality: suburbia now held a majority of the U.S. population, but the Republicans no longer held a majority of suburbia. The polls showed that Clinton led among suburban voters by about five points nationally, the Democrats' first edge since Lyndon Johnson's 1964 landslide. Those suburban victories had proved transient; the gains of 1992 had more social, economic and demographic depth, although it was premature to say that suburbia had a Democratic future.

A further demographic change could be seen in the increasing political role of women and minorities visible in 1992. The political culture of the 1980s, one could argue, had a definite male or aggressive coloration—getting tough on crime, whipping inflation, curbing government, regaining world respect, idealizing Darwinian economics, de-emphasizing welfare and the safety net, and reversing defeat in Vietnam, the Panama Canal treaties and the 1979 hostage-taking of the U.S. embassy staff in Iran by a decade of gunboat diplomacy from Grenada to

Tripoli and Panama. White males liked it and went almost two to one for Ronald Reagan in 1984; women split more evenly. The "gender gap" of the 1980s, then, was pro-Republican because it reflected male ideological enthusiasm and female ambivalence. The 1990s began with signs of a very different political culture. White males, many of them under economic pressure, had less command, while women and minorities enjoyed more influence as the broader national emphasis shifted from gunboat diplomacy and Darwinian economics toward more concern with domestic problems, national and household budgets, pressures on families, repair of the safety net, and more concerns for those who lost ground during the 1980s. The new gender gap, which helped Democrats in 1992 because women were lopsidedly in favor of new-agenda politics and men were divided, also supported the thesis of a sea change.

While all these changes encouraged the Democrats, the central caution remained: the favorable trends could dissipate quickly if the new administration failed to revitalize and sustain the economy—and the lessons of history and of past great powers were more cautionary than encouraging.

The Lessons of Great-Power History

As we have seen, the magnitude of frustration voting in 1992 reflected how middle-class Americans worried not just about recession but about the signs of a *larger* decline: stagnant incomes and loss of the economic cushion the United States had gained in World War II, the troubling emergence of the United States as a lower-wage manufacturing nation, and speculation that the next generation's standard of living might fall.

When candidate Clinton blamed part of the U.S. decline on lack of a national economic strategy, Republicans grumbled about the Democrats running America down, contending that things were not that bad. Ironically, when one compares the circumstances of the United States with those of previous economic powers as they began to decline—seventeenth-century Spain, eighteenth-century Holland and turn-of-the-century Britain—*both* sides had a point.

Overall, America clearly *was* slipping. Despite GOP denials, the late 1980s and early 1990s revealed serious and continuing declines: real hourly wages were in a steady downtrend, infrastructure was wearing out, car-jackings and drive-by shootings were increasing, public debt was expanding and U.S. air and naval bases were being dismantled around the world, just as the legions of the Roman and British empires had departed in their day. Yet if Democrats were correct in framing the broad facts of America's ebb—a tide the general public, too, felt and feared—optimists also had a case. Unlike Holland and Britain in their heydays, the United States was not a relatively small maritime power lacking great natural resources or a large domestic market and thereby vulnerable. On the contrary, because of its size, resources and the possibility of a larger North American economic union, the United States had no reason to expect the Dutch and British fate, provided its policymakers learned from earlier downturns that imperial overreach, mushrooming debt and increased emphasis on finance, money and the interests of rentiers rather than on manufacturing were more than a source of great-power decline. These circumstances were also clues to possible remedies.

Understanding is not enough, though. Indeed, Clinton and Perot between them raised many of the needed perspectives in the 1992 campaign, and some Spaniards, Dutchmen and Britons, debating their nations' predicaments, had also understood what was going wrong. We have seen in Chapter 8 how, as Spanish gold shipments from the New World were about to decline, the early-seventeenth-century economic reformers known as *arbitristas* explained that Spain was destroying itself through excessive bureaucracy and debt, overreliance on importing gold and indifference to manufacturing and the middle class. One prime minister, the Count-Duke of Olivares, proposed a plausible reform agenda, only to see it overwhelmed by the Thirty Years War. Many in Holland circa 1750 could see that financial speculation and a preference for overseas investment had subordinated concern about decaying Dutch manufacturing and growing poverty; no Dutch government, however, implemented any remedy. Even before Britain's economy peaked relative to the rest of the world, Matthew Arnold had warned of the danger of becoming a second Holland, and by the 1890s, books worrying about the German and U.S. challenges had become best-sellers. In 1903, as we have seen, Prime Minister A. J. Balfour put the case for helping British manufacturing before Parliament and the electorate, only to see it rejected.

As the results of the U.S. presidential election of 1992 sank in, the question for the new decade and the upcoming century was whether the United States could go beyond a vague debate to concrete remedial action. Despite America's greater size and broader renewal opportunities, it did suffer from many of the same weaknesses that had eventually crippled earlier great economic powers. The dangers deserved attention.

Take the process of financialization, with its favoritism to upper-bracket elites and financial interests. This had proceeded apace in the late 1980s and early 1990s, as the salaries of corporate CEOs soared from 30 times that of the average worker in 1980 to 130 to 140 times as much in 1991 while real hourly wages declined, and the income of investment firms' set records while unprecedented numbers of ordinary Americans fell back on public assistance. But the most crippling corollary of financialization has always been the expansion of debt and government deficits. Although profligacy in modern public finance has so far typically involved left-liberal politicians and their constituencies, a variation occurs in leading economic powers as they move past their zenith: then conservatives, too, discover the convenience of government debt in helping them maintain a military presence around the world, in letting policymakers borrow instead of raising taxes on the rich, and in sustaining a large rentier class dependent on safe, profitable returns on investments. Moreover, as debt serves these functions, old political and moral restraints break down: ignoring the inevitable risks becomes easier.

Loose financial practices, in turn, create entrenched dependents and constituencies. The Hapsburgs drowned Spain in debt, but in 1622, when the government proposed to cap the interest on bonds at 5 percent, the rentiers and foreign bankers who had grown accustomed to much higher rates balked and proposed to let some other class bear the consequences.[2] After Holland increased its public debt sixfold in the wars of the early eighteenth century, holding and trading debt instruments became a financial life-style for wealthy Dutchmen, even though by the 1760s and 1770s many Dutch financiers were sure that the country's speculative bubble would soon burst.

The financialization of early-twentieth-century Britain, in turn, proceeded rapidly even as the nation slipped in manufacturing and technology. That the national debt had expanded tenfold during the Great War didn't seem to matter during the go-go years of the 1920s. London remained the capital of international finance, but further borrowing would soon end that, because after the national debt tripled again to £25 billion during World War II, Britain found itself dependent on U.S. monetary support. The general economic recovery of the 1950s and 1960s helped, but by the time of the next currency devaluation in 1967, one economic historian described the extraordinary transformation: In fifty years, the capitalist superpower of 1914 had become "the ward of the other developed countries of the non-Communist world. They constituted a creditors' club exercising the same watchful concern over the British economy that the Aid Consortia exercised over those of India, Indonesia or Turkey."³

As Americans, too, would discover by the late 1980s, the early stages of major chronic indebtedness are more numbing than energizing. Former U.S. commerce secretary Peter Peterson, who in 1991 described America's passivity toward rising domestic and foreign debt as "pathological," invoked Britain's precedent. Even in the 1950s and 1960s, said Peterson, "most Britons did not seem too sensitive to the crushing burden—either on their pockets or on their consciences. Their regret seemed a trifle perfunctory, their concern superficial, and their appreciation of the scale and urgency with which the creditors required repayment very vague indeed."⁴ Late-twentieth-century American attitudes were surprisingly similar, abetted by the profitability of debt, leverage and speculation to the financial community.

Meanwhile, the overindulgence of financial elites and investors by the political right is often countered by the left's overenlargement of the welfare state. In rich countries starting to fade, politicians have often turned to welfare statism and expanded public payrolls to avoid or cushion working-class or middle-class income losses. Consider the European-settled nations of the Southern Hemisphere—Australia, New Zealand, Argentina and Uruguay—that quickly grew rich at the turn of the century from producing grain and meat. As their relative wealth faded in the 1920s and 1930s, they embraced welfare-state solutions: cradle-to-grave security, family allowances, bloated government payrolls and high pensions. So, too, had the great economic powers: government and church payrolls maintained a veritable welfare state in seventeenth-century Spain, likewise swollen provincial and municipal payrolls in eighteenth-century Holland, and, no one can ignore the mid-twentieth-century British welfare state. While such policies can mitigate unfairness, they do not result in long-term revitalization. The challenge for middle-class renewal is to curb the several sources of excessive debt: the abuses sponsored by financial elites, interest groups and welfare statists alike.

In all these respects, historical precedents offer little encouragement. The extent to which Washington of the early 1990s was an "iron triangle" of lobbies and influence wielders was matched in many state capitals, and the documentation was weighty: inch-and-a-half-thick directories of Washington representatives listing fourteen thousand names, cynical surveys ranking the fifty states by their ratios of lobbyists to elected legislators. Kindred buildups had been a stifling presence before. Four hundred years earlier the flow of New World gold to Spain helped Madrid's population grow from 4,000 in 1530 to 100,000 a century later, luring bankers and moneymen from all parts of Europe, supporting a huge Hapsburg court and a massive church establishment in which every religious order and faction imaginable was represented. By 1611 the government was ordering the great nobles to leave Madrid and return home, according to one historian, in hopes of reducing the ranks of parasites, but the attempt failed.[5]

Mancur Olson, the contemporary U.S. historian who has linked the sclerosis of great nations to high interest-group ratios, explains the decline of twentieth-century Britain by its much larger number of associations than any other country except the United States and a network of interest groups so powerful that it gave rise to the term "establishment."[6] The United States of the 1990s, in turn, probably ranked as the greatest interest-group concentration in world history— and in Washington some of the most influential agents represented foreign masters. None of the previous great economic powers had been able to clear out the sclerosis of entrenched elites and interest groups; the United States, with its populist traditions, would have to be the first.

A related challenge lay in America's entrenched and complex geographic subdivisions from states down to counties, municipalities and even water districts and special tax districts. Like the Hapsburg empire, the United Provinces of the Netherlands and the United Kingdom of Great Britain and Ireland, the United States got an explosive boost from the way its territories, markets and population came together—even the names reveal the geographic fusion processes that have helped each great economic power to its zenith. The problem, however, is that as great powers have matured and then begun to decline, once-vital geographic boundaries have calcified into regional interest groups and expensive duplicative bureaucracies. Here, too, the precedents are glum, but the opportunities of a North American economic union could give the United States a rare re-energizing.

There are other areas where late twentieth-century U.S. policymakers may learn from history, not least the accumulating political demands of 1991–92 to replace yesteryear's internationalism with a narrower set of U.S. interests and a greater emphasis on domestic problems. Beyond the overt nationalists like Buchanan, Harkin and Perot, even Paul Tsongas, whose demands for sacrifice in his brief 1992 presidential campaign endeared him to the upper-middle-class intelligentsia, bragged about buying an American automobile "because I think like an economic patriot"—and he struck a chord by proclaiming that "the Cold War is over—Japan and Germany won."[7]

In 1991, Peter Peterson, chairman of both the Council on Foreign

Relations and the Institute for International Economics, wrote a paper entitled *Rethinking America's Security: The Primacy of the Domestic Agenda*, and its demand for emphasizing domestic affairs was promptly endorsed by the bipartisan American Assembly. William G. Hyland, editor of *Foreign Affairs*, the nation's best-known foreign policy journal, had broken the ice a few months earlier by declaring, "What is desperately needed is a psychological turn inward. . . . We need to start selectively disengaging abroad to save resources."[8] The editor of another journal was even more blunt: "A new isolationism focused on domestic reform and intent on strictly evaluating our foreign commitments has much to commend itself to the American people."[9]

Ohio professor Alfred Eckes, former chairman of the International Trade Commission under Ronald Reagan, pointed out that since World War II U.S. policymakers had relentlessly subordinated domestic economic considerations, jobs and even industries to please allies and advance diplomatic and military objectives. Even with the Cold War over, Eckes said, "Officials in Washington continue to play the old game of trading access to the U.S. market for cooperation on non-trade issues." The United States, he said, could no longer afford that.[10]

The plans announced by Clinton in 1992 to emphasize rebuilding the U.S. infrastructure and high-value-added, high-wage jobs also drew on what history said about the past failures of declining economic powers. The Republicans, argued Democratic theorists, had favored investors and investment too much for their own sake, witness George Bush's repeated calls for reduction of the capital gains tax on virtually every kind of asset, not just new ones but also old assets bought years ago. New York governor Mario Cuomo, campaigning for Clinton, charged that in the Reagan-Bush era, too many investors had put their money in Taiwan, junk bonds or BMWs instead of in Ohio, Pennsylvania or other parts of the United States.

The nation's need for investment had become a cliché, but government statistics showed that the top 1 percent of Americans—the investing class by any definition—had already formed huge sums of capital during the 1980s boom. Stock prices had soared, but so did the price of French Impressionist paintings, English antique furniture, classic automobiles, rare Burgundies, seaside mansions and Park Avenue triplexes for the rich, as well as the similar but less costly items demanded by $150,000- or $250,000-a-year doctors, lawyers and corporate vice presidents. Speculation and lavish consumption flourished, but too little was ultimately invested in ways that would rebuild Middle America's fading high-wage jobs base. Lobster salad tasted better, Ferraris were more fun, junk bonds paid higher interest, plants in Tijuana returned more dividends than those in Terre Haute and paper entrepreneurialism produced the quickest capital gains. What was missing wasn't capital but its productive investment in the national interest— and the wise men of the previous great economic powers could have cited chapter and verse about that, too.

The Democrats proposed guidelines. Wealth, in general, would be taxed more, and long-term investments would be treated better than short-term investments; so would funds invested in high-technology start-ups. Multinational companies would be more closely scrutinized; foreign multinationals operating in the United States would face higher taxes, while U.S. multinationals would no longer get tax breaks for moving jobs overseas. "Trickle-down" Republican economics, which Clinton derided, would be replaced by more investment in public infrastructure, from schools to transportation, and more investment in people through increased outlays for health insurance, education and job retraining.

Greater controversy surrounded a national industrial policy to promote the high-technology sector. The lack of statist traditions made the United States more like Britain and Holland, which could not manage such strategies and transformations, and less like Japan or Germany. Moreover, there was a second roadblock: the enormous role and power of interest groups and the likelihood they would warp any national strategy to suit their own purposes. A more limited national-interest and competitiveness agenda should have been pursued a decade earlier; by the 1990s, strategic coordination and decision-making still made sense, but interest groups, political considerations and bailouts for politically favored groups were sure to figure more prominently in the outcome.*

The most important strategy of all was obscure—how to reduce the U.S. budget deficit and high level of international indebtedness. Neither blueprint, Democratic or Republican, had been taken seriously by economists during the 1992 presidential election. Only the independent Perot had spoken to that predicament. And perhaps more than any other circumstance of America's global decline during the previous

---

*In 1984 I published a book entitled *Staying on Top: The Business Case for a National Industrial Strategy*, which argued for what was then a relatively limited competitiveness agenda. Eight years later the likelihood of distortion by interest groups seemed much higher, an argument I set forth in the July/August 1992 *Harvard Business Review*.

two decades, it hung like a sword over U.S. prospects for renewed economic growth—and over the new Democratic administration's prospects for consolidating a true watershed.

Economic Decline, Middle-Class Renewal and the Future of the Party System

Economic decline sours voters, curdles the public psychology and changes political systems. It is a tale that has been told since Greece and Rome, and most recently in the Great Britain of the first half of the twentieth century which, as its people lost their confidence, exchanged the politics of optimism that had characterized the nineteenth-century party system of Liberals versus Conservatives for what soon became class-conscious competition between capitalist Conservatives and socialist Labourites.

Democrats quickly claimed that the 1992 presidential election in the United States, by drawing frustration politics into the two-party system, represented a renewal of the same populist-progressive traditions that had marked the previous upheavals of the industrial era in the administrations of Theodore Roosevelt and Woodrow Wilson and then Franklin D. Roosevelt. Nineteen ninety-two was, they claimed, another such moment. But under the unusual circumstances of the 1990s, that possibility remained as much a question as an answer.

Not only does economic decline curdle voter psychology, it consumes politicians and national leaders, as it had from Rome down to a between-the-wars Britain managed by little-remembered prime ministers who could not stop the tide. The same could be true of the United States since the war in Vietnam and its haunting theme song, "Bye-Bye Miss American Pie." Presidents Lyndon Johnson, Richard Nixon, Gerald Ford, Jimmy Carter and George Bush were all defeated for reelection or forced to step down before completing two terms. Only Ronald Reagan, apostle of "America is back," the debt-laden shadow empire of the 1980s, managed two terms before reality set in again.

The careful historian will note that the U.S. political system has survived such problems before. From 1876 to 1892, none in a series of weak presidents, almost all single-termers, could win a majority rather than plurality of the popular vote. Politics did not regain a firm base until the Democratic fusion with the Populists in 1896. Before that there were the ineffective pre–Civil War presidencies of 1840–60, six men in twenty years, none of whom served more than a single term, partly because the party system was breaking down as the Civil War approached.

That the unsuccessful or thwarted presidencies since the 1960s pointed to another larger upheaval—and not toward a simple watershed replacement of Republicans with Democrats—also seemed conceivable in 1992, a possibility dramatized by the extraordinary independent candidacy of Ross Perot, who in May and June achieved the hitherto unimaginable: national polls showed him passing the presumptive Democratic and Republican presidential nominees even before he entered the race. Several commentators noted in June that by a number of important yardsticks, Perot's third-party candidacy stood to be the most broadly based since John C. Fremont won 33 percent for the fledgling Republican party in the election of 1856. At its peak, Perot's movement was stronger than Fremont's in the polls, and in contrast to previous third-party contenders, his support was not just in one angry region, cultural group or among an ideological fringe, it was *national.* His appeal was not to a periphery with peripheral issues but to the angry, radicalizing middle—the people whose frustrations and circumstances we have been examining. In June, private polls gave Perot a stunning 60 percent backing in Orange County, California, famous as the archetype of heavily Republican high-tech suburbia.

The formerly Republican billionaire businessman's decision to leave the contest in July, with a partial nod to Clinton, sent his supporters flooding into the Democratic nominee's column and gave the Arkansas governor a lead over Bush that he never lost. That was Perot's principal near-term effect: to help realign Republican and Independent voters in Clinton's direction. Even when he returned to the race in October, ultimately pulling more or less evenly from Bush and Clinton, his overall effect was twofold; first, to attack Bush on grounds of both economic failure and personal integrity, partly neutralizing the incumbent's attacks on Clinton; and, second, to provide an alternative ballot choice to anti-Bush Republicans and independents, especially in the suburbs, where a huge 20–25 percent vote for Perot did its greatest—and fatal—damage to the Republican presidential coalition.

Nevertheless, if Perot had simply wanted to beat Bush, whom he regarded as having failed the American people, he would not have reentered, for Bush was about to lose. The importance of his reentry was that by winning one or two of the three presidential debates, he regained much of the reputation he had lost after July's withdrawal. And by doing so, he was able to win 19 percent of the vote on Election Day, not the best showing by a third-party nominee since 1856, as might have been possible earlier, but the best since 1912, when Theodore Roosevelt tried to reclaim the White House on the third-party Progressive ticket—and TR was an ex-president at the time.

The major third-party candidates have generally seen the valid part of their critique absorbed by one of the two major parties, except in the 1850s, when that was not possible. In July 1992 Clinton seemed to have absorbed the Perot constituency at little relative cost; by November 1992 that was no longer true. Perot's message and constituency would have to be preempted by actions and achievements in the cause around which Perot had based his candidacy: restoration of the American Dream, serious reduction of the deficit that hung over America's children, reduction of interest-group control in Washington and adoption of a national strategy to rebuild manufacturing and the larger U.S. economy.

Many Americans thought Perot suffered from egotism and more than a hint of paranoia, but polls showed that three quarters of voters were glad that he had run. Perhaps more important, as Election Day closed in on a weary electorate, late-October Time/CNN polls showed that 63 percent of Americans favored the formation of "a third political party that would run candidates for president, Congress and state offices against the Democratic and Republican candidates." Even in June, at Perot's zenith, a lower 59 percent had thought so, and the October support included 62 percent of Republicans, 76 percent of Independents and 58 percent of Democrats. While some looked to Perot, others were talking about third parties and new centrist movements. The existing party system was weaker, much further removed from its Civil War roots, than when Theodore Roosevelt had tried to breach it in 1912.

Much of the burden of upholding the nation's two-party tradition and making economic and political renewal work was on Bill Clinton and the Democrats, despite their own encrustation with interest groups, but that was just one part of the equation. From the frontier vitality of Jacksonian Democracy in 1828 to the electoral revolution of 1992, ordinary Americans—whether they be called yeomanry, the "middling sort" or twentieth-century middle class—have made the U.S. system of politics and government one of the world's most effective. It is they who have made democracy work. As we have seen in Chapter 3, the United States has successfully used watershed elections to manage economic and cultural upheavals that have torn other nations apart. Swing voters have made national politics a reliable process of renewal by repeatedly turning against unpopular elites and rebuilding what historians have called the "vital center." The 1990s, however, looked as if they might be different.

Despite the validity of ordinary Americans' economic concerns, there were signs that the middle class, which had come to rage against "special interest groups," could become the biggest economic interest group of them all. In previous eras, expanding income, increasing national wealth and greater opportunity and mobility had under-pinned the ability of the great mass of the population to be a force for national renewal. However, it had now begun to seem that middle-class decline and frustration could no longer be rectified in this man-ner. And although voters knew that federal budget deficits would make some economic sacrifices necessary, they also knew that reducing or taxing middle-class entitlement programs—from Medicare to Social Security and even children's eligibility for college loans—would fur-ther diminish what were for many already-eroding incomes or living standards. Politicians would have to generate an agenda of shared sacrifice and renewal that rested more heavily on those who had made so much money from the speculations and abuses of the 1980s before the general public would accept retrenchment.

The United States was not alone in watching its politics and eco-nomics of the 1990s turn away from the speculative and ideological excesses of the prior decade. Even as George Bush lost the presidency, the conservative leaders of most of the other G-7 governments were also worrying about upcoming elections and the difficulty of survival with their job ratings in the 20s and 30s. New tides were coming in Britain, Canada, Germany, Japan and elsewhere, not just in Washing-ton. But the United States *was* alone in the trauma of a great power sliding from its increasingly distant zenith. What was at stake in the revitalization of the United States economy and the middle class was nothing less than the remaining belief—and perhaps now more the hope—in American exceptionalism.

Notes

Chapter 1

1. For example, the U.S. Census Bureau in 1992 reported a decline in the percentage of persons with "middle" incomes from 71.2 percent in 1969 to 63.3 percent in 1989 ("U.S. Says Middle Class Shrinking," *New York Times,* February 22, 1992). The University of Michigan's Panel Study of Income Dynamics found a 15-point shrinkage from 1978 to 1989 ("America's Middle-Class Meltdown," *Washington Post,* December 1, 1991).
2. "U.S. Underestimated Job Losses," *Los Angeles Times,* February 2, 1992.
3. "Kids Count," Survey Release and Data Sheet, Annie Casey Foundation, Greenwich, Connecticut, January 1992.
4. "Index of Social Ills Shows U.S. Woes," *Chicago Tribune,* January 14, 1992.
5. "U.S. Society Called in Decline," *Chicago Tribune,* February 23, 1992.
6. "New Suburbs," *Wall Street Journal,* March 26, 1987.
7. "Backlash Hits Growth-Loving Moreno Valley," *Los Angeles Times,* January 13, 1992.
8. Frank S. Levy and Richard C. Michel, *The Economic Future of American Families: Income and Wealth Trends* (Washington, D.C.: Urban Institute Press, 1991), p. 101.
9. "Study Finds Income Growth Rate of Two-Parent Families Declined in 1980s," *Washington Post,* January 17, 1992.
10. "Rich Get Richer, the Middle Class Poorer," *Philadelphia Inquirer,* December 12, 1991.
11. "The Incredible Shrinking Middle Class," *American Demographics,* May 1992, pp. 34–38.
12. "Rich-Poor Gap Is Widening," Associated Press, *Boston Globe,* December 3, 1990.
13. Cader, Rainwater and Smeeding, *American Economic Review,* May 1989.
14. "Consumers Draw Down Value in Their Homes," *Wall Street Journal,* August 5, 1991.
15. "The Other Suburbia," *Newsweek,* June 26, 1989, pp. 22–24.
16. "Jobless, Their Affluence Ebbs Away," *Boston Globe,* December 30, 1990.

17. "Once Welfare Meant Someone Else," *New York Times,* March 11, 1991.
18. "Tough Times Hit Home for Those Who Lose Theirs," *Los Angeles Times,* January 28, 1992.
19. "Suburban Homeless Seek Shelter," *Chicago Tribune,* February 5, 1992.
20. "Country Club Helps Members Find Work," *Los Angeles Times,* May 18, 1991.
21. "Signs of Distress Are Rising in the Suburbs," *Philadelphia Inquirer,* March 22, 1992.
22. Ibid.
23. "Welfare Line No Longer Just for Hardcore Poor," *Chicago Tribune,* January 19, 1992.
24. "Recession Impacting Family," Rocky Mountain Poll release, March 12, 1992.
25. "New Poor Swelling State's Welfare Rolls," *Dallas News,* February 9, 1992.
26. "Reality of Homeless Teens Sinks In," *Chicago Tribune,* October 9, 1990.
27. "Hunger Rears Head in Affluent Suburbs," *Denver Post,* March 10, 1991.
28. "Record Numbers of Americans Enlist in Food Stamp Program," *Boston Globe,* February 2, 1992.
29. "Food Pantries on the Rise in Affluent Areas," *Boston Globe,* July 12, 1991.
30. "School Lunch Numbers Testify to Hard Times," *Washington Post,* December 14, 1991.
31. Patricia Calhoun Bibby, "Is the Yuppie Era of Buying Spent?" *Louisville Courier-Journal,* February 24, 1991.
32. "U.S. Workforce Gets Bludgeoned," *Philadelphia Inquirer,* December 7, 1991.
33. "Bye-Bye America's Pie," *Washington Post,* February 11, 1992.
34. "U.S. Workers on Job Longer for Less Pay," *Christian Science Monitor,* May 15, 1992.
35. "Graduates Facing Worst Prospects in Last Two Decades," *New York Times,* May 12, 1992.
36. See Katherine S. Newman, *Falling from Grace* (New York: Free Press, 1988).
37. Frederick Lewis Allen, *The Big Change: 1900–1950* (New York: Bantam Books, 1961), p. 127.
38. Ibid., p. 128.
39. Ibid., p. 184.
40. "The New Rich," *Fortune,* January 1952, p. 62.
41. Ibid., p. 184.
42. Ibid., pp. 185–86.
43. Ibid., p. 183.
44. Simon Schama, *The Embarrassment of Riches* (Berkeley: University of California Press, 1988), p. 4.
45. Ibid., p. 323.
46. C. R. Boxer, *The Dutch Seaborne Empire, 1600–1800* (London: Pelican Books, 1988), p. xxiii.

47. F. Crouzet, *The Victorian Economy,* quoted in Paul Kennedy, *Rise and Fall of the Great Powers* (New York: Random House, 1987), p. 151.
48. E. J. Hobsbawn, *The Pelican Economic History of Britain: From 1750 to the Present Day: Industry and Empire,* Vol. 3 (Baltimore, Md.: Penguin Books, 1968), p. 154, Appendix 10.
49. Abbé Coyer, *Nouvelles Observations sur l'Angleterre* (1779), p. 15.
50. "The New Rich," p. 62.
51. Allen, op. cit. p. 204.
52. Allen, op. cit., p. 187.
53. Various speeches by Joseph Chamberlain in Aaron L. Friedberg, *The Weary Titan: Britain and the Experience of Relative Decline, 1985–1905* (Princeton, N.J.: Princeton University Press, 1988), p. 75.
54. Ibid., p. 72.
55. Walter Russell Mead, "Why the Roller-Coaster Only Goes One Way: Down," *Los Angeles Times,* April 14, 1991.
56. Donald H. Straszheim, *Merrill Lynch First Quarter 1991 Economic Analysis,* p. 14.
57. "Not Getting Ahead," *New York Times,* December 16, 1990, Section 4, p. 1.
58. "Downward Mobility Is Stalking Baby Boomers," *Business Week,* January 29, 1991, p. 22.
59. "Consumer Spending: From Spur to Drag," *Wall Street Journal,* January 21, 1991.
60. "Hours of Work Up," *Christian Science Monitor,* August 31, 1990.
61. Katherine Newman, "Falling from Grace" (New York: Free Press, 1988), p. 21.
62. "America's Middle-Class Meltdown," *Washington Post,* December 1, 1991.
63. Shares of pretax adjusted family income from Congressional Budget Office tax simulation model, House Ways and Means Committee 1992 Green Book, p. 1521.
64. Denny Braun, *The Rich Get Richer* (Chicago: Nelson-Hall, 1990), p. 246.
65. Ibid., p. 249.
66. Benjamin Friedman, *Day of Reckoning* (New York: Random House, 1988), p. 38.
67. Barry Siegel, "Crises of Pessimism Part of U.S. History," *Los Angeles Times,* April 4, 1982, p. 10.
68. Ibid.
69. In 1975, close to the peak of U.S. economic confidence, the Gallup Poll, in its last question of this sort, found 72 percent of Americans putting themselves into the middle class (release, July 21, 1975).
70. Frank Levy, *Dollars and Dreams: The Changing American Income Distribution* (Russell Sage Foundation, 1987), p. 206.
71. Levy and Michel, op. cit., p. 54.

Chapter 2

1. "Rich-Poor Gap Is Widening in Western Nations," *Boston Globe*, December 3, 1990.
2. "Cardboard Citizens," *Financial Times*, April 30, 1991.
3. "Thatcher's Poll Tax," *Philadelphia Inquirer*, April 24, 1988.
4. "Fight Over British Tax Shift Imperils Thatcher Ideology," *New York Times*, April 23, 1990.
5. "By-election Jolts British Conservatives," *Washington Post*, March 9, 1991.
6. "Canada Decides to Introduce New Sales Tax," *Wall Street Journal*, April 25, 1989.
7. "Mulroney Could Pay Dearly for Canada's New Tax," Reuters, *Boston Globe*, December 16, 1990.
8. "Canada Bites the Budget Bullet," *Washington Times*, February 14, 1991.
9. Gallup Poll Canada, October 1991.
10. "Rich Man, Poor Man in Japan," *New York Times*, December 26, 1988.
11. Statement of Senator Daniel P. Moynihan to U.S. Senate Finance Committee, December 13, 1991.
12. "An End to the 80% Tax," *U.S. News & World Report*, March 9, 1992, p. 70.
13. 1991 Handbook, Advisory Commission on Intergovernmental Relations, pp. 122–30.
14. Ibid.
15. "Some Worry Plan to Cut Tax Credits May Spur New Backlash," *Los Angeles Times*, April 24, 1990.
16. David Broder, "Who's the Fairest of Them All," *Washington Post*, February 13, 1991.
17. *Tax Features*, November 1990, p. 5.
18. "Once-Proud British Rail System," *Chicago Tribune*, May 12, 1991.
19. "Triumph of Capitalism Rings False," London *Observer*/Cleveland *Plain Dealer*, December 31, 1989.
20. "Suburbs Staggered by Cuomo Budget Cuts," *New York Times*, February 6, 1991.
21. "Budget Cuts Begin to Hit Where It Hurts," *Los Angeles Times*, September 30, 1991.
22. Warren Brookes, "The New Deficit Dynamic," *Washington Times*, December 3, 1990.
23. "Law and Economics: A New Order in the Court?" *Business Week*, November 16, 1987, p. 93.
24. Statement by the President, July 3, 1987, the White House Press Office.
25. "Study Assails Values of the New Right," *Los Angeles Times*, January 25, 1985.
26. Bob Kuttner, "The Fraying of America's Communal Thread," *Boston Globe*, March 8, 1985.
27. "Conservative One-Worlders," *Wall Street Journal*, April 3, 1989.

28. E. J. Dionne, "Economic Inequality Becoming the Norm," *Washington Post,* May 13, 1990, p. 1.
29. Benjamin DeMott, "The Myth of Classlessness," *New York Times,* October 10, 1990.
30. Ibid.
31. Kuttner, op. cit.
32. "Books on Greed Worry Wall Street," *New York Times,* February 12, 1990.
33. "The Cutting Edge: Wealth Issues, Tax Fairness Themes and Populist Public Opinion," *American Political Report,* May 24, 1991.
34. "Rich Man, Poor Man in Japan."

Chapter 3

1. See, in particular, Margaret Canavan, *Populism* (New York: Harcourt Brace Jovanovich, 1981).
2. Interview, National Conference of State Legislatures, September 10, 1992.
3. NBC/Wall Street Journal poll, April 11–14, 1992.
4. *Washington Post,* July 8, 1992, p. 1.
5. "California Budget Agreement Forged," *Investors Daily,* July 23, 1991.
6. "A Brewing Revolt Against the Rich," *Fortune,* December 17, 1990, p. 90.
7. "Democrats Coalescing on 1992 Strategy," *Washington Post,* July 26, 1991.
8. Washington Outlook, *Business Week,* October 7, 1991, p. 45.
9. "The Greening of Corporate Executives," *Dallas News,* November 10, 1991.
10. "Roper's the Public Pulse," Research Supplement, June 1991, p. 4.
11. "On the Eve of '92: Fault Lines in the Electorate," Times-Mirror Center for People and the Press, December 4, 1991.
12. William Safire, *The New Language of Politics* (New York: Collier Books, 1972), p. 387.
13. *Third Barnhart Dictionary of New English* (New York: H. W. Wilson Co., 1990).
14. Lawrence Goodwyn, *The Populist Moment* (New York: Oxford University Press, 1978), p. 281.
15. Fingerhut-Granados Opinion Research, "Post-Election Poll Shows Mondale Could Have Won Vote of Reagan Democrats with Populist Economic Appeal," November 8, 1984, p. 2.
16. Ibid., p. 3.
17. Kevin Phillips, *The Politics of Rich and Poor* (New York: Random House, 1990), p. 29.
18. "The Electronic Election," *Boston Globe,* November 13, 1988, p. B12.
19. "To Broaden Political Base, Dukakis Must Keep Running," *Christian Science Monitor,* November 14, 1988.
20. "Liberalism Reconstructed," *The Commonwealth Report,* April 1989, p. 1.

21. Ibid.
22. "Democrats Coalescing on 1992 Strategy."
23. "Wofford Pulls Even with Thornburgh in Pennsylvania," *Wall Street Journal,* October 31, 1991.
24. "U.S. Report Says Voters Feel Shut Out of Political Process," *Financial Times,* June 11, 1991.
25. Mancur Olson, *The Rise and Decline of Nations* (New Haven, Conn.: Yale University Press, 1982).

Chapter 4

1. "Millionaires," *The Nation,* January 18, 1928, p. 57.
2. Ibid.
3. Geoffrey Perrett, *America in the Twenties* (New York: Touchstone Books, 1982), pp. 321–22.
4. Stuart Chase, *Prosperity: Fact and Myth* (New York: Charles Boni Paper Books, 1929), p. 116.
5. Charles F. Holt, "Who Benefitted from the Prosperity of the Twenties?" *Explorations in Economic History,* 14, July 1977, pp. 277–89.
6. William Greider, *Secrets of the Temple: How the Federal Reserve Runs the Country* (New York: Simon and Schuster, 1987), p. 692.
7. Ibid., p. 245.
8. U.S. Census Bureau, *The Statistical History of the United States* (New York: Basic Books, 1976), p. 1112.
9. "Sensitive Issues Reportedly Kept Poverty Study Quiet for Months," *Boston Globe,* May 13, 1991.
10. "Economists Question Accuracy and Value of U.S. Statistics," *Washington Post,* July 5, 1990.
11. Ibid.
12. Ibid.
13. "Did Economy Trip on False Statistics?" *Charlotte Observer,* June 5, 1991.
14. "U.S. Jobless Figures Fail to Add Hidden Unemployed," *Los Angeles Times,* April 11, 1991.
15. "Official Decries Gap Between Rich and Poor," *Los Angeles Times,* October 30, 1991.
16. "U.S. Underestimated Job Losses, State Finds," *Los Angeles Times,* February 3, 1992.
17. "Jobless Figures Don't Add Up," *Philadelphia Inquirer,* July 5, 1992.
18. "Inflation May Be Worse Than Data Show," *Wall Street Journal,* May 10, 1990.
19. "How Accurately Does the Government Measure the Pinch of Inflation?" *New York Times,* April 7, 1991.
20. Ibid.

Chapter 5

1. "The Ides of Taxes Are Upon Us," *Washington Times,* April 12, 1992.
2. Release, February 5, 1991.
3. The data on the different effective state tax rates on middle-class and rich families comes from *A Far Cry from Fair,* Citizens for Tax Justice, April 1991.
4. Ibid., p. 12.
5. "Unpopularity Tax," *Forbes,* June 24, 1991, p. 88.
6. "High-Taxes New Yorkers Face Milking," Associated Press, *Washington Times,* September 19, 1991.
7. Brad Sherman, revised statement of March 22, 1991, p. 3.
7A. "They're Not Called Taxes, But Fees to Rise," *Los Angeles Times,* August 31, 1992.
8. "Making Tax Code Family-Friendly," *Miami Herald,* June 2, 1991.
9. Ibid.
10. *The Tax Fairness Index,* Progressive Policy Institute Report, July 1990, p. 4.
11. Unpublished data from the Urban Institute.
12. "The New Rich," *Fortune,* January 1952, p. 63.
13. Robert Shapiro, "Invest," *The New Republic,* December 23, 1991, p. 17.
14. "How Hefty a Tax for Millionaires?" *Washington Times,* January 22, 1991.
15. Ben J. Wattenberg, ed., *The Statistical History of the United States* (New York: Basic Books, 1976), p. 1112.
16. "States and Cities Fight Recession with New Taxes," *New York Times,* July 27, 1991.
17. " 'Soak the Rich' Fallacy," *Christian Science Monitor,* May 10, 1991.
18. Release, February 5, 1991.
19. Ibid., pp. 20, 51.
20. "States Take Up New Burdens," *New York Times,* May 21, 1990.
21. "Cuomo: U.S. Must Alter Course," *Christian Science Monitor,* August 12, 1991.
22. Neil Peirce, "Hard-Hit States Pass Bill Down the Line," *Philadelphia Inquirer,* April 22, 1991.
23. "Cries for Help Go Unheeded," *Los Angeles Times,* February 4, 1991.
24. "The Natives Are Restless," *Forbes,* April 16, 1990.
25. Jon Margolis, "Government Closest to the People," *Chicago Tribune,* July 23, 1991.
26. *A Far Cry from Fair,* Citizens for Tax Justice, April 1991, p. 11.
27. "Tax Charade Hits Rural Areas," *Des Moines Register,* June 11, 1989.
28. "Hidden Taxes Set to Deluge New Yorkers," *New York Times,* May 22, 1990.
29. "Are State Courts Becoming Tax Collectors?" *California Journal,* September 1991, p. 425.
30. Ibid.

31. "Mapping Options as Court Takes Up Prop. 13," *Los Angeles Times,* October 27, 1991.
32. "Business Fees Replace Overt Tax Hikes," *Human Events,* May 23, 1992, p. 15.
33. "Higher and Higher," *Dallas News,* October 1, 1991.
34. "State's Water Rate under Attack," *Boston Globe,* February 8, 1992.
35. "The Natives Are Restless."
36. "As Realty Taxes Go Up, Up," *New York Times,* February 4, 1991.
37. "Poor Towns Taxed More to Get Less," *Chicago Tribune,* July 22, 1990.
38. "Beyond the Property Tax," *U.S. News & World Report,* August 6, 1990, p. 39.
39. "Red Tape Kills an American Dream," *Los Angeles Times,* July 8, 1991.
40. "Who's That Taxing at Your Door," *Chicago Tribune,* May 7, 1991.
41. "Beyond the Property Tax," p. 40.
42. "Nationline," *USA Today,* August 13, 1991.
43. "Legacy of Anti-Tax Fervor: Levies, But with a Purpose," *New York Times,* November 27, 1990.
44. "Not a Big Tilt in Tax Policy," *New York Times,* October 27, 1990.
45. "Budget Pact Creates New Bubble," *Investor's Daily,* November 27, 1990.
46. "Budget Tricks and Treats," *Washington Times,* October 31, 1990.
47. "Budget Deadlock Is Not about Whether to Tax the Wealthy But How to Do It," *Wall Street Journal,* October 24, 1990.
48. "Bush Considers Taxing Worker Health Benefits," *Chicago Tribune,* April 26, 1991.
49. Steven D. Gold, "A New Twist for State Tax Policy in 1991," *State Legislatures Magazine,* December 1991.
50. Ibid.
51. "Business Fees Replace Overt Tax Hikes," p. 15.
52. "Unpopularity Tax," *Forbes,* June 24, 1991, pp. 88–89.
53. "Colleges Fear Proposed Tax on Students," *Los Angeles Times,* June 2, 1990.
54. "For Travelers, It Seems Nothing Is Certain Except Taxes," *Wall Street Journal,* March 14, 1991.

Chapter 6

1. "Cries for Help Go Unheeded," *Los Angeles Times,* February 4, 1991.
2. "Eighties Leave States and Cities in Need," *New York Times,* December 30, 1990.
3. "Suburbs Staggered by Cuomo Budget Cuts," *New York Times,* February 6, 1991.
4. "An Era of Abundance Ends in Nassau County," *New York Times,* December 16, 1991.
5. "New Cuts Sap Feeble School Districts," *New York Times,* April 11, 1991.

6. "Recession Leaving State Governments More Efficient," *New York Times,* April 22, 1992.

7. "Governors Say States Face Increasing Pinch," *Boston Globe,* April 22, 1992.

8. Henry J. Aaron, "Why States, Cities Are in Such a Sorry State," *Boston Globe,* June 23, 1991.

9. "Fat Paychecks Got States and Cities Deep in Hock," *Business Week,* September 23, 1991, p. 26.

10. "As Libraries Face Cuts, Supporters Plan a Protest," *New York Times,* July 8, 1991.

11. "Many Public Libraries Suffer Major Blows," *Wall Street Journal,* February 13, 1991.

12. "Study: U.S. Ranks Low in Spending on Schools," *Chicago Tribune,* April 9, 1991.

13. Interview with American Federation of Teachers, June 1992.

14. "Gains at Private Primary Schools," *USA Today,* December 28, 1991.

15. Jane Bryant Quinn, "Squeezed by Tighter Budgets," *Chicago Tribune,* April 15, 1991.

16. "Cal State System Crippled," *Los Angeles Times,* October 11, 1991.

16A. "At U Conn, Costs Squeeze Its Students," *New York Times,* August 16, 1992.

17. Quinn, op. cit.

18. "Are College Costs Out of Line," *Investor's Daily,* Nov. 12, 1991.

19. "Bush Seeks Limits on U.S. Aid to Students," *Chicago Tribune,* May 29, 1991.

20. "Dallas Students Protest Teacher Layoffs," *Philadelphia Inquirer,* September 4, 1991.

21. "Millionaires' Tax Urged for Student Loan Fund," *New York Times,* July 31, 1991.

22. "Rich Tactic for the Poor," *Los Angeles Times,* July 20, 1991.

23. "Budget Cuts Ravage Hospital Care," *New York Times,* October 22, 1991.

24. "State Mental Health System Deterioration," *Chicago Tribune,* November 18, 1991.

25. "An Investment in America," *Boston Globe,* February 7, 1990.

26. "Economists Warn of Third Deficit," *Dallas News,* September 28, 1989.

27. "Shoddy Infrastructure Gets Scant Attention," *Boston Globe,* April 11, 1990.

28. "Infrastructure Poses Trillion-Dollar Problem," Cleveland *Plain Dealer,* June 4, 1989.

29. "States Pay Bigger Share for Highways, Bridges," *Los Angeles Times,* April 17, 1990.

30. "Federal Cuts Derailing Mass Transit," *Christian Science Monitor,* April 8, 1991.

31. Ibid.

32. See, respectively, Fred Barnes, "Planes, Migraines and Automobiles,"

Business Month, August 1990, and "Shoddy Infrastructure Gets Scant Attention," *Boston Globe*, April 11, 1990.

33. Barnes, op. cit.
34. "Stuck in Traffic," *California Journal*, August 1991.
35. "Taming the L.A. Traffic Monster," *Christian Science Monitor*, November 28, 1990.
36. Ibid.
37. "The Public Fat Cats," *Wall Street Journal*, December 28, 1990.
38. "Rising Costs Force Towns to Share Various Services," *New York Times*, July 15, 1991.
39. "School Fundraisers: Rich Areas Prosper, Poor Suffer," *Los Angeles Times*, June 17, 1991.
40. "Many Are Buying Their Own Security," *Philadelphia Inquirer*, June 23, 1991.
41. Ibid.
42. "Legacy of Anti-Tax Fervor," *New York Times*, November 27, 1990.
43. Milton Goldin, *Ronald Reagan and the Commercialization of Giving* (Tarrytown, N.Y., 1990), pp. 31–33.
44. "U.S. Charities See Increase in Gifts," *Boston Globe*, December 16, 1990.
45. "Look Who's Being Tightfisted," *Business Week*, November 5, 1990, p. 29.
46. Ibid.
47. Ibid.
48. "Pul-eeze! Will Somebody Help Me?" *Time*, February ?, 1987, pp. 48–56.
49. Ibid., pp. 49, 52.
50. Ibid., p. 55.
51. "Poultry, Yes, Hospital Care, No, Consumers Say," *Birmingham News*, June 10, 1990.
52. Jane Bryant Quinn, "The Middle Class Melt," *Newsweek*, December 17, 1990.
53. Ibid.
54. "Lower Tuition Becomes an Enticement," *Boston Globe*, January 13, 1992.
55. "Big Chill on Campus," *Time*, February 3, 1992, p. 61.
56. Ibid., p. 63.
57. "Cost of Cable Service Up 56%," *Washington Post*, July 19, 1991.
58. "Cable on Defensive," *Los Angeles Times*, November 23, 1991.
59. "Ticket Flap: What Price Convenience?" *Los Angeles Times*, May 10, 1991.
60. "It's Slippery at the Top," *Forbes*, September 30, 1991, pp. 113–22.
61. Ibid.
62. "High Attorneys' Fees Are Coming under Attack," *Philadelphia Inquirer*, September 9, 1990.
63. "Activists Want to Pry Open Lawyers' World," *Wall Street Journal*, August 31, 1990.
64. "Banks Revise Fee Structures," *Wall Street Journal*, May 13, 1991.

65. "Interest on Deposits Falls," *New York Times,* April 19, 1991.
66. Ibid.
67. "Ills of the Nation's Health Care System," *Wall Street Journal,* June 24, 1991.
68. "Soaring Medical Costs," *Business Week,* October 28, 1991, p. 24.
69. "Doctors' Pay Up 73% in Three Years," *Des Moines Register,* May 5, 1991.
70. This was the usual estimate Canadians gave to the U.S. press in 1991–92.
71. "Successful System Focuses on Controlling Doctors' Costs," *Boston Globe,* May 13, 1991.
72. "In Canada, a Government System That Provides Health Care for All," *New York Times,* April 30, 1991.
73. "Successful System."
74. "Germans' Health Care Model," *Boston Globe,* May 5, 1991.
75. "Why Health Care Costs Are Tough to Cure," *USA Today,* March 11, 1991.
76. "Why Drugs Cost More in the U.S.," *New York Times,* May 24, 1991.
77. "Drug Costs under Fire," *USA Today,* September 25, 1991.
78. "Are Soaring Medical Costs Sinking Employee Morale?" *Investor's Daily,* June 21, 1991.
79. "Part-time Work a Full-time Chore," *Chicago Tribune,* March 31, 1991.
80. "The New Bragging Rights," *California Business,* July/August, 1991, p. 61.
81. "Part-time Work a Full-time Chore."
82. Chris Tilly, *Short Hours, Short Shrift* (Washington, D.C.: Economic Policy Institute, 1990), p. 3.
83. "Unprepared for Recession," Economic Policy Institute, March 1992, press release, p. 1.
84. "Beware: Pensions Are an Endangered Species," Reuters New Service, *Los Angeles Times,* July 30, 1990.
85. "Retirement Prospects Grow Bleaker for Many as Job Scene Changes," *Wall Street Journal,* August 26, 1987.
86. Jane Bryant Quinn, "Lost: Another Health Benefit," *Newsweek,* June 17, 1991.
87. Stephen Rose and David Fesenfest, *Family Income Changes in the 1980s* (Washington, D.C.: Economic Policy Institute, 1990), p. 17.
88. "The American Family Isn't Mom, Dad and the Kids Anymore," *Atlanta Constitution,* November 13, 1988.
89. "For Many Women, One Job Isn't Enough," *New York Times,* February 15, 1990.
90. "Two Income Couples Earn More," *Investor's Daily,* November 18, 1988.
91. *Families on a Treadmill in Staff Study of the Joint Economic Committee,* January 13, 1992, p. 18.
92. "Child Care Costs Hit Poor Hardest," *Boston Globe,* August 15, 1990.
93. "Census Report Shows a Rise in Child Care," *New York Times,* August 16, 1990.

94. "Options Help Lower Child Care Costs," *Chicago Tribune*, February 4, 1991.
95. "Home Ownership Dream Fading for Middle Class," *Chicago Tribune*, October 3, 1989.
96. "Home Ownership for Young Buyers Dropping," Associated Press, *Birmingham News*, June 25, 1989.
97. "Americans Less Likely to Own Homes Now," *Investor's Daily*, December 21, 1990.
98. "Foundations of Homeownership Crack," *Wall Street Journal*, June 14, 1991.
99. "Homebuying by Unmarrieds Surges in State," *Los Angeles Times*, January 10, 1991.
100. "Foundations of Home Ownership Crack."
101. "America: What Went Wrong," *Philadelphia Inquirer*, October 20, 1991.
101A. "Boom Decade Rang Faintly," *Boston Globe*, April 19, 1992.
102. "Baby Boom Faces Care of Aging Relatives," *Wall Street Journal*, September 26, 1991.
103. Ibid.
104. "Hours of Work Up, Hourly Pay Down," August 31, 1990.
105. "Shift of Women into Labor Market," *Baltimore Sun*, September 11, 1988.
106. "When It Comes to Cutbacks, Little Things Now Mean a Lot," *Philadelphia Inquirer*, September 6, 1991.
107. "The New 'In' Vacation: Shorter, Closer to Home," *Chicago Tribune*, September 1, 1991.
108. "Stagnant Pay: A Delayed Impact," *New York Times*, June 18, 1991.
109. "Two-Career Families Face Dilemma," *Los Angeles Times*, August 12, 1990.
110. "Americans Would Take Cut in Income to Gain More Leisure Time, Survey Says," *Christian Science Monitor*, June 20, 1991.
111. "Stagnant Pay: A Delayed Impact."

Chapter 7

1. "What's a Deb to Do?" *New York Times*, December 16, 1990.
2. "Looking Downscale Without Looking Down," *Business Week*, October 8, 1990, p. 62.
3. "Restaurants Go Downscale to Draw Families," *Investor's Daily*, December 11, 1990.
4. "Sweatshops Are Found Resurging and Spreading," *New York Times*, September 4, 1988.
5. "Welfare Rolls in Illinois Largest Since Depression," *Chicago Tribune*, February 28, 1991.
6. "1980s Gravy Train Left Most Behind," *Chicago Tribune*, May 12, 1991.

7. "Tremendous Trend," *Forbes*, September 2, 1991, p. 23.
8. Ibid.
9. "Dream of Striking It Rich Fading in Silicon Valley," *Los Angeles Times*, September 9, 1991.
10. "California Population Surprise," *Washington Post*, December 17, 1991.
11. "Lavish Homes Seen Losing Luster in New Jersey," *New York Times*, October 9, 1991.
12. "Jobs Vanish and May Not Return," *Los Angeles Times*, November 28, 1991.
13. Robert Reich, "The Unprepared American," *Christian Science Monitor*, April 11, 1991.
14. Lawrence Mishel and Rudy Texeira, "The Myth of the Coming Labor Shortage" (Washington, D.C.: Economic Policy Institute, 1991).
15. "Narrowing a Wage Gap," *New York Times*, June 26, 1987.
16. "California Is No. 1 in Taxes on Rich," *Los Angeles Times*, July 25, 1991, p. D4.
17. "Americans Are Just Simulating the Good Life," *San Francisco Chronicle*, June 18, 1991.
18. "85% of All Households in Hock," *Investor's Daily*, April 22, 1991.
19. "An Excess of Plastic," *Forbes*, February 4, 1991, p. 52.
20. Robert Pollin, *Deeper in Debt: The Changing Financial Conditions of U.S. Households* (Washington, D.C.: Economic Policy Institute, 1990).
21. These are the estimates of Susan Sterne of Economic Analysis Associates Inc. of Stowe, Vermont.
22. "Wealth of U.S. Households Stayed Flat," *Wall Street Journal*, January 11, 1991.
23. "The Richest People in America," *Forbes*, October 21, 1991, p. 145.
24. "Even with Less Consumers May Spend More," *Business Week*, July 29, 1991, p. 20.
25. "The Richest People in America," p. 145.
25A. Mortimer Zuckerman, "Washington's Nasty Addiction," *U.S. News & World Report*, May 4, 1992, p. 100.
26. "Wealth of U.S. Households Stayed Flat."
27. William Greider, *Secrets of the Temple: How the Federal Reserve Runs the Country* (New York: Simon and Schuster, 1987), p. 591.
28. "The 1980s Surge in Home Prices Was Mostly a Mirage," *Business Week*, September 23, 1991.
29. "Eighties Pounded State Renters, Homeowners," *Milwaukee Journal*, September 14, 1991.
30. Phillips, *Politics of Rich and Poor*, p. 194.
31. "Vacation-House Sales Slow to a Standstill in Some Parts of U.S.," *Wall Street Journal*, June 21, 1991.
32. "Wealth of U.S. Households Stayed Flat."
33. "Consumers Draw Down Value in Their Homes," *Wall Street Journal*, August 5, 1991.

34. "1992 Roundtable," Barron's, January 20, 1992, p. 15.
35. "Winning Bid for Exec Comes at a Key Moment," Los Angeles Times, October 25, 1991.
36. "Firms' Failures Leave Lives in Ruin," New Orleans Times-Picayune, October 27, 1991.
37. Howard C. Weizmann, "Safe Annuities or Federalized Annuities," Wall Street Journal, October 24, 1991.
38. "Title Insurers' Reserves Stir Worry," New York Times, November 9, 1991.
39. "Shortfall Doubles for the Country's Top Pension Plans," Washington Times, November 26, 1991.
40. "Retire or Bust," Newsweek, November 25, 1991, p. 50.
40A. "Private Pension Funds in Peril," Washington Times, July 29, 1992.
41. "Warning Given on Public Employee Pensions," Philadelphia Inquirer, November 21, 1991.
42. "Social Security Faces Crisis, Former Official Warns in Book," Miami Herald, January 5, 1992.
43. "Stockman: The Economy Is Now Out of the Woods," Philadelphia Inquirer, July 14, 1991.
44. Public Citizen, Who Robbed America? (New York: Random House, 1990).
45. "RTC May Try to Redo Some Costly Deals," Chicago Tribune, July 22, 1990.
46. "Taxpayers' Nightmare," San Francisco Examiner, June 16, 1991.
47. Peter Passell, "Economic Scene," New York Times, February 12, 1992.
48. Who Robbed America? p. 149.
49. "Taxpayers' Nightmare."
50. "Changes Sought in S&L Bail-out," Chicago Tribune, July 31, 1991.
51. "Fed's Fat Cat Insurance," Washington Times, October 20, 1991.
52. "Bank Rates Hit," Washington Times, October 9, 1991.
53. "Economic Diary," Business Week, September 16, 1991.
54. "Economic Scene," New York Times, June 5, 1991.
55. "Earning Plight of Baby Boomers," New York Times, September 21, 1988.
56. "Many Young Families Face '30s Living Standards," Portland Oregonian, April 1, 1990.
57. "Downward Mobility Is Stalking Baby Boomers," Business Week, January 28, 1991.
58. "A Generation's Vast Wealth Is Baby-Boomer Windfall," Philadelphia Inquirer, May 26, 1991.
59. Ibid.
60. "The Windfall Awaiting the New Inheritors," Fortune, May 7, 1990, p. 72.
61. "Generation to Inherit Uneven Riches," Boston Globe, October 6, 1991.

Chapter 8

1. Report of Genesee Economic Area Revitalization (GEAR), 1990, p. 7.
2. "Pittsburgh Shakes Off Rust," *Los Angeles Times,* October 9, 1991.
3. "Imports, Immigrants Hurt the Unskilled," *Christian Science Monitor,* September 6, 1991.
4. This paragraph is based on the survey "Rust Belt's Recession Cushion" published by the *Los Angeles Times* on January 7, 1991. A kindred examination of much more distressed Peoria, Illinois, was published by *The New York Times* on November 17, 1991.
5. "Rust Belt's Recession Cushion."
6. J. H. Elliott, *Imperial Spain 1469–1716* (New York: Mentor Books, 1966), pp. 194–95.
7. González de Cellorigo, quoted in ibid., pp. 306–7.
8. C. R. Boxer, *The Dutch Seaborne Empire, 1600–1800* (London: Penguin Books, 1965), p. xxiii.
9. Jonathan I. Israel, *Dutch Primacy in World Trade, 1585–1740* (Oxford: Clarendon Paperbacks, 1991), p. 357.
10. Ibid., p. 402.
11. Fernand Braudel, *The Perspective of the World, Civilization and Capitalism 15th–18th Centuries,* p. 197.
12. Boxer, op. cit., p. 328.
13. Asa Briggs, "Middle Class Consciousness in British Politics, 1780–1846," *Past and Present,* Vol. I (1956), pp. 65–74.
14. Ibid.
15. Samuel H. Beer, *British Politics in the Collectivist Age* (New York: Knopf, 1961), p. 45.
16. Aaron L. Friedberg, *The Weary Titan* (Princeton: Princeton University Press, 1988), pp. 38–40.
17. Ibid., p. 75.
18. G.D.H. Cole and Raymond Postgate, eds., *The British Common People, 1746–1946* (London: Methuen & Co./University Paperbacks, 1961), p. 497.
19. John Stevenson, *British Society, 1914–45* (London: Penguin Books), p. 38.
20. E. J. Hobsbawm, *The Pelican Economic History of Britain: From 1750 to the Present Day: Industry and Empire,* Vol. 3 (Baltimore, Md.: Penguin Books, 1968), p. 273.
21. Stevenson, op. cit, p. 119.
22. Ibid., pp. 130–31.
23. Ibid., p. 123.
24. Michael Sissons and Philip French, *Age of Austerity* (London: Penguin Books, 1964), p. 38.
25. Ibid., p. 42.
26. Elliott, op. cit., p. 313.
27. Ibid., p. 204.

28. Boxer, op. cit., pp. 34–35.
29. Braudel, op. cit., p. 197.
30. Boxer, op. cit.
31. Braudel, op. cit., pp. 274–75.
32. Hobsbawm, op. cit., p. 119.
33. Cole and Postgate, op. cit., p. 498.
34. Ibid.
35. Joseph S. Nye, Jr., "Before Fall," *New Republic,* February 13, 1989, p. 37.
36. Charles W. Boyd, ed., *Mr. Chamberlain's Speeches* (London: Constable, 1914), Vol. 2, pp. 535–36.
37. "Democratic Campaign Issue: Jobs," *Washington Times,* July 5, 1991.
38. Economists from Japan's Nomura Institute and elsewhere made this point in several international publications.
39. George F. Will, "What Dukakis Should Be Saying," *Washington Post,* September 15, 1988.
40. Elliott, op. cit., pp. 200–201.
41. Simon Schama, *The Embarrassment of Riches: An Interpretation of Dutch Culture in the Golden Age* (New York: Knopf/University of California Press, 1988), p. 166.
42. Stevenson, op. cit., p. 124.
43. Roger Milliken, "Power, Wealth and Protectionism," speech delivered to National Conference of Christians and Jews, New York, December 6, 1985.
44. Paul Kennedy, *The Rise and Fall of the Great Powers* (New York: Random House, 1987), pp. 151–52.
45. Boxer, op. cit., pp. 324–25.
46. Friedberg, op. cit., p. 39.
47. Ibid., p. 64.
48. Ibid., p. 63.
49. Hobsbawm, op. cit., p. 166.
50. "For Sale: America," *Time,* September 14, 1987, p. 53.
51. John B. Judis, "Show and Tell," *New Republic,* January 20, 1992, p. 15.
52. Boxer, op. cit., p. 118.
53. Kennedy, op cit., p. 319.
54. Elliott, op. cit., pp. 326–29.
55. Friedberg, op. cit., pp. 116–18.

Chapter 9

1. Christopher Matthews, "From One Who Warned of Hitler," *Washington Times,* November 12, 1991.
2. Max Lerner, "Enduring Qualities of Evil," *Washington Times,* November 24, 1991.
3. Seymour Martin Lipset and Earl Raab, *The Politics of Unreason* (New York: Harper Torchbooks, 1970), p. 95.

4. Ibid., p. 80.
5. Richard Hofstadter, *Social Darwinism in American Thought* (Boston: Beacon Press, 1955), p. 119.
6. Richard Hofstadter, *The Age of Reform* (New York: Knopf, 1955), p. 132.
7. Ibid.
8. Lipset and Raab, op. cit., p. 167.
9. Ibid., p. 190.
10. Ibid., p. 169.
11. James A. Farley, *Behind the Ballots* (New York: Harcourt Brace, 1938), p. 250.
12. Lipset and Raab, op. cit., p. 169.
13. Richard B. Morris, ed., *Encyclopedia of American History* (New York: Harper & Row, 1976), pp. 417–18.
14. Ken Bode, "Hero or Demagogue?" *New Republic,* March 3, 1986, p. 37.
15. *Papers of Franklin D. Roosevelt,* 1938. Vol. 5, pp. 69–69.
16. William Leuchtenburg, *Franklin D. Roosevelt and the New Deal* (New York: Harper & Row, 1963), pp. 53–54.
17. Arthur M. Schlesinger, Jr., *The Politics of Upheaval* (Boston: Houghton Mifflin, 1960), p. 68.
18. Lipset and Raab, op. cit., pp. 176, 194.
19. Alan Brinkley, *Voices of Protest* (New York: Knopf, 1982), p. 198.
20. Ibid.
21. This paragraph was largely taken, with some rephrasing, from p. 198 of my book *Post-Conservative America,* published by Random House in 1982.
22. Eugene Litwak, Nancy Hooyman and Donald Warren, "Ideological Complexity and Middle American Rationality," *Public Opinion Quarterly,* Fall 1973, p. 320.
23. See Seymour M. Lipset, *Political Man* (New York: Anchor Books, 1963), pp. 131–73.
24. See "KKK Leader's Race Stirs Dismay," *Los Angeles Times* (May 29, 1980), and "White Supremacist's Vote-Getting Talent Stuns His GOP Detractors," *Washington Post* (November 15, 1980).
25. "Angry Voters Send Message," *Washington Times,* November 14, 1991.
26. See, in particular, Lowell Streiker and Gerald S. Strober, *Religion and the New Majority,* 1972.
27. NBC/Wall Street Journal poll, April 1992.
28. "On the Eve of '92: Fault Lines in the Electorate," Times-Mirror Center for People and the Press, Washington, D.C., December 1991, pp. 2–3.

Chapter 10

1. "Clinton's Stand on Middle-Class Tax Hike," *Human Events,* November 7, 1992, p. 3.

2. "Imperial Spain," p. 311.
3. Peter Peterson, "Rethinking America's Security: The Primacy of the Domestic Agenda," privately printed, May 11, 1991.
4. Ibid., p. 7.
5. "Imperial Spain," p. 311.
6. Mancur Olson, *The Rise and Decline of Nations* (New Haven, Conn.: Yale University Press, 1980), pp. 77–80.
7. Bob Kuttner, "Tsongas' Plea for Economic Patriots," *Boston Globe,* June 7, 1991.
8. "Shift to Domestic Concerns Urged," *Washington Post,* July 19, 1991.
9. "Time for a New Isolationism," *Christian Science Monitor,* June 18, 1990.
10. Alfred Eckes, "Trading American Interests," *Foreign Affairs,* Fall 1992, pp. 135–54.

A P P E N D I X   A

The Converging Income Shares of the Middle Quintile and the Top 1 Percent of the U.S. Population

Shares of Pretax Adjusted Family Income (AFI)

(In percent)

All families (by income group)	1977	1980	1985	1988	1989
Lowest quintile	4.7	4.3	3.7	3.5	3.6
Second quintile	10.8	10.5	9.5	9.1	9.2
Middle quintile	16.3	16.0	15.1	14.6	14.7
Fourth quintile	22.9	22.9	22.2	21.7	21.7
81 to 90 percent	15.6	15.7	15.7	15.3	15.4
91 to 95 percent	10.1	10.1	10.4	10.1	10.3
96 to 99 percent	11.6	11.7	12.4	12.6	12.7
Top 1 percent	8.3	9.2	11.6	13.4	13.0
Overall	100.0	100.0	100.0	100.0	100.0
Highest quintile	45.6	46.7	50.1	51.4	**51.4**
Top 10 percent	30.0	31.0	34.4	36.1	36.0
Top 5 percent	19.9	20.9	24.0	26.0	25.7

Note: Table reads for boldface figure that 51.4 percent of all adjusted pretax family income in 1989 belonged to families in the fifth or highest quintile. Quintiles are weighted by persons.

Source: Congressional Budget Office tax simulation model, cited in U.S. House Ways and Means Committee 1992 Green Book. p. 1521.

Important Changes in the Tax Burden

The Declining Importance of the Personal Exemption

Federal Income Tax Personal Exemption, as a Percent
of U.S. Individual Income

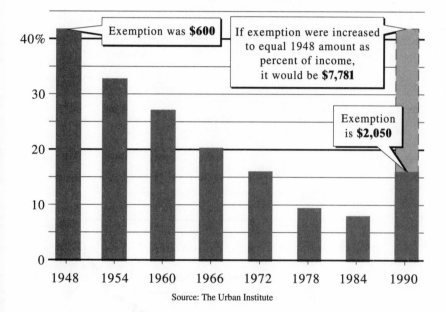

Source: The Urban Institute

The Rising Social Security (FICA) Tax

Year	Tax Rate	Tax Base	Max Payment
1980	5.80%	$25,900	$1,502
1981	6.65%	$29,700	$1,975
1982	6.70%	$32,400	$2,170
1983	6.70%	$35,700	$2,391
1984	7.00%	$37,800	$2,646
1985	7.05%	$39,000	$2,749
1986	7.15%	$42,000	$3,003
1987	7.15%	$43,800	$3,131
1988	7.51%	$45,000	$3,379
1989	7.51%	$48,000	$3,604
1990	7.65%	$51,300	$3,924

Source: Social Security Administration

Tax Changes and the Benefit to the Top 1% and Top 5% (1977–1989)

Total Federal Effective Tax Rates for All Families

All families (by income group)	1977	1980	1985	1988	1989	Percent change 1977–1989
Lowest quintile	9.3	8.1	10.3	9.3	9.3	0.1
Second quintile	15.4	15.6	15.8	15.9	15.7	1.4
Middle quintile	19.5	19.8	19.1	19.8	19.4	-.4
Fourth quintile	21.8	22.9	21.7	22.4	22.0	.7
81 to 90 percent	24.0	25.3	23.4	24.6	24.2	.9
91 to 95 percent	25.2	26.3	24.2	26.0	25.6	1.5
96 to 99 percent	27.0	27.9	24.3	26.5	26.2	-2.9
Top 1 percent	35.5	31.7	24.9	26.9	26.7	-24.7
Overall	22.8	23.3	21.7	22.9	22.6	-.7
Highest quintile	27.2	27.5	24.1	26.0	25.6	-5.8
Top 10 percent	28.8	28.6	24.5	26.5	26.2	-9.0
Top 5 percent	30.6	29.6	24.6	26.7	26.5	-13.5

Note: Table reads for boldface figure that, for the lowest 20 percent of income of the population in 1977, total Federal taxes were 9.3 percent of income. Quintiles are weighted by families.

Source: Congressional Budget Office (CBO) tax simulation model, cited in 1992 Green Book of House Ways and Means Committee, p. 1510

The Rising Burden of Real Estate Taxes

Property tax revenue outpaces inflation in New Jersey

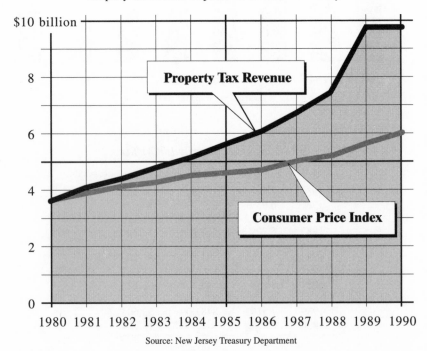

Source: New Jersey Treasury Department

The Rising Burden of Real Estate Taxes (continued)

The Ten U.S. Counties with the Highest Per Capita Property Taxes (1990)

County	Property Tax Revenue Per Person	Property Tax As Share of Total County Revenue
Fairfax, Va.	$1,185	74%
Prince William, Va.	770	67%
Montgomery, Md.	627	42%
Henrico, Va.	623	43%
Baltimore, Md.	502	44%
Anne Arundel, Md.	459	37%
Prince George's, Md.	395	42%
Mecklenburg, N.C.	376	57%
Westchester, N.Y.	356	30%
Onondaga, N.Y.	313	36%

Source: *City & State newspaper, U.S. News and World Report*

The Soaring Cost of Services and the Weakening Health and Pension Safety Net

The Inflation in Health Costs

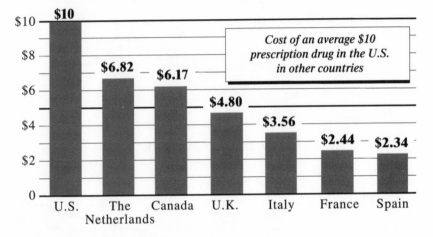

> Cost of an average $10 prescription drug in the U.S. in other countries

Source: 1989 Annual Survey of Farmindustria, Italian Pharmaceutical Association

Doctors' income

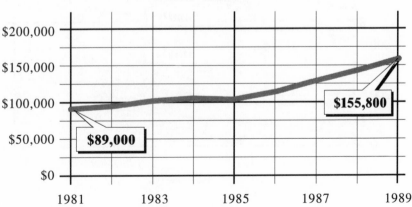

Source: American Medical Association

Prices and Profits for 20 Prescription Drugs

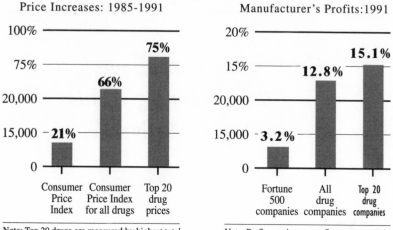

Price Increases: 1985-1991

Consumer Price Index: **21%**
Consumer Price Index for all drugs: **66%**
Top 20 drug prices: **75%**

Note: Top 20 drugs are measured by highest total expenditures.

Manufacturer's Profits:1991

Fortune 500 companies: **3.2%**
All drug companies: **12.8%**
Top 20 drug companies: **15.1%**

Note: Profit margins are profits as a percentage of sales

Source: Families USA Foundation

Health Care Contributions

Average Annual Employee Contribution for Health Care Coverage and Percent of Plans Requiring Contributions

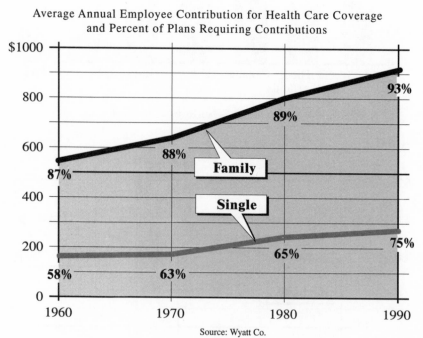

Source: Wyatt Co.

The Rising Cost of Attending College

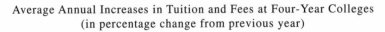

Average Annual Increases in Tuition and Fees at Four-Year Colleges
(in percentage change from previous year)

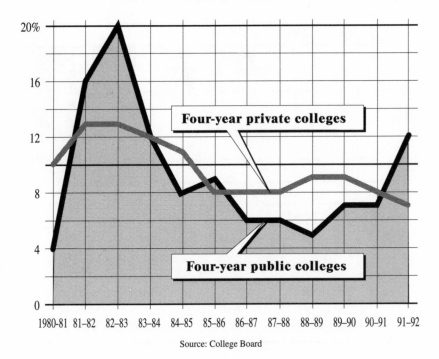

Source: College Board

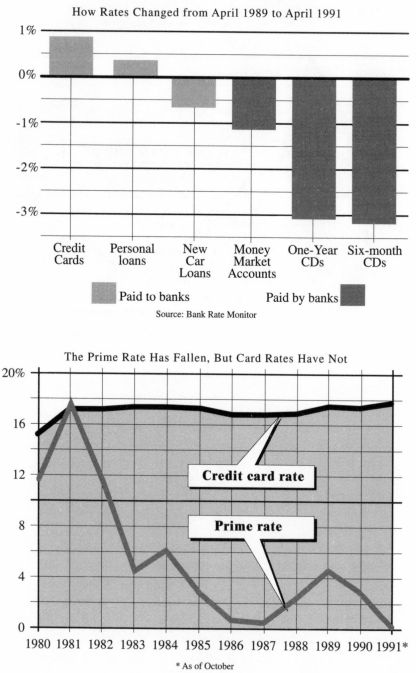

Banks Pay Less Interest—and Charge More

How Rates Changed from April 1989 to April 1991

Paid to banks   Paid by banks

Source: Bank Rate Monitor

The Prime Rate Has Fallen, But Card Rates Have Not

Credit card rate

Prime rate

* As of October

Source: Bancard Holders of America

Soaring Cable Television Charges

U.S. Cable Rates

Average Basic Monthly Service Charge per Subscriber

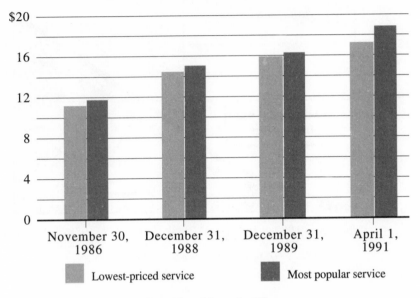

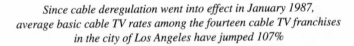

Source: General Accounting Office

Soaring Cable Rates in Los Angeles

*Since cable deregulation went into effect in January 1987,
average basic cable TV rates among the fourteen cable TV franchises
in the city of Los Angeles have jumped 107%*

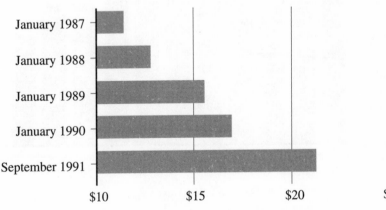

Source: Office of Telecommunications, *Los Angeles Times*

Surging Automobile Premiums

Accelerating Costs since 1980

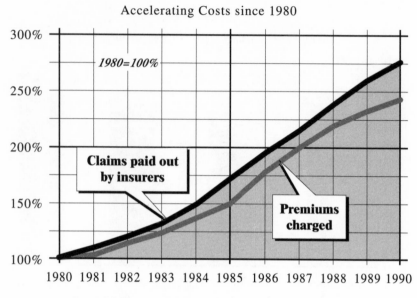

Source: *U.S. News & World Report*, Basic data: A.M. Best Company, Inc.

Shrinking Vacations

Vacation Length
Average number of nights

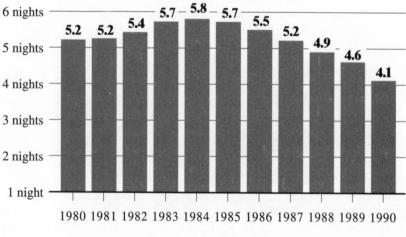

Source: U.S. Travel Data Center

Declining Pension Coverage and Safety

In the 1980s, employers by the thousands terminated pension plans, cut back on their contributions, or claimed pension fund assets.

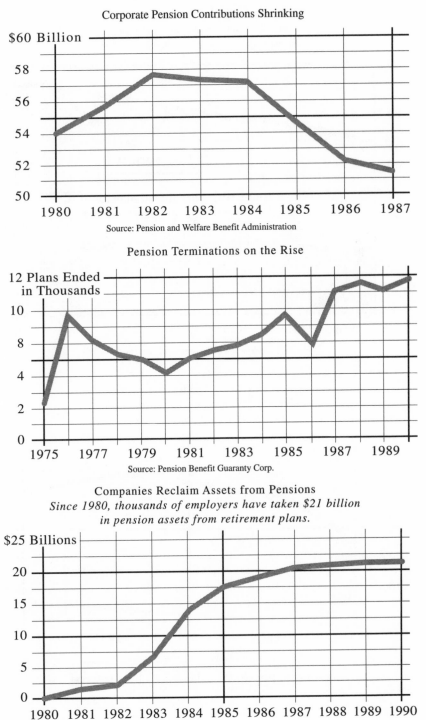

Corporate Pension Contributions Shrinking

$60 Billion
58
56
54
52
50

1980 1981 1982 1983 1984 1985 1986 1987

Source: Pension and Welfare Benefit Administration

Pension Terminations on the Rise

12 Plans Ended
in Thousands
10
8
4
2
0

1975 1977 1979 1981 1983 1985 1987 1989

Source: Pension Benefit Guaranty Corp.

Companies Reclaim Assets from Pensions
Since 1980, thousands of employers have taken $21 billion in pension assets from retirement plans.

$25 Billions
20
15
10
5
0

1980 1981 1982 1983 1984 1985 1986 1987 1988 1989 1990

Source: Pension Benefit Guaranty Corp., Newhouse News Service

Declining Pension Coverage and Safety (continued)

Workers and Pensions
While the number of workers is growing,
the number of those with pensions is not

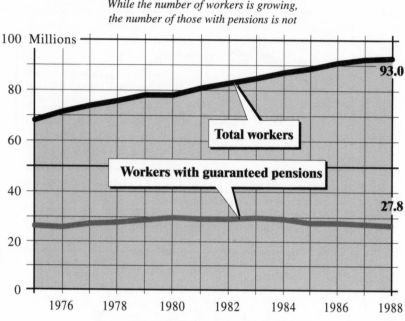

Sources: *Philadelphia Inquirer*, Bureau of Labor Statistics

Less Coverage
Percentage of private-sector workers,
16 and older, covered by pensions

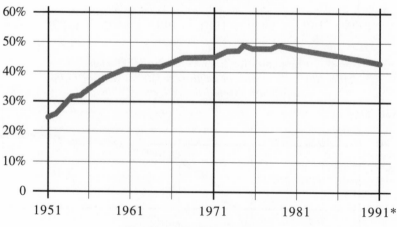

*Note: Figures after 1988 are estimates.

Sources: David E. Bloom of Columbia University and Richard B. Freeman
of Harvard University, *The New York Times*

Index

ABOUT THE AUTHOR

KEVIN PHILLIPS was chief political analyst for the 1968 Republican presidential campaign and later served as assistant to the attorney general. Since 1971 he has been the editor-publisher of *The American Political Report*. Phillips is a contributing columnist to the *Los Angeles Times*, a member of the political strategists' panel of *The Wall Street Journal*, and a regular commentator for National Public Radio. He served as a commentator for CBS Television at the 1984, 1988 and 1992 Republican and Democratic presidential conventions. He is also a periodic contributor to the Op-ed page of *The New York Times* and the Outlook section of *The Washington Post*.

Phillips's first book, *The Emerging Republican Majority*, was described by *Newsweek* as "the political bible of the Nixon Era." It predicted the coming conservative era in U.S. national politics.